THE BOOKRUNNER

A History of Inter-American Relations—
Print, Politics, and Commerce in the United States
and Mexico, 1800–1830

Mathew Carey. Engraving by Samuel Sartain. Printed by John Neagle in 1825.

THE BOOKRUNNER

A History of Inter-American Relations—
Print, Politics, and Commerce in the United States
and Mexico, 1800–1830

Nancy Vogeley

American Philosophical Society
Philadelphia • 2011

> Transactions of the
> American Philosophical Society
> Held at Philadelphia
> For Promoting Useful Knowledge
> Volume 101, Part 1

Copyright ©2011 by the American Philosophical Society for its Transactions series.
All rights reserved.

Library of Congress Cataloging-in-Publication Data

ISBN: 978-1-60618-011-2
US ISSN: 0065-9746

Library of Congress Cataloguing-in-Publication Data

Vogeley, Nancy J.
  The bookrunner : a history of inter-American relations : print, politics, and commerce in the United States and Mexico, 1800-1830 / Nancy Vogeley.
    p. cm. — (Transactions series, ISSN 0065-9746 ; v. 101, pt. 1)
Includes bibliographical references and index.
ISBN 978-1-60618-011-2 (alk. paper)
1. Booksellers and bookselling—Pennsylvania—Philadelphia—History—19th century. 2. Booksellers and bookselling—United States—History—19th century. 3. Booksellers and bookselling—Mexico—History—19th century. 4. Carey, Mathew, 1760-1839. 5. Booksellers and bookselling—Pennsylvania—Philadelphia—History—19th century—Sources. 6. Booksellers and bookselling—United States—History—19th century—Sources. 7. Booksellers and bookselling—Mexico—History—19th century—Sources. 8. Carey, Mathew, 1760-1839—Correspondence. I. Title.

Z478.6.P5V64 2011
381'.45002097309034—dc23
                              2011017447

CONTENTS

Acknowledgments vii

Introduction 1
   Communication, Commerce, Books 5
   The Business of Ideology 11
   American Book History 16
   My Journey from Archives to Book 28

Chapter 1: Philadelphia 35
   The Beginnings of an Hispanic Vogue
      in the United States 42
   Business and Politics 50
   Valentín de Foronda 57
   Translation Business 62
   Growth of the Export Business and the Myth
      of Philadelphia 71
   Las Casas 78
   Philadelphia's Spanish-Speaking Community 83

Chapter 2: The Letters 109

Chapter 3: Mexico 155
   Juan Germán Roscio 159
   Literary Style 167
   Commerce 170
   Freemasonry 176
   Robeson and Veracruz 184
   Book Culture in Mexico 191
   The Philadelphia/Mexico Trade:
      A Summary 206

CONTENTS

Conclusion 223
    United States/England/France 224
    Additional U.S. Influence 234
    Books as Commodities 239
    American Readers 243
    Commerce and Books: Postcolonialisms 248

Appendix A: Books Mathew Carey Offered for Sale in the *Aurora General Advertiser*, April 7, 1815 263
    Books Listed for Sale 263

Appendix B: Suplemento Al *Noticioso General*, Núm. 52 Del Miércoles 1° de Mayo de 1822 267

Appendix C: Spanish-Language Books Printed by Ackermann, Advertised in 1826 in *Curiosidades para Los Estudiosos*, Sold in London in Su Repositorio de Artes, and in Mexico, Colombia, Buenos Aires, Chile, Peru, and Guatemala 277
    En Prensa 279

Appendix D: Catalogue of Spanish Books and Manuscripts, Printed in William Robertson's *History of America*, 1803 Edition 281

Bibliography 297

Index 329

ACKNOWLEDGMENTS

Paul Rich, Guillermo de los Reyes, and Antonio Lara must be credited with discovering the Robeson letters in the Historical Society of Pennsylvania. Following their preliminary findings and on a tip from David Szewczyk of the Philadelphia Rare Books and Manuscripts Company, I went to the HSP. My thanks are due, then, while I worked in Philadelphia, to David, to the staff at the HSP, to James Green of the Library Company and his people, and to Glenys A. Waldman and Cathy Giamo of the Masonic Library.

I also gratefully acknowledge the help, over years, from librarians at the John Carter Brown Library (Brown University), the Clark Library (UCLA), the Bancroft Library (University of California, Berkeley), the Darlington Library and Latin American Office (University of Pittsburgh), the Heinz History Museum (Pittsburgh), the Rare Book Room at the Library of the University of Pennsylvania, the Hagley Museum and Library (Wilmington, Delaware), the American Antiquarian Society, the British Library (Colindale), the Biblioteca Nacional (Madrid), the Bibliothèque Nationale (Paris), and the Biblioteca Nacional and Archivo General de la Nación (Mexico). I am particularly grateful to Martha Whittaker at the Sutro Library (San Francisco, California State System) for the many favors she has shown me over years of working there. Research in those wonderful libraries was a joy and gave me an appreciation of similarities among the early book cultures in the United States and Mexico.

For insightful readings of early versions of this work, I owe thanks to Michael Mathes, Harold Sims, and Ralph Bauer. David S. Shields and Brian Connaughton have encouraged my research into Llorente, and have read the manuscript in its later stages. The comments of all these scholars have helped immensely, yet I alone am responsible for errors.

The HSP has graciously given permission to quote from the Robeson letters, as well as to reproduce other materials from their collection. The HSP, the Masonic Library, the Library Company, the American Antiquarian Society, the Library of Congress, and the Sutro Library have also given permission to use materials for purposes of illustration. At the American Philosophical Society

ACKNOWLEDGMENTS

I am most appreciative of the interest Roy Goodman, Pam Lankas, and Mary McDonald have taken in this project. Last but not least, I must mention other kindnesses—the willingness of Mexicana Airlines to lug books back home for me, and the attentiveness of the many bookdealers who have sold me books, Alfonso Vijil of Libros Latinos being one of the most valuable. In many ways this study of the spread of books is my tribute to booksellers.

INTRODUCTION

SOME TIME IN JULY OF 1822, Thomas W. Robeson sailed from New Castle, Delaware, downriver from Philadelphia, bound for Mexico with a load of books. Robeson was acting as agent for Mathew Carey, a prominent bookseller and publisher in Philadelphia to whom he would write some twenty letters detailing his trip from the United States to the port of Alvarado on the Gulf Coast and on up to the highlands of Mexico City. In the first letter, dated July 17, Robeson reported that he was still in New Castle packing the ship; on August 15 he told of his arrival at Alvarado; on January 25 he described Santa Anna's *golpe* against the government of Agustín de Iturbide and the probable close of his business. On May 31 correspondence from the firm of Carey and Lea advised Robeson to wind things up and clear the account because political upheaval in Mexico did not promise stable conditions for sales and thus adequate return on their investment. Robeson's lists of titles sold, and in what quantities, are the most revealing documents we have yet for telling how the writings of Rousseau, Paine, and other social philosophers whose names we should know, got to and inflamed a newly independent Mexico. In describing an early trade link between the two parts of the Americas, the letters document a U.S.–Mexican relationship that would grow as the postcolonial nations sought new alliances and international status, free from parental restrictions.

Although the time span of the letters is brief, the Robeson/Carey exchange—the basis for this study—is a valuable find. Cached in the Historical Society of Pennsylvania (Philadelphia), the letters provide the material collateral for knowing about cultural transfer. They anchor airy theories of intellectual indebtedness in specific data. They situate the movement of men's thought, often connected to high motives and conjectures of a communion of souls, in an economic context. Rather than portraying Robeson as an adventurous hero, the letters, which emphasize the routine of business, instead focus attention on the books and their physicality; their detail, which could seem dull in describing inventories and duties, is a refreshing addition to the field of book history. Coming at a time when the two American societies were developing their political consciousness, the letters highlight how attitudes toward reading, literacy, patterns of spending and book ownership, press freedom, and so on, contributed to that consciousness. This study of two American book worlds, at similar times in their histories, then, helps to show how ideas shaped postcolonial lives, at one level going into men's minds but at another going into their pockets as a source of wealth. It aims to prove that not only did Enlightenment thought on paper affect those men and women, and jolt them into new thinking, but that the practice of commerce—the means by which the books were made available to readers—was a new, accessory factor that contributed to their decolonizing development as its freedoms opened up old colonial restrictions.

Although one sparrow does not make a summer and one cannot conclude from Robeson's letters a larger trade, one can surmise from them several impressions relative to the state of the U.S. print world in the early days of the republic, recognition in the United States and throughout the hemisphere of the need for, and benefits of, American interdependence, and, in Mexico, openness to U.S. influence. Many Mexicans thought that they could learn from the U.S. model how to move from the hatreds of revolution to peaceful nationhood. There was initial admiration for men like George Washington and warm praise for documents like the U.S. Constitution. By 1822, its revolution behind it, the United States seemed to be moving on to the world's stage. War with England was over with the Treaty of Ghent (1814), thus bringing some measure of peace and relief from war-time expenditures. U.S. territory had been extended with the Louisiana Purchase (1803) and acquisition of the Floridas (1819). The Monroe Doctrine had not yet been promulgated (1823); but U.S. seamen, mapmakers, explorers, and maverick soldiers were making sorties throughout the hemisphere, securing contacts in preparation for new trade and political alliances. Spanish American revolutionaries in the United States invited involvement in their struggles for independence, visiting businessmen and officials at the highest levels of governance; their pleas deepened U.S. consciousness of possible leadership in prospects for change there. South America would not win its independence wars until 1825, but Mexico, having won its independence in 1821, beckoned. So that former Spanish possession, on the southern border of the United States, now seemed to be a likely field for U.S. involvement; if it no longer needed soldiers and arms, it did need ideas.

In Mexico remnants of war meant that arguments roiled as to what form of government to adopt. The new nation had inherited Spanish preferences for monarchism and centralism; and some members of the elite class wanted the Spanish king to come to Mexico, just as the Portuguese king had reinvented his empire in Brazil. But another faction—the principal backers of the Carey/

Robeson initiative—argued for definitive separation from Spain and republicanism. Taking advantage of their support, Robeson slipped his books through cracks that postcolonial indecisiveness and corruption permitted. Established booksellers quickly bought from him. The political content of Robeson's books, then, can be seen to have been an important means by which Mexicans improved their range of vision and plotted another phase of their development. But the very fact of foreign paper in their world also contributed to Mexican liberation. Witnessing the dealings of the U.S. bookseller in their midst, and taking books from his hands, Mexicans learned to participate in a new economic system. The business seemed to be a partnership between two nations advancing toward international status. Yet the trade, in which one became provider and the other client, also foreshadowed an unequal power relationship that would have implications for the future.

North/south relations have usually been explained in terms of diplomacy. But the commercial nature of the Robeson/Carey correspondence opens up another view, parallel but contradictory to that history of guarded and often hostile exchanges. The letters tell of an initial optimism that friendship between the two countries might work. They confirm that financial exigencies in the United States were pushing businessmen to come up with products that could create new demand; books were cheap to produce, requiring little or no raw material, and Mexico looked to be a logical market for ambitious publishers. The fact that Robeson's cargo was made up of Spanish-language books is perhaps surprising because today we think of the United States as English-speaking in its early days. Yet the Spanish books point to a cultural pluralism in the United States. Booksellers already carried stock in their warehouses for a multilingual U.S. population. As we will see, U.S. printers published then for a diverse readership, which was often regional. English would later emerge as the East Coast's *lingua franca* but, in the meantime, printers printed entertaining books, newspapers, political pamphlets, religious literature, and so on, in several languages. Thus, export of these books was the logical next step.

Beyond the apparent benefit of new markets for U.S. books, however, an expansionist spirit was pushing the United States south and west, causing many to look toward Mexico and the Caribbean as possible fields for takeover. They saw Mexico as a partner in a hemispheric union, resistant to European encroachments; but more covetously, they recognized Mexico's tenuous hold on its northern territories and thought that the mining wealth and territory there could be annexed. In particular, southern interests envisioned extending slavery to those areas.

The book traffic between Philadelphia and Mexico, then,—in its very fact and in the titles provided—goes far toward revealing historical attitudes in the two American nations as regards political and economic development. It casts light on the role print played in both countries in this first phase of their respective developments; the comparative (and contrastive) measure of this resource—as it behaved domestically and internationally—will be the first part of my inquiry. Recent studies of print, following Benedict Anderson's theory that printing allowed for communities to be imagined, have emphasized its role in nation-building.[1] Yet the Robeson/Carey letters push scholars toward an international consciousness, an understanding that U.S. printers were interested not only in local or even national markets, but also in foreign ones. The term "antebellum," commonly used to describe the period in U.S. history between 1815 and the Civil War, as Edward L. Ayers persuasively argues, elides much of what those years really were and is more properly labeled "postbellum" or "the Era of American Expansion"; Ayers here not only corrects a view that everything in the country's development pointed to the later War but usefully remembers how those generations dreamed beyond the nation's borders.[2]

Although the Robeson/Carey letters would seem to say that U.S. printers, as suppliers to Mexico, were superior to the Mexicans, that conclusion is false. Printing had a long history in Mexico so this study of transferal is not a finding for U.S. technological superiority.[3] Printers came into Mexico and Peru in the mid-sixteenth century to service the early missions, seminaries, and universities that were founded then for those urban centers (Mexico in 1553 and Peru in 1578) and which early on fostered an academic culture.[4] Harvard College was not established until 1636 amid a population that was still dispersed throughout New England and along the Eastern seaboard. Isaiah Thomas in *The History of Printing in America* (1810), in discussing U.S. printing throughout the colonial years, emphasizes the dependence of the British colonies on foreign imports and minimizes the importance of domestic print shops.[5] Yet Spanish-American colonial print production, though it flourished, was controlled by the Inquisition until late in the eighteenth century, and educated taste prescribed religious, classical, and professional literature.[6] To get around these restrictions, Mexicans had to rely on manuscript and oral forms of communication for news and access to contradictory opinion. With this background, then, in the first years after independence when Mexicans were groping for ideas beyond the fixed ideologies that colonial authorities and taste had insisted on, Mexican bookdealers looked to import the Enlightenment texts that travelers could not adequately summarize, the long political treatises that letters could not repeat, the print forms that somehow conveyed recognition of their substance beyond what a fleeting word or ink jotting suggested.[7]

Printing was a tool for political consolidation, and an economic boon, in both of the former colonies; and commonalities suggest equalities. But the two, at different stages of their development, were unequal. In 1822 the United

States was further along on its path toward economic, political, and cultural viability, whereas Mexico had only recently stopped fighting and would not decide on a constitution until 1824. Entrepreneurship in Mexico was tainted by memories of colonial monopolies and cultural inhibitions regarding vile money-making; racial divisions made political union problematic. English and Spanish colonialisms had left different modes of government, notions of civic arrangement, and social attitudes in the populations. Thus the coming together that some might characterize as a marriage of unequals—remembering Jerry Brown's description of the NAFTA (North American Free Trade Agreement) accords—is better thought of as romantic first love. The partners were equal in their Americanness; parents had kept them apart but now they yielded to the pull that prohibitions resulting from viewing one another from across boundaries had built up; starry-eyed, with dreams in common, they thought they could embrace despite differences.

This early attempt at reaching beyond the self to another, with whom one seeks some exogamous relationship outside the family structure, points to an evolving maturity. The rapprochement as both American nations broached internationalism is an intriguing example of long-distance idealism, but also of hard-headed realism as the two countries met and attempted to negotiate differences. For a short time, the United States and Mexico came together fraternally; and, although that interlude of good will soon came to an end as animosities set in and European powers edged out the United States as suppliers to Spanish America, that period in the early 1820s when the United States and Mexico acknowledged their similar colonial pasts and a common American future deserves a new look.

COMMUNICATION, COMMERCE, BOOKS

The letters tell that the book trade was an important means by which the two parts of the Americas sought to communicate with one another. "Communication" in the discourse of the eighteenth and early nineteenth centuries was often described in terms of "commerce," exchange in both public and private intercourse.[8] Commerce suggested new economic practices but also new interpersonal relationships in salons, coffee houses, Masonic Lodges, and so forth. As political realignments appeared in post-Napoleonic Europe and colonialisms fell away in the Americas, new industrialization with its attendant technology, use of labor, and search for international suppliers and markets required that attitudes characteristic of small-scale transactions be left behind. New national economies, dependent on exchange, demanded changes in thinking about how commerce worked. Formerly, in colonial Spanish America, "commerce" had been a derogatory term, connoting the monopolistic policies the metropolis had imposed on American and Pacific colonies, and even the slave trade for which Cuba was the central market; now for Americans commerce meant freedom from that relationship which had kept them poor and dependent, and an end to that hideous business. Formerly, it suggested illegal contacts that subverted royal privileges; now it alluded to opportunities for many men to seek wealth. Formerly, at the familiar level, it suggested secret exchanges; now it meant open relationships and the warmth of friendship that society approved of.

Thus the term was being recast positively. Books benefited from being associated with commerce; rather than being devalued as they were absorbed into a market system, they were more highly prized—though perhaps for new reasons. Books were trading counters in impersonal venues but they were also instruments of interpersonal linkage; thus they were appreciated because they functioned at both levels of communication. Books facilitated commerce in the sense that their production stirred specie and permitted exchanges of money and goods, but books also meant commerce as they introduced one individual to another in a manner free of the performances of personalities. Books transmitted the wisdom of one mind to another in a way that suggested an authority dictating orders to a subordinate. But the physical act of reading, in the comfort of one's own reading space and at his own pace, also suggested the reader was somehow asserting his power and controlling the relationship. New literary genres were putting books in the hands of many more persons than previously. The political essay seemed to reveal secrets that only privileged persons knew about; the novel authorized a release of emotion that was both private and public as the reader connected with a community of other readers and opened up to human feelings of compassion. Men were breaking with the formulae of court hierarchies, families were rupturing as romantic attitudes toward love provided new reasons for marriage, and notions of sentiment were disturbing old behavioral boundaries.[9] Books—particularly recent publications—addressed these new concerns.

Books were one of the most attractive of the new commodities U.S. businessmen thought to produce. They were small and portable, desirable as more people aspired to greater learning. Copyright laws still had not arrived in the Americas so that European works could be reproduced freely with no payment to the author. Booksellers were often both printers and publishers, but they also distributed for printers in other cities thus building an interstate commercial system.[10] As they extended their business, booksellers helped to found the first national banks and were players in international credit networks. Yet it was a challenge for American booksellers, and the authors whose works they printed, to make a success of the business because, far from the aristocratic patrons of Europe, American books competed with the necessities of life. Many Americans preferred European writers to their own, forcing publishers to go abroad for merchandise.

Entrepreneurship, or risk-taking, was behind Carey's "adventure" to Mexico, as well as behind the cooperation of sympathetic Mexicans. The fact that the item traded was books, a good that Mexicans were familiar with, allowed Mexicans to accept the new business more easily. Spanish printers in the late eighteenth century had begun to take an antiquarian interest in the country's literary inheritance, printing old manuscripts and thus teaching Mexicans to accept fresh reading material.[11] Yet the warnings of heterodoxy the Inquisition had thrown up around foreign-produced books deterred some. And the self-interest behind the mercantile transactions, which Anglo economists saw as a positive incentive for market equilibrium, offended others who saw in them Catholic sins of greed and egoistic pride. Nevertheless Robeson's letters show that those Mexicans who participated in the business seemed to overcome their qualms, sponsoring the endeavor and buying the materials that on some days were in the bookstalls but on other days were prohibited as immoral and seditious.

Beyond the limits of the United States, Robeson entered uncharted waters. Within the United States, book peddlers moved freely. But once an agent went outside and onto so-called neutral seas and then into another country's legal system, he took on another character. His ship competed with pirates and freebooters.[12] His activity was similar to that of filibusterers, men who with a private army invaded a country under the secret sponsorship of a government and the agreement that the action would benefit it (the excuse being that wartime conditions authorized that infringement on the laws of neutrality). Thus I have called him a bookrunner, suggesting he was like gunrunners who crossed with their illegal goods into uncertain territory. If books sold freely in the United States, in independent Mexico they were subject to the whims of the government, still controlled by an ecclesiastical court that held out for an official Catholicism, and a residual colonial morality which believed that monitoring of public discourse was necessary. Outsiders, from a Protestant country like the United States, were suspect—particularly in Mexico City where the few who came were generally Spaniards or representatives of nations acceptable to Catholic Spain. Ports along the Mexican Gulf coast like Veracruz were more accustomed to seeing men of other nations, itinerant traders or managers of established commercial houses that represented authorized countries. Robeson's books, then, circulated on the border between open, legal business and clandestinity. Both Anglo and Spanish America professed faith in commerce—their ability to trade freely beyond the rules and monopolies of their former imperialisms symbolized their equality with other mature nations. But how these new liberties were to be interpreted, whether as free trade or freedom of speech and the press, was a dilemma that both parts of the Americas confronted.

The second part of my inquiry concerns the kinds of books Robeson sold. Two features stand out: they were mostly political tracts and they were written in Spanish. Printers had a history in both Anglo and Spanish America of servicing the powerful state. Only in the eighteenth century did they begin to abet revolution. Rousing men to understand their common interests and either to support the status quo or to rally in protest of grievances, printers published the political pamphlets and newspapers that deepened division. After independence, these media continued to flourish and went from instilling the lessons of power to operating in a more egalitarian society in which they simultaneously stirred and calmed debate. In the United States, throughout the eighteenth century and into the first decades of the nineteenth, printers mediated across an increasingly diverse population. Immigrants (Frenchmen moving in to contest British controls and later fleeing Napoleonic upheavals, Germans brought initially to the United States to fight as mercenaries in Britain's war with the colonies) added to the original population. Within this range, printers helped to develop common ground by creating a shared political discourse that still, in many cases, was communicated in separate, parallel languages. They promoted equality among speakers from across the British Isles (English, Welsh, Scottish, Gaelic), users of Dutch, German, French, Spanish, and Italian; they printed in Latin, Greek, and Hebrew for an educated elite, and even in Indian tongues for indigenous peoples. By printing the mysterious religious literature each preferred, their unique secular materials and local concerns, printers gave respectability to each little speech community and social class and made it seem open to the other. Books and other printed materials reached out across distances to join the groups in what could seem to be the word-less, conceptual world where books transported them. Thus printers served a purpose that is seldom recognized—uniting the populace even as they sold to separate markets. By reprinting imported books, booksellers kept alive ties that immigrants had to their countries of origin, reminding them of events back home even as new ties were forged in this hemisphere. Then, as the population began to ask for literature beyond the elitist colonial fare, democratic political publishing flourished. Readers wanted political books that set out new thinking; and although those books often demarcated differences and had the potential for fomenting hatreds, they also brought men together in imaginative and intellectual worlds where words might stand in for weapons. Other literary categories—science and technology, religion, travel, school texts, entertainment, journalism—would increasingly interest readers. But politics—personalities, principles, issues, questions—was a staple of booksellers in both the United States and areas to the south in the first decades of the nineteenth century.

Books played different roles in Anglo and Spanish America, though, and this is where this study finds an important set of problems to be explored. Differences are often explained in terms of the Protestant/Catholic identities of the respective areas; and this characterization, which deserves greater precision, will be examined later. Literacy is another yardstick according to which the two areas are measured. Percentages were higher in Anglo America, it is true, thus supposing greater demand for printers' output. But the elite requiring the sophisticated political essays that we see in Robeson's inventories would have been approximately the same size in the two areas, albeit each of a different class and educational formation. Gentlemen in each world would have had roughly the same classical education; their money, depending on the region, would have come from the same agricultural production and mercantile exchange. After independence Mexico continued to develop its extensive mining economy, whereas the United States derived its revenue from trading, and also from the sea—fishing and whaling. Journalism, perhaps a literary mode a notch below the political essays in Robeson's cargo, which proliferated in both areas in the nineteenth century, certainly correlated with literacy. By the 1820s the U.S. population was beginning to be more extensively literate, although at a more basic level, than Mexico's, which, confined to the cities, more stratified racially, and with historically more reverential expectations for books, had a somewhat different character. In both Americas, however, an intermediate level emerged that is hard to classify—semi-literates like farmers and some women, but also schoolchildren and adults eager to learn the vocabulary for talking about the new sciences, Masonry, and so on. Thus the calculation Carey made to supply appropriate reading material for people he did not know and whose cultural condition he could only guess at is an intriguing example of early globalization problems.

Carey guessed correctly—probably on the advice of Mexicans with whom he was in contact—that Mexicans, like readers in the United States, wanted literature that would help them in their decolonizing thinking. Consequently, though some of his titles were newly printed, the demand for which was still unknown, his cargo was largely made up of works, proven to have been useful in Europe, the United States, and those areas of Spanish America where Carey had contacts. Robeson's letters report what Mexican customs permitted or he smuggled in, and then, once there, what he might import in the future—legal treatises and codes, Masonic handbooks, scientific materials, and some novels. A central message of the books in the Robeson cargo, however, one of the first large shipments of books we can guess entered Mexico after independence, was decolonization; and this feature will be a principal concern here. Nationalism has often absorbed historians as they track the consequences of independence in Anglo and Spanish America. Yet decolonization—that parallel phase describing colonies that detached from the mother country, left behind loyalist and monarchist modes of behavior, and struck out justifying criminalities of regicide and fratricide so as to enable nationalism—has often been erased. Thus the decolonizing function of Robeson's books, and the model of his entrepreneurial venture, will be a major question in this study.[13] Mexicans needed the angry rhetoric of Thomas Paine that had helped U.S. Americans a generation before to declare independence. Mexicans needed to have on hand the intellectual arguments of Jean Jacques Rousseau so as to rethink their social contracts. Mexicans needed to hear the anti-English sentiments of Barère de Vieuzac and his dissertation on freedom of the seas so as to begin to distance themselves from imperialistic thought. They needed models of American state constitutions so as to write their own. And they particularly needed the perspective of one author, the Catholic Venezuelan, Juan Germán Roscio, whose work we will see in detail later, in helping them to disconnect from a Spanish mind-set.

Central to this book bridge that Carey was building between the two societies is the question of translation. I understand "translation" literally as the passage of a text from one word system to another. But I also consider translation to be the adaptation of one cultural artifact to another's understanding, the uprooting and transposition of that artifact to foreign soil where readers might not have the background to appreciate the author's departures from traditional thought and conceptual innovations, let alone his subtleties of language. Roscio's treatise was written in Spanish. But other books that Carey sent had their origins in other languages; and literary scholars who deal with textual matters will understand that not only did simple substitution of words betray the first iteration but that the translator often took liberties with the original text by adding or subtracting passages where he thought it appropriate.

Finally, all the factors that went into making Philadelphia the cultural and economic center of the United States at that moment fed into the persona of Robeson and his actions, the books he selected and their messages of modernity and cosmopolitanism, so that that city's character was imprinted on Mexico's imagination. Philadelphia's location midway between New England and Virginia helped to make it a meeting place for competing factions. New York had not yet emerged as an important financial center; Washington, though designated as a capital, was not yet built up. Instead diplomats, businessmen, and expatriates clustered in the already-established city of Philadelphia, on the easily accessible Atlantic coast. Pennsylvania's Quaker history of tolerance attracted some, just as nearby Maryland's Catholic history drew others. Like Bordeaux on the French coast, islands in the Caribbean, and later London, the city was part of a network of authors, publishers, and customers that extended to Spanish America. Printers in this Atlantic consortium enlarged their business by providing materials for readers whose own presses were not yet free. Their motives ranged from ideological sympathies with insurgents and republicans to a desire for profit. They projected an American design, even before the Monroe Doctrine was proclaimed. Americans could not depend on European printers to provide the ideas they needed after independence. Most European printers were too controlled by their monarchies after the Congress of Vienna; and, although a few renegade European presses, away from the supervision of authorities in the capitals, supplied them with helpful literature, Americans relied on one another for the declarations of independence and constitutional models that would set out and sustain their beliefs.

THE BUSINESS OF IDEOLOGY

Robeson, whose business depended on retailing politics, was a new breed of international traveler. Philadelphia-based and English-speaking (with some apparent familiarity with French), he traded in the new pragmatism, which would have represented a change from old-fashioned Spanish philosophy and even some of the newer Enlightenment forms. Even though he called himself a republican while distastefully witnessing the monarchic panoply of the Mexican court, he does not appear to have been a salesman for republicanism. His letters do not self-indulgently express ideological sympathies or antipathies as earlier adventurers might have done so as to win favor back home. He kept to himself his motives for running risks in a world where laws were up for grab. He only reported the facts, useful for business success. He coldly trafficked in new ideologies and seems not to have operated out of idealism or personal conviction. Although we are dealing with his letters, rather than a diary, we have the impression that his actions were quick responses to challenges, friendships were business alliances. He conveniently seems to have forgotten moral rules. Thus, while revealing a new man, the letters display a new, uniquely American economic philosophy—a set of practices that individuals make up as they go along rather than any prescribed theoretical system.[14]

"Ideology" is a term that I have used and now requires definition.[15] By it I intend not a hard-and-fast set of philosophical principles but rather, in the context of the period, someone's personal opinion, or animus. The eighteenth-century writers of the new ideological books Robeson was selling—called "thinkers" or "journalistic writers" in the parlance of his day[16]—took over from the theologians and speculative philosophers of a previous period and vied in the Enlightenment marketplace for adherents. They were not metaphysicians nor did they produce elaborate systems or absolute ethical yardsticks. Instead they usually attacked specific historical problems and confronted political dilemmas. American ideology was of necessity tentative; for example, writing in Chile in 1812, an essayist for a newspaper being started up there by U.S. editors invited by the new Chilean government, asked in the prospectus: "What government is most advisable in the Americas in the present circumstances? Without a doubt a provisional one because uncertainty is one of our circumstances."[17] He then went on to ironize the difficulty of adapting one culture's invention to another's uniqueness (thus showing the inherent capacity of philosophical systems for betrayal).

> France, which had an ancient and powerful nobility, an opulent clergy, a great number of public functionaries, where the Catholic religion dominated from the days of Clodovicio and where reformers were only sustained at the cost of much blood and sacrifice, where ruled luxury, dissipation, corruption, ambition, united to a fickle and inconstant character, tried to adopt the governmental system of the United States of America. . . . Paris, under the same constitution as frugal, tranquil and philosophical Pennsylvania![18]

"Philosophical Pennsylvania" had now replaced France as a source of ideas. Even French philosophers like Raynal, the essayist stated, had recently confessed that they had tried to give laws to the whole world from the sanctuary of their studies but had had to repent of their effrontery, realizing that they had not taken circumstances into account. Ideas had to be chosen and applied carefully since events were changing every day (in 1812 Americans in Chile and Mexico were fighting to free themselves from 300 years of imperial rule yet who in Madrid they were actually rebelling against was confused. Spain, with the help of the English, was itself struggling to throw off Napoleonic rule and that would not happen until the battle of Vitoria in 1813).[19]

The economic literature of this period in the history of the Americas is thought to be well known—for example, Adam Smith's *Wealth of Nations* and treatises by French physiocrats. The impact of their ideas on U.S. leaders like Alexander Hamilton and Thomas Jefferson has been studied. Less well known, however, is the imprint that entrepreneurial practice left on societies opening up to foreign trade, where entrepreneurship usually meant illegal operations of men on the ground. In the Americas, where imperial controls and treaty regulations still pretended to operate in the first decades of the nineteenth century, de facto business enacted this new commerce. In the case of Mexico, free-trade practices were crudely introduced by outsiders yet they tucked into the quiet receptivity of locals who desired change; Robeson's way was facilitated by Mexican backers whose views had led them to invite importation of controversy. Although they had probably read the essays of Spanish political economists like Gaspar Melchor de Jovellanos[20] and Valentín de Foronda (whom we will meet later), their primary objective—to get rid of Agustín de Iturbide, who had proclaimed himself emperor when Mexico became independent in 1821[21]—forced them into considering economic deregulation as a first step toward political change. Jovellanos and Foronda had theorized in a vein the period called "political economy"; however, their books, useful as they were, did not serve the Mexicans because they were rooted in Spanish considerations and did not openly criticize the monarchy. Therefore, the books coming out of Philadelphia, because they were designedly antimonarchical and antiimperial, were more pertinent and more helpful. Mexican readers might have read their political message passively, but the book agent's backers and customers learned new economic lessons as they actively participated in the risky business.

Economics informed two concerns—decolonization and nation formation—at the forefront of American minds. Although British America had won its political independence in 1783, in the early 1800s it was still casting about for political security and economic viability; and so the concerns there could be thought of as successive processes. However, Spanish America was struggling to accomplish both goals simultaneously, and we have a sense that the U.S. publishers of the *Aurora de Chile*, whom we have seen, understood that dilemma. Without preaching excessively about U.S. advances, they held out as ideals to be aimed at political liberty, the rule of law, and equitable property arrangements. In an unsigned editorial, published on August 20, 1812, the paper stated:

> Colonial dependence and political nullity are one and the same thing. A people that depends on a metropolis does not figure among the nations; it is no more than a province... a piece of real estate out in the country (*fundo*), a patrimony of the metropolis, destined to enrich it. Inasmuch as the luxury of the owner always grows in proportion to that plenty..., the wealth of the court of Spain grew immensely with the possession of its American patrimony.[22]

The real estate is characterized by vast territories over which the population is scattered. The essayist—who probably was the Chilean Camilo Henríquez who wrote most of the material—quotes Fray Bartolomé de las Casas who in 1542 foresaw the same destruction of the land and butchery of the indigenous population on the Spanish-occupied mainland that had already occurred on the island of Hispaniola. Then, through years of colonial occupation, Spain kept its American possessions dependent by means of an economic system that transferred their wealth immediately to the metropolis, and obedient by means of a deliberate policy of ignorance. The colonies were denied the Enlightenment that Europe enjoyed. The essayist interprets Spain's present occupation by English and French troops to be punishment for that violent and unjust colonialism, and a propitious moment for American peoples to seize their liberty. Realizing that tyranny and old thinking still blinded many and prevented them from revolting, he urges reluctant Americans to gratefully acknowledge the heroes who were avenging the Indians killed by Spaniards in the Conquest years and already beginning to create a "glorious homeland." Chileans should not stop with assassinating their tyrant king, however, thinking like Oriental peoples that that deed assured their future; instead they had to continue on to overcome anarchy and found a state in which impartial law protected everyone, and industry and enlightenment assured happiness.

Mexico was the only Latin American country, aside from Brazil, to embrace monarchy after independence. Many believed that that European model best served the new nation; even if they went along with independence, they were so accustomed to a king's personality and the bureaucratic structures associated with that form of authority that they persisted in their retrograde convictions. Yet Iturbide, who had set himself up as an emperor, was overthrown in 1823. Why did his regime fail? I believe that the economic literature of Jovellanos and Foronda, which would have been the most influential in Spain's colonies because it entered legally, was one contributing factor; their prescriptions of new modes of social organization and order, their recommendations for trade apart from colonialist policies, implicitly indicted the authoritarian controls monarchism implied.

Another factor was the commercial acceleration, which Spain itself initiated in the last years of its imperial rule, that had begun to undercut older beliefs that the colonies existed to return their extractive wealth to the king's coffers according to a highly regulated system. Although the Spanish Academy of Language had resisted for many years admitting commercial vocabulary to its dictionaries, the terms, which were usually French borrowings and conveyed notions of decentralized and unauthorized trade (if not exactly free trade), acquired currency because they described the traffic that was actually taking place.[23] In the last years of the empire, economic developments had begun to change Mexico despite Spain's consular oversight and bureaucratic paperwork. Trade within the colony, Caribbean exchanges, inter-American commerce, and deals with non-Spanish merchants behind the backs of inspectors were beginning to train Mexicans to rely on themselves. Iturbide's fall was already being prepared for by men who were taking charge of their own lives and creating networks apart from government-mandated ones.

A third factor emerged, however, when Iturbide came to power and authorized a certain openness in his desire to create a new economic base for Mexico and win the recognition of other nations. His policy brought outsiders into the country; when U.S. agents, Englishmen and Frenchmen, arrived in Mexico to invite Mexican partners and vend goods, old colonial mentalities began to change. Iturbide knew his state-building task would be difficult. After years of war he needed loans to rebuild the country; he was faced with reconciling factions from hard-and-fast Spanish traditionalists, intent on preserving their economic security, to new opportunists who embraced republicanism as a way to free up old restrictiveness. Agriculture, cattle-raising, and trading carried on in distant regions were increasingly a source of income, competing with mining wealth, which historically had flowed through the capital. Hard currency, rather than old-fashioned credit from Spanish trading houses, was necessary. Commerce, which justified self-interest and envisioned a mechanism in which multiple self-interests balanced one another according to an exchange principle, was gradually replacing the self-abnegation that religion taught. Thus, the economic model, put forward by the presence on the ground of the U.S. agent, related to the book trade but separate from the titles themselves, turned out to be an important antiauthoritarian blow to Iturbide. The U.S. bookseller enacted individual freedom and sharp Yankee capitalism; he represented a civil government that had begun to think about wealth in manufacturing terms, apart from land holdings, concessions from a king and aristocratic privilege. This personal contact between two differently structured American economies and cultures—although the contents of his Philadelphia-produced books mattered, too—underlies this and later versions of inter-American exchange.

When placed alongside other documents of the time that tell of state plans and controls, the bookseller's letters show an individual spirit. Contrasting views will be seen later in two other commercial documents from the same period—one by Joel Poinsett, an emissary from the United States to Mexico, and another by Juan Schmaltz, a Frenchman sent by the French king to assess the possibilities of that country's trade with Mexico. Both Poinsett and Schmaltz, who were not themselves businessmen, in their respective reports reveal how governments were beginning to co-opt business in neo-colonial ways. Carey's agent, on the other hand, operates independently, dealing free of centralized dictates and unconcerned with setting up a trading company. Conscious that his book business, in that period of ecclesiastical inspections, if not Inquisition strictures, may be viewed by many Mexicans as illegal, he superficially abides by Mexican rules (paying duties and going through the motions of inviting ecclesiastical oversight). Operating on the borders of changing laws and sidestepping partisanship, he invents his business as he goes along. From the evidence of the letters, we assume that his partners in the business are only Carey; the ship captains; and trading houses in Veracruz, New Orleans, and the U.S. consul in Havana. Despite the participation of the latter, it does not seem that the government of the United States figures in the arrangement.

The Mexican book business was like the slave trade and opium traffic, which merchants in the United States engaged in at that time and which brought great wealth.[24] It attracted extraordinary men who were willing to deal in merchandise that others shunned, men who could think internationally and bet on success. Connected to the growing shipping trade, books that had circulated before only surreptitiously were now, in a changing political climate, promising profit. Their production was open in the United States but in Mexico books were a niche business that some invited, whereas others, considering authors like Rousseau and Paine morally dangerous, tried to stop. The story of this Carey business, then, is part of the history of ideas in Mexico; valuably it adds to that history precise information as to the flow of those new books, and documentation as to the factors favoring or obstructing their sale.

Official histories have not always recorded the volume of that trade in imported books. Or, if they have, the amount reported is not always trustworthy. For example, a Mexican history of imports arriving in Veracruz, and then transported on to Mexico City, omits entirely any statistic for 1822, a year of great internal turmoil.[25] The history recognizes "paper and books" as a category, along with textiles, wines and liquors, foodstuffs, glassware, machinery, and so on. It says that in 1821 books and paper in the amount of 436,138 pesos were sold (6% of total imports) and in 1823, 175,406 pesos (5% of total imports). Although the percentage of total sales between the two years remained roughly the same, the total worth of books sold in 1823 is considerably lower, causing one to wonder if the second figure is accurate. Thus, the statistics provided by Carey's agent, a private record that has not been factored into official summaries, are a welcome addition to our knowledge of Mexico's book consumption in 1822.

AMERICAN BOOK HISTORY

In 1987, a conference at the John Carter Brown Library, underwritten in part by the Library of Congress, invited Americanists from throughout the hemisphere to a dialogue. Its purpose was to find commonalities in their respective colonial histories yet also to explore differences between their print cultures.[26] The conference was unusual in its early date[27] and the fact that it recognized that most national studies of printing and distribution had omitted these larger questions. In Latin America, book historians were often bibliographers such as José Toribio Medina, who in the late nineteenth and early twentieth centuries gathered together a country's or a city's imprints. Such studies, as valuable as they were (and continue to be), had the effect of suggesting the presses only distributed within national boundaries and that readers only consumed their output; thus these bibliographers worked to reinforce the message of the political state (Mexico, Chile, Venezuela, etc.).[28] It is true that some scholars of the colonial period considered larger viceregal administrative units, the movement of printed materials from the metropolis to the colonies, and unofficial if not illegal practices apart from print records such as manuscript writing. Irving Leonard, one of the most important, documented how Spain controlled its American colonies through supervision of books. Dipping below the level of print culture into manuscript, and anonymous oral sources that often found their way into print in eighteenth-century Mexico, Pablo González Casanova and José Miranda studied satire; although they worked beyond the parameters of printing licenses, their work still reflected boundaries set by Spain.

It is only lately that investigators have begun to build on the hemispheric vision that scholars at the John Carter Brown conference introduced. In the United States the emergence of studies variously called Atlantic, trans-American, and comparative has helped to develop that consciousness;[29] Doris Sommer, Kirsten Silva Gruesz, Ralph Bauer, Anna Brickhouse, and Jorge Cañizares-Esguerra are among the most prominent who have gone far to enlarge that vision. The multicultural, Latino, and borderland studies of Nicolás Kanellos and Werner Sollors—emphasizing diversity within the United States—have extended it.[30] Globalization theories have so normalized the larger vision that national literary and cultural histories are coming to seem parochial and old-fashioned.

What U.S. scholars view as the "book," however, is still a topic that sets them off from their Mexican counterparts. Bibliographic studies remain a corner of U.S. scholarship; and although the "history of the book" has seemed to cast a wider net, rallying scholars to pursue questions of the economics and politics of the printing industry, books' modernizing and democratizing functions, and the cultural shifts that books contributed to such as literacy development and the structuring of taste distinctions among classes, and so on, the newer topic still seems antiquarian and remote from more popular critical theory. Robert Darnton, David D. Hall, Hugh Amory, and David S. Shields have labored mightily to examine a book's sociological ramifications. However, a recent issue of the *PMLA* (*Publications of the Modern Language Association of America*, January 2006), with essays on the topic "The History of the Book and the Idea of Literature," reveals a prevailing theorizing in the United States of the book; essays there treat it as an abstraction, a medium or middle state in which orality passes into print and writing is reduced to typography, a device that absorbs its surroundings encyclopedically or separates reality off from aesthetic categories, an object that becomes obsolete as new technologies appear. These definitions reveal a totalizing desire to talk about the book as one phenomenon in all times and places, a preference for talking about a virtual book rather than a real one, an understanding of it as a generic concept, well controlled in scholars' hands, without regard for the multiple copies in the hands of others whose differing perceptions and interpretations create many versions of the same book.

In Spanish America, bibliography has only slowly yielded to the history of the book. Scholars there still are cataloging archives; and even though there have been studies of the role of books in education, particularly examining how, in the case of Mexico, schoolbooks encouraged indigenous peoples to leave behind their native languages and merge into the dominant cultural system, and on reading as a socializing tool, scholars have mostly stayed within the narrative line of one country's print world. Political demands still make national histories of literature, and national cultural studies, useful.[31] Methodologically, the influence of the social sciences has been great on these scholars, causing them to rely heavily on what they have access to and can prove. Thus they generally have not considered foreign books whose origins are obscure; they have avoided questions of distribution and text. Once they recorded an imprint, they considered that their labor was done.[32] Following books' trails into the hands of readers seemed like guess-work, so they left that work to literature specialists. The latter were the only ones who, often caring less about statistical verifiability, dared to tackle the questionable science of "influence" so as to surmise books' impact on readers and then their possible recycling as the thinking of others in new utterances and writings. This tracking was often messy because words and ideas were frequently transmuted in such a way that original sources were obscured. Although in a free society this may happen because a writer wants to proclaim originality and conceal plagiarism, in a closed one the writer is often forced to maintain this obscurity because he is reading clandestine books or talking to dangerous friends. Consequently, the connections traced by literature specialists were frequently dismissed as inconclusive and dubious.

Nevertheless, Latin American scholars have generally preserved a sense of the book's social circumstances that often has eluded Anglo-Americans. Historical methodological preferences may explain the differences. In the United States the Britisher D.F. McKenzie has been an influential voice in determining an understanding of the nature of the book. McKenzie, often labeled a bibliographer, in the two texts that comprise his *Bibliography and the Sociology of Texts*, sets out parameters for that study; unlike bibliographers in Spanish America he does not define bibliography as the accumulation of imprints. Instead in that 1986 work he focuses on "printed books . . . [studying] whether or not the material forms of books, the non-verbal elements of the typographic notations within them, the very disposition of space itself, have an expressive function in conveying meaning" (1999, 17). In situating the development of bibliographic studies alongside formalist analysis of literature, New Criticism and semiotics in the 1940s and onwards, and media studies later, McKenzie has helped to make this self-referential focus appear to be paramount in U.S. book studies. In emphasizing how print fixes the text, he and his followers have tended to disregard external considerations such as authorial intention, the book's content, variants of reception, and so on.

"Reception," a literary notion au courant for a while in the Anglo–U.S. world, would seem to have awakened scholars to a book's social functions. However, reception theory had its roots in European phenomenology so that its followers in the United States—systematizing rather than seeing diversity—mainly equated the notion with determining how the text dictated its readers, how genre conventions determined tacit agreement between author and reader, how a homogenous interpretive community shared attitudes toward that category of writing called "literature," and so on. Their thinking imagined consumers in terms like "the ideal reader" and "implied readers."[33] So, as promising as this notion was for highlighting a book's trajectory after it left the hands of its author and printer, it failed to disclose the conditional, material realities that govern books' lives. Although Anglo-American critics sometimes used "response" in their analyses, which should have suggested individual differences in reacting to a text, "reception" absorbed their attention and made them seem blind to the sociology of literature.[34]

Although British studies have largely influenced U.S. attitudes toward "the book," Latin Americans have mainly gotten their impetus to go beyond their bibliographic studies from French historians of the book—Roger Chartier, Lucien Febre, and Daniel Roche. The emphasis of these scholars, deriving as it does from research into European religious differences and printing connected with the French Revolution, has mainly caused Mexicans like Carmen Castañeda and Laura Beatriz Suárez de la Torre in their recent collections to emphasize the social nature of the book. They have even embraced as a guiding figure the U.S. scholar Robert Darnton, perhaps because his work has focused on eighteenth-century France. The Mexican collections indicate that, as books ceased to be an elite commodity there in the early nineteenth century, they circulated in stores and bookstalls alongside food, candles, rope, and soap (Castañeda 2001, 245–257; Guiot de la Garza 2001, 233–243), political literature and instructional materials were as important to the culture as pleasurable reading, and graphic design for semiliterate peoples was a necessary part of book production. The collections do include some information about the arrival in Mexico in the nineteenth century of foreign printers and booksellers (often French and Spanish), and report that translations, such as the novels of Walter Scott and Eugène Sue, entered the country (Suárez de la Torre 2001, 9). Yet acknowledgment of Mexican consumption of foreign books and cultural borrowing is still infrequent.

It must be noted, however, that Latin Americans have always mentioned in their histories of literature the fact that the Philadelphia printer William Stavely published one of Spanish America's first novels, *Jicoténcal*, there in

1826. Yet they have not pursued the mystery of why that Spanish-language work was published extraterritorially, instead disputing who the anonymous novelist was and failing to trace the book's circulation.[35] Thus, although they knew of the city's relevance to their history, they customarily passed over that source of books as an oddity and did not ask why a U.S. printer was involved.[36]

Continuing research into the "history of the book" holds promise that scholars in the United States and Latin America may extend the possibilities of that field. In the United States the globalizing, hemispheric, Atlantic, and multicultural studies mentioned earlier have helped to push toward recognition of this country's cultural diversity, in the past and in the present, and its interconnectedness with other nations even as it developed its own distinctiveness. Journals like *Early American Literature* have recently extended their understanding of "American" to include Hispanic America. Historians of immigration like David Hackett Fischer, who in his study of Britishness in the United States in *Albion's Seed* explored regional varieties in attitudes toward literacy and the book, and researchers like Janice Radway, who have affirmed as essential to appreciating the country's reading culture the popularity of noncanonical literary forms like *Reader's Digest*, have made scholars aware that the United States is far from uniform in its use of English or in its appreciation of "literature." Linguistic and discourse theories have caused U.S. scholars to rethink the sociology of a text. In Latin America the boom in colonial studies has renewed appreciation of manuscripts, and nonliterary forms, though Latin America's earlier bibliographic tradition, in which distinctions of secular/religious, literary/nonliterary never mattered in the recording of an imprint, facilitated this turn. The work of cultural anthropologists like Néstor García Canclini has recast readers as consumers, thus opening up another view of book history in Latin America.

"Anglo America" often stands in opposition to "Latin America." In continuing to use the "Anglo" label, I use it for its ready reference, though I worry that in doing so I extend the misconception. Repeating it, however, I mean to question it, to challenge the way in which historians have subsumed the multilingualism of the early United States into a later English-language policy, a national history that affirms only British origins. The general public (and not a few history specialists) has the impression that U.S. history began with revolt against British colonial rule. Schoolbooks tell that New England and Virginia, the first colonies, were English-speaking, and we conclude from that too-easy generalization the country's original nature.[37] We fail to realize that many early arrivals spoke varieties of English or some other continental language, and that the country's first documents, though written in English, did not set that language out as a defining mark.[38] Print records show that Dutch-, German-, and Welsh-speaking settlers across New York and the Delaware

River valley demanded their own language materials; and studies of emblems like liberty poles, in the pre-Revolutionary War years, which wordlessly rallied support in those various communities, testify to the fact of the country's regional cultures and multilingualism.[39] After the French and Haitian revolutions (1789, 1791–1804), French speakers came to the eastern seaboard cities in great numbers; if the black slaves who accompanied their white owners did not require the printed word, their presence, for example, in Philadelphia, created a francophone oral underclass with experiences of revolt that differentiated them from Negroes already in the city.[40] With Napoleonic disturbances in Europe, more Frenchmen, more Germans, and Italians and Spaniards arrived—some as short-time utopianists and curious travelers, but others to stay. With the acquisition of Louisiana, French-speaking New Orleans and towns along the Mississippi River basin entered the linguistic mix. Scottish and Irish immigrants went west.[41] At the upper end of the social scale erudition and sacred communication was conducted in Latin, Greek, and Hebrew; at the other end, Indian tongues marked communities.[42] When in the late 1820s Noah Webster's campaign for a standardized English began, his effort can be seen to have reflected a desire to defend the power of the New England English-speaking elite from growing heterogeneity elsewhere. Yet Webster also recognized that the country was beginning to need dictionaries to pull together the varieties of English, and codify which was the norm and which could be discarded; new needs dictated new vocabularies. As English gained currency, other speakers were assumed to either have returned home or to have been absorbed into a majority English-speaking culture; of those who stayed, their frequent Catholicism or Jewishness was marginalized by the dominant Protestantism (although its churches were often linguistically different, that fact has been forgotten). However, today we know that a variety of tongues persisted into the nineteenth and twentieth centuries; Germans in the Midwest, for example, kept separate schools and subscribed to German-language newspapers (printed in the United States as well as abroad), and oral communities in the Far West (among them many Chinese miners and railroad workers) retained their distinctiveness.[43] Unfortunately, these "minor" cultures are still often categorized as "ethnic" rather than "American."[44]

Yet "American" is often a misused signifier. When we in the United States call our part of the hemisphere "America," and lump all the countries to the south into "Latin America" or relegate them to no-name status as "south of the border" or "developing nations," we appropriate the term. In so doing, we not only do our neighbors a disservice but we also forget the complexity of our own nation's birth. It is not clear when the United States began to appropriate "American" and "Atlantic."[45] It may be that the usage began when new nationals in Anglo America simply continued with the parent's label.[46] Certainly this happened in Mexico where insurgents first cried out that they were Americans, rebelling against European injustice; only later did they call themselves "Mexicans."[47]

Recently, calling into question this U.S. selfishness, historians like John H. Elliott and Felipe Fernández Armesto have raised the question as to whether the Americas have a common history.[48] The question implies its answer—yes. These historians recall that European imperialisms for centuries named their colonies in this hemisphere "American," similarly provoked independence there by their respective maladministrations, and set postcolonial development in Anglo and Latin America on parallel courses that really are only different solutions to the same problem. Though the north and the south seem to be separate and of no interest to the other, the fact that others historically have viewed us as a common entity, that is, the Indies, the Americas, the New World, should make us aware of the original imposition of the label and thus its problematic nature as an assignment of Europe. We may have different cultures but both parts of the Americas have invented their identities from the remnants of their respective colonization. "American," then, is a geographical denomination; yet it also has historical significance in referring to a cluster of imperial formations and then, processes of decolonization and nation-building.

My insistence on this definition of "American" is vital to understanding the Robeson/Carey book trade. The correspondence underscores suppositions of "American" that were recognized then and are often forgotten today—that the half of the world whose origins were grounded in submission to a dominant foreign power had come to an enlightened consciousness, had fought for independence, and was now searching for a different self. "American," as the region freed itself from Europe, was a term that was no longer past-looking and deconstructive; instead it was forward-looking and reconstructive. Robeson's cargo was not made up of old colonial books but rather of contemporary essays enabling political refashioning; handlers at both ends of the book circuit looked to them for help in this process.

The Robeson/Carey letters help to restore awareness of the role printers in both the United States and Mexico played in developing not only a national consensus but also an international consciousness. If U.S. historians still remember that at the time of the revolution and in the postwar years printers sensitized the populace to political concerns and brought it to the point of action, they have regularly passed over their importance for succeeding decades, absorbing that industry's contributions into larger surveys. As we have seen they have tended to confine their narratives of the 1800s to domestic issues like slavery and the lead-up to the Civil War. Printing disappeared from their purview, in favor of a focus on manufacturing, banking, and so forth. The Europeanized taste of the urban east coast was elided into a melting-pot experience; and printers' earlier multicultural business and political activism seemed to be irrelevant. Once revolutionary rhetoric subsided and national principles began to be affirmed, U.S. printing became a business like any other, trading diversification for a more lucrative, single language. If thought of at all, printers were considered to be producers of useful reading material for backcountry settlers. This literature (schoolbooks, songbooks, tracts, pious sheets, how-to farming manuals, etc.) was easily passed over; among other reasons it did not fit with belle-lettristic definitions of "literature." The newspapers and magazines they printed were considered to be ephemera. Printers became invisible, servants of nativist authors like James Fenimore Cooper, Washington Irving, and William Cullen Bryant.[49] The print industry's production of partisan speeches, position papers, journalism, and so on, dropped out of the history books as politics was separated from the mainstream and professionalized.

Professionalization also helped the country's multilingualism to disappear. When men like Henry Wadsworth Longfellow entered academia to teach romance languages, foreign languages left the mainstream.[50] Specialists whose reading was work-related (politicians, lawyers, doctors, professors, theologians, historians, etc.) took over from the previous generation's generalists (gentlemen who had their own libraries and cultivated elite pastimes ranging from reading the classics to growing grapes). A new concept, "the general reading public," emerged, which forgot the country's early diversity and made the century's novels, periodic collections like *Harper's Weekly* and *Harper's Monthly*, and the publications of the American Tract Society, appear to be one national "literature." The "general reading public" leveled the market, making believe that English was standard in the United States and absorbing class differences, which had always existed and were growing, into a seemingly classless field of communication.

However, a Spanish-language presence in the United States was probably erased for other reasons. The unilaterally proclaimed Monroe Doctrine emptied the United States of any doubt as to its dominance in the hemisphere and eliminated any thought of pulls-and-tugs with other powers. Spanish, of all the languages the Philadelphia printers offered in the years from 1800 to 1830, which at first was prestigiously attached to a European power but was later diminished by association with Spain's former colony and now a rival, Mexico, would become politically sensitive. As the U.S.–Mexican border fell into dispute, it was expedient to say that the United States was English-speaking and its was the only voice in the hemisphere.

The Carey/Robeson letters, then, help to correct the myth of an English-speaking U.S. nation, immersed in domestic concerns throughout much of the nineteenth and twentieth centuries. They provide evidence of an early realization in both the United States and Mexico that books in common could cement friendly relations.[51] The letters, in their documentation of the fact that political and economic books were those in demand, challenge those literary historians who have built their narratives exclusively around poetry, theater, the novel, and perhaps the essay. The fact that this type of "literature" made up the cargo, and not items of exquisite taste, tells that in the eighteenth and early nineteenth centuries, nonfiction made up much of what readers consumed, and that literary histories have often only partially recorded readers' taste. Devotional literature, instructional manuals, popularizations of scientific discoveries, dictionaries, periodicals, and almanacs were staples of the book market in both the United States and Mexico. Although scholars have sometimes acknowledged the importance of religious materials to a population's mental formation, particularly if the materials were satirical and therefore supposedly imaginative, or if they had a political dimension such as sermons promising "a city on a hill," literary histories have often ignored this important chunk of print production and readers' intake. This narrow focus has also limited scholars as they have traced the travels of major authors, and friendships across borders, only to conclude literary exoticisms.[52] In a comment that suggests a reevaluation of materials, judged to be nonliterary, and translated works, Carmen Castañeda quotes Darnton in wishing that academics would go beyond studies of "el gran-libro" and "el gran-autor" (2002, 8).

It is important to note that the Carey/Robeson letters call into question what Enlightenment literature is often considered to have been, and what path that supposedly international movement took.[53] One interpretation, which sees in that time frame the "nature of the book" emerge as an analogue of the history of science, sweeps Europe's varying developments into the growth of London's print world and scientific community. Adrian Johns, a student of D.F. McKenzie, argues in his magisterial and thought-provoking *The Nature of the Book, Print and Knowledge in the Making* that "early modern Europeans put printing to use to create and maintain knowledge about the natural world." Johns envisions his study "as contributing to the discipline known, rather anachronistically, as the history of science" (1998, 6). Although Johns acknowledges that translations aided in that dispersal of knowledge, he defines them in terms of authorized or unauthorized and pirated, thus suggesting that authorization (and confirmation of authorship by means of government licensing) satisfactorily carried the original text to another country and into another language. It appears that Johns has chosen to understand the Enlightenment as "science," in which data and mathematical symbols can transparently carry "knowledge" from one language community to another, thus enabling him to argue for essential qualities of the book. Although he says that competition between English and Dutch publishers never did outlaw pirating, his sense is that the dependability that the new scientific literature required caused England to try to control its printing industry by standardizing book runs.

Yet, as we will see with the evidence of the political books in Robeson's cargo, Johns's thesis leaves out a good portion of what Enlightenment publishing was, the conditions under which books traveled, and then what grafting one culture's learning and taste onto another's involved. Assertions of veracity as "scientific" discoveries were made, or of fixity, as print was supposed to lock in as fact the results of experiential testing, or of reliability as identical book copies repeated the original, are made moot by the political books and their bootlegged circulation. Their personal opinion-making calls their "knowledge" into question. Mexicans could hardly have considered the books authoritative, rationally inspired, or weighted with "knowledge." Rather, it seems that Mexicans wanted the terminology and venturous thought (not "knowledge") that those foreign political books provided them with so as to write their republican constitutions. As Nicholas Canny and Anthony Pagden have written, underscoring American's need for new expressive categories: "For the rebels, the language of contractualism was morally the only valid one" (1987, 276).

Writing in Spain in 1762, José Clavijo y Fajardo described how traditionalists tried to control the entry of foreign print into the country. Spanish travelers who had been exposed to non-Spanish thought and who might be bringing in dangerous books were cordoned off.[54] Clavijo said that "patriotism, morality and religion" were invoked by narrow-minded Spaniards to condemn books whose origins in liberal France and Protestant, materialistic England they distrusted. Calling attention to the difficulties of transferring thought from an enlightened society to a traditional one, he said that even the new terms required in the physical sciences were thought to be injurious to the faith of persons who did not understand them—for example, "oscillation" and "elastic fibers." "Books," therefore, in Clavijo's view, were suspicious by their very nature, representing a threat to old-fashioned, unquestioning belief.[55] Some books obviously got through to eager Spanish readers, however, so that "books" in that period and place became a measure of a reader's exposure to foreign thought and political persuasion. If, in London as Johns claims, the Royal Stationers were charged with overseeing the publication of books for reasons of proprietary concern, in Spain the Inquisition was still supervising printing and reading for reasons of morality and dogma.

It must be noted parenthetically here that Mexico was ahead of Spain in embracing "the sciences." In the last decades of the eighteenth century, mining technology had entered the colony with the arrival of men trained in Germany. Reversing the Enlightenment spread we normally think of, Mexicans sent their own news of medical, botanical, astronomical, and anthropological finds to Europe, influencing developments in learned circles throughout the continent;

that news traveled via private correspondence but also through communiqués to scientific journals. Yet Mexico stood to learn from British, continental, and U.S. thinkers the political and economic ideas that Spain had generally forbidden in the colony, not only their applicability to home problems but also their example of free expression. This is where Robeson's letters show that, instead of Mexico's understanding of Enlightenment literature being "scientific" in the sense that they were exposed, one by one, to the lessons of new physical discoveries, rather the country's political leaders, the book buyers, learned of the epistemology behind the modern sciences—speculative and pragmatic.

The letters highlight the complexities often surrounding a book's reception. In a closed society readers usually do not get a book in a bookstore, but instead from a friend, who may himself have procured it via a clandestine network. Overviews of state and Inquisition controls, studies of bookstore inventories, and textual comparisons made so as to guess at influence are good places to begin research into a book's life. Yet circumstances of a book's arrival in the bookstore, or the friend's library, and then its hand-off to another—even a guess as to whether its contents have been communicated verbally, or some assessment of the reader's education if a name is inscribed in a volume—are essential considerations before textual critics take over. Paper trails are few and far between, thus blocking measurement of a book's circulation. In societies in which record-keeping is done to please inspectors, even that paper trail is suspect. However, collateral sources may help. For example, advertisements in the *Diario de México*, a Mexico City daily that published from 1805 to 1816, reveal a lively person-to-person trade in books, apart from bookstores yet still open to the scrutiny of ecclesiastical inspectors; newspaper readers offered books for sale and others listed titles they wanted to buy.[56] Inventories in wills, which may be considered to be truthful, can tell what books people owned.

The Robeson/Carey letters identify an often-overlooked category in the corpus of Latin American literature. Robeson's books were written in one country, translated in a second country, and then passed by their handlers to a third country. In carrying the residues of these various cultures, they acquired a flavor that labels like "translated, "foreign," or "international" do not quite capture. Historians of national literatures, who began to write their domestic narratives after independence from Spain, have often not known quite what to do with these peripheral books, either ignoring them, or relegating them to a subcategory called "subversive." These national historians have diminished their importance, perhaps reproducing colonial attitudes that books not vetted by Church authorities and smelling of sedition, Masonry, agnosticism, and Protestantism were best destroyed by forgetting. The books' broad perspectives, like the worldviews of the universal histories of the late-eighteenth, early-nineteenth-century period, were replaced by new nationalistic historiographic practices.[57] For a brief moment in the 1820s and 1830s, works like the Spanish translation of Walter Scott's *Waverley* were read in Mexico.[58] Yet Mexican historians today regularly omit this fact, failing to consider how that story of Scottish revolt against English imperialism resonated with Mexicans. Instead they affirm that domestic books became Mexicans' preferred reading, passing quickly over the moment when Mexicans borrowed ideas and stories from Europeans and North Americans so as to sort out and imagine their own development. They resent "influence," which they feel denies Mexican originality and creativity. After independence military and political events required Mexico's own historicizing; and so, this initial borrowing, as well as later cosmopolitan taste, tended to disappear from their national literary narratives.

Postcolonial critics often write off borrowing or cosmopolitanism as an elite's prolonged, unhealthy dependency on distant culture. These critics are perpetuating the distaste for foreign imports that theories of colonial studies have produced. These have emphasized the control of metropolitan books on colonial thought, suffocating any native creativity. Spain, they say, taught obedience not only by means of didactic and regulatory books but also through the enforcement of a standard language; Spain sought to prescribe correct Castilian usage as sometimes badly educated conquistadores reported back to a court where Castilian was still fighting for dominance with Aragonese. Spanish soldiers and friars, who were coming into contact with Indian languages and instructing new converts in concepts such as "a soul," needed to have Indian speech written down and codified in dictionaries and grammars according to a Latin-based format. Spain restricted entry into its American colonies of imaginative books such as fantastic romances of chivalry and novels, fearing that their reading endangered impressionable minds. Thus, postcolonial critics, in looking to the emergence of native authors and literature as healthy signs of a country's independence, have usually suspected any continuing importation of foreign books of more brainwashing.

In this light residents of today's so-called Third World have often been considered to be unthinking consumers of the output of foreign businessmen — "unthinking" because elites there have been conditioned to believe that their cultures are not yet capable of producing worthy literature and, envious of seemingly advanced civilizations, have preferred foreign works as symbols of their separation from inferior indigenousness. Or they are labeled "unthinking" because populaces there fill their minds with cheap borrowings of the First World's entertainment industries. Both groups have been thought to be victims of First World advertising and campaigns of political clientelism — manipulated into dependence.

I agree that this interpretation of colonial indebtedness is often accurate. However, I am also finding in this study of the arrival of U.S.-printed books in Mexico that the domestic leadership was far more astute in its importation of foreign cultural material than has been recognized. That elite knowingly asked for books that would help the country in its development. In that first phase of self-government, when men were still trapped in their thinking by colonial language, foreign books expressed what they could not yet articulate. At a moment when press restrictions still made some expression impossible, already-printed books took the blame for saying things that Mexicans themselves did not dare say. Mexican presses, far from being intimidated by production from abroad, sold these books and went on to thrive by printing domestic authors who had been inspired by these works.

Thus the Robeson/Carey letters add to postcolonial debate. They correct suppositions regarding the use of imported cultural materials, suggesting that that importation did not just mean dominance. The letters credit the Mexican elite with self-knowledge and judgment that knew when to begin and when to stop importation. They point to a healthy mind-set on the part of a literate elite, desirous of replacing Spanish colonialism with thinking from another source. The letters, in their evidence of U.S. and Mexican desires to engage with one another, reveal an early historical precedent. They place contact between the United States and Mexico at an earlier date and in a different relationship than the border conflict at mid-century; the peaceful business contrasts with hostilities at the Alamo and the U.S. invasion of Mexico in 1846.[59]

——— MY JOURNEY FROM ARCHIVES TO BOOK ———

Knowing of *Jicoténcal* for the primacy of Spanish American letters, I traveled to Philadelphia to explore archives there. In the Historical Society of Pennsylvania, I learned of the Robeson letters. In the Society's collection of Carey business records I found another set of letters—written to Robeson from Carey and Lea, Carey's son and son-in-law to whom he had turned over the business in 1822. The two sets of letters provide a view of early inter-American trade and the role of printing in those postcolonial worlds.

In the first chapter I focus on Philadelphia, studying the city's international flavor and its Hispanic character, in the period from 1800 to 1830. In the second chapter, I reproduce the letters in condensed form. In the third I discuss Mexico and that book world in the light of political turmoil, economic stringencies, and new but still-not-firm press freedoms. In the conclusion I look at the larger picture of influences. In the 1820s the United States, England, and to an extent France, intervened in Spanish America. Authors and printers in England mainly affected South America, whereas the United States had a greater influence on Mexico. This finding should help to correct histories of

Spanish American nationalisms that usually subsume independence movements and early governance into one narrative. Finally, appendices provide lists of Spanish-language books offered for sale in the United States, England, and Mexico, and specify titles that were available.

The records I have consulted do not tell the whole story of Spanish-language publishing in the United States in the nineteenth century; nor do they reveal a complete picture of literary culture in Mexico in the 1820s. But this reporting is a first step in rediscovering ties between their postcolonial American worlds.

NOTES

1. See Anderson. For the United States, see Loughran; for Latin America, Castro-Klarén and Chasteen.

2. Ayers, 37–38.

3. Neither is it a story of one country's literary influence on another since the United States was only then developing its own literature and did not have much to export of its own production. For an excellent example of this type of study, see Fabian on "English Books and Their German Readers." I say this mindful of Davidson's claim in *Revolution and the Word* that "approximately one hundred novels were written between 1789 and 1820" in the United States (viii). Despite this large number, Davidson emphasizes the preponderance in the early republic of British novels (19), omitting, however, consideration of translated French or Spanish novels. "America" in her title is the English-speaking United States. For a history of printing in the Americas, see the original edition of Thomas, in which he discusses printing in Spanish America.

4. On "academic culture" in Spanish America, see Lanning.

5. Hall makes this point in analyzing Thomas's *History*. Hall calls Thomas's description of U.S. printers' and booksellers' dependence on English imports "cultural cringe... before the mother country." Yet Hall says: "American imprints often relied on European authors for their texts and on European presses, paper, and type for their production" (7).

6. On Mexican colonial book history, see Iguíniz. On Inquisition controls in the eighteenth century, see Pérez Marchand and Torres Puga.

7. For discussion of the passage from manuscript to print, see McKitterick, Johns, and in the case of Mexico, the introduction to my *Un manuscrito inédito*.

8. See, for example, *The Commerce of Everyday Life, Selections from The Tatler and The Spectator*, ed. Erin Mackie (Boston: Bedford/St. Martin's, 1998).

9. Henry Mackenzie's *The Man of Feeling* (1771), reissued in an edition by Kenneth C. Slagle (New York: Norton, 1958), presents sentiment, which

is often only considered to be limited to women's experiences and love stories, as proper to men.

10. Remer is valuable for her description of how printers became publishers and booksellers. She valuably concentrates on Mathew Carey and lists all Philadelphia printers and booksellers for 1790, 1795, 1799, and 1805. However, in discussing distant markets, she stays within the borders of the territorial United States.

11. See López.

12. Popular studies of piracy abound but the most serious I have found on the subject are by Baker and Davis.

13. I have studied "decolonizing discourse" in the introduction to my *Lizardi and the Birth of the Novel in Spanish America*.

14. For background on Europe's trade policies, prior to American independence, see Parry and Tracy.

15. For a discussion of contemporary French understanding of the term, and a description of the French ideologues, friends of Franklin and Jefferson, see Echeverria.

16. These distinctions derive from Menéndez y Pelayo, who attributes the taste for this kind of writing to England and the essays of Addison and Steele.

17. "¿Qual govierno comvendrá [sic] à las Americas en las actuales circunstancias? Sin duda el provisorio, por que la incertidumbre es una de sus circunstancias".

18. "La Francia que tenía una nobleza tan antigua, y tan poderosa, un clero opulento, un tan gran número de funcionarios públicos, donde dominaba la religion católica desde Clodovicio, y donde los reformados se habían sostenido a costa de tanta sangre, y tantos sacrificios; donde estaba el imperio del luxo, la disipación, la corrupción, la ambición, unidas a un carácter de ligereza, e inconstancia:: quiso adoptar el sistema guvernatibo [sic] de los Estados Unidos de América.... París baxo la misma institución que la frugal, tranquila y filosófica Pensilvania!" The essayist and brains behind the newspaper was Camilo Henríquez. Samuel B. Johnston, William H. Burbridge and Simon Garrison were the printers of the *Aurora de Chile*. When Johnston returned to the United States, he had published *Letters written during a residence of three years in Chili, containing an Account of the Most Remarkable Events in the Revolutionary Struggles of That Province, with an Interesting Account of the Loss of A Chilian Ship, and Brig of War, by Mutiny, and the Consequent Imprisonment and Sufferings of Several Citizens of the United States, for Six Months, in the Dungeons of Callao* (Erie, PA: R.I. Curtis, 1816). For a study in Spanish see Hernández.

19. Lovett is good on the confusion in Spain's intellectual class as a result of Napoleon's invasion and modernizing reforms; many sided with Napoleon

and thus were vilified and forced to emigrate when the Spanish king returned in 1814. As a result that class was emptied of leadership when Spanish Americans sought direction from Spain, as they mostly had done.

20. Three of Jovellanos's works had recently been reprinted in Mexico: "Pan y toros (oración apologética en defense del estado floreciente de la España, dicha en la plaza de toros el año de 1794 por . . .)" (México: Ontiveros, 1820); "Libertad del comercio" (México: Ontiveros, 1820, 20 pp.); and "D. Gaspar de Jovellanos a sus compatriotas: memoria en que se rebaten las calumnias divulgadas contra los individuos de la junta central. Se da razón de la conducta y opiniones del autor desde que recobró su libertad. Con notas y apéndices" (Puebla: Imprenta del Gobierno Imperial, 1821).

21. For an overview of the man and his government, see Anna.

22. "La dependencia colonial, y la nulidad política son una misma cosa. Un pueblo que depende de una metrópoli, no figura entre las naciones; no es más que una provincia; y si es una colonia, no es más que un fundo, un patrimonio de la metrópoli, destinado a enriquecerla. Como el luxo de un propietario crece a proporción de lo opimo, y rico de sus fundos, las proporciones de la corte de España crecieron inmensamente con la posesión del patrimonio americano".

23. See Gómez de Enterria.

24. On Philadelphia's participation in the opium trade, see Lee.

25. See Rees and Florescano Mayet.

26. See the catalogue for the exhibition by Greer Johnson, addition by Newbury.

27. In May 2002, the Society of Early Americanists' initiative in Early Ibero-/Anglo-American Studies held a summit meeting in Tucson, Arizona, to exchange ideas regarding the comparative histories of early America. Bauer summarizes their results of this conference (2003). Later related conferences have been held at the John Carter Brown Library (Brown University) and the American Antiquarian Society.

28. Although seemingly limited in its focus, the project "Recovering the U.S. Hispanic Heritage," under the direction of Kanellos, has valuably pointed to interrelationships in the Americas.

29. See Taylor's argument that "hemispheric" studies are a more satisfactory label than "American" for rounding up a complete history.

30. Shoemaker's list of American (U.S.) imprints is fundamental. For Spanish-language materials, see also Theroux, Colón, Simmons.

31. The genre of the history of Mexican literature began with Carlos González Peña. Recently the series by centuries of the *Historia de la literature Mexicana*, under the general editorship of Beatriz Garza Cuarón (UNAM y Siglo XXI), has begun a rewriting. For studies of literature in a cultural context,

see the collections edited by Castañeda y Cortés and by Suárez de la Torre. The focus on bookstores by Zahar Vergara is also interesting.

32. A notable exception is the work done by the Seminario de Historia de la Educación en México. Members (Anne Staples, Dorothy Tanck Estrada, and Josefina Zoraida Vázquez) have centered their studies of reading around the topic of education.

33. See my summary of reader response theory in "Defining the 'Colonial Reader'."

34. The Britisher McKitterick, in his valuable discussion of the history of the book and the history of reading, nevertheless asserts the importance of print when he concludes: "theories of reading, like theories of authorship and of textual development, must derive from bibliographical analysis, even if they can never be wholly dependent on such analysis" (223).

35. The debate is primarily between Leal and Cortina, who argue that the author was Félix Varela, and González Acosta, who is equally convinced that it was José María Heredia. Bueno discounts the Heredia theory. Brickhouse believes that several might have collaborated in the work—Heredia, Vicente Rocafuerte, and Varela.

36. An exception was Onís who worked in the United States. As valuable as his study is, he did not consider the market for Spanish-language books.

37. This impression has been enhanced in the modern period by H.L. Mencken's work.

38. Scholars are recently retrieving the importance of other U.S. languages. See Roeber for German and Dutch books, and Baer-Wallis for Irish and German language usage.

39. Fischer says in *Liberty and Freedom*: "The Liberty Pole had a meaning that suited the condition of New York, where many ethnic groups lived side by side but never quite together. Their strongest bond was a common desire for liberty to keep their own customs, to worship in their way, and to be secure in their property" (42).

40. See Dessens. Branson and Patrick in Geggus make the point that the several Catholic churches in Philadelphia permitted these coloreds to assimilate into their congregations, though the city's almshouses often refused them help.

41. Fundamental for this appreciation are the works by Fischer.

42. See Shoemaker; H.A. Salisbury published in Buffalo, NY, *Kiansa, Hymns in the Seneca Language*, compiled by Jabez Backas Hyde (40 pp.) in 1819.

43. For German Americans, see Peterson.

44. Sollors's collection, useful in its spread, tends to concentrate on the diversity of language usage in the United States, particularly in the late nineteenth century. Its essayists mention some writing in those different languages;

for this see in Sollors "Worlds of Difference, Lin Yutang, Lao She, and the Significance of Chinese-Language Writing in America" by Xiao-huang Yin (176–187). Spanish is considered to be limited to the Southwest and to Ladino (Jewish-Spanish) newspapers in the first half of the twentieth century. Yet coverage of the cooperation of U.S. publishers and booksellers in furthering this bilingualism is slim.

45. For example, Kraus focuses on the ties between England, northern Europe and the U.S. For a critical examination of Atlantic studies, see Colley.

46. Confirming my hypothesis are studies by Shields, and Amory and Hall.

47. See Jiménez Codinach, 1997, 103–122. Officially, in 1824 when the first constitution was promulgated, the country's name, Estados Unidos de México (United States of Mexico), was modeled after the federation of states to the north. This formulation first appeared in the bilingual *Gaceta de Texas*, and Jiménez Codinach speculates on whether the idea came from José Alvarez de Toledo, one of the editors who was Cuban, or the other editor, the U.S. agent, William Shaler.

48. See the several works by Elliott. For the topic in terms of literature see Chevigny and Laguardia; Pérez Firmat. Earlier historiography done in the 1940s, which promised such an approach— for example, Whitaker— is only now beginning to yield results.

49. For example, Jackson's study of authorship largely sets aside questions of printers despite its consideration of "economies."

50. Hispanism today is still considered to be an English-language discipline, confined to literary studies and the university. See Kagan.

51. Rodrigo Lazo has valuably studied how Cubans in the United States published more than seventy newspapers for Cuban readers during the nineteenth century (3). Yet, as astounding as that fact is, he does not say who these printers were and what carriers took their goods to the island.

52. See, for example, the study of the maritime channel for the novel (between England and France), by Cohen and Dever. Brickhouse is a notable exception in her coverage of distribution.

53. See Torre's collection, *The Enlightenment in America, 1720–1825* for a valuable examination of its reach in America. However, Torre defines "America" as the emerging United States and does not consider Spanish America.

54. Quoted in Sarrailh, 384.

55. Clavijo (1730–1806) was editor of *El Pensador*, a Madrid paper that ran from 1761 to 1767; the paper helped introduce Rousseau into Spain. Clavijo had been educated in France, translated Buffon's *Histoire naturelle* into Spanish, and advocated modernization in Spain according to the French model. He was persecuted during the Inquisition.

56. Studies of that nineteenth-century book world in Mexico include Wold, Delgado Carranco, Guerra, and my two books.

57. See my study of the universal history, written by the Cuban José María Heredia, who emigrated to the United States and then later moved to Mexico. Heredia's book was a translation (and adaptation for Mexico's reading public) of the work by the Scot, Alexander Fraser Tytler, *Elements of General History, Ancient and Modern*, to which are added a table of chronology and comparative view of ancient and modern geography.

58. Scott published the novel anonymously in 1814, thus beginning a series of novels described as the *Waverley* novels, and only acknowledging authorship in 1827. The translator to Spanish, Heredia, probably acquired copies of Scott's novel and Tytler's history when he was in the United States between 1823 and 1825. He published his translation of *Waverley* in Mexico in 1833 (3 vols.).

59. Spanish-language publishing was already beginning in 1823 in San Antonio, Texas (called Béxar). The following are listed in Shoemaker: "Manifiesto del Supremo poder executivo a la nación. Reimpreso en Béxar, en la imprenta del govierno de la Provincia de Texas, June 10, 1823" (Asbridge, impresor, 8 pp.); "Noticias de gobierno de Texas. Oficio dirigido al Supremo poder ejecutivo" (Imprenta del gobierno de Texas, 11 junio 1823, Asbridge impresor [broadsheet]); "Junta gubernativa de la Provincia de Texas . . . Dios y liberta, Béxar, 8 de julio 1823" (Imprenta del gobierno de Texas, en San Antonio de Béxar, 1823); Texas Courier. Prospecto. To the advocates of Light and reason, the friends of the Provinces of Texas (San Antonio de Béxar: Imprenta del gobierno de Texas, Abril 9, 1823 [broadsheet, parallel Spanish and English columns]).

1

PHILADELPHIA

1816 WAS AN IMPORTANT DATE FOR U.S. publishers. In that year the duty on books imported from England was raised from 5% to 15%. As a result, Mathew Carey began then to print his own editions of all the English and continental books he could get his hands on. Copyright laws in those years protected U.S. authors but did not extend to foreign books. As William Clarkin writes in describing Carey's 1821 reprint of Lord Byron's *Marino Faliero, Doge of Venice*:

> This is an example of the outrageous piracy and piratical competition engaged in by American publishers of that time. America would not accept international copyright until 1891. Until then, American publishers could and did steal literary material from any source—but especially from Britain. Scott, Byron, Hunt, and the other British writers were very much the rage in the United States. Carey had his agents in England and Scotland who would buy a copy of a newly published work and ship it post-haste to him in Philadelphia. Arrived there, Carey would have it printed up and bound—to be shipped to his booksellers throughout the Union. He did this with all speed because, of course, his rivals, the Harpers in New York City, were doing the very same thing. Whoever got the work out first would make great profit. It is small wonder, then, that these books often got themselves published in a sloppy, slam-bang manner. It wasn't very moral, but it was legal. (1984, 211)

However, it is worth noting that Carey was generous with his own materials. For example, in 1822 Carey wrote and published a long pamphlet on the present economic condition of the United States in which he declared "any bookseller desirous to republish it, from motives of public spirit or profit, has the writer's Permission."[1]

Carey (1750–1839) had come to the United States from Ireland in 1784. He had begun his printing career in Dublin where the pamphlets he wrote and had published antagonized both Catholics and Ireland's Protestant English overlords.[2] To escape his father sent him off to France where the youth met Benjamin Franklin and the Marquis de Lafayette, whose friendships would later benefit him. He returned to Ireland but then had to flee again, this time to the United States. In Philadelphia he began his business by publishing a newspaper that quickly gained circulation when in it he reproduced debate from the state's General Assembly. He was, then, first a printer, though later he left printing to others, concentrating on publishing and selling books. A "printer" was just that, a craftsman who was often a jobber who contracted for a single item; a "publisher" backed authors by taking on the financial risk, securing copyright, calculating the total cost by arranging for typesetting, paper, bookbinding, and so on; a "bookseller" marketed the book, either by wholesale or retail.[3] Carey's shop on Chestnut St. grew to be a center for the book industry. Printers and booksellers in other places in the United States, principally New York and Boston, also flourished in the last decade of the eighteenth century and the first decades of the nineteenth; Carey cooperated with some, jointly publishing and exchanging books for sale, but other times he competed with them. Several of these U.S. printers were also Irish expatriates.

Rosalind Remer tells how during the colonial period American printers did business by printing newspapers, cheap pamphlets, almanacs, as well as service items such as legal forms. American booksellers mainly got books from England, as did England's other colonies, Scotland and Ireland. Some books did come to the American colonies as Scottish and Irish reprints of London editions. But London printers were their principal suppliers, exporting probably half their production to America. Yet London usually ignored the wishes of American readers. Rather than an assortment, the printers sent many copies of one book; and these were often the books that had remained unsold in London, dumped on the U.S. market. London decided which authors would be printed and assumed the financial risk of those decisions. With independence, U.S. printers developed the newspaper and political pamphlet business they had already begun; and, cut off from London, they looked elsewhere for book imports.[4]

One logical source was the Irish print shops. In 1788 Carey began a business relationship with a Dublin friend, Patrick Byrne, which lasted over 25 years and was firm enough to allow for insurance and Carey's return of unsold merchandise.[5] Over one two-and-a-half-year period, Byrne supplied Carey with fourteen shipments of books, whose value totaled over 2,000 Irish pounds. Initially, Carey warned Byrne about American taste:

> The people here are by many degrees more enlightened than on your side of the Atlantic. [There are] Few, even of the farmers, who have not a taste for Milton, Thompson, Young, &&. The vile tales & burton books, whereof thousands are annually disseminated throughout Ireland, & which corrupt the taste, (and may I not add, the morals) of the youth of both sexes, find here no circulation.... When, therefore, you mean to supply the American market with literary food, let it be of the most solid and substantial kind;

history, voyages, philosophy, science, and well chosen school books. (Kinane 1994, 317–318)

At first sales were slow. Religious books, law materials, dictionaries and school texts comprised much of the demand, whereas novels and "elegantly bound" volumes mostly remained unsold. The Carey–Byrne correspondence also tells of Carey's continuing interest in Irish politics; Byrne reported that Mathew's brother, William, had been arrested and committed to Newgate (presumably for Catholic radicalism). This early partnership between Carey and an overseas bookseller helps explain the Carey firm's later willingness to undertake business with Mexico. Carey's efforts to experiment with sales, his recognition of the viability of transatlantic trade and rejection of U.S. insularity so as to internationalize a home readership would be hallmarks of his shop. The correspondence documents Carey's abhorrence of smuggling; when Byrne suggested in one letter that he could undervalue the value of one shipment for purposes of duty avoidance (Kinane, 1994, 322), Carey refused. This detail regarding Carey's scruples is pertinent for thinking that Carey did not consider Robeson's later activities in Mexico to be illegal, although he certainly knew of Robeson's deceptions along the same lines.

Carey's business was associated with anti-English, pro-American sentiment. Catholic, he published the first Catholic Bible in the United States in 1790. His faith, his Irish background and contacts, and immigrant experience set him apart from established, mainly Protestant U.S. printers. He was active in a Hibernian Society and apparently, as we will see later, appreciated the needs of Catholic readers. Between 1785 and 1822, when his son and son-in-law took over the firm and it became H.C. Carey and I. Lea,[6] he published almost 1,100 books. He and other printers were kept busy in those years publishing the new country's first government documents, newspapers, political pamphlets, school books (atlases, dictionaries, primers), almanacs, stationery and forms, and so forth. A sign of Carey's entrepreneurial spirit is his proposal in 1801 that printers from Boston, New York, and Philadelphia hold a yearly book fair, on the model of Frankfurt and Leipzig.

Philadelphia's appetite for reading in those years is documented in James Mease's *Picture of Philadelphia*, published there in 1811. Mease says that Philadelphia had 51 printing offices, containing a total of 153 presses, and that these produced annually 500,000 volumes. "There are upwards of sixty engravers in Philadelphia, and twenty more would find constant employ" (86–87). Philadelphia had eight daily papers (four in the morning and four in the evening), nine weekly papers, two semi-weekly, two tri-weekly, three periodical works monthly, and four quarterly.

Carey's firm stood out from this array for several reasons. Although many printers used their newspapers and pamphlets to promote political factions and parties, Carey tried to keep a distance from politics. Instead he soon became identified with Bible printing, and with supplying "literature." The concept emerges in the manifesto of the Philadelphia Company of Booksellers, formed in 1802 to which Carey was a party:

> The growing interests of LITERATURE in this rising Empire, have, for some time, appeared to the Booksellers of Philadelphia to demand a vehicle to communicate literary information, as well of Books already published, as of those contemplated to be executed. Under this idea, they have commenced the present Paper, printed at their joint expense, and to be distributed to persons likely to afford patronage to the production of the Press - whether those merely calculated to afford amusement to the passing hour, or those which unfold the doors of the Temple of Learning. (quoted in Remer 1996, 61)

Literature as amusement or instruction represented a new category for printers. It promised a readership beyond the political press, and materials beyond ephemera. Consequently, Carey increasingly began to focus his business on books rather than on timely newspapers and pamphlets; and, in addition to importing books from Ireland after independence, he turned to the continent.

The United States signed a peace treaty with Great Britain in early 1815, thus somewhat regularizing sea traffic with London and opening up trade with other countries. Philadelphia then began to enjoy the availability of "fancy goods" from London and Paris, hides from Russia, and fine woods from Campeche, tea and nankeen from India and Canton—as well as books. In those months the Philadelphia newspaper, *The Aurora, The General Advertiser*, was filled with ads for the luxury commodities that Philadelphians apparently had the income to purchase—either as consumers or as speculators and middlemen. J.L. Fernagus and V. de Gelone regularly announced French books for sale; and Carey advertised that he, too, was selling imported books. On April 7, 1815, the *Aurora* said that Carey had 28 Spanish items for sale.[7] One was authored by a Spanish American; another, a schoolbook written by one of Carey's contract writers in Philadelphia and published by Carey in 1811, would already have been in Carey's warehouse; one told of a European Masonic trial; the rest were Spanish imprints, classics from Spain's Golden Age (1550–1680) or works by more recent Peninsula writers.

This list of Spanish books that Carey was selling in his shop, included here in Appendix A, testifies to his interest in foreign-language publishing (in French, Italian, Spanish, German, Latin, etc.). It shows his reliance on imports but also his patronage of non-English-speaking writers in Philadelphia. Reprinting foreign books that had acquired a reputation in Europe guaranteed sales; however, putting into print works by unknown domestic authors was riskier and Carey sometimes shared the risk of printing and marketing with others. For example, in 1805 the Philadelphia firm of Thomas and George

Palmer printed *Catèchisme contenant les elements de la Foi Catholique-Romaine, avec les priers de matin & du soir, les Litanies du S. Nom de Jesus, Celles de la S. Vierge, & et le Cantique de M. de Fénelon sur la passion de N.S.J.C.*[8] Carey sold the catechism in his bookstore.

In 1808 Carey published Bernardin de Saint-Pierre's novel, *Paul et Virginie*, in a Spanish translation by Josef Miguel Alea.[9] The publication is significant for its linkage of two non-English-speaking cultures via a U.S. medium. Carey clearly was gambling that a Spanish-speaking readership — whether within the geographical confines of the United States or without in Mexico and the Caribbean — would welcome this recently published work of French literature (1787) whose tropical love story takes place in the French colony of Mauritius in the Indian Ocean. In 1786 Mauritius was declared a free port, thus allowing access to India's rich markets, and giving Spaniards another route to their colony in Manila.[10] Thus the story of commerce and black slavery, apart from its love angle, might have had contemporary meaning for U.S. readers. It is not known how that book might have reached distant markets; but readership for another is more obvious — students of the Spanish language, either children or adults: In 1809 the Philadelphia printers Thomas and William Bradford published a collection of readings in Spanish, *Rasgos históricos y morales: sacados de autores célebres de diversas naciones y destinados para la instrucción y entretenimiento de los estudiantes del idioma español*,[11] gathered together by the Philadelphian, Santiago [James] Matthias James O'Conway; Carey would later employ O'Conway as a translator.

Carey may have been led to recognize that translations among the foreign languages and translations (often adaptations) of continental works into English might be lucrative when he brought several religious works into English. In 1808 Carey printed *The Old Testament, translated out of the original* and *The Psalms of David, in metre, translated and diligently compared with the original text and former translations: more plain, smooth, and agreeable to the text than any hereto fore: allowed by the authority of the Kirk of Scotland, and appointed to be sung in congregations and families*. Translations from exotic places — probably fiction masquerading as "translation" — also interested Carey. In 1816 he published *Gulzara, princess of Persia; or The Virgin Queen*, described as "collected from the original Persian"; the following year he published a work whose translation path seems tortuous — *The hero; or The adventures of a night [sic]; a romance translated from the Arabic into Iroquese [sic] and From French into English*. Indeed, the fiction of contemporary writers like Robert Southey and Leigh Hunt, some of whose works Carey printed, was often a mixture of pretended translation, travel exoticisms, and evocations of ancient myth and history.[12]

Carey gradually left off printing religious literature to focus instead on publishing entertaining secular works, which could be made available in translation—works brought into English from other languages, or translations from one foreign language to another. In 1811 he printed the English translation of a Spanish play by Lope de Vega, "The Father Outwitted."[13] In that same year he published in Spanish three novels by the controversial Atanasio Céspedes y Monroy: *El desafío, La paisana virtuosa,* and *La presumida orgullosa* (*La paisana virtuosa* shows that Carey thought that cultural differences did not much matter to his readers because he illustrated it with a plate he had for his edition of *Charlotte Temple*).[14] "Céspedes y Monroy" was a pseudonym for the Peruvian Pablo de Olavide y Jáuregui (1725–1803) who had gone to Spain, where he was imprisoned by the Inquisition. He escaped and fled to France where he attracted the support of writers like d'Alembert, Voltaire, and Marmontel. In 1797 Olavide plotted with Francisco de Miranda and other Spanish Americans in their rebellion against Spain. Olavide's story reached the United States when an account of his persecution by the Inquisition was appended to the end of a work published in Baltimore in 1803—"The Adventures of Joseph Pignata."[15] We will learn more of this high-visibility writer later.

Suggesting a category of Spanish-language reader besides native Spanish-speakers that Philadelphia publishers might also have aimed for is a curious publication that Carey put out in 1810: *La Galatea de Miguel de Cervantes, imitada, compendiada, concluída por Jean Pierre Claris de Florian* (*The Galatea by Miguel de Cervantes, an imitation, abridged and with an ending provided by Jean Pierre Claris de Florian*).[16] Florian (1755–1794), a Frenchman who had ties to Spain because his mother was Spanish,[17] seems to have taken the original Spanish text into French; Casiano Pellicer translated it back into Spanish; and then Florian rewrote the whole thing, giving it another ending.[18] Florian's works were popular in France and Spain, and also in the United States, where several of his novelettes were published in English translation: *Claudine, or, The Savoyarde* (1800, 1813);[19] *Gonzalvo, or, The Spanish Knight, A Romance* (1801);[20] *William Tell; or Swisserland Delivered* (1810, 1820, 1823).[21] In 1811 a play by George Colman, "The Africans, or War, Love and Duty," based on Florian's novelette, *Selico*, was performed in a Philadelphia theater.[22]

Carey's publication of Florian's take-off of *La Galatea*, rather than Cervantes's original, points to a market composed of English speakers who wanted to learn Spanish—or at least become familiar with Spain's culture. This watered-down version of an intellectually rich and linguistically complex classic suggests a budding interest in the language in the United States, and thus buyers among new recruits. Indeed Thomas Jefferson had studied Spanish while he was in Paris and wrote part of a Greek grammar in that language, believing that Spanish would be important to the future of English-speaking Americans. His example, as well as that of Henry Clay who also advocated the importance of Spanish America for the United States, probably inspired others to study Spanish.

In fact, several Spanish-language study books appeared in the United States in those years. In 1810 O'Conway had published in Philadelphia by Thomas Dobson his *Hispano-Anglo Grammar*.[23] In 1811 Carey published Charles Le Brun's *El director de los niños para aprender a deletrear y leer; o método para facilitar los progresos de los niños quando se mandan por la primera vez a la escuela*;[24] the work was richly illustrated. In 1820 the New York printer Guillermo (William) Grattan published *Elementos de la lengua castellana, fundados en los principios establecidos por la Academia española*, written by Mariano Velázquez de la Cadena.[25] In 1822 Carey and Lea published—as we will see later—*The elements of Spanish and English Conversation; with new, familiar, and easy dialogues, designed particularly for the use of schools*, written by Edward Barry. In 1823 Carey and Lea published two books by Henry Neuman—*A new dictionary of the Spanish and English languages*[26] and its translation, *Diccionario nuevo de las dos lenguas, español e inglés*.[27] In 1822 Mariano Cubí y Soler had published in Baltimore two Spanish textbooks: *Extracto de los más célebres escritores y poetas españoles en dos partes*,[28] written for the Spanish school there, Colegio de Santa María; and *A new Spanish grammar, adapted to every class of learners*, for English speakers of all ages.[29] In 1823, conscious of the needs of English-speaking businessmen who were looking to expand their interests into Spanish-speaking areas, he had published in Baltimore *The English and Spanish Conductor, being a series of familiar dialogues and commercial letters*[30] and *A new pocket dictionary of the English and Spanish languages, wherein the words which are subjected to two or more spellings are written in their different orthographies. Compiled from Neuman, Connelly &*.[31] In 1824 Cubí y Soler had published in Baltimore his *Gramática de la lengua castellana, adaptada a toda clase de discípulos, a todo sistema de enseñanza*.[32] Maryland's Catholic history had drawn Spanish speakers, and some were also living in the formerly Spanish-held Louisiana and Florida. Many, however, were settled in the Philadelphia and New York areas.

After 1816 Carey accelerated the publication and sale of foreign-language books. An 1816 catalogue of books available at his shop lists 199 works in German, presumably for German speakers, particularly in the region around Philadelphia.[33] The size of this German-speaking community—and a measure of the interconnectedness between the various language groups in the United States—is the fact that a work by the Spaniard José Clavijo y Fajardo (whom we have seen) was published in 1816 in Philadelphia in a German translation by Thaddeus Spottvogel—*Der deutsche mann und der patriot im streit; oder, Das literarisch-politisch halsgericht*.[34] French speakers had come into Philadelphia in great numbers in 1793 in the wake of the slave revolt in Santo Domingo, thus creating a sizeable community and market for French-language novels, catechisms, and so on; understandably, these ousted members of the nobility did not want to read republican literature but rather news of the French court and Napoleonic reverses.[35] In 1822 Carey published a French grammar to be used in classes at the newly founded West Point.[36] In 1818, a Philadelphia press called "Stamperia delle provincie unite" published Niccolò Machiavelli's *Opere istoriche e politiche*, and in 1819 the same press published Gaetano Filangieri's *La scienza della legislazione* in five volumes.[37]

THE BEGINNINGS OF AN HISPANIC VOGUE IN THE UNITED STATES

Here I concentrate on the Spanish-related materials that Carey and other U.S. printers and booksellers made available—English-language materials that pertained to Spain and her empire, and those written in Spanish. Generally, I will consider only pamphlets and books, omitting newspaper articles and exchanges, and broadsides. It is the logic behind publishing these items, and the evolution of that business for domestic markets to include an export trade, that I want to explore.

Interest in Spain was part of the concern for international affairs that the United States began to show around 1800. As Napoleon's armies pushed back established monarchies in Europe, and the Caribbean became a theater where English, French, and Spanish forces struggled for dominance and even threatened U.S. territorial sovereignty on its northern, southern, and western borders, U.S. publishers responded with political reporting for a readership increasingly concerned with those changes. Treaties were signed; the Louisiana Purchase in 1803, though it seemed to be a boon to the United States by doubling its size, nevertheless involved the nation in a dispute with Spain that was only resolved with the Adams–Onís treaty in 1819. As its ships ventured into the Mediterranean, the Atlantic, and the Gulf, the United States confronted new enemies. Travelers and immigrants brought news of their respective homelands that both threatened U.S. stability but that also gave U.S. businessmen reason to think they could cash in on those disruptions.

Carey's publication record in the period from 1800 to 1830 allows measure of that developing international consciousness. As we have seen, Carey seems to have begun his notice in 1810–1811 with the publication of a few Spanish-language novels. Around 1819–1820 he began to publish political works (though they seemed to avoid topicality, their references to tyranny and freedom contrast with the neutrality Carey preferred in his English-language publications). In 1822, when his book agent went to Mexico with these political titles, Carey seems to have been at his most optimistic. When that venture apparently failed, he (and his firm) seem to have lost interest in Spanish-language publishing, concluding that U.S. demand was too small and the risks of selling in Spanish America too great. He then retreated to English-language publishing for the domestic market. Yet other U.S. printers went on publishing in Spanish and putting out English-language materials that pertained to the Spanish-speaking world until the 1830s.[38]

In studying the U.S. Revolutionary War and the postwar years U.S. historians have mainly focused on the relationship with Great Britain; England was seen to threaten the United States as it controlled Caribbean shipping and extended its interests in Central America. However, Thomas Chávez has recently argued that Spain played a greater role in U.S. life during that period than has previously been acknowledged. The Spanish royal family, allied with France in Bourbon family pacts so as to counter English power in Europe and in the Americas, contributed to the U.S. war with gunpowder and Mexican silver paid to U.S. rebels via Havana. That silver, which came into banks in New Orleans and Philadelphia, helped the United States but it also made its way from Philadelphia to Paris, thus aiding in that country's later revolution.[39] The Spanish governor in New Orleans, Bernardo de Gálvez, averted his eyes when supplies entered the Mississippi River to go upriver to Natchez, St. Louis, and Pittsburgh. Spain entered the U.S. war against Britain, then, for reasons of loyalty to France but also to try to protect its American shipping, which England was interrupting. Chávez claims that Spain's help to the U.S. colonists was kept quiet so that Spain's own colonies would not resent what could seem to them to be Madrid's hypocrisy and themselves rebel. He shows that diplomacy between U.S. representatives and Spanish officials was carried out in Paris, Madrid, Cádiz—and in U.S. cities like Philadelphia.

Although the United States never really left behind its cultural allegiance to England, in the last decade of the eighteenth century and the first decades of the nineteenth, the young nation began then to open up to trade and diplomatic contact with other European countries. France's Enlightenment innovations and revolutionary sympathies with the United States, promoted by famous friendships between U.S. diplomats and Frenchmen, are well known. Print records, though they tell of a predominating English influence on U.S. culture, nevertheless also reveal an appreciation among the U.S. population of Spanish history and artistic accomplishment. In the 1790s plays by Miguel de Cervantes and Pedro Calderón de la Barca, classic writers from Spain's Golden Age, were performed in Philadelphia theaters. Visitors' narratives also tell of a cosmopolitanism that went beyond Englishness. A Spanish priest, Antonio José Ruiz de Padrón, claimed to have visited with Franklin at his Philadelphia home where he discussed religious freedom with Protestant ministers. (Franklin had returned to Philadelphia by 1785 so the meeting, which the priest failed to date, would have happened after that.) Ruiz de Padrón said he had been shipwrecked off the coast of Pennsylvania and that Franklin had invited him to a *tertulia* where the Catholic learned that quiet dialogue with knowledgeable men was better than the rages against impious Protestants he had been accustomed to delivering. He bragged that then Franklin invited him to preach a sermon in Spanish in "the" Catholic church in Philadelphia to a congregation made up of Spaniards on the frigates of war, *La Héroe*, *La Loreto*, and eight or ten ships from Florida that were in Philadelphia's harbor. In that sermon, which was quickly translated into English, he criticized the Inquisition; and that version, he said, caused more than 80 Protestant families to have their children baptized Catholic, now understanding that the Inquisition was not part of essential Catholic doctrine. He said that his was the first sermon of the Roman Catholic Apostolic faith to have been preached in the United States and that he also gave sermons in New York and Baltimore. Ruiz de Padrón later became an outspoken delegate to the Cortes de Cádiz, leaving Spain for London after the despotic Spanish king, Fernando VII, returned in 1814.[40]

The liberalism and tolerance that Ruiz de Padrón found in Philadelphia is apparent in the output of Philadelphia's print shops. In the 1790s U.S. printers bootlegged to Europe works that printers there were forbidden to publish; for example, Madrid Inquisition records for 1805 list the Philadelphia-printed Marquis de Sade's *Justine* (1791, 1794).[41] In fact, "Philadelphia," as a true but also fictitious attribution, was notorious in Europe for its liberal printing. A document that became the credo for Spanish American independence appeared with that imprint in 1799, though it was really printed in London. "Lettres aux espagnols-americains," written by the Peruvian Jesuit, Juan Vizcardo y Guzmán, circulated widely throughout Europe, Spanish America, and the United States. A Spanish version, "Carta a los españoles americanos" came out in 1801, printed in London by P. Boyle.[42] The ruse for printing it initially with a false Philadelphia imprint was the brainchild of Francisco de Miranda, a Venezuelan patriot, who saw in Vizcardo's call to arms the lessons of Rousseau's *Social Contract*, adapted to Catholic America. Miranda, who had toured in the United States in 1783–1784 and had important contacts here and in Europe, facilitated the document's printing and distribution—in both its print and manuscript forms.[43] "Philadelphia," then, whose printers conceivably could have published the inflammatory work because they were known for such printing and export, deflected attention away from the author, patron, and London printer.

Contemporary politics, understood in the context of ongoing European imperial designs and burgeoning American independence movements throughout Spanish America, was the stimulus for much U.S. publishing. In

1801 the Philadelphia printers Joseph and James Crukshank published *Voyages of Don George Juan and Don Antonio de Ulloa to South America*;[44] that account by Spanish explorers of their inspection tour in 1735–1746 had earlier quickened European interest in the Americas that Spanish governance had closed off. For example, William Robertson had relied on the account for his 1777 *History of America*, which combined the histories of British and Spanish America. In 1808 James Biggs, a U.S. officer who had accompanied Miranda in a failed attempt to incite rebellion on the Venezuela coast, had had published in Boston his *History of D. Francisco de Miranda's attempt to effect Revolution in South America in a series of letters, by a gentleman who was an officer under the General, to his friend in the United States. To which are annexed sketches of the life of Miranda and geographical notices of Caracas*. Biggs's work was so popular that re-editions followed in 1809, 1811, 1812, and 1819.[45]

U.S. interest in international politics intensified when Europeans came and debated one another in the U.S. press. For example, Joseph Priestley, living then in the United States, took on C. F. Volney regarding the latter's *Ruins, or Meditations on the Revolution of Empires*. Priestley, a Deist, attacked him as an "unbeliever" and criticized the work. Volney was in the United States from 1795 until 1798 when John Adams, who considered him a French agent preparing for the invasion of Louisiana, made his stay uncomfortable and he returned to France. Volney's *Ruins* had been published originally in Paris in 1791. Three English translations soon followed—one published in London, one in Philadelphia, and then one in Paris in which Volney helped the U.S. writer, Joel Barlow, to smooth out the language of the others.[46] The work was immensely popular in its story of a traveler to Syria who witnessed there the decline of the great Asian empires and meditated on the probable fall of the European empires "on the banks of the Seine, the Thames, or the Zuy-der-Zee." Rather than fate or the hand of God, Volney claimed, "civil and religious tyrants" caused empires to die. Volney's combination of moral philosophy, comparative anthropology, and political commentary, which to some extent borrowed from Rousseau's notions of inequality and property in its analysis of the principles of society, was a valuable corrective to the work of the French naturalist, the Comte de Buffon. The latter had compared animal and human life in the Old and New Worlds in his *Histoire naturelle* (1749–1804) and said that the New was inferior. Volney, on the other hand, who found decay and corruption in the Old and had come to the United States to escape, was widely read in the Americas.

In 1821 Carey published the Spanish translation of another work by Volney, *La loi naturelle ou Catéchisme du Citoyen Français* (*Natural Law or Catechism of the French Citizen*), which Volney had had published in France in 1793. A resident translator in Philadelphia who worked for Carey, Santiago Felipe

Puglia, took this work, a synthesis of some of the ideas of *Ruins* in a question-and-answer format, into Spanish. The shorter *Catequismo* was a logical import into Mexico where, at that moment, intellectuals were rethinking their ties with Spain; and, although the title did not go into Robeson's shipment, we will see that he requested it for the future. Like the Catholic catechism, Volney's was arranged according to virtues and vices. But its emphasis on morality as social utility and its explanation of natural law in the secular Enlightenment language of peace and tolerance of the rights of others (though the Deist author did acknowledge God) seemed to be an attractive supplement to religion's system.

Napoleon's advance into Spain in 1808 deepened the interest of U.S. readers in Spain and its empire. When the French took the Spanish king prisoner, when the Spanish people rebelled and England joined with them in a war against the French, when with Napoleon's defeat and the Congresses of Vienna (1814) and Aix-la-Chapelle (1818) European powers reestablished monarchism and traded territories, U.S. readers were shaken by the changing world order. As kings reasserted their powers and claims, Americans could understand a threat to their own security. They read the Abbé Dominique Georges Frédéric de Pradt's several reports on the European congresses for what they might tell of the plans of the European monarchs to reinvade the Americas and take back their former possessions.[47] Readers asked for news of Napoleon's military expeditions, which ranged over the European continent. Almost immediately after the Spanish campaign began, the New York printer, Ezra Sargeant, published the 46-page *An Exact and Impartial Account of the Most Important Events which Have Occurred in Aranjuez, Madrid, and Bayonne; from the 17th of March until the 15th of May, 1808. Treating of the Fall of the Prince of Peace; and of the Termination of the Friendship and Alliance between the French and Spanish Nations*; the author was Pedro de Cevallos, first secretary in the government of Carlos IV. One 179-page item, printed in 1809 in Boston by Munroe, Francis, and Parker, *The Intrigues of the Queen of Spain with the Prince of Peace and others, Written by a Spanish Nobleman and Patriot*, presented Spanish politics in terms of the peccadillos of the Spanish queen and the prime minister. A 65-page account of the battles of Talavera, written by John William Croker, was published in Philadelphia by J. and A.Y. Humphreys in 1811. Written in Spanish and published in New Orleans in 1808 by Juan Mowry was the 59-page *España ensangrentada por el horrendo corzo"* (*Spain Bloodied by the Horrendous Roebuck* [the roebuck was Napoleon]).

Particularly interesting for the several readerships it points to is the essay by the Spaniard Antonio Capmany y de Montpalau, *The Anti-Gallican Sentinel ... Dedicated to all nations, Translated from the Spanish by a Gentleman of this City*. The essay appeared in New York in 1809, printed for Ezra Sargeant;

the second part in Philadelphia in 1810, printed by Fry and Kammerer.[48] Capmany wrote this violently anti-French, anti-Napoleonic essay in Spain in Spanish, addressing Spanish Americans:

> To you I address myself, O noble inhabitants of the opposite hemisphere; illustrious children of Spanish blood, descendants of the first colonists, defenders of the new world, followers of the gospel, whose first light was extended in those regions by the piety and zeal of the catholic monarchs! Since nature has removed you to such a distance from your mother, to whose succour, in her perilous struggle, you cannot come with your hereditary strength and valour; do then, to the good intentions and wishes you have manifested, unite the powerful aid of your gold and silver; and let it be said, for the first time, that those metals, which have caused so many evils in the world, shall serve for the benefit of the human race. Now they cannot fall into the hands of the rapacious French, that ungrateful people, who so often availed themselves of those precious treasures to shed our blood. The Pyrenees are guarded, the ports are closed, all friendship at an end, commerce interrupted, and those hands cut off, by which the treasures of both worlds were wantonly consumed. Defend, by the powerful aid of those riches, so liberally bestowed upon you by bountiful nature, the native land of your venerable ancestors, about to be imbrued in the blood of your brethren. An insolent Corsican threatens to convert our land into a wilderness, to extirpate the present race, and to introduce a new and motley tribe drilled and clothed a la François. This Attila promised to have you wedded with his adoptive brats, without considering that three centuries of trials prove your aversion to an alliance with a heterogeneous race. He might believe that besides the Spaniards, whom he deceived in the peninsula, the number of those still to be deceived and conquered, was very inconsiderable; but let the impostor know that Ferdinand can count upon twenty-four millions of loyal vassals in the old and new worlds. Let him wipe away the tears of the wretched deputies from the merchants of Bordeaux and Bayonne, who bewailed their misery, imploring his protection and favour. Hearken to his reply: "Have patience. In order to attain happiness, one must first endure privations and hardships; you shall have trade in the Spanish and Portuguese colonies."

Capmany was a noted economist and philologist, later a delegate to the Cortes de Cádiz, a rump government that claimed legitimacy in Spain while Fernando was in a French jail. In this essay he was talking to Spanish Americans, undecided whether to retain ties to Fernando, to declare loyalty to regional juntas in Spain that also claimed legitimacy, to support Napoleon's deputy in Spain, José Bonaparte, or to seize the moment and form their own American governments. These men, many of whom were in London or the United States, were most easily reached through the English-language press. However, Capmany's promise of American trade and wealth in the Spanish and Portuguese colonies, translated into English, would also have alerted British and U.S. businessmen to the benefits to be gained if France were expelled from the Peninsula and commerce could commence, free of interference from Bordeaux and Bayonne merchants.

Capmany's essay, that someone took the time to translate into English for this double market, explains the appearance in U.S. bookstores of other English-language translations of works by Spaniards and Spanish Americans. The following is a sample: Miguel Ramos Arizpe's *Memorial on the Natural, Political and Civil State of the Province of Coahuila, One of the Four Provinces of the East, in the Kingdom of Mexico* (Philadelphia: printed by G. Palmer for John Melish, 1814); Manuel Torres's *An Exposition of the Commerce of Spanish America: with some Observations upon Its Importance to the United States* (Philadelphia, G. Palmer, 1816, 199 pp.);[49] *Outline of the Revolution in Spanish America, or An Account of the Origin, Progress and Actual State of the War Carried on Between Spain and Spanish America (written by "A South American")* (New York, J. Eastburn & Co., 1817, 219 pp.);[50] Francisco Javier Clavijero's *The History of Mexico, Collected from Spanish and Mexican Historians, from Manuscripts and Ancient Paintings of the Indians* (Philadelphia, T. Dobson, 1817, 3 vols.); Simón Bolívar's address to the Congress of Angostura (reprinted in Washington, D.C., in 1819 by Byron S. Adams, translated by Francisco Javier Yanes). Related to these books by Spanish or Spanish American authors is James Yard's publication, *Spanish America and the United States; or, Views of the Actual Commerce of the United States with the Spanish Colonies, and of the Effects of a War with Spain on that Commerce. Also some observations on the probable influence of the emancipation of the Spanish colonies on the agriculture and commerce of the U.S.* (Philadelphia, M. Carey & Son, 1818, 58 pp.). Yard signed himself "A Merchant of Philadelphia."

These works—particularly those by Ramos Arizpe and Clavijero—show how U.S. printers were beginning to appropriate texts written for other venues for U.S. readers. Ramos Arizpe originally had his work published in Spanish in Cádiz in 1812; it was written as an earnest report on Mexico's northern territories for purposes of correcting Spanish maladministration. However, its detail was probably read in the United States as a guide to U.S. expansion there. Clavijero's history appeared first in Italian in 1780 as a defense of Mexico's indigenous culture but also as an intervention in European historiography (answering William Robertson and the naturalists Buffon and de Pauw by protesting the truth of Spanish histories and codices). Most probably its information on Mexican geography, plant and animal life, and its argument that syphilis did not originate in America, endeared the book to U.S. readers.

Besides an interest in Spanish and Spanish American politics, though, a vogue for Hispanic culture beyond an appetite for economic, military, and political news seems to have flourished in the United States then. Publishing records prove the point: In 1807 the Philadelphia printers Fry and Kammerer printed Joel Barlow's *The Columbiad*, based on Columbus's discovery of America.[51] In 1808 an unknown New York publisher printed Alonso de Ercilla's *Sketch of the Araucana with copious translations from that poem* (translated by William Hayley and the Rev. H. Boyd). In 1808 Thomas and Whipple in Newburyport, Massassachusetts, published the two-volume *Female Quixotism* by Mrs. Tabitha Tenney; the story had nothing to do with Spain except that it showed the author's familiarity with Cervantes's *Quijote* as it criticized the pernicious effects of reading Romantic novels. In 1809 August Friedrich Ferdinand von Kotzebue's *Pizarro* was printed in Boston by E.G. House for John West and Co. In 1810 Matthew Gregory Lewis's *Alfonso, King of Castile, A Tragedy in Five Acts* was printed in Philadelphia by Smith and M'Kenzie for Bradford and Inskeep. In 1814 the New York publisher D. Huntington printed Miguel de Cervantes's *The History and Adventures of the renowned Don Quixote*. In 1815 Robert Southey's *Roderick, the Last King of the Goths* was printed in Philadelphia by William Fry for Edward Earle, Eastburn, Kirk and Co. In 1816 Richard Graves's *The Spiritual Quixote* was printed in Providence by Robinson, Howland, Miller and Hutchens. Also in 1816 Barlow's *The Vision of Columbus* was printed in Baltimore by Z. Harman (this version of *The Columbiad* had first been published in 1787 by Hudson and Goodwin in Hartford). In 1821 a *Spiritual Guide*, written by the seventeenth-century Spanish priest and theologian, Miguel de Molinos, was published in Philadelphia by J.H.A. Skerrett for Benjamin and Thomas Kite; Molinos had been censured by the Inquisition as a heretic because his quietism sounded too much like Protestantism. Yet this may have been what endeared him to U.S. readers, largely Protestant but, if Catholic, willing to confront unorthodox ideas.

The editions of *Don Quijote*-related titles are noteworthy. The Spanish book appears to have been read at that moment, not as a literary fantasy but as a commentary on modern Europe. It is reported that *Don Quijote* was the only novel that Thomas Jefferson read twice, considering that it satirized feudalism.[52] Thomas Paine in *Rights of Man*, responding to Edmund Burke's lament in *Reflections on the Revolution in France* that the age of chivalry was dead ("the nurse of manly sentiment and heroic enterprise is gone"), delighted that the book signaled the end of the aristocratic order (20). *Don Quijote*, only recently rediscovered in Spain and acclaimed a national classic,[53] appears to have been admired internationally for reasons other than comic entertainment.[54]

Other developments interested Philadelphians in Spanish culture. Two marriages united well-to-do Philadelphia women with Spanish diplomats: Mathilda Stoughton and Josef de Jaudenes y Nebot,[55] and Sally McKean and Carlos Martínez de Irujo.[56] After Fernando VII was restored to the Spanish throne in 1814, José, Napoleon's older brother who had governed in Spain since 1808, came to Philadelphia under the name Count Survilliers. In 1815 he rented a house in the city from Stephen Girard and bought a property of almost 1,000 acres in Bordentown, New Jersey, where he set up court and became friends with some of Philadelphia's most prominent citizens—Girard, General Thomas Cadwalader, and Joseph Hopkinson, president of the Pennsylvania Academy of Fine Arts. Bonaparte introduced Philadelphia to European culture and classical taste, particularly in the context of his experiences in Naples and Spain; for example, Nicholas Biddle named his estate on the Delaware River "Andalusia."[57] The Philadelphia painter, Charles Willson Peale, painted Bonaparte's portrait.[58] In 1816 Bonaparte even had published in New York his novel, *Moina, or the Peasant Girl of Mount Cenis*, which he signed "Joseph, king of Spain."[59]

However, Spanish exoticism was also beginning to be felt beyond that elite. Washington Irving was already traveling in Spain and in 1832 would publish his "Tales of the Alhambra." He had begun his interest in Spain early, though, when in 1806 he helped to translate from the French François Raymond Joseph Depons's *A voyage to the eastern part of Terra Firma, or the Spanish Main in South America during the years, 1801, 1802, 1803 and 1804*;[60] in 1813–1814 Irving wrote for the *Analectic Magazine*, published in Philadelphia, a series of naval biographies whose protagonists (like David Porter) sailed in Spanish waters.[61] At Harvard in 1823, George Ticknor drew up a syllabus for a course on the history and criticism of Spanish literature.[62] Opera, at first English and then increasingly Italian, was beginning to introduce audiences in the United States to Mediterranean music, stories, and themes. [63]After the initial English, Dutch, Irish, and German immigration waves that had settled New England, Virginia, New York, and eastern Pennsylvania, the populations of the large cities saw the arrival of Frenchmen, Italians, and Spaniards, many of whom had been wealthy and influential in their homelands and who began to alter taste. Even a face cream, the "Balm of Iberia," was marketed to the ladies of Philadelphia. The product, which sold for two dollars at Dr. Dyott's Family Medicine Warehouse, was claimed to have originated in a harem in Georgia, the "ancient Iberia in Asia" where Lady Mary Montagu got it from the sultana.

BUSINESS AND POLITICS

Nevertheless, business and political news largely dictated the Spanish-related fare that U.S. publishers put out. As insurgencies meant that Spain was beginning to lose control of its American colonies, U.S. businessmen and politicians saw opportunities for trade and territorial expansion into Florida, the Caribbean, Mexico, and South America. However, a few major publishing events, which had caused a sensation when they were published in Europe, had already awakened them to that potential. When Alexander von Humboldt, who had been granted access to Spanish possessions in the Americas that Spain had previously closed off to foreigners, published his *Essai politique sur le royaume de la Nouvelle-Espagne du Mexique* in Paris in 1808, competitors' eyes were opened to Mexico's great mineral wealth. A U.S. edition soon followed: *Political Essay on the Kingdom of New Spain* (New York, I. Riley, 1811).[64] In 1815 Carey published another book by Humboldt, *Personal Narrative of Travels to the Equinoctial Regions of the New Continent during the Years 1799–1804*.[65]

Documents in the Archivo General de la Nación (Mexico), written by William Davis Robinson (whom we will see later), help with an understanding of U.S. attitudes toward Mexico in those years.[66] Robinson had gone to Mexico in 1816 at the request of President James Monroe to gauge the extent of that insurgency. Mexican rebels had several times come to the United States to request aid, thinking to recruit the soldiers and get the arms left over from the War of 1812. When José Manuel Herrera arrived semiofficially as representative of José María Morelos and with a constitution in hand, the U.S. president and Congress felt they needed information on the state of affairs there so as to decide whether to support the rebels or to remain neutral and affirm Spanish rule. In Mexico Robinson was captured by royalist forces, and in the several letters pleading his case to the Spanish viceroy he argued that he was there to assess to what extent other European powers were aiding the insurgency. Mexican historians call Robinson a nefarious conspirator; and reports the Spanish ambassador to the United States sent back to Madrid seem to confirm that, despite what Robinson told the viceroy, he was hardly an impartial observer.[67] As we will see, Robinson is representative of several U.S. actors who, on their own but also with the permission of the U.S. government, helped the rebel cause. They used the U.S. press to defend their personal motives and to publicize their meddlings as "adventures"; their memoirs and travel narratives had the effect of further stimulating U.S. interest in lands to the south. Their writings also made U.S. citizens aware that European power politics was being carried out on their doorstep and that the United States self-interestedly should intervene in Mexico and the Caribbean so as to keep other Europeans out. Robinson, as a result of travels to London, Amsterdam, Hamburg, and to Venezuela as a tobacco trader, especially understood English and French designs on Spanish America. After the Congress of Vienna (1814) with its purported "balance of power," England had emerged as the real force in Europe, determining policies in the continent's other monarchies. After the Peninsula War and Napoleon's defeat, England's navy and armies were preeminent and threatened the United States. if they intervened in Mexico.

Thus, even though England had lost the War of 1812 and signed the Treaty of Ghent (1814) with the United States, its new policy of commercial imperialism meant new designs; England particularly coveted Cuba, Central America, and Mexico. The Louisiana Purchase of 1803 had excluded England from the Louisiana/Texas region as well as the whole Mississippi Valley, though its influence there competed still with residual French and Spanish cultures. (In 1818 the New Orleans attorneys at law, L. Moreau and Henry Carleton, published a legal guide for businessmen in the region, based on a Spanish code of law—*A Translation of the Titles on Promises, Obligations, Sale, Purchase, and Exchange; from the Spanish of Las siete partidas*.) In 1819, when the United States acquired east and west Florida from Spain with the Adams–Onís Treaty and so seemed to resolve boundary disputes with Spain and France, England, which had owned the Floridas from 1763 to 1783 and whose settlers still determined the slave culture in west Florida, which in 1783 had passed to Spain, refused to back off. England stirred Indian factions in the area where runaway black slaves sought refuge in the lawlessness; agents (often double-agents) in the pay of European powers operated, and piracy in the Gulf threatened U.S. shipping. Spain governed west Florida from 1783 until 1819, a territory that extended from the Atlantic coast west to the Mississippi River (excluding New Orleans); and official paper regulations created numbers of Spanish speakers. For example, the first Spanish-language newspaper in the United States, *El Misisipí*, was published in New Orleans from 1808 to 1810.[68]

Aaron Burr's 1808 conspiracy for control of the Mississippi River region and then takeover in Mexico (for which the U.S. vice-president was tried for treason) often is made to stand for all U.S. relations with Mexico in the first decades of the nineteenth century. Once Burr's case is dismissed as aberrant adventurism, the U.S. government could appear to be exonerated from blame. For that reason, Robinson's letters, which tell of European struggles for dominance in the Americas, and U.S. meddling in Mexico once the Floridas were acquired, are valuable.

The Burr connection with Mexico is significant here, however, because one of the players in Burr's scheme, James Wilkinson, figures in the Robeson/Carey correspondence. Wilkinson, a Revolutionary War general, was at that time governor of the Louisiana Territory. However, he was a double or even triple agent, working for the U.S. government, Burr, and also for the Spanish king—who paid him an annual pension of two thousand dollars for services. Jefferson, whose vice-president Burr had been, stood by Wilkinson during Burr's trial in which Wilkinson was implicated; and in a flurry of publications in 1809, Wilkinson attempted to clear his name.[69] He never succeeded, and at the close of the War of 1812 he was further disgraced when a general court martial accused him of errors in moving his troops, "neglect of duty and unofficerlike conduct" (drunkenness).[70] Although the charges were dropped, this failed hero moved to Mexico where he died in 1825.

South America also interested U.S. businessmen and politicians. In 1817–1818 Henry Marie Brackenridge traveled there on a U.S. government mission and, as secretary, compiled a long report. Published in London in 1820, the analysis recognized gaps in earlier Spanish and English descriptions of that region and attempted to provide a truer history. It updated events and traced the impact of U.S. revolution on the region that Spanish policy had cordoned off so as to prevent that example from inspiring similar revolt.[71] But now that that area had indeed begun to rebel, the United States could argue for American rights to independence, freedom from further European encroachments, and hemispheric unity. Works like William Robertson's *History of America* (1777), and later Richard Snowden's *The History of North and South America* (1815),[72] also taught U.S. readers to think of large American commonalities.

The English-language readership that U.S. publishers aimed for in putting out political and military news of Spain and Spanish America is perhaps easy to determine.[73] The Spanish-speaking market, on the other hand, is difficult to gauge. However, the numbers of those readers, where they resided, their political heft, and reading preferences are, to some degree, indicated by the quantities and varieties of Spanish-language books Carey and other U.S. printers provided them with between 1800 and 1830. Current events and politics predominated, and I will first describe the books containing those. But histories, legal treatises, Masonic handbooks, religious studies, and novels were also being made available to them; and that range suggests a plan by U.S. printers to go beyond satisfying domestic demand so as to supply Americans in other parts of the hemisphere.

The authors of the political books and often book-length pamphlets are sometimes hard to identify because they signed their works anonymously or pseudonymously. Some were Spaniards or Spanish Americans in Philadelphia on business—like Valentín de Foronda, chargé d'affaires for Spain, and Manuel Torres, chargé d'affaires for Gran Colombia. Some were diplomats in the city like Luis de Onís, ambassador from Spain. Others were visitors or refugees, and we will see several of them. These men wrote original works but they also served as translators of the writings of others.

Some who had been delegates to the Spanish Cortes in Cádiz summarized discussion taking place there to draft Spain's first constitution (1811–1812). In 1812 José Alvarez de Toledo had published in Philadelphia his *Manifiesto o satisfacción pundonorosa a todos los buenos españoles europeos, y a todos los pueblos de la América, por un diputado de las Cortes reunidas en Cádiz*.[74] The 83-page publication provoked refutations and rejoinders—one 91 pages long from as far away as Charleston.[75] Anonymous writers penned *El amigo de los hombres a todos los que habitan las islas y el vasto continente de la América Española, obrita curiosa, interesante y agradable seguida de un discurso sobre la intolerancia religiosa* (1812);[76] *Manual de un republicano para el uso de un pueblo libre* (1812).[77] (Luis de Onís judged that *El amigo de los hombres* was more inflammatory than *Manifiesto* in furthering rebellion in Spain's American colonies.)[78] A pseudonymous writer signing himself "El patriota sensible," wrote *El triunfo de la libertad y del patriotismo* (1813);[79] and another, who self-identified as a Spaniard in the United States, wrote *Examen crítico del decreto de las cortes de 13 de febrero de 1813. Escribíalo un Español residente en los E.U. Agosto de 1813* (1815).[80]

Alvarez de Toledo was a well-born Cuban, formerly an officer in the Spanish Navy and later in the British Navy. In 1811 he was named a delegate to the Cortes from Santo Domingo. He was variously a monarchist (he proposed a wild scheme to rescue the Spanish king from Napoleon's jail in Bayonne), defender of American representation in the Cortes, outright enemy of Spain in fighting for Mexican and Cuban independence, and then, finally, Spanish loyalist again. When he first fell into disfavor in Spain, he fled to Philadelphia with the help of the U.S. agent in Cádiz, Richard Meade, whom we will meet later. One month after arriving in the United States in September 1811, Toledo had published his *Manifiesto*, thus attesting to his quick use of the U.S. press to publicize his personal defense and communicate with like-minded Spanish American malcontents in the United States and elsewhere. Immediately, too, he sought an interview with James Monroe, claiming he had evidence that England planned to take over Cuba, Santo Domingo, and Puerto Rico, and assuring Monroe that the American delegates in the Spanish Cortes would approve of such a plan because the delegates were resentful of their disproportionate representation in the Cortes. The delegates, he claimed, had authorized him as their representative to organize an army in northern Mexico to begin revolution.[81]

Monroe apparently approved of Alvarez de Toledo's plan to work for Mexican and Caribbean independence. He provided him with money and a letter of introduction to William Shaler, a U.S. agent in Havana (who, Onís claimed, was on the island to stir revolt).[82] However, Toledo delayed leaving Philadelphia claiming that ice on the Delaware River impeded his departure (though a Spanish diplomatic report says that he was deterred because he and his contacts in Cuba feared what black slaves might do there if an uprising occurred).[83] Meantime he allied himself with revolutionaries in the city, principally Juan Mariano Bautista de Picornell y Gomila who was trying to get support for insurgency in Venezuela, and the Mexican Bernardo Gutiérrez de Lara. Yet Toledo never went to Cuba, instead going to Texas in December 1812. On the frontier conflicts arose between him and Gutiérrez de Lara, and when his division of the army suffered a huge loss in 1812 at the battle of Río Medina, he left Mexico for New Orleans. In 1813 Toledo and Shaler published in Louisiana one issue of a Spanish-language newspaper, *La Gaceta de Texas*, to be followed by one issue of *El Mexicano* in English and Spanish.[84] Alvarez de Toledo is mentioned as having fought in the U.S.–British battle in New Orleans in December 1814.

From then on Alvarez de Toledo's career is cloudy. He was reviled by Luis de Onís, who tried to block his *Manifiesto* from distribution throughout the Americas, and circulation of his other writings in U.S. newspapers by direct intervention and by employ of the Portuguese priest Miguel Cabral de Noroña (who used the pen name "Un Americano")[85] to challenge Toledo in the press. Later Toledo became an ally of Onís when he sought a pardon from the Spanish king; Toledo also was known to have been a friend to the secret Spanish agent, Fray Antonio Sedella. Called variously a turncoat, freebooter, or filibusterer, opportunist, and liberal, he was a hero to some and villain to others. Yet in this discussion of the Spanish-language press in Philadelphia, he was typical of the plotters who recognized the press's value in influencing opinion.

After 1814, when Fernando returned to Spain and proved to be a despot, the tone of U.S. Spanish-language publications changed. Monarchist sentiment, sympathy for keeping the empire intact, and hope of liberal reform vanished. Three Spanish Americans, working for Philadelphia printers as house authors and advisors, set out plans for independence: the Ecuadorean Vicente Rocafuerte (1773–1847), the Venezuelan Juan Germán Roscio (1763–1821), and the Mexican Fray Servando Teresa de Mier (1765–1827). Rocafuerte, in and out of the United States from 1819 until late in the 1820s, made important contacts with government officials and businessmen in Philadelphia, New York, Baltimore, and Washington, and traveled frequently to Cuba and Mexico with boxes of books and petitions for loans. Later Rocafuerte became commercial attaché for Mexico in London, returning finally to Ecuador where he became its first president. Rocafuerte is said to have been responsible for having printed in Philadelphia in 1821 Fray Bartolomé de las Casas's *Destrucción de las Indias*.[86] This sixteenth-century indictment of Spanish mistreatment of American Indians was republished in the first decades of the nineteenth century as proof of Spain's illegal conquest and destructive colonial policies, thus adding to colonial anger toward Spain (details of the flurry of interest in Las Casas will be given later). In 1821 Rocafuerte had published one of his own works—*Ideas necesarias a todo pueblo americano independiente que quiere ser libre*[87] and then in 1822, *Bosquejo ligerísimo de la revolución de Mégico* (this collection of anti-Iturbide materials for Mexican consumption, though appearing with a Philadelphia imprint, was probably published in Cuba).[88] In

1823 he authored *Ensayo político: El sistema colombiano, popular, electivo y representativo es el que más conviene a la América Independiente*,[89] and the introduction to a U.S.-printed book for export to schoolchildren in Spanish America.[90] Rocafuerte was not an original thinker but rather a collector of documents; for example, *Ideas* included selections from Thomas Paine's *Common Sense*, a speech by John Quincy Adams (July 4, 1776), the U.S. Declaration of Independence, the Articles of Confederation, the U.S. Constitution, and the Bill of Rights.

Roscio, in Philadelphia from 1817 to 1818, had published there his *El triunfo de la libertad sobre el despotismo en la confesión de un pecador arrepentido de sus errores políticos, y dedicado a desagraviar en esta parte a la religión ofendida con el sistema de la tiranía* (1817, 1821).[91] This important work, which Robeson included in his shipment of books to Mexico, will be discussed later. In 1817 he also had published in Philadelphia in a bilingual Spanish–English edition his translation from the French of a papal homily, *Homilía del Cardenal Chiaramonte, Obispo de Imola actualmente Sumo Pontífice Pío VII*.[92] The homily threw the support of the Church behind the Spanish king, rebuking Americans for their insurgency; the pope's words infuriated Spanish Americans and Roscio refuted the homily in a second part of the publication. When Roscio returned to Venezuela, he became the country's vice-president, dying there in 1821 (he had been gravely ill in Philadelphia, dictating his will there).

Mier, whom we will see later, was in and out of Philadelphia between 1820 and 1822, where he had published his *Memoria político-instructiva* in 1821.[93] It is known that that work, advice to the leaders of the new nation Mier called Anáhuac, did enter Mexico. As of today we do not know how, but we do know that Mexico did get U.S. goods from New Orleans via the Mississippi River system and northern towns.

Throughout the 1820s Carey and other U.S. publishers pumped up this political flow, mainly through reprints. Some of these were blueprints for governance that Spanish Americans themselves were coming up with. Independence throughout most of Spanish America was becoming an accomplished fact, and emerging leaders were searching for models of self-rule. They had to sort out the theories of the French philosophes from the liberalism of the Spanish Cortes and the republicanism of the United States. The French theories were vague and seemed contaminated by France's violent experience with Robespierre and Napoleon; Spanish liberalism, as expressed in merchant terms in Cádiz, still implied colonial trade policies; and U.S. republicanism, which taught federalism and religious tolerance, was unacceptable to many. Thus, in 1822, the Philadelphian Juan F. Hurtel printed for the bookseller Robert Desilver, *Constitución de la República de Colombia, impresa en la villa del Rosario de Cúcuta, en agosto de 1821*.[94] In 1823 Hurtel also printed several works by the Peruvian Manuel Lorenzo de Vidaurre: *Cartas americanas, políticas y morales* in two volumes, *Proyecto de un código penal*, and his *Plan del Perú: defectos del gobierno español antiguo, necesarias reformas, u obra escrita . . . a principios del año 10 en Cádiz, y hoy aumentada con interesantes notas*.[95] In 1824 Hurtel published *Los ilustres americanos*. In 1823 in New York Abraham Paul printed a *Cartilla para los gefes y los pueblos en América*—a primer for leaders and peoples in America. Joseph Desnoues, who variously called his New York bookstore "a Spanish" and "a French, Spanish and Italian shop," published a catalogue of the books he had for sale in 1824—thus suggesting volumes in those languages. In that same year Desnoues published Joachim Heinrich von Campe's *El nuevo Robinson Crusoe, historia moral e instructiva* (though seemingly a novel the work suggested guidelines for building social relationships where none existed).[96] In 1824 in New York Guillermo (William) Grattan published a work printed the previous year in Guatemala by Fernando Valero—*Lecciones de retórica que dió a los pasantes de la Academia de Derecho teórico práctico su presidente . . . .*[97] In 1825 in Philadelphia, Stavely and Bringhurst published the text of the Mexican president Guadalupe Victoria's address when he took office after Iturbide fell on October 20, 1824—*Manifiesto del Presidente de los Estados Unidos Mexicanos, a sus compatriotas*.[98]

When the Cubans José María Heredia, Félix Varela, and Domingo del Monte arrived in the United States in the mid-1820s, fleeing Spanish rule, their publications added a plea for independence and antislavery arguments to the Spanish American political debate. Stavely and Bringhurst published Varela's *Lecciones de filosofía* in 1824 and seven numbers of Varela's newspaper, *El Habanero*, between 1824 and 1826. That paper apparently was written for export and is known to have gotten to its Cuban readership because Varela tells, midway through the run, that he was reviled not only by the Spanish government on the island but also by factions who were seeking to invite invasion by alliances with new American nations (Mexico and Colombia).[99] Varela's perspective is unique in assessing Cuba's fortunes relative to the rest of Spanish America but also in recognizing how the colony was hurt by being joined still to Spain (which he called "a dead body attached to a living organism"—the living organism being the Holy Alliance, which was actively furthering the interests of France and Austria).[100] In 1825 a Cuban, Juan Gualberto Ortega, called on Cubans to revolt against Spanish rule in a Philadelphia pamphlet "A los cubanos."[101]

VALENTIN DE FORONDA

Philadelphia was a refuge for Spanish American revolutionaries in the years between 1810 and 1830. But to explain their reception we must go back to the first decade of the nineteenth century, when opinion in the United States favored Spain, thought to be a buffer against the possible aggressions of England and France. Two of Spain's ministers in the United States, Carlos Martínez (the marqués de Casa Yrujo) and Luis de Onís, contributed to this perception in pamphlets aimed at the U.S. public. Casa Yrujo wrote three "letters" in English, two of which he signed and in the third of which he claimed to be "Verus." He also wrote in Spanish "Reflexiones sobre el comercio de España con sus colonias en America" (Baltimore, 1799, printed by Mathew Carey's brother James); the work was published a year later in English, translated by "another Spaniard."[102] Onís was first posted in New Orleans and then came to New York and Philadelphia where he monitored the activity of Spanish dissidents and Masons. Onís, too, penned some pamphlets in English. Also using the pseudonym "Verus" and pretending to be a U.S. citizen, he had published in 1813 "Observations on the Conduct of Our Executive Towards Spain." Three other pamphlets followed in 1817.[103] He encouraged the Portuguese priest Cabral de Noroña (whom we have seen) to write two Philadelphia-published works: "Diálogo sobre la independencia de la América Española entre un entusiasta liberal y un filósofo rancio"[104] and "Reflexiones imparciales sobre la franc-masonería."[105] Onís, officially concerned with protecting Spanish interests but also thought to have had pro-Napoleonic leanings, meddled in other ways. Described by a contemporary as "as *wicked* a man in his situation can be," Onís was implicated in an 1810 attempt to assassinate Manuel Torres, the commercial agent from Gran Colombia we have seen before who had the ear of both John Adams and James Monroe.[106]

Another Spaniard, however, Spain's consul general in the United States, Valentín de Foronda (1752–1822), contributed a great deal to extending Spanish awareness in the United States[107] Foronda, a workaholic, had special duties for commercial representation in consulates in Boston, Newport, New York, Baltimore, Norfolk, Charleston, and New Orleans.[108] His responsibilities extended to arranging for Spain to pay tuition for Cuban students in Baltimore schools.[109] Appointed by Carlos IV in 1801, he was later confirmed as chargé d'affaires by Fernando VII. Born in Vitoria in the Basque region of Spain, Foronda belonged to the Sociedad de Amigos del País (an Enlightenment philanthropic organization headquartered in the Basque provinces)[110] and to the Real Academia de Bellas Artes y Ciencias in Bordeaux. These contacts away from Madrid, as well as study in France and travel in Belgium, Holland, and Italy, led him to enlightened views. In Spain, before coming to the United States, he published several important essays on economic theory and plans for social order; he translated the Baron de Bielfeld's *Instituciones Políticas* (1781)[111] and Condillac's *Lógica* (1794, 1800),[112] treatises that were widely read. He also is supposed to have translated the novel by Jean François Marmontel,

Belisario, whose publication the Spanish censor, however, prohibited.[113] In the United States Foronda enjoyed considerable prestige in the diplomatic community (although he and Yrujo did not get along).[114] In 1804 he wrote a report, in manuscript, of his views of the United States; among other opinions he said that freedom of the press there was not "liberty, but out-of-control license, a frenzy."[115] A polymath, he had published in London in 1807 the literary study, "Observaciones sobre algunos puntos de la obra de *Don Quixote*."[116] In 1809, he corresponded with Thomas Jefferson with respect to plans for a Spanish constitution; a surviving letter from Jefferson to Foronda (October 4, 1809) disclaims any U.S. "connivance" in supporting Miranda during the time he was in the country. Foronda also had connections with the business community in Mexico. Records of Foronda's correspondence with Gabriel de Iturbe, a Mexican with ties to a Basque trading company known for its free-trade policies, provide a clue as to how Philadelphia-printed items might have been passed on to Mexico—the two men's Basque origins and their business interests might have introduced them and diplomatic pouches might have facilitated their exchanges.[117] Foronda left Philadelphia, probably in 1809, for Spain, where he continued contact with Mexico; in a letter to the *Diario de México* (November 11, 1812), he argued for a freedom of the press that did not extend to defaming respectable men.[118] The Peninsula War still raged in Spain when he arrived home and an absolutist government would prevail in 1814. Foronda was soon jailed for his liberalism when he had published, in La Coruña, an edition of Rousseau's *Social Contract*.[119]

Foronda published actively while he was in Philadelphia, and those publications deserve attention because they provide insight into the city's independent thinking, public debate, and tolerance of foreigners. In "Carta sobre lo que debe hacer un príncipe que tenga Colonias a gran distancia" (1803),[120] which he signed with an "F," he attacked traditional colonialism in which the European power imagines its colonies to be sheep whose wool it cuts and whose milk it devours.[121] With heavy doses of fiction to disguise the criticism (Foronda invents a "friend" with whom he dialogues, a "dream" he had, and an "imaginary prince" to whom the remarks are directed), Foronda rethinks Spain's operative political and economic philosophies. European maintenance of distant colonies results in piracy, war with other sea-faring nations, expense, and so on. Instead, Foronda praises the wealth of the new United States, listing the many products of its internal economy. Because it is content in its borders, it does not have the outlay that European nations do; its wealth, because it is inexhaustible like foodstuffs, is superior to the Mexican silver mines on which Spain prides itself and which may soon give out. In this essay Foronda distinguishes between "comerciantes" and "traficantes." The former are creators of true wealth because they produce and manufacture the products that are sold on the market; the latter are only middlemen who profit from the labor of others. Josefa Gómez de Enterría has studied the concern that Foronda and others were showing for the use of new commercial language then; words like "capital," for example, were fighting with old-fashioned terms like "caudal," Somehow—perhaps via Foronda's correspondence with Iturbe—this letter advising a prince on colonial policy reached Mexico because the Mexican writer, José Joaquín Fernández de Lizardi, who published in 1816 what is universally seen as Spanish America's first novel, mentions it in one of his 1812 essays, where he credits it as a source for the utopia he sketches there.[122]

In his "Cartas presentadas a la Sociedad Filosófica de Philadelphia" (1807),[123] Foronda gives evidence of the extent to which he and his fellow Spaniards had merged into Philadelphia's cultural life. In the pamphlet, again in the form of a letter, Foronda addresses another member of the American Philosophical Society, the Spanish-speaking "Señor Vaughan" [John Vaughan]. Like other such Enlightenment academies and societies in Europe devoted to the discovery and dispersal of useful knowledge, the Society, founded in Philadelphia in 1743 by Benjamin Franklin, included in its Philadelphia circle corresponding members. For example, Franklin nominated the Spaniard, Pedro Rodríguez, Count of Campomanes, for membership, thus recognizing advancements in Spain and internationalizing Philadelphia's scientific culture. In "Cartas" Foronda introduces topics that he imagines of interest to members: the discovery, published in a Mexican gazette, of the use of quinine for curing yellow fever, and guaco for counteracting snake bite; his offer to help Philadelphia improve its already excellent public health; suggestions for a new English grammar that would provide better rules and improve translations; his analysis of the inherent musicality of English (his example, drawn from a speech in the English Parliament whose content dealt with the seizure of neutral ships, disguised complaint of England's treatment of Spanish vessels); and recommendations for updating the 1780 edition of the dictionary of the Real Academia Española by accepting new usages (this item was surely intended for fellow Spanish-speakers in the United States and Spanish America).

Foronda's comments regarding the respective qualities of the French, English, and Spanish tongues are particularly interesting. Translation, the essay's principal concern, reveals how these European languages, removed from the worlds that created them, might mix, how modernizing influences such as commerce and politics might challenge official rules for correctness, how new needs might dictate the need for practical texts in these vernacular languages. It displays Foronda's sense, as the Peninsula was falling apart into old regionalisms as a result of the war, that the pretense that "Castilian" equaled "Spanish" did not allow for the separate languages of Galicia and Cataluña (he does not mention Basque). Although Foronda cites earlier studies of the Spanish language by Benito Feijoo[124] and Capmany, it is clear that, in Philadelphia, he was confronted with a confusing language world. If Foronda, who admits he does not know English, is daring to analyze that language's poetic qualities, and (as we will see) a Frenchman, an Italian, and an Englishman were translating works into Spanish for Philadelphia printers, it is obvious that a spirit of easy cross-over prevailed and that many translators were self-promoters who were less than adequate. (We will read later that Mexicans objected to the Spanish translations of some of the books for sale. Charles Le Brun's translation of *Libertad de los mares* displeased them. They did not like the accents he placed over every word so as to aid students of Spanish in pronunciation. Despite the fact that the Buenos Aires gazette endorsed the work, the feature bothered them. Robeson will report to Carey: "You can tell Mr. Le Brun that his work is highly spoken of" but also that "*Liberty of the Seas* is not relished here.")

On October 9, 1809, Foronda had published "Apuntes ligeros sobre la nueva constitución, proyectada por la Magestad de la Junta Suprema española, y reformas que intenta hacer en las leyes."[125] In that pamphlet, in which he confesses he is torn between orders of the French invaders of Spain and loyalties to the now imprisoned Fernando VII, Foronda refers to letters received via Caracas and Havana. Finally he decides the following, which sounds like he has been reading Rousseau: "I am persuaded that the people, that is the nation, is the true sovereign—a truth as undeniable as the Rock of Gibraltar, and that is found in the hearts of all, although buried under bayonets [but] to Spain's good fortune, potentially resurrected from there soon."[126] The reference to the Rock of Gibraltar would have sounded patriotic since Spaniards still lamented the loss of Gibraltar to England in the early eighteenth century. Surreptitiously, then, into what seemed like a promise that Spain might soon reclaim the Rock, Foronda inserted a revolutionary definition of nationhood.

In "Cartas para los amigos y enemigos de Don Valentin de Foronda, encargado de negocios y cónsul general de S.M.C. Fernando VII, cerca de los Estados Unidos de la América Septentrional, relativas a lo acontecido en España con el motivo de haber nombrado el emperador Napoleón I a su hermano Joseph rey de las Españas e Indias" (1808),[127] Foronda reveals how Spaniards and Spanish Americans in his jurisdiction were beginning to divide in their loyalties. The 1808 pamphlet is the second version of his address to friends and enemies; a third edition would come out in 1809. When, initially, Foronda had refused to recognize José Bonaparte as king in Spain and resign in favor of the French-appointed consul sent to replace him, when he also refused to acknowledge the legitimacy of the Junta de Sevilla (Spaniards who had fled French troops and formed a provisional government in that southern city), eleven other Spaniards in Philadelphia wrote to him publicly, asking him to step aside. These men, one of whom was secretary of Foronda's legation, expressed their allegiance to Fernando VII, but so also did Foronda, who declared he was still a monarchist despite his statements about popular sovereignty and liberal views on commerce. Upset that they had formed a quasi-Spanish government without consulting him, Foronda challenged their "patriotism" and they, in turn, challenged his. In these "Cartas" we read of Foronda's appeal to Philadelphia's Spanish-speaking community for support. But we also understand the existence of a larger network when he tells that he customarily sent on to Spanish-language gazettes throughout the United States for republication letters and circulars that he received from Spain (1809, 18).

Thus we see confusion as to who spoke in the name of "Spain" in the years between 1808 and 1814—whether José Bonaparte, the various juntas scattered throughout Spain, overseas Spaniards suddenly bereft of official status yet still obliged to perform duties, or renegades in various Spanish American locations who were using legal excuses to press their own independence demands. In fact, Philadelphia was an important space where these rivals contested for authority. An 1810 document from Mexican Inquisition records tells that José funneled his edicts through Philadelphia into Mexico; his Philadelphia agent, charged with fomenting rebellion in Mexico among 500 sympathizers, was "Mr. Dumoland."[128] Because Mexican monarchists kept his diplomats out, José retained representatives in the United States to press his interests.

Later in the 1820s, Spaniards, disgruntled because of politics in Spain and/or desirous of earning a living in Philadelphia, came and had their works published. Félix Megía (or Mejía) had his *No hay union con los tiranos*[129] and *Pizarro, o los peruanos*[130] published in the city in 1824; his *La Fayette en Monte Vernon, en 17 de Octubre 1824. Drama en 2 actos* in 1825;[131] and in 1826 his *Guillermo Tell, o, La Suisa libre*.[132] In 1826 Megía took on a complicated project for the Philadelphia publisher William Stavely: Jean Pierre Claris de Florian, whom we have seen, had translated from Hebrew into French the four-canto poem "Eliezer y Nephtaly," and Megía took the poem a step further translating it into Spanish verse.[133] The project is significant for what it tells about the commercial viability of a work of such sophistication. In 1826 Megía had published in Mexico in the Masonic newspaper, *El Sol*, a curious item—a refutation of DeWittt Clinton's approval of a papal encyclical backing the tyrannical Spanish king (which we have seen).[134] Megía died in 1853 but little else is known about him.

——— TRANSLATION BUSINESS ———

It appears that Carey and other printers initially printed Spanish translations of entertaining French and English plays and novels for Foronda's Spanish-speaking community in the United States. These, however, were soon replaced by political materials; and readership was extended by selling these abroad. Europe had returned to monarchy but Spanish America was still in flux, in need of political wisdom. The following titles suggest readers there: *Constitución de los Estados Unidos de América* (1810),[135] Manuel García de Sena's *La independencia de la costa firme justificada por Thomas Paine treinta años ha* (1811),[136] Garcia de Sena's translation of John M'Culloch's *Concise History of the United States from the Discovery of America up until 1807—Historia concisa de los Estados Unidos: desde el descubrimiento de la América hasta el año de 1807* (1812),[137] Charles Le Brun's translation of Bertrand Barère de Vieuzac's *La libertad de los mares, ó el govierno Inglés descubierto* (1820; see Figure 1.1),[138] James Philip Puglia's translation of Paine's *El derecho del hombre* (1821, 1822),[139] Jean Jacques Rousseau's *Contrato social* (1821, 1822; see Figure 1.2) by an unidentified translator,[140] and Edward Barry's translation of Vicesimus Knox's *El espíritu del despotismo* (1822; see Figure 1.3).[141]

Knox published his *Spirit of Despotism* secretly in London in 1795 during the war with France; he said that a few copies circulated then "with the greatest stealth" (*con el mayor sigilo*). For a broader readership it was reprinted in London in 1821, although some of the same repression obtained then. Carey's publication of it in 1822, which the translator Edward Barry dedicated to Simón Bolívar, takes advantage of anti-British sentiment even as it explores the conditions favoring despotism. Knox's work is a kind of Machiavellian tract showing how the spirit of despotism works—it takes advantage of common peoples' indifference to public affairs, favors royal privilege, and discourages commerce. Knox analyzes loyalty and demonstrates mistaken ideas surrounding it.

García de Sena, a Venezuelan, is known to have arrived in Philadelphia, where his brother resided, in 1810. Given his knowledge of English and his familiarity with the city's printers, however, he may have been in the country earlier.[142] In addition to his translation services, he was a conduit for the receipt of Venezuelan newspapers and pamphlets in the United States, and for the transmission of U.S. materials to Caracas.[143] In *La independencia de la costa firme* he was both compiler and translator of selections from Paine's *Common Sense, Dissertation on the First Principles of Government, Dissertation on Government, the affairs of the Bank and Paper Money*, as well as the texts of the U.S. Declaration of Independence; the Articles of Confederation; the U.S. Constitution; and constitutions of Connecticut, New Jersey, Pennsylvania, and Virginia. In the introduction he instructs his brother, now back in Venezuela, to tell everyone there about the happiness in the United States that these legal advances have procured; he also hopes that his message will reach Puerto Rico so that readers there will be helped in throwing off colonial despotism (Spain was using Puerto Rico to thwart revolution in its mainland colonies).

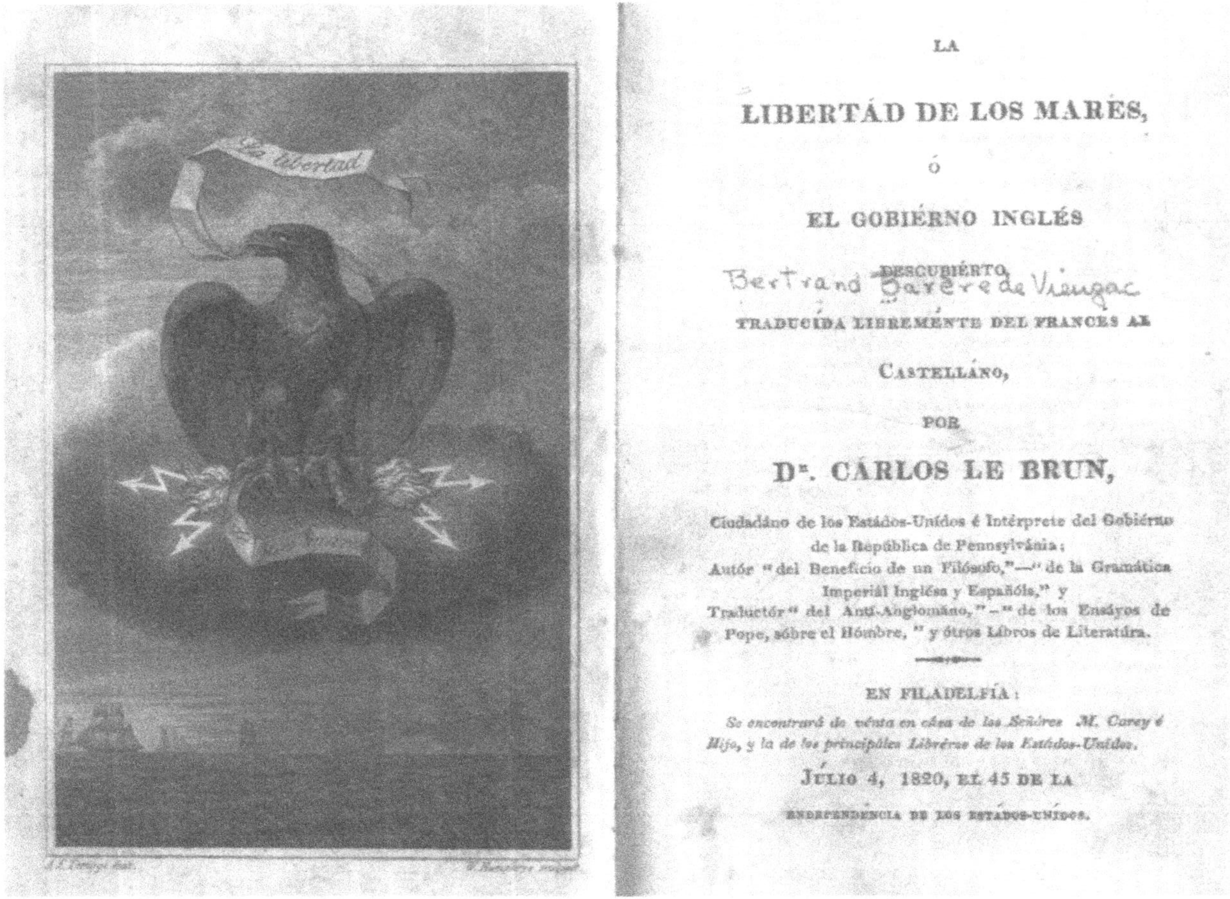

LA
LIBERTÁD DE LOS MARES,
ó
EL GOBIÉRNO INGLÉS

DESCUBIERTO Bertrand Bayere de Vieuzae
TRADUCIDA LIBREMENTE DEL FRANCÉS AL
CASTELLANO,

POR
Dn. CÁRLOS LE BRUN,

Ciudadano de los Estados-Unidos é Intérprete del Gobiérno
de la República de Pennsylvánia;
Autór "del Benefício de un Filósofo,"—". de la Gramática
Imperial Inglésa y Española," y
Traductór "del Anti-Anglománo,"—". de los Ensáyos de
Pope, sóbre el Hómbre," y ótros Líbros de Literatúra.

EN FILADELFÍA:
Se encontrará de vénta en cása de los Señóres M. Carey é
Híjo, y la de los principáles Libréros de los Estádos-Unídos.
JULIO 4, 1820, EL 45 DE LA
INDEPENDENCIA DE LOS ESTADOS-UNIDOS.

FIGURE 1.1 Title page of *La Libertad de los Mares.*

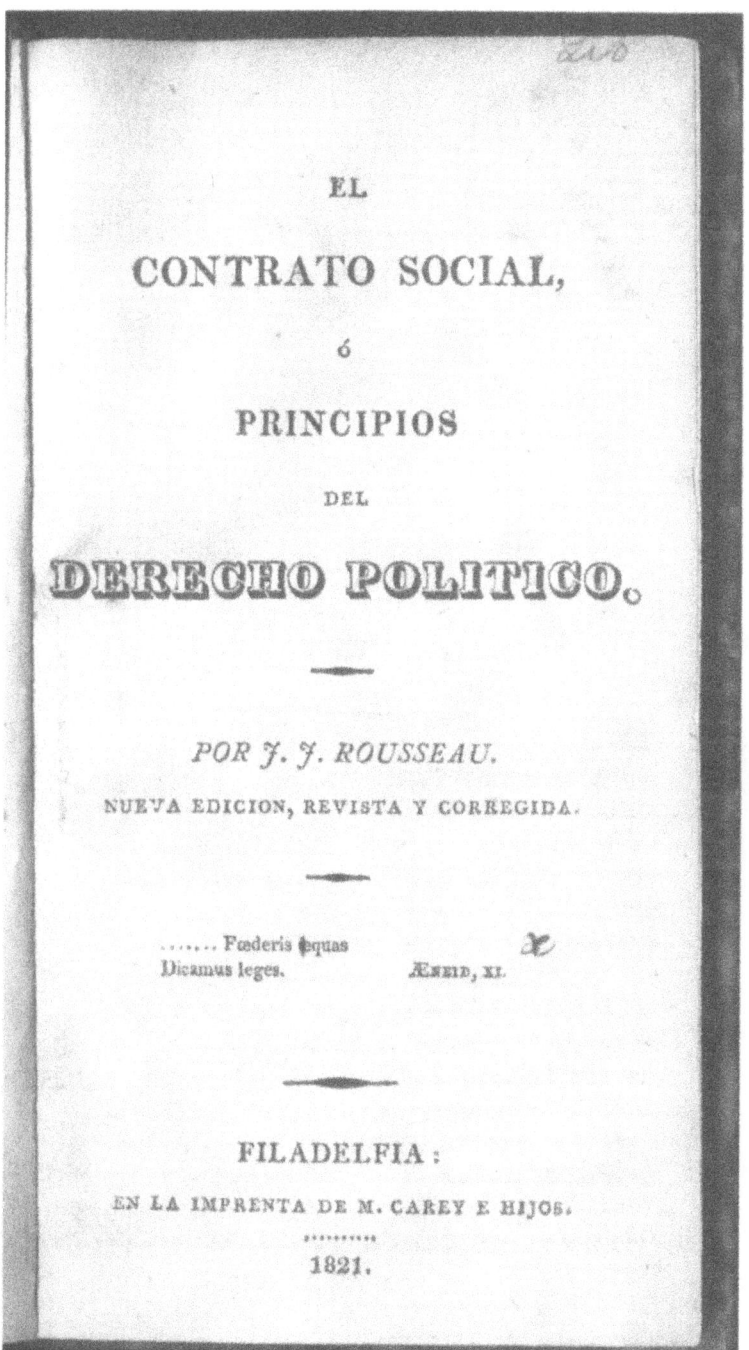

FIGURE 1.2 Title page of Rousseau's *El Contrato Social ó Principios del Derecho Politico*.

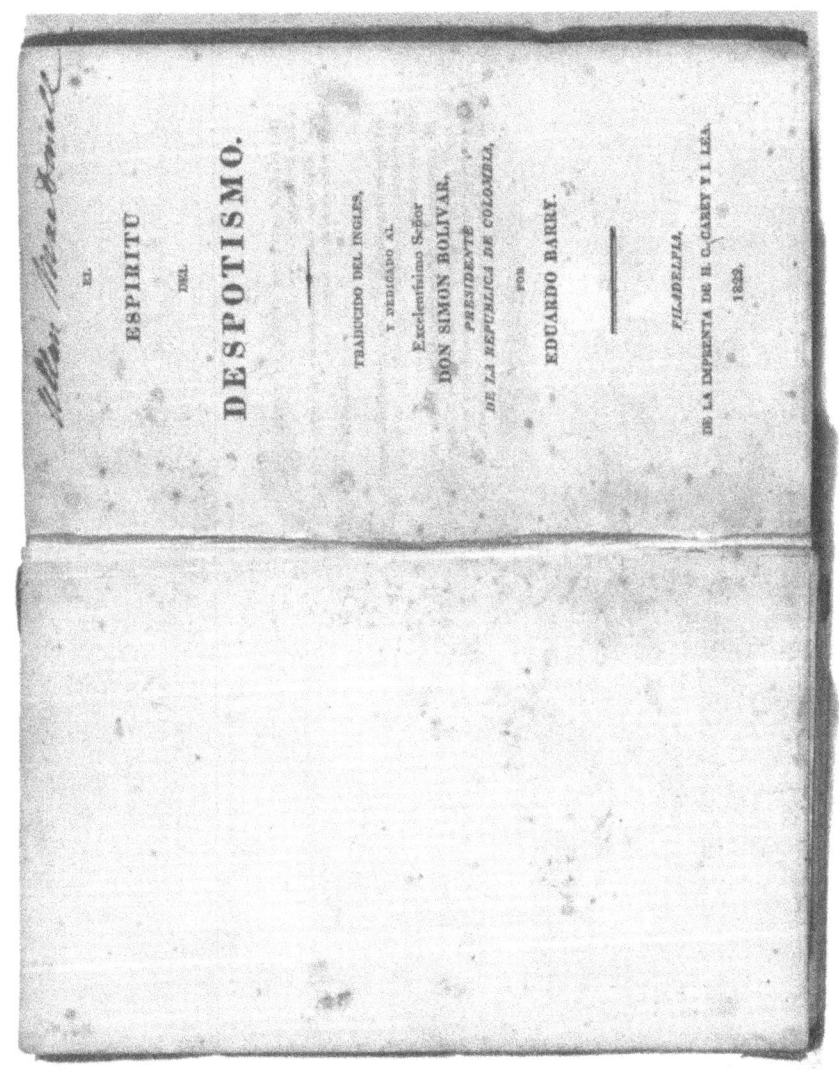

FIGURE 1.3 Title page of *El Espíritu del Despotismo*.

It is not clear if Rocafuerte used García de Sena's translations of these U.S. documents for his *Ideas necesarias* in 1821. In García de Sena's translation of M'Culloch's history of the United States he included much of M'Culloch's synthesis but he also transcribed legal materials for constitutionalists in Spanish America.[144] García de Sena's works are important because there is testimony that they reached Spanish America (particularly Venezuela) in great numbers, documenting the influence of Paine's ideas and the language of U.S. state constitutions there (in fact, Spanish diplomatic sources tell that 5,000 copies of *La independencia de la costa firme* were printed, to be exported to Spain's American colonies).[145] In letters to Secretary of State James Monroe in 1815 García de Sena intervened in behalf of the insurrectionist government of Cartagena, requesting guns.

The other translators who worked for Philadelphia publishers were an assortment of foreign visitors and residents.[146] Here I single out Charles Le Brun, James Philip Puglia, and Edward Barry. One has to dig to find out about them since they frequently kept their pasts quiet as they merged into U.S. society. For example, biographies of Le Brun's son, a prominent architect in the Philadelphia area, tell that his father came to the United States as Napoleonic ambassador. However, Le Brun never mentioned this fact in the advertisements he provided as part of the titles of his translations; there he only called himself a citizen of the United States and interpreter of the state of Pennsylvania.[147] We know that he was in Philadelphia as early as 1811 when Carey published his *El director de los niños para aprender a deletrear y leer*.[148] In 1815 Le Brun and his wife advertised in the Philadelphia paper, *Aurora General Advertiser*, schools that each operated. Le Brun translated "from the Anglo-Maniac," from Pope's *Essays on Man* a French version that he published himself,[149] and "other books of literature." He authored (in French) "Theodore or The Peruvians" (1814), as well as "For the Benefit of a Philosopher" and "On the Imperial English and Spanish Grammars." In 1826, he had printed two works reflecting politics in Spain— *Retratos politicos de la revolución de España* and *Vida de Fernando Séptimo*.[150] *Retratos* is interesting because, in addition to sketching political figures, the author asks why the U.S. revolution succeeded but Spain's 1820 popular revolt failed. It is not clear if Le Brun wrote these latter works or merely paid for their printing.

Barère's *Libertad de los mares*, printed by Juan F. Hurtel in 1820 and sold in Carey's bookstore, deserves attention here because the title went into Carey's shipment to Mexico.[151] Several features of that work might have recommended it: A Buenos Aires gazette enthused over the edition. The reviewer lauded LeBrun's translation, the appeal for freedom of the seas, but also the handsome edition, commenting especially on the frontispiece's excellent engraving.[152] Also attractive to Carey was Barère's and Le Brun's anti-English sentiment.

Le Brun took advantage of Barère's diatribe to impose on it his own hatred of England. In a four-page preface, a 58-page introduction and abundant footnotes, Le Brun says that England's spies hounded him for his loyalty to France. He describes England's "crimes" in India, Ireland, North America, Europe (Denmark), and on the sea. Then, textually, England is made to boast of its dominance:

> Italy will no longer extend its already limited commerce; Spain will not improve its already weakened trade; Holland will be stripped of its fishing which has made it so powerful. Portugal will be cultivated by myself alone. Denmark and Sweden will be confined to their internal trade. The Baltic will be watched over by Russia to my advantage; and the Russian people will be no more than my auxiliary navy, or commercial arm.... In expectation of this great revolution [commercial take-over] that I am organizing silently, my manufacturing and commercial companies assure me of the mines of Brazil. My plotting will give me entire possession of Mexico and Peru, which my treatises and squadrons are preparing in advance. My trinkets assure me the scalpings of savages in North America against the Americans. My intrigues allow me to monopolize the commerce of the United States and direct their uncertain politics.[153]

Then Barère: "The British government trafficks like a conqueror, sails like a pirate, colonizes like a despot, trades like a [wretched] merchant, administers like a tyrant, does business like a lord."[154] Le Brun complains that "freedom of the seas" is different from neutrality and should be considered as rather escape from the British yoke (1820, lvii).

Puglia, who claimed to have been the translator of Paine's *Rights of Man*,[155] Volney's *Catechism of the French Citizen*, and author of other works, was born in Genoa.[156] After a period in Cádiz where his business failed and he was jailed, he came to the United States in 1790. In Philadelphia he taught Spanish, French, Italian, and English. He also authored *El desengaño del hombre* (1794, 1822) — a work that we will see filled the Mexican inquisitors with fear.[157] Also published in 1822 in Philadelphia by H.C. Carey & I. Lea was the "historical novel" *Reynaldo y Elina, o La sacerdotisa peruana*, translated into Spanish from the French by Antonia Tovar y Salcedo, about whom we know nothing.[158]

Key to Carey's translation business, however, was Edward Barry, whom scholars of Masonry have identified as an English Mason living in Philadelphia.[159] We have seen that, in 1822, Barry translated from English to Spanish Knox's *El espiritu del despotismo*.[160] In 1826 he translated to Spanish David Ramsay's *La vida de Jorge Washington*.[161] But Barry seems to have specialized in translations of Masonic materials. He translated into Spanish *El solitario, o el misterioso del monte* (1822),[162] *Jachin y Boaz; o una Llave Auténtica para la Puerta de la Francmasonería* (1822, 1826),[163] Thomas Smith Webb's *El monitor de los Masones Libres; o Ilustraciones sobre la Masonería* (1822),[164] and Samuel Cole's *La librería Masónica y general Ahiman Rezon* (1823).[165] In 1826 he translated from Spanish to English Valentín Llanos Gutiérrez's *Sandoval, or The Freemasons: A Spanish Tale*[166] and, in 1828, *Observations on the political reforms of Colombia*.[167] Barry himself authored *The elements of Spanish and English Conversation, with new, familiar and easy dialogues, designed particularly for the use of schools* (1822).[168] In addition, he worked for Carey correcting proofs; an undated bill submitted to Carey and Lea tells that he worked on editions of *Rights of Man, Atala, Rinaldo* (probably Tovar y Salcedo's translation from the French to Spanish, *Reynaldo y Elina, o La sacerdotisa peruana*), *Ruins, La verdadera Masonería de adopción*, Henry Newman's *A New Dictionary of the Spanish and English Languages*, and Walter Scott's *Fortunes of Nigel*.

To explain the appearance of four Spanish translations of Masonic works that Carey and Lea printed in 1822—though there were Spanish printings by other printers in the United States from around 1818 until 1827—it must be noted that Freemasonry was entering Spanish America rapidly in the first decades of the nineteenth century. Scottish and English Masons and their literature influenced the United States at perhaps an earlier date; Spanish Americans, on the other hand, were at first indoctrinated by French and Spanish Masons and word-of-mouth contact. Later, as France lost control in the Caribbean and most of Spain's American colonies gained independence, the United States moved into those areas, taking there its earlier Masonry and English organization. Records in the Masonic Temple of Philadelphia tell that that city's Grand Lodge soon became the center for granting patents to Spanish- and French-speaking Lodges in New Orleans, but also in Cuba and Mexico. It also received their minutes and reports.[169] We will see Mexican Masonry in greater detail later, but here we remark on the importance of Barry's translations into Spanish of English-language Masonic materials. These often 200-page books confirmed, but also challenged, the version of Masonry that Mexicans had earlier gotten from the short pamphlets published in Cádiz, and through contact with French and Spanish Masons.[170]

Barry is listed in Philadelphia directories of the period as "gentleman" and "teacher," and in 1829, as "consul for Colombia."[171] In the latter role he was consulted by the Philadelphia painter Charles Willson Peale, who wanted to settle his son in South America and required contacts there.[172] He apparently was well-connected because a letter to Tench Coxe, dated August 21, 1823, reveals that Coxe had called on Barry, who was not at home.[173] However, in two letters to Carey and Lea (December 9, 10, 1822), we learn that Barry must have been young and impecunious; he ashamedly implored the loan of $250 to avoid an "execution" at two o'clock. He said that his family was ignorant "of the blow impending." Despite his various services to Carey and

Lea, Barry must not have been working for them when Robeson was traveling to Mexico because he wrote: "Perhaps a day will come when you may wish to employ me, and of course it is useless for me to say that I am ready to undertake anything that you may wish." (This suggests that Barry knew of this potentially lucrative Carey and Lea project, and wanted in on it instead of just doing hack translation and copy-editing.)

Barry's concern in his letter that his family not know of his indiscretion is significant; more than just a youth's embarrassment in the face of a parent's displeasure, it suggests that "family" was a business and his conduct, representing them in Philadelphia, improper. In fact, his family may have been the Trinidad trading company of Edward Barry that William Davis Robinson names in his *Memoirs of the Mexican Revolution*, saying that the Spanish king had granted it trading privileges and that, in 1803, he had been their agent for a tobacco contract in Venezuela.[174] When the privileges were suspended and Robinson lost money, he launched a lawsuit against the king. In the *Memoirs* Robinson also mentions James Barry of Baltimore, flour merchant in the Cuban trade who died in Cuba in 1798.[175] This Barry and a brother were partners with the Marqués de Casa Yrujo with contracts to provision Spanish troops in the Caribbean; and this contingent pressed the Vatican to name John Carroll the first Catholic bishop in the United States. Thus, if the young Philadelphian was related to this Trinidad Barry family network, it would explain his financial anxieties, his knowledge of Spanish, and his desire to participate in the Mexican book trade. However, other information suggests that the Barrys were not English but instead Irish. Many Irish immigrated to the Canary Islands in the eighteenth century, among them was a Diego (James) Barry.[176] The Irishmen put down roots there, marrying and forming trading companies that took advantage of the islands' position as a way-station, handling the shipping between Spain and Spain's American colonies in the Caribbean, Mexico, and South America. The Trinidad company may have been an extension of this Canary Island business.

Adding to the Barry story is the fact that another Barry worked in London in Spanish-language publishing. In 1826 David Barry published in London *Noticias secretas de América*, a report that Jorge Juan and Antonio Ulloa had compiled for the Spanish king, Fernando VI, in the eighteenth century.[177] These agents for the Crown traveled from Panama south to Chile to report on the misconduct of Spanish governors, priests, miners, and so on. Although a sanitized version of their trip had been published immediately on their return and, as we have seen an English-language version of their trip had been published in Philadelphia in 1801, the more devastating manuscript had lain in secret in Spanish archives since 1735. Barry found it and had it published, saying it identified conditions he himself had witnessed. In the preface, he explains that he spent part of his youth in Spain, then in 1820–1822 traveled to Venezuela, Argentina, Chile, and Peru. In 1823 he returned to England and then on to Madrid. We know no more about David Barry. But his interest in Spanish America and his use of the London press to influence attitudes toward Spanish American independence parallel Edward Barry's life in Philadelphia.

——— GROWTH OF THE EXPORT BUSINESS AND THE MYTH OF PHILADELPHIA ———

After the war with Great Britain concluded in 1815, the U.S. economy was in ruins. Some entrepreneurs worked to extend internal markets, developing, for example, the Erie Canal between 1817 and 1825. Philadelphia, which previously had had important links to the West Indies, England, and cities in Europe, sought to expand the trade it had early on established with the Orient. In *Philadelphia and the China Trade, 1784–1844,* Jean Gordon Lee describes these profitable routes and the products involved. Some Philadelphians took opium from Turkey to Canton where it was exchanged for "rhubarb, tea, silk, porcelain, cassia, nankeens, furniture, lacquerware, fans and floor matting" (1984, 14); these goods were taken back to the United States and sold profitably. Other Philadelphia merchants, notably the Quaker Nathan Dunn, abjured the opium connection and exported from America "ginseng, copper, quicksilver, lead, glass, stoves, dyes, and tobacco." Dunn also displayed an interest in conveying to the American public knowledge of Chinese culture, and he collected a number of Chinese objects for a museum in Philadelphia (which opened in 1838).

Thus, I believe that Carey's entry into the Mexican market reflected this mood of economic expansion. When we read Robeson's account of opening up Mexico to book sales, the possibilities for future trade by exporting more books and importing from Mexico cochineal and spices, gold and silver, we learn of the breakdown of Spanish colonial controls and the rush by agents of other countries to enter that market. Carey's enterprise may have stemmed from his desire to spread Masonry and subvert a ruler with increasing monarchical designs, as some have argued. These ideological motives may have played some role in his thinking. But, first and foremost, I believe economic factors determined his move.[178] Philadelphia and New Orleans were poised on the brink of the Atlantic and the Gulf, in propitious positions to harbor Spanish American revolutionaries, but also to supply new nations with their needs.

Testimony to the Carey firm's decision to open up the business to foreign markets is found in their business ledger from 1822. Mathew's son, Henry Charles, and his son-in-law Isaac Lea, took over Mathew's bookshop on January

1, 1822; and there one reads of 22 such "adventures" besides the one to Mexico—to the West Indies (Cuba, Puerto Rico, Port-au-Prince, Curaçao, Cape Haitien, Aux Cayes, St. Thomas), to South America (La Guaira, Pernambuco, Buenos Aires, and Valparaíso), as well as to Calcutta and Canton. Cargo for these other adventures is unrecorded. During the months of 1822 the number of Spanish-language books that the firm published jumped. At first the venture to send books to Mexico could have seemed to be advantageous— some of the books were already published and in the warehouse; U.S. publishers did not have to pay foreign authors for their work; and writers like Mier and Roscio who had been in Philadelphia for a while were gone by then (and presumably had been paid). However, once Robeson got to Mexico, Carey and Lea realized that political upheavals meant that they were having trouble getting their money back and quickly drew back from further Spanish-language publishing and overseas marketing. They did publish in 1828–1829 a Spanish-language literary annual, *El Aguinaldo*, though its distribution is unknown.[179] Wherever it went, it was hugely popular because they printed 1,500 and 2,500 copies. They paid an unknown editor for his work; he drew most of the contents, including the plates, from the contemporary *Atlantic Souvenir*.[180]

When Henry and Isaac first took over, they maintained the same business practices as Mathew, who remained active as a writer. For the sake of convenience, I will refer to the firm as "Carey." Their relationship with Robeson was similar to an arrangement Mathew had with Mason Locke Weems, described as "a strange and brilliant character who roamed the countryside in Virginia and Maryland selling curious little books in areas with no bookstores."[181] Weems created a market where none existed; he traveled, displaying sample books in taverns and taking orders. He then deputized men in those outlying areas to act as his agents in the network he created. He reported back to Mathew what books men required and he himself wrote books for popular taste—among them *The Life and Memorable Actions of George Washington* (Baltimore, 1800). In 1809, after "some 16 editions of as many as 5,000 copies each had been sold . . . Carey bought the copyright and began to publish it" (J. Green 1985, 12). Carey, then, understood the publisher's need to hire salesmen who, rather than just distributors to existing outlets, were themselves entrepreneurs.

There is no suggestion in the archives I consulted that the U.S. government subsidized Carey, or any other of the U.S. publishers we have seen, in the development of foreign markets. This contrasts with British practice where the Foreign Office provided money for the publication of magazines helpful to that country's interests, and carried copies in diplomatic pouches into Cádiz when England was fighting there against French occupation.[182] Instead Carey and other publishers seem to have relied on their own pluck and ingenuity in dreaming up ways to earn a living. Mail service had not yet been regularized in the United States so that travelers personally carried friends' letters and commercial papers; the U.S. Navy had only recently been funded but, after the Revolutionary War and on into the period of the War of 1812, individual merchant mariners bore the burden of furthering U.S. trade and eluding pirates and enemy ships;[183] diplomatic relations were still being negotiated between the United States and Mexico. Robeson depended on the U.S. consul in Havana for getting his money home. But it is not clear if the U.S. Navy protected his ships.[184]

We have seen that U.S. publishers widened their business by contracting out with printers for that portion of their work and exchanging with publishers in other cities copies of their output, which they would then sell. Carey also followed these practices. George Phillips printed for Carey Humboldt's *Personal Narratives of Travels to the Equinoctial Regions of the New Continent*. In 1816 the Philadelphia printer Lydia R. Bailey printed for Carey Henry Salt's *A Voyage to Abyssinia* (Bailey inherited her husband's business and operated it, also printing tracts for Philadelphia's Female Tract Society). In 1816, together with Wells and Lilly in Boston, Carey published John Howe's *Travels in the Interior of Brazil, particularly in the gold and diamond districts* and Etienne Jouy's *Paris Chit-Chat*. He maintained an office in Baltimore where Henry had learned his trade, and in New York where he kept the agent, Daniel Arden, during 1822–1823. He dealt with the New Orleans company Morgan Dorsey, which we will see later; a bill from that company to Carey, dated February 4, 1822, charges Carey with the storage of twelve boxes of books for five months. (One wonders whether these were the Spanish-language books that Carey had printed in 1821 and which were ready for Follin and Malsain, whom we will see, to pick up and take on to Mexico in the Spring of 1822.)

Carey's business was facilitated by the establishment in Philadelphia in 1816 of the United States' first paper-making machine. The Gilpin brothers, Joshua and Thomas, brought a copy of the English Foudrinier machine to the city; and Carey quickly advertised that he was using their machine-made paper. In 1819 Carey printed a series of addresses by the Philadelphia Society for the Promotion of National Industry on this paper; the addresses proclaimed "To be independent for the comforts of life, we must fabricate them ourselves. We must now place the manufacturer by the side of the agriculturalist."[185]

How much Carey paid his translators and proofreaders is suggested in a letter Matthias O'Conway wrote to the company on March 7, 1822. There he agrees to translate the unidentified work for $200 in a period of three months. He continues: "If I correct the proofs, I must be paid at the rate allowed for foreign languages. The work is arduous, the price moderate. Merchants pay me one dollar per page, without the drudgery of correcting proofs. Such are my terms from which I shall not swerve."

An indication of how Carey contracted with authors is provided by the record of his dealings in 1820 with William Davis Robinson, a fellow Philadelphian whom we have seen.[186] Robinson was an established author; he had already had published in Georgetown, D.C. *A Cursory View of Spanish America, particularly the neighbouring vice-royalties of Mexico and New-Grenada, chiefly intended to elucidate the policy of an early connection between the United States and those countries* (1815, Richards and Mallory), and in London *Memoir addressed to persons of the Jewish religion in Europe on the subject of emigration to, and settlement in, one of the most eligible parts of the United States of North America* (H. Hay, 1819).

Robinson proposed to Carey publication of a manuscript that "has been put into my hands written by a British officer who accompanied Mina to Mexico." Francisco Javier Mina was a Spaniard who had fought in the Peninsular War to expel Napoleon; but when Fernando returned, he decided to come to the Americas to fight there for reform (see Figure 1.4). Mina went first to London where he met Fray Servando Teresa de Mier, who sympathized with his plan, and then came to the United States to raise money and recruit men for an invasion of Mexico, where he expected to be well received. In the United States he got help especially in Catholic Baltimore, and in 1817 his army of British, U.S., and Spanish Americans left New Orleans for Mexico. Within months he was shot by royalist forces, and members of his army—Mier and John Bradburn, whom we will later see—were imprisoned.

In Robinson's first letter to Carey (February 26, 1820), he writes enthusiastically that this manuscript "will create no common sensation among the Dons ... [because it shows on] what a slender thread hangs Mexico." However, Robinson did not want to put up any of his money in the publication and instead he asked Carey to publish it and then time to pay off his debt. On April 2, Carey offered to print 1,500 copies for $750; Robinson would sell the work to subscribers in Philadelphia, Washington, and Baltimore (there is no mention of a Spanish-language edition for Mexico although in an undated letter Robinson asked that 200–300 copies be sent to New Orleans). The exchange of letters went on throughout 1820 with Robinson increasingly pessimistic about the book's sale. On October 23, Robinson wrote that he did not want to be bothered with selling the books and offered to sell the copyright. In fact, demonstrating how quickly books were rushed into print, in December 1820, another Philadelphia printer, Lydia Bailey, put the book out as *Memoirs of the Mexican Revolution*.[187]

It must be noted that Robinson's contemporary history, written for consumption in the United States and England, is not just the story of a British officer. As we have seen, Robinson had traveled in Mexico at the height of the insurgency so he augmented the Britisher's story with his own views of events

FIGURE 1.4 Portrait of General Xavier Mina.

and the country's commercial promise if independence was successful. The book also incorporated, without naming the author, material from Mier's *Historia de la revolución de Nueva España*, published in London in 1813 under the pseudonym José Guerra. Mier had drawn together in his *Historia* documents he was daily receiving from friends in Spain and Mexico so that his "history" was more like a journalistic summary, written to defend the Mexican rebels and refute Spain's propaganda. However, Robinson must not be seen as a plagiarist but rather as a disseminator in the English-speaking world of a point of view not understood there. If he did not name Mier it was to protect him. Robinson's book also included details of a plan for constructing a canal across the Isthmus of Tehuantepec so as to link the Atlantic and the Pacific. Then, in a long section, Robinson told his story. Imprisoned in Mexico in San Juan de Ulúa (where Robinson coincided with Mier and Carlos María Bustamante, whom we will meet later) and Cádiz, and threatened with banishment to an African jail, Robinson had his own exciting personal experience to narrate. In addition, Robinson probably also met Roscio in Philadelphia before Roscio returned to Venezuela (in *Memoirs* Robinson points out the irony of monarchical Spain seeking to negotiate a truce with "one of its most illustrious victims").

Although other U.S. cities published Spanish-language books in this period, Philadelphia seems to have been the center for foreign-language publishing. Despite some nativist jealousies in the Delaware River valley, print records tell of the city's welcoming character. In 1796, Morgan Rhees's sermon, "The Good Samaritan: An Oration delivered on Sunday evening, May 22, 1796, in behalf of the Philadelphia Society for the Information and Assistance of Persons Emigrating from Foreign Countries" was published by the Philadelphia printers, Lang and Ustick. Responding to this hospitality, the Spanish-speaking community grew.[188] Between 1790 and 1810 the mostly Peninsula-born Spaniards in Philadelphia were largely diplomats and businessmen. The first three rows of pews in St. Mary's Roman Catholic Church were reserved for the Spanish delegation, and St. Augustine Church was another place where Spaniards met important Philadelphians like Stephen Girard.[189] The city's Quaker freedoms, as well as the example set by Pennsylvania's payment to the Indians for their lands (thus seeming to ratify property rights and the rule of law), also made life there seem agreeable.[190] In fact, Philadelphia's Quaker culture was written into a widely read Spanish novel and educational treatise, *Eusebio*, by Pedro Montengón, a secularized Jesuit in Italy. In the work, published in Madrid between 1784 and 1788, the hero is shipwrecked off the Pennsylvania coast, saved by a Quaker couple, and educated in an idealized Philadelphia.

The myth of Philadelphia as a peaceful center where freedom of the press permitted publication of what the Spanish American countries themselves could not print and circulate may explain one publication mystery. "Philadelphia," as I have said, appears as the place of publication of Rocafuerte's *Bosquejo ligerísimo de la revolución de Mégico*. Yet the strange name of the publisher, Teracrouef y Naroajeb (in which Rocafuerte's name is hidden), has led some scholars to doubt that that attack on Iturbide was published in Philadelphia and instead argue that it came out in Havana. "Charleston" as the imprint of an edition in 1813 of Rousseau's *Social Contract* is also generally thought to be a blind attribution to conceal its publication from Spanish and Spanish American censors. Scholars mention this work but nobody seems to have a copy of it.[191]

Philadelphia's printers themselves attracted Spanish Americans who wanted to learn the trade. José G. Ricardo in his book on printing in Cuba tells that the Trinidad printer, Cristóbal Murtra, sent his son Francisco to Philadelphia in the 1820s to study typesetting and business methods with James Hardig (1989, 48–49). Cuba, still under Spanish colonial control, was increasingly looking to North American markets for its manufacturing development; Philadelphia's superiority in printing was well known in the Caribbean. We have seen that the Philadelphia printers Thomas and George Palmer published several Spanish-language books;[192] another "Palmer" printer in Cuba—Pedro Nolasco Palmer, who began business in Havana in 1791 and whose firm in 1814 became Pedro Nolasco Palmer e Hijo—printed a work for Rocafuerte in 1820.[193] Pedro Nolasco, a member of the Cuban Palmer family, lived in New York for a while as a correspondent of the newspaper *El Triunfo*.

One more Philadelphia publisher with ties to Spanish America was William Stavely, also an Irish Catholic immigrant. Stavely was not a high-volume publisher like Carey, but he published several works in Spanish. In 1826 Stavely printed for an unknown author the Spanish-language novel *Jicoténcal*. That work, one of Spanish America's first novels, is recorded in all of the histories of Spanish American literature as an early appearance of the genre; and, marking its importance in English-language circles at the time, William Cullen Bryant reviewed it in his *The United States Review and Literary Gazette*.[194] However, *Jicoténcal*'s Mexican story suggests that it was meant to be exported to Mexico, as well as to the Spanish Caribbean, Central and South America, because its narrative of Hernán Cortés and his soldiers advancing into Mexico with the aid of republican Indians and an Indian woman interpreter told Conquest history from an American perspective. The retelling, which revealed weakened defenses as tribes were split between imperial loyalists and republicans, would have resonated both historically and contemporarily. Thus the novel corrected metropolitan versions of that sixteenth-century invasion, which often featured European superiorities; and its story of internal politics presented the dilemma of present-day Americans, torn between traditionalism and republican reform. It is significant that *Jicoténcal* was published in Philadelphia, where the author could freely express his American views.

Mario Vargas Llosa, the modern-day Peruvian novelist, is the latest of the Spanish and Spanish American novelists to remark that the novel is often the only means whereby dissidents in a controlled society can voice their thoughts. "If you live in a country where there is nothing comparable to free information, often literature becomes the only way to be more informed about what's going on."[195] Consequently, *Jicoténcal* must be seen not only as historical retrieval or Romantic nostalgia but rather as an indictment of the authoritarian Iturbide's contemporary suppression of republicanism. The novel, then, was apparently an innocent literary artifact with a higher pedigree than journalism, but it was also a political screen. Stavely, then, who often published with Bringhurst, was a news reporter and political publisher; but he was also, as this novel shows, a literary purveyor. In 1821 Carey published the sixteenth-century picaresque novel *La vida de Lazarillo de Tormes*; and this work went in to Robeson's cargo for Mexico. However, it did not sell well and this miscalculation might have been one of the reasons his firm drew back from Spanish-language publishing. Stavely, however, continued his work with apparent success.

Other Philadelphia and New York publishers who specialized in Spanish-language publishing in the years from 1800 to 1830, besides Stavely, the Palmers, Hurtel, and Carey, were William Duane, Abraham Small, Thomas and William Bradford, Andrew Blocquerst, D. Huntington, William Grattan, Robert De Silver, and then later, the immigrant Spaniard Cayetano Lanuza (see Figure 1.5).[196]

—— LAS CASAS ——

We have seen that, in 1821, the Philadelphia printer, John F. (Juan Francisco or Jean-François) Hurtel, printed Fray Bartolomé de las Casas's *Breve relación de la destrucción de las Indias, presentada a Felipe II, siendo príncipe de Asturias*. Hurtel was the son of French colonists who had come to Alabama. The story of this Spanish-language republication of a sixteenth-century work in Philadelphia is significant here because it demonstrates relationships between printers in Paris, London, Philadelphia, and Mexico City. We begin in Paris in 1800 when the Abbé Grégoire read to the National Institute his "Apologie de Barthélemy de Las Casas, évêque de Chiappa" (later published as *Apologie de Barthélemy de Las Casas, évêque de Chiappa, par le citoyen G.; lu à l'Institut National le 22 Florel al an 8*).[197] Las Casas was a Spanish Dominican who went to the Americas in the sixteenth century, soon after their discovery, seeing firsthand Spain's cruelty toward the Indians. At midcentury, at a council in

Libros de fondo que se encuentran en casa de Lanuza y Mendia de Nueva York.

Diccionario filosófico de Voltaire, traducido por C. Lanuza, 10 tom. en 18o N. York 1825.
Cuentos y Sátiras de Voltaire, puestos en verso castellano por M. Domiuguez, un tom. en 18o N. York 1825.
El Vicario de Wakefield, por el Dr. Goldsmith, traducido por M. Domiuguez, un tom. en 18o N. York 1825.
Vida de Jorge Washington, por Ramsey, 2 tom. en 18o N. York 1825.
Compendio de la historia de los Estados Unidos, un tom. en 18o N. York 1825.
Auxiliar Vocabulario de bolsillo español ingles, por J. L. Barry, un tom. en 16o N. York 1825.
Fábulas de Samaniego, un tom. en 18o N. York 1826.
Fábulas de Iriarte, un tom. en 18o N. York 1826.
Ortografia de la lengua castellana, por la Academia española, un tom. en 18o N. York 1826.
Jicotencal, 2 tom. en 18o Filadelfia 1826.

EN PRENSA,

Vida de Benjamin Franklin, escrita por él mismo.
Clotilde, ó el Médico Confesor, por Victor Ducange.
Pérsiles y Sigismunda, última obra de Cervantes.

Tambien se hallará un gran surtido de libros españoles antiguos y modernos, y toda clase de encuadernaciones.

FIGURE 1.5 Page from *Jicoténcal* showing the list of books for sale at the New York bookstore of Lanuza y Mendia.

Valladolid, he participated in a theological debate, with legal overtones, with the Aristotelian Juan Ginés de Sepúlveda. Sepúlveda argued that indigenous Americans were "ignorant, unreasoning, and totally incapable of learning anything but the mechanical arts" and that natural law allowed Spain to forcibly convert them to Christianity. Las Casas defended the human nature of American natives and said that Spanish treatment of the indigenous population was the real barbarism. He called for protection for the Indians and instruction in the Catholic faith since they indeed had souls; well-meaning, he at first suggested that Africans might substitute for Indian labor—an idea that he quickly repudiated but which many took to be justification for the Atlantic slave trade. His *In Defense of the Indians*, a summary of his argument with Sepúlveda, was published in Latin in 1552. Before he died in 1566, Las Casas was named bishop of Chiapas, a southern region of present-day Mexico, where he lived and wrote.

Grégoire noted the Spanish priest's attempt to defend the human nature of American natives, and his defense of Las Casas draws on Las Casas's notion of several kinds of human nature in Europe, Africa, and the Americas. The 1791 slave rebellion in Haiti, which ousted the French, abolished slavery, and established black rule on the island, challenged France's policy of colonialism at a time when French legislators had just proclaimed men's essential freedoms and equality. Grégoire's focus on Las Casas, therefore, reflects political pressures to review earlier definitions of human nature, in the contexts of Christian and ancient belief but also in light of new anthropological findings and the experience of European travelers and colonial administrators.

London quickly seized on Las Casas's pertinence to international politics. England in those years was at war with France, fighting Napoleon across the European continent and waging an antislavery campaign in the Atlantic by intercepting slaving ships of various European powers. In 1812 the London printers Schulze and Dean published Las Casas's *Breve relación de la destrucción de las Indias Occidentales*, said to be a reprint of the sixteenth-century Sevilla edition. Their Spanish-language edition was probably designed for export to Spanish America where intellectuals, smarting at the assessments of eighteenth-century French naturalists of American nature as inferior, were in the process of gathering evidence of other views so as to justify their fight against European domination. This London book was carried to Philadelphia, probably by Fray Servando Teresa de Mier, who had known Grégoire in Paris and who was in London from 1811 until early 1815.[198] Indeed Mier, rather than Rocafuerte as has been claimed, was responsible for having engaged Hurtel to print the work. Proof of this exists in Mier documents in the library of the University of Texas (Austin) that reveal he paid $158 U.S. for the printing and for ten copies to be bound, and the fact that the Philadelphia edition includes a speech by Mier. This speech figures in an Austin letter that Mier wrote to Pedro Gual, dated September 12, 1821, in which he recommended that Gual have it read at Masses in Colombia; Mier claimed that when he read it at a Mass in Soto-la-Marina in 1817, the populace had been stirred to revolt.

In 1821 *Breve relación* was printed in Mexico by Mariano Ontiveros. Mier probably also carried the Philadelphia edition to Mexico. He had been in the United States from June 1821, until February 1822, returning to Mexico with Mina. When that invasion effort failed and Mier was captured, he was held in the Spanish prison of San Juan de Ulúa until May of that year before being allowed to proceed on to Mexico City. Ontiveros acknowledged that the work had previously been printed in Sevilla and Philadelphia. This admission, as well as the fact that the Philadelphia and the Mexico City editions both run to 164 pages, clinches the fact that Ontiveros based his edition on the Philadelphia text. Given recent colonial orthodoxies prohibiting foreign books, his confession of the text's Philadelphia origins seems strange until we think that under Iturbide's postcolonial government, it probably was intended to advertise that no Spanish official had interfered with its contents.

Thus we see Philadelphia's importance as a handover point in a route funneling European books to Mexico. In 1821 in Puebla, along the road from Veracruz to Mexico City, two editions of Las Casas's work were also printed; the Imprenta Liberal de Moreno Hermanos put out a 90-page work called *El Indio esclavo*, identified as authored by Las Casas,[199] and the 126-page *Brevísima relación de la destrucción de las Indias*.[200] Puebla had a separate cultural and printing history from Mexico City; its location allowed it to receive news from abroad more quickly and it prospered with its own business and important library. Its archbishop exercised considerable power, often challenging the viceregal government in Mexico City. In 1822 Ontiveros reprinted a 24-page version of what he claimed was the Puebla 1821 publication of *Destrucción de las Indias, o sea su conquista publicada en Sevilla el año de 1552*.[201] In 1822 Ontiveros republished his 164-page edition of the work from the previous year; an editor signed the preface "F.M.F." but indications are that this was Fray Servando Teresa de Mier. The Sutro Library's copy of this 1822 edition is bound together with six other works. It is not clear when the binding occurred, and whether the gathering was deliberate or accidental. The Sutro copy includes "The Supreme Governing Junta of the Kingdom to the Spanish Nation" (Valencia, J. de Orga, 1808),[202] "Political and Instructive Memorandum" (México, M. de Ontiveros, 1822; Mier is not identified as the author of this work),[203] "Hidalgo from Dolores" (México, Ontiveros, 1822),[204] "Blessing that our mother the Holy Church gives to the new king or emperor on the day of his coronation" (México, Valdés, 1822),[205] "Ceremonies of the Church" by Andrés Casaldo (México: Valdés, 1822),[206] "In honor of the great patriarch Saint Augustine" by Mariano Luis Estrada (México, Ontiveros, 1818).[207]

Before we leave Mexico, however, two other Mexican editions of *Breve relación* must be mentioned. An edition was published in 1822 in Guadalajara by D. Urano Sanromán; and in 1826 a version, *Crueldades que los españoles cometieron en los indios mexicanos*, was published in Mexico City by the Oficina de la testamentaría de Ontiveros with emblematic devices suggestive of Freemasonry on the frontispiece.

In Paris, interest in Las Casas was heating up again. There, in 1822, the printer Moreau printed for the bookseller Rosa Las Casas's collected works in Spanish, *Colección de las obras del venerable Obispo de Chiapas, Don Bartolomé de las Casas*. The editor was Juan Antonio Llorente, an exiled Spanish priest in Paris, who translated Las Casas's original Latin text and gathered unpublished documents into the printing. Llorente had the work published in French in Paris and in Brussels in that same year. His collection is remarkable, not just for the fact that it makes Las Casas's work available but also because it publishes hitherto-secret or generally inaccessible documents: "Letter written to Father Bartolomé Carranza de Miranda, resident in England by the Spanish king, Felipe II, in 1555, on the perpetuation of the Indian *encomienda* system";[208] "Response by Las Casas to an inquiry regarding the conquest of Peru in 1564";[209] "On the sovereign power of kings to dispose of the rights of vassals, peoples and jurisdictions" (written originally in Latin and published finally in Germany because it was forbidden in Spain);[210] "Apology by Grégoire, bishop of Blois, in which he tried to argue that Las Casas had no part in introducing African slaves into America";[211] "Dissertation of Doctor Gregorio de Funes, dean of Córdova in Tucumán (Argentina) in the form of a letter to Grégoire on the same topic";[212] "Report from Doctor Mier, native of Mexico, confirming the apology of Bishop Casas, written by the bishop of Blois, in a letter relating to the reports of Grégoire, Mier, and Funes."[213] The latter from Argentinean and Mexican theologians make clear American involvement in European debate, and a communication network apart from Madrid.[214] The fact that both the Mexican and Paris publications of Las Casas's *Destrucción* added related materials suggests that Las Casas was an author under whose umbrella critics of Spanish colonialism took refuge.

The Philadelphia imprint of *Breve relación*, then, shows the city to have been a vital link in the chain transmitting British and European materials to Mexico. The Spanish-language printing suggests that it was published for the export trade since no English edition appeared in the United States for many years.

PHILADELPHIA'S SPANISH-SPEAKING COMMUNITY

Perhaps the first Spanish speakers in the eastern United States date from the early eighteenth century.[215] Sephardic Jews who had fled Spain and Portugal and gone on to Holland and the West Indies came then to Philadelphia, as well as to New York, Newport, Charleston, and Savannah. Merchants and bankers, they helped to finance the Revolutionary War; and in their communities and synagogues continued a Ladino culture that made use of the fifteenth-century brand of the Spanish language that they spoke when they were expelled from the Peninsula in 1492. What documents exist show that they wrote their Spanish tongue in Hebrew characters and that they relied on printers in Amsterdam for the Hebrew religious and legal texts they required. However, their business dealings seem to have dictated that they generally merged rapidly into English-language society.[216]

In the first decades of the nineteenth century, as we have seen, Peninsular Spanish diplomats and businessmen predominated in cities and towns along the east coast of the United States. After 1814 when European monarchies reestablished their power at the Congress of Vienna and quashed republican movements throughout the continent, Spanish, French, and Italian republicans — and Spanish American revolutionaries — arrived. A Mexico City newspaper in 1814 published a piece of doggerel in which an ousted republican speaks of fleeing to Philadelphia to escape punishment by the Spanish king: "I intended to escape, with my luggage ready, to go to Philadelphia."[217]

Servando Teresa de Mier is typical of those political adventurers who came on to Philadelphia then and who made use of the city's print shops to criticize the Spanish king and advocate republicanism.[218] The Mexican Dominican priest, somewhat of a busybody, arrived after years in prisons in Mexico and Spain, and travels through France, Portugal, Italy, and England. In Paris he ran a language school and collaborated with Simón Rodríguez, Bolívar's tutor, in translating to Spanish Chateaubriand's *Atala* (Rodríguez took credit for it as "Samuel Robinson"). He met the Abbé Grégoire, who wrote letters of introduction for him and with whom he later corresponded. He observed in Paris, and in Rome and Spain, disputes in theological views and varieties of ecclesiastical practices. He was curious and open to difference; for example, in Bayonne across the Spanish border in France, he found a community of exiled Jews and participated with them in their Spanish synagogue rites. Thus he brought with him to Philadelphia a wealth of experience, familiarity with Europe's breakdown of authority, and a personal example of tolerance.[219]

In Mexico, he had antagonized authorities by preaching that St. Thomas had preceded the Spaniards in bringing Christianity to Mexico and so the Spanish claim that its power was responsible for evangelizing the country, justifying the takeover of indigenous peoples, was invalid. He was in Cádiz at the time the Cortes met there to write a constitution, entering into debate and joining a Masonic Lodge. Although he later claimed he never was a Mason,[220] he immediately entered Philadelphia's Masonic community, lodging with an influential Mason, Manuel Torres, chargé d'affaires for Gran Colombia—from whose private library Mier stole books under the pretext of borrowing.[221] In London, as we have seen, he had his *Historia de la revolución de Nueva España* published and made important contacts with Englishmen and exiled Spaniards. He joined Mina's 1817 invasion of Mexico and was returned again to a Mexican prison. In 1821, back in Philadelphia (from June 1821 to February 1822), he had his *Memoria politico-instructiva* published with the intent that it go to Mexico to Iturbide and his cabal who in the last stages of the insurgency were undecided as to what postwar government they should form. Many wanted a monarchy. But Mier, having experienced the duress of the Spanish monarchy and the disadvantages of a constitutional monarchy such as he witnessed in England, advocated a republic. He warned that, though Spain might sacrifice the rest of Spanish America, it would not give up its wealthiest colony. Fernando, along with his fellow monarchs in Europe, was planning to send a royal to govern in Mexico. Iturbide's insistence on instituting a monarchy only played into Europe's schemes for American dominance.

Memoria, then, was a republican tract. But into it Mier inserted selections from Paine's *Common Sense* (which he had translated previously) and late-breaking news from the gazettes he had access to in Philadelphia from London, Paris, Bordeaux, Madrid, and Veracruz. He told of Spain's sale of the Floridas to the United States, thus revealing the mother country's shameful willingness to trade for her own advantage the American possessions it had always described as beloved children. Hearing in Philadelphia of the interventionist politics of the Holy Alliance with regard to Spain's imminent loss of its American colonies but also with the Turkish presence in Greece, Mier relayed news of European monarchs' increasing solidarity and aggressiveness. By repeating what he heard from his Mexican sources, he advised Mexican rebels of the extent of the enemy's forces and the chances of their revolt's success. Reporting on general Mexican dissatisfaction with Spanish rule by citing the increasing use of anonymous broadsides to publicize disgust, he encouraged the insurgents who were operating in the provinces and would not have known of the scale of their support. Fearing that internal communications were disrupted, he told that independent troops took Alvarado in March or April but that by June no ships had left from there. Thus Mier, in postscripts to his book-length essay, sent news to Mexico. Philadelphia was a listening-post that gathered news and then, in turn, transmitted it back to American outposts. Mier, like Robinson, used his Philadelphia-printed book as a kind of newspaper.

Print records tell of another addition to Philadelphia's Spanish-speaking community. In "Manifesto que hace el Coronel Español, José Coppinger, demostrando el injusto y violento proceder que se ha observado en San Agustín de Florida, despojándole de Orden de la Autoridad gobernante, de los Archivos de su Gobierno y otros papeles, después de la Entrega de la Provincia a los EEUU,"[222] we learn that disgruntled Spaniards found their way to Philadelphia from Florida in 1819 after Spain sold the property to the United States. However, Joseph Coppinger Connor, who had been governor of St. Augustine and the person appointed by the captain-general of Cuba to deliver Florida to its new owners, was apparently not a Spaniard but an Irishman who worked for Spain. Coppinger must have retained his loyalty to Spain though, because in 1825 we see him fighting again for Spain as the military governor of the fort of San Juan de Ulúa in the bay of Veracruz where he surrendered this last Spanish holdout to Mexico.

Philadelphia's Spanish-speaking community, which can be called "international," "stateless," "expatriate," or even "drifting," was integrated into the city in several ways, the most important of which was through its use of Philadelphia's printers and publishers. The fact that Foronda and Mier did not speak English did not stop their participation; they not only sent their materials abroad but they also entered into dialogue with Philadelphia's intellectuals. Two items, again connected to Mier, prove this point. Although Foronda and Coppinger had written in Spanish, Mier, an ordained Catholic priest who claimed to have a doctorate in sacred theology from the University of Mexico, published his two 12- and 11-page pamphlets in Latin (to be translated later into English).[223] The first, "The opinion of the Rt. Rev. Servandus A. Mier . . . on certain queries proposed to him by the Rev. William Hogan," is dated July 11, 1821; the second, "A word relative to an anonymous pamphlet printed in Philadelphia, entitled 'Remarks on the opinion of the Rt. Rev. Servandus A. Mier,'" is dated August 17, 1821. No publisher is recorded for either. In the first Mier answers Hogan, the priest of St. Mary's Church in Philadelphia who had asked his help in a debate over a bishop's right to excommunicate a cleric under his jurisdiction; in the second Mier responds to an anonymous criticism of the theological arguments in the first pamphlet.[224] Mathew Carey, under the signature "A Catholic laymen," also entered this debate, publishing several pamphlets in defense of Hogan.[225] This was more than a local dispute. The Roman Inquisition took note of Hogan's and Mier's discussion and put their published works on the Index of Prohibited Books.[226] That fact suggests the oversight of Catholic authorities in the United States at that time—and their concern that privileges conceded to the Spanish king were up for grabs in Catholic areas of the Americas where independence was being declared. It also suggests that the Church was aware of the export of U.S.-printed works to Mexico and points beyond.

One gathers, then, that these Spanish speakers, although many were in the United States briefly, readily merged into that society. Printers invited their business. Catholic churches took them in. Philadelphia's welcoming spirit fostered their participation in local events. A liberal, republican spirit was also a universalizing principle that made them feel at home. Commercialism, key to new international relationships, promising harmony, made these travelers feel connected to one another despite their changing geography. Masonry offered them introductions, friendships, and protections.[227] Despite Mier's disclaimers, most believe he did join a Lodge in Cádiz, called the Sociedad de Caballeros Racionales, which has been variously labeled "Masonic" and "para-Masonic."[228] Torres's books helped to wean him away from English monarchism and convince him of American republicanism. Torres was a friend and father-figure to many like Rocafuerte. Torres paid the publishing costs for Mier's *Memoria* and Las Casas's *Brevísima relación*.[229]

One more source affords a glimpse into that Spanish-speaking community. Writing to John Quincy Adams, then Secretary of State, on December 17, 1822, Richard W. Meade, a Philadelphian whom we will meet again, tells that Torres had been accused of using his advantageous position to plot an invasion of Puerto Rico. Meade exculpates Torres by blaming others; but these, he says, were responsible for no more than petty schemes and mere selfish gain. Furthermore, their plans did not directly involve the United States. Meade and William Duane, publisher and editor of the paper *Aurora*, whom we have seen, were executors of Torres's estate after his death.[230] Meade writes:

> For many months prior to the declaration by this Government of the independence of the Spanish Americas, a set of adventurers existed in this country, holding their rendezvous in this city, Baltimore, and New York, watching their opportunity to undertake any adventure which could furnish them the means of living at the expense of their neighbors. Many of them were foreigners of desperate fortune, who, in their imaginations, fancied any project lawful which should put them in possession of the means of seizing on a portion of the Spanish colonies, under the pretence of establishing independent Governments, but, in fact, with no other view but that of enriching Themselves.[231]

Meade's letter goes on to quote the Mexican "Col. Cortés," whom we will also meet, in saying that these Spanish Americans shifted their loyalties according to the fortunes of factions back home; therefore, Spanish American politics in Philadelphia were increasingly hostile as rival parties vied for support. By 1822, although many Spanish speakers were upstanding members of Philadelphia society as they participated in the activities of the American Philosophical Society, various church parishes, and business alliances, others were rancorous transients.

The letter provides other insights. In mentioning a "Baptist Irvine" who "came to this city for the express purpose ... of procuring Spanish authors on the Americas, in order to complete a work which he had announced as being about to publish on those countries,"[232] Meade, who had been U.S. consul in Cádiz from 1806 to 1816, reveals that he lent Irvine, U.S. agent to Venezuela to whom Simón Bolívar had written an important letter ("Carta de Angostura," August 20, 1810),[233] a number of "valuable" books from his own library. Thus, this connection, if not friendship, between Meade and Irvine, two U.S. commercial agents with ties to Spain and Spanish America, helps us to understand how authors found their sources, and how sponsors such as Meade facilitated contacts and publication arrangements. Indeed, copies of two pamphlets by the Spanish Americans Roscio and José María Salazar, held in the Library Company of Philadelphia, bear dedications by their authors to the Philadelphia businessmen, William Duane and William White Chew, respectively.

Meade's letter to Adams also reveals the haste with which experience was being converted into literature for an avid reading public. The testimony of travelers, soldiers, and diplomats was increasingly fascinating not only the curious but also informing a new social class in the peacetime United States—businessmen who were seeking new markets and assessing the risks of overseas trade. If the political books by foreign authors were weapons to be exported to the propaganda wars and diplomatic campaigns in Spanish America, narratives of contacts abroad by knowledgeable compatriots (and maps and language instructional materials) were useful for U.S. tradesmen.

Philadelphia publishers of Spanish-related materials, then, served several markets: An English-speaking public in the growing United States interested in foreign culture and business opportunities; Spanish-speaking communities within the United States; and still another spread of readers in the West Indies, Mexico, and Central and South America. The populations of those lands were caught up in their respective rebellions against Spain; after 300 years of colonial rule, all, with the exception of Cuba and Puerto Rico, would gain their independence between 1821 and 1826–1827. Mexico would be the first; South America would not conclude its wars until later.

The Carey/Robeson letters found in the next chapter throw light on the U.S. book traffic to those Spanish American markets. In transcribing the letters, I have abridged the sometimes repetitive material to get at the essential story, introduced punctuation, and modernized the old spelling.

NOTES

1. "Desultory Facts, and Observations."
2. For background on Carey, see James N. Green's studies; Bradsher, Rowe —also Carey's several publications.
3. Remer is excellent on these distinctions.
4. Discussion here is drawn from Remer, Chapters 1 and 2.
5. The following discussion relies on Kinane.
6. See Kaser.
7. There is no publication information for these titles so one assumes they are foreign imprints.
8. "Catechism containing the elements of the Roman Catholic faith, with morning and evening prayers, Litanies of the Name of Jesus, those of the Holy Virgin, and the song of M. de Fénelon on the Passion of Our Lord Jesus Christ."
9. This was followed by a second edition in 1810. Montesinos describes Alea as a supporter of José Bonaparte, forced to leave Spain with the change of government. He committed suicide in France.
10. *Documentos relativos a la Independencia de Norteamérica*, Vol. 5 (2), p. 656.
11. "Historical and Moral Pieces Taken from Celebrated Authors from Various Countries and Destined for the Instruction and Entertainment of Students of the Spanish Language, 195 pp.
12. For example: Carey's printing in 1813 of Miss Cuthbertson's *Santo Sebastiano, or the Young Protector* (the author had also written *The Romance of the Pyrenees*); in 1816 of Mrs. Bridget Bluemantle's *Monte Video; or, the officer's wife and her sister, a novel* (in two volumes) and Leigh Hunt's "The story of Rimini, a poem"; and in 1818 the printing in Philadelphia by William Greer for Benjamin Warner of the third edition of Robert Southey's *Letters from England, by Don Manuel Alvarez Espriella, translated from the Spanish* (in two volumes).
13. This 14-page "interlude" does not identify the Lope play it borrows from. However, a note at the end says that it inspired Molière in "L'Ecole des Maris," Wycherley in "The Country Wife," and Sheridan in "The Duenna."
14. "The Challenge," "The Virtuous Country Maid," "The Prideful and Vain Girl." These three exemplary novels, whose U. S. publication by Carey has been overlooked by scholars, were published originally by Josef Doblado in Madrid in 1800.
15. Published by G. Douglas, 72 pp. On Olavide, see Núñez, Alonso Seoane, Perdices Blas, Valle, Unzueta, Berruezo León. For identification of the pseudonym, I consulted Aguilar Piñal.
16. Menéndez y Pelayo says that Olavide helped Florian with this reworking (refundición) (140). An English translation was published in Boston in 1798,

"printed and sold by W. Spotswood, and C.P. Wayne": *Galatea, A Pastoral Romance; imitated from Cervantes, by M. de Florian; translated into English; To which is added, Amelia, or The Faithless Briton; Amelia or Malevolence Defeated; and Miss Seward's Monody on Major Andre; Embellished with Engravings.*

17. Florian in *La Jeunesse de Florian, ou Memoires d'un Jeune Espagnol; Ouvrage poshume* (Paris: J. Gratiot, 1807) fictionalizes his youth by setting events in Spain. In that work he disguises his love life but also his relationship with Voltaire. Florian's uncle and guardian had married a niece of Voltaire and Florian visited the writer in Ferney. Madrid stands in for Paris, and El Escorial for Versailles.

18. The story of this rewrite does not stop with Florian. Cándido María Trigueros took Florian's version and made other touches so that when it was published in Madrid in 1798 he claimed to be the author. See Aguilar Piñal, *Cándido María Trigueros*, pp. 248–255.

19. Whitestown, NY: Warren Barnard; Georgetown: Richards and Mallory.

20. New York: D. Longworth.

21. Baltimore: Ph. H. Nicklin and Co.; Philadelphia: Fry and Kammerer, 1810; Boston: James Loring, 1820. In the 1820 edition it is described as "a posthumous work to which is prefixed 'The life of the author' by Jauffret and translated from the French by William B. Hewetson."

22. Carey published this play in 1811.

23. Full title under his Spanishized name, Santiago Matthias O'Conway: *Hispano-Anglo Grammar, containing the definitions, structure, inflections, references, arrangement, concord, government and combination of the various classes of words in the Spanish language. An appropriate vocabulary, familiar phrases, dialogues, and a complete index* (399 pp.).

24. "Guide for Children to Help Them Learn to Spell and Read; or Method for Aiding the Progress of Children When They Are Sent to School for the First Time."

25. "Elements of the Spanish Language, founded on the principles established by the Spanish Academy." Republished in a second edition in 1824.

26. Philadelphia: A. Small and H.C. Carey and I. Lea, 2 vols.

27. "New Dictionary of the Two Languages, Spanish and English" (Filadelfia: Impreso a costa de Abraham Smith, 2 vols.).

28. "Extracts of the most celebrated Spanish writers and poets, in two parts, printed by J. Robinson and sold in the bookstore of Fielding Lucas.

29. Also printed by J. Robinson and sold by Fielding Lucas.

30. F. Lucas, Jr., 155 pp.

31. F. Lucas, Jr., J.D. Toy, printer, 2 vols.

32. "Grammar of the Castilian Language, Adapted to All Classes of Students and to Every System of Teaching" (printed by José Robinson, 219 pp.).

33. Many Germans had come to the United States as a result of the British Crown's Hanoverian connection. They established print shops (with special print fonts) in Philadelphia and Germantown. But at the time of the independence war, they were accused of siding with the British and many of their properties were confiscated. See the 1810 edition of Thomas for this and Spanish American printing.

34. A measure of Clavijo's fame is the fact that he was the subject of Goethe's *Clavigo* (1774).

35. Branson and Patrick, Dessens. The Philadelphia *Aurora*, in issues for 1815, regularly printed a separate category of "Poste restante" for the city's French speakers.

36. Claudius Berard, *Leçons Françaises a l'usage des commençans et surtout des cadets de l'Académie Militaire des Etats-Unis a West-Point*, 236 pp.

37. A Spanish translation of Cesare Beccaria's *Dei Delitti e delle Pene* (*Disertación sobre los delitos y las penas*) was published in Philadelphia in 1823 by Robert Wright (x, 148 pp.). However, Simmons in "Spanish and Spanish American Writer Politicians" quotes Francisco P. Laplaza to the effect that "Philadelphia" may be a false attribution and that the work may have been published in Spain, London or France since it had been prohibited in Spain (39).

38. Shoemaker lists many such works, particularly for 1826.

39. See Stein and Stein.

40. Spell in "An Illustrious Spaniard in Philadelphia, Valentín de Foronda," reports this detail without giving any more specifics. However, a full description is provided in the reprint of "Dictamen del doctor don Antonio Josef Ruiz de Padrón, Ministro Calificado del Santo Oficio, Abad de Villamartín de Valdeorres, y diputado en Cortes por las Islas Canarias, que se leyó en la sesión pública del 18 de enero sobre el Tribunal de la Inquisición, con algunas notas añadidas por el Pensador Mexicano" (México, Imprenta de don Mariano Ontiveros, 1820) in the *Obras* of Lizardi (Vol. 4, 285–328).

41. Cited in Defourneaux. For a description of foreign books in Spain then, see Herr; see also Spell's *Rousseau in the Spanish World*.

42. For a long discussion, see Stolley.

43. Miranda in his *Diary* describes his U.S. travels; see Racine on Miranda's life and career.

44. 108 pp. Who the editor and translator of what purports to be an account of their 1735–1746 voyage is unclear. He seems to have been a Londoner who says he got the manuscript from Ulloa who stopped in London on his way home to Spain. He says that in England Ulloa showed his materials to scientists and was rewarded by membership in the Royal Society. He also says that Ulloa's papers were immediately published by the Spanish king on his

return—it is true that a sanitized version of the report was published in Madrid in 1748. However, as we will see, David Barry's 1826 London edition is the first to print the full report of Spanish abuse and mismanagement in the colonies.

45. The second edition was published in Boston by Oliver and Munroe; the third in Boston by E. Oliver; and the fourth also in Boston by Edward Oliver.

46. Barlow used as the basis for his translation some work that Thomas Jefferson had already begun. This translating process is recorded in the 1835 edition of Volney's *Ruins* (Boston: Charles Gaylord), along with some of the controversy between Volney and Priestley. For Barlow's role in the translation, see also Mulford.

47. *The Congress of Vienna, trans. from the French* (Philadelphia: M. Carey; Boston: Wells, Lilly, 1816); *Europe after the Congress of Aix-la-Chapelle, Forming the sequel to the Congress of Vienna.* Trans. and with notes by George Alexander Otis (Philadelphia: M. Carey, 1820).

48. First part also printed in Baltimore by Benjamin Edes, 1810. Capmany (1742–1813), a philologist, is noted for his *Teatro histórico-crítico de la elocuencia española* (1786–1794), *Filosofía de la elocuencia*, as well as a French–Spanish dictionary in which he was concerned with the number of Gallicisms entering the Spanish language. He was policitized by the French invasion of Spain and participated in the debates at the Cortes de Cádiz. One speech was later printed as "Discurso pronunciado en sesión pública de las Cortes el día 9 de agosto del corriente denunciando el impreso intitulado 'El Defensor acérrimo de los derechos del pueblo, núm. 1" (Cádiz: Imprenta de De. Vicente de Lerna, 1813).

49. Full title: *An Exposition of the Commerce of Spanish America, with some observations upon its importance to the United States. To which are added A correct analysis of the monies, weights and measures of Spain, France, and the United States. With tables of their reciprocal reductions, and of the exchange between the United States, England, France, Holland, Hamburg, and between England, Spain, France and the several states of the Union.*

50. The author is generally thought to have been Manuel Palacio Fajardo, a Venezuelan who had accompanied Miranda and Bolívar and who was in London, seeking aid for the independence cause. The work was also published in London in 1817 by Longman, Hurst, Rea, Orme and Brown; in 1818 in Hamburg in a German translation by Hoffman und Campe; and in 1819 in Paris in a French translation by P. Mongie l'aine.

51. For background, see Wertheimer, Chapter 2.

52. Cited in Van Wyck Brooks, 225.

53. French Bourbon aesthetics, which had forced neoclassical rules of verisimilitude onto Spaniards in the eighteenth century, caused the country

to repudiate many of its Baroque fantasies from the Golden Age and rewrite many of the plays of Lope and Calderón. Thus Don Quijote was read as a hero who could be admired and imitated; he only erred in not understanding the age in which he lived and imagining that chivalry still existed. See Rodríguez Cepeda, Alvarez de Miranda, Schmidt; and for the United States, Wood.

54. For example, the burlesque of *Don Quijote* permitted a Spanish author, José Clemente Carnicero, to depict Napoleon as the Don Quixote of Europe, a foolish knight: "Napoleón o El verdadero Don Quixote de la Europa, o sea Comentarios Crítico-Patrióticos Burlescos a varios decretos y párrafos de las Gazetas de Napoleón y su hermano José. Escrito por un español amante de su Patria y Rey. Desde primeros de febrero de 1809 hasta principios de enero de 1810" (Madrid: Imprenta de Ibarra, 1813).

55. Gilbert Stuart painted their portraits, reproduced in *American Art: 1750–1800, Towards Independence* (111).

56. Spell, "An Illustrious Spaniard in Philadelphia," 136–140. McKean was the daughter of the governor of Pennsylvania, and her son was born in Philadelphia in 1802.

57. See Cooper, *Classical Taste in America, 1800–1840*, especially 68–71. However, Wainwright says the name came from the original owner, John Craig, who had a partnership with the Spaniard, Francisco Caballero Sarmiento, to trade with Spanish properties in the Americas (3).

58. See Wainwright, *Paintings and Miniatures at the Historical Society of Pennsylvania*.

59. Printed by H. Hall and J. DeJeane. Stroud in her biography of Bonaparte does not mention this work.

60. This work, said to be by "an American gentleman," was published in New York by I. Riley and Co. Grases discusses Irving's contribution in *El viajero Francisco Depons*.

61. For further discussion of Irving's interest in Spain, see Adorno.

62. "Syllabus of a course of lectures on the history and criticism of Spanish literature" (Cambridge: Printed at the University press by Hilliard and Metcalf, 84 pp.).

63. Indeed, sheet music for the piano and guitar was an important means by which Spanish-related themes entered the U.S. imagination. "General Bolivar's Grand March" and "March in Pizarro" were published in New York in 1821.

64. Humboldt had stopped in the United States. on his way home from Mexico and Cuba in 1804, visiting Jefferson.

65. This work detailed the travels of Humboldt and Aime Bonpland.

66. Ríos has published them in a Spanish translation.

67. *Documentos relativos a la Independencia de Norteamérica*, León Tello (Vol. 3, 2).

68. Kanellos and Martell. For background on the Floridas, see McMichael; for Spanish borderlands history in general, see Weber.

69. Daniel Clark, "Proofs of the Corruption of Gen. James Wilkinson; and of His Connexion with Aaron Burr" (Philadelphia: William Hall Jun. & George W. Pierie, 1809, 199 pp.). For background see Adams; Rydjord, Ch. 7, 12, 13; Isenberg; Dunkerley, Second Case. Charles Willson Peale painted Wilkinson's portrait in Philadelphia in 1796–1797.

70. "At a General Court Martial (of which Major General Henry Dearborn was president) convened at Utica, in the state of New York, on the 3d day of January, 1815 . . . Major General James Wilkinson was tried on the following charges and specifications. . . . " n.p.

71. "Voyage to South America: Performed by Order of the American Government in the years 1817 and 1818 in the Frigate Congress" (London: T. and J. Allman, 1820).

72. Philadelphia: Printed by William Greer for Johnson and Warner.

73. My discussion of the commercial interest of English speakers in the United States in Spanish-related materials is meant to augment studies of the printing industry that focus on production and ignore readership. For some appreciation of what U.S. readers actually read in the late eighteenth, early nineteenth century, see the dated but useful study by Van Wyck Brooks; and works by Davidson.

74. "Manifesto or honorable satisfaction to all good European Spaniards, and to all the peoples of America, by a deputy of the Courts gathered together in Cádiz," printer unknown, 83 pp.

75. "Objeciones satisfactorias del mundo imparcial; al folleto dado a luz por el marte-filosofo de Delaware, Don José Alvarez de Toledo, reimpreso con notas explanatorias" "Satisfying objections from the impartial world to the pamphlet put out by the war-time philosopher from Delaware . . . with explanatory notes" (no printer).

76. "The Friend of Men to All Those Who Inhabit the Islands and the Vast Continent of Spanish America, A Small Curious, Interesting and Agreeable Work, Followed by a Discourse on Religious Intolerance" (Philadelphia: Printed by Andrés José Blocquerst, 25 pp.).

77. "A Republican's Manual for the use of a free people" (Printed by T. y J. Palmer, 35 pp.). Simmons says this is "a dialogue between a teacher and a student wherein the former tries to instill republican ideas in the mind of his questioning pupil" (32).

78. *Documentos relativos a la Independencia de Norteamérica*, León Tello (Vol. 3, No. 1, 429). This six-set guide to documents in Spanish archives was

put out on the occasion of the U.S. Bicentennial and is a useful addition to what is known in the U.S. and Mexican libraries.

79. "The triumph of liberty and patriotism, written by 'The Tender-hearted Patriot'" (Printer unknown, 11 pp.). Simmons says this was "an exhortation to Mexicans to resist the military expedition that Alvarez de Toledo was by this time actively directing against San Antonio de Béxar" (32).

80. "Critical Examination of the Decree [issued by] the Courts on Feb. 23, 1813, written by a Spaniard resident in the U.S., August, 1813" (New York: Printed by Quadrante).

81. Studies of Alvarez de Toledo are many. See Sevilla-Soler (42–43); Santana; Kanellos "José Alvarez de Toledo y Dubois"; Dykstra; Palmer; and the documentation provided by Luis de Onís in *Documentos relativos a la Independencia de Norteamérica*, León Tello (3, 1). On the Monroe meeting, see Santana, 14..

82. León Tello (3,1, 605).

83. *Documentos*, León Tello (3, 1, 605).

84. See Kanellos, *Hispanic Periodicals in the U.S.*

85. Cabral had published the Cádiz newspaper "El Duende Cosmopolita" and, when he got to Philadelphia, started "El Cosmopolita Sensible, o El Duende en la América." See Solís and also Guzmán who fictionalizes these characters in his novel.

86. *Breve relación de la destrucción de las Indias Occidentales . . . Impresa en Sevilla. Reimpresa en Londres y ahora en Filadelfia* (Brief Account of the destruction of the West Indies . . . printed in Sevilla. Reprinted in London and now in Philadelphia, Juan F. Hurtel, 1821, 164 pp.).

87. "Ideas necessary for every American People which desires to be free" (Philadelphia: D. Huntington, 180 pp.), republished in Puebla in 1823 by Pedro de la Rosa. On Rocafuerte, see Rodríguez O. (1975), particularly Ch. 3; Cordero Aroca.

88. *Bosquejo ligerísimo de la revolución de Mégico, desde el grito de Iguala hasta la proclamación imperial de Iturbide. Por un verdadero americano.* "Quick Sketch of the Revolution in Mexico, from the Cry of Iguala to the imperial proclamation of Iturbide. By a True American" (Philadelphia: Imprenta de Teracrouef y Naroajeb). I have used the facsimile edition. Labastida in the prologue questions whether a Philadelphia printer printed the work (42–46, 52–55).

89. "The Columbian System Is the One Most Advisable for Independent America" (New York: Imprenta de A. Paul).

90. "A la juventud americana" in *Lecciones para las escuelas de primeras letras, sacadas de las Sagradas Escrituras, siguiendo el texto literal de la traducción del Padre Scío, sin notas ni comentarios* "To American Youth" in "Lessons

for primary schools, taken from Holy Scripture, following the literal text of the translation by Father Scio, without notes or commentary" (New York: A. Paul).

91. "The triumph of liberty over despotism in the confession of a sinner repentant of his political errors, and dedicated to redress in this part of the World the wrongs done to religion by the system of tyranny" (Filadelfia: Thomas H. Palmer, 406 pp), (Filadelfia: Imp. de M. Carey e Hijos, 1821, 365 pp.). I have used the facsimile edition.

92. "Homily of Cardinal Chiaramonte, Bishop of Imola, Presently His Holiness Pius VII' (Filadelfia: J.F. Hurtel). His translation is based on the Abbe Grégoire's French translation from the Italian (Gerona, 1800). Miliani considers Roscio's refutation to be a separate work, saying that it was not published until 1820 and that no copy survives (xxiv).

93. See Mier, *Memoria politico-instructiva enviada desde Filadelfia en agosto de 1821 a los gefes independientes del Anáhuac, llamado por los españoles Nueva España* "Instructive Political Memorandum" (Juan F. Hurtel, 12 & 4 pp.)

94. "Constitution of the republic of Colombia, printed in the town of Rosario de Cúcuta, August, 1821."

95. "American Letters, both political and moral," "Project for a Penal Code," and "Plan for Peru; defects in the older Spanish government, necessary reforms, or a work written ... at the beginning of the year 1810 in Cádiz, and today augmented with interesting notes" (225 pp.).

96. Translated by Don Juan de Olero. This work was published in a translation by Tomás de Iriarte in several editions in Madrid (1798, 1803, 1820).

97. "Lessons in rhetoric that the president of the Academy of Theoretical and Practical Law gave to graduates ... " 240 pp.

98. "Manifesto of the President of the United Mexican States to his Compatriots," 14 pp. Note that Mexico's name is now modeled after that of its northern neighbor.

99. *El Habanero* is available in a modern edition.

100. "un cadáver unido a un ser viviente" (120–121).

101. "To Cubans" (n.p., Sept. 10, 1825).

102. "Observations on the commerce of Spain with her colonies, in time of war, by a Spaniard in Philadelphia. Translated from the original manuscript by another Spaniard" (Philadelphia: James Carey, 1800, vii, 63 pp.). Remer describes the less-successful James (48–49).

103. "Observations on the Existing Differences between the government of Spain and the United States" (Philadelphia: n.p., 20, 25, 52 and 8 pp.). Simmons in "Spanish and Spanish American Writer Politicians" attempts to solve problems of their chronology.

104. "Dialogue on the independence of Spanish America between an enthusiastic liberal and an old-fashioned philosopher" (T. y J. Palmer, 1812, 18 pp.).

105. "Impartial reflections on Freemasonry" (Thomas H. Palmer, 1818, 30 pp.).

106. Letter of George W. Irving to James Monroe (Jan. 4, 1816). Quoted by Whitaker, 58–59.

107. For background on Foronda, see Garate, Benavides y Rollán, Barrenechea. These studies correct the common error that "Foronda" was a pseudonym for Juan Valentín Matías Fabbroni.

108. See Pradells Nadal.

109. Legajo 1706, *Descriptive Catalogue*.

110. Shafer studies such societies, founded to promote Enlightenment ideas of progress.

111. *Instituciones Políticas. Obra en que se trata de los Reynos de Portugal y España, de su situación local, de sus posesiones, de sus vecinos, y límites, de su clima, y producciones, de sus manufacturas, y fábricas, de su Comercio, de los habitantes, y de su número, de la nobleza, de la forma de su gobierno, de sus Departamentos, del Soberano, y de sus Títulos, y en que se fundan; de la sucesión al Trono, de sus Exércitos, y Marina, de sus Rentas, de la política general de cada Corte, y de la política particular para con otras Potencias. Escrita en idioma francés por el Varón de Bielfeld. Y traducida al castellano aumentada de muchas notas por Don Valentín de Foronda.* (Burdeos: Casa de Francisco Mor, 1780, viii y 156 pp.).

112. Madrid: Don Benito Cano, 1800.

113. Montesinos, 21.

114. However, a curious publication by Josef Bruno tells another story. In *Privada y oficial correspondencia de . . . Secretario de Legación de S.M.C., cerca de los E.U. de la América Septentrional, con el Marqués de Irujo* (Philadelphia: William Duane, 1806, viii, 179 pp.), Bruno writes that, after initially enjoying hospitality in Foronda's home, he had a falling out with him and engaged Duane to have 25 copies of this complaint printed and distributed. Foronda also seems to have been at odds with Irujo, and then later with Onís.

115. Onís, "Valentín de Foronda's Memoir on the United Status of North America, 1804," *The Americas* 4 (1948): 351–387, quoted in Benavides y Rollán (129).

116. The U.S. Hispanist, George Ticknor, is convinced that this 74-page work, published under the pseudonym T.E., was Foronda's. A copy with Ticknor's manuscript notes is in the Library of Congress.

117. Torales Pacheco, 154–155. Torales has studied the Iturbe family in her "La familia Yraeta, Yturbe e Ycaza". She notes that the Iturbe daughters married foreigners.

118. Delgado Carranco, *Libertad de imprenta, política y educación*, 94.

119. Spell documents this edition in *Rousseau in the Spanish World: Cartas sobre la obra de Rousseau titulada: Contrato social, en las que se vacía todo lo interesante de ella, y se suprime lo que puede herir la religion católica apostólica romana. Por el ciudadano Valentín de Foronda.* (Coruña: Oficina de Don Antonio Rodríguez, 1814, 228 pp.). Spell says that because all copies were ordered destroyed, existing copies are rare (284).

120. "Letter on what a prince should do who has colonies at great distance" (Philadelphia: n.p., 15 pp.). The essay includes a letter dated March 1, 1800. Barrenechea mentions another 1803 pamphlet that he says was printed in Philadelphia, "Carta sobre los efectos productores de la educación. Escrita a un príncipe imaginario" (Letters on the productive effects of education). I cannot find documentation for this. Benavides y Rollán mention still another "Carta" from 1803, for which Foronda requested permission to publish from Irujo. It was denied and so the fiction of "Carta que se supone escrita en Boston por un comerciante en Filadelfia" was never published. In it Foronda sets out the disadvantages for Pennsylvania as a result of the Lousiana Purchase; the northern state will not be able to compete with the agricultural output of Kentucky nor with the port of New Orleans.

121. "suponer las Colonias como una oveja que debe conservar su amo para cortarle la lana y chuparle la leche."

122. *Obras*, Vol. 3, 399.

123. "Letters presented to the Philosophical Society of Philadelphia" (Philadelphia: Thomas y Guillermo Bradford, 56 pp.).

124. Feijoo (1676–1764), a Spanish Benedictine, was a prolific writer on various social topics. He analyzed national languages and temperaments.

125. "A Few Slight Notes on the New Constitution Projected by the Supreme Spanish Junta, and Reforms that It Is Attempting to Undertake in Law" (Philadelphia: Thomas y Jorge Palmer, 1809, 15 & 1 pp.).

126. "Como estoy persuadido a que el Pueblo, esto es la Nación es el verdadero Soberano: verdad tan incontrastable como el Peñón de Gibraltar, y que se halla en el corazón de todos; aunque enterrada baxo de las Bayonetas, y que por fortuna de España puede desenterrarse en el día"....

127. "Letters for the friends and enemies of Don Valentín de Foronda, business representative and cónsul general for His Royal Catholic Majesty Fernando VII, regarding the United States of North America relative to what has happened in Spain with respect to the emperor Napoleon I having named his brother Joseph king of Spain and the Indies." (Philadelphia: Thomas y Jorge Palmer, 10 pp.). A third edition was published the next year, 39 pp. with additional material, also printed by Palmer.

128. "Expediente formado de una Proclama de José Bonaparte, y otros papeles, que remitió a este Tribunal El Exmo. E Illmo. Sr. Arzobispo Virrey

Dr. Francisco Xavier de Lizana. Se prohibió en Edicto de 22 de Abril de 1810". (File formed on the basis of a proclamation by José Bonaparte, and other papers, that His Most Excellency the Archbishop and Viceroy Dr. Francisco Xavier de Lizana sent to this Tribunal. It was prohibited in an edict on April 22, 1810). This document is housed in the Bancroft Library (University of California, Berkeley), Vol. 21:4, No. 2749). See Rydjord, Ch. 17–18, particularly p. 299, for further discussion.

129. "No hay unión con los tiranos, morirá quien lo pretenda; o sea, La muerte de Riego y España entre cadenas. Tragedia en cinco actos por F.M., autor del periódico que se publicó en España con el título de Zurriago en los años de 1821-1822 y 1823. La da a luz el P.J.J.M.X. del R. [Juan José Manuel Ximénez del Río" (There is no union under tyrants, anyone will die who tries [to attempt it]; that is, The Death of Riego and Spain in chains. A tragedy in five acts by F.M., author of the newspaper published in Spain with the title "The Whip" in the years 1821–1822 and 1823. It is published by P.J.J.M.X. del R" (Philadelphia: Stavely and Bringhurst), republished in Mexico in 1825 by J. Cabrera, 56 pp.

130. "Pizarro and the Peruvians."

131. "La Fayette at Mount Vernon, Oct. 17, 1824. Drama in two acts" (Philadelphia: Stavely y Bringhurst, 30 pp.).

132. "William Tell, or Free Switzerland."

133. "Eliezer y Nephtaly, poema en quatro cantos traducido del hebreo al frances por Mr. Florian, y puesto en verso español por Felix Megía" (Filadelfia: Imprenta de Guillermo Stavely, 1826), [7] 93 pps.

134. "Encíclica del Papa Leon XII, en auxilio del tirano del Español Fernando VII [24 September, 1824]. Con una disertación en sentido opuesto por F. Megía. Discurso del señor De Witt Clinton, gobernador de Nueva York, a El Sol de la Verdad [translated from the English by C. de Oviedo] (Filadelfia: 1826). This item is held in the British Library.

135. Traducido del inglés al español por Jph. Manuel Villavicencio. (Philadelphia: Imprenta de Smith & M'Kenzie, 28 pp.).

136. "The Independence of the Mainland Justified by Thomas Paine Thirty Years Ago" (Filadelfia: T. y J. Palmer, 255 pp.).

137. (Filadelfia: T. y J. Palmer, 405 pp.) The English-language original had gone into a third edition by 1807.

138. *La libertad de los mares; o, El gobierno inglés descubierto. Traducido libremente del francés al castellano por dr. Carlos Le Brun* ("Freedom of the seas; or the government of England exposed." Filadelfia: Juan F. Hurtel, lvi, 325 pp.). On the cover: "To the philosopher of Montecello. Thomas Jefferson, ex-president of the United Statuses." Barère de Vieuzac (1755-1841), an important member of the French Assembly after the Revolution, had been consul in La Coruña.

139. *El derecho del hombre para el uso y provecho del género humano. Compuesto por Don Tomás Paine, Miembro de la Convención nacional de Francia; Secretario del Congreso, durante la Guerra de América; autor de la obra, intitulada* Common Sense *(Sentido Común, &&)*. Traducida del inglés por Santiago Felipe Puglia ("Rights of Man for the use and benefit of humankind") (Filadelfia: Matías Carey e Hijos, 1821, 168 pp.; Filadelfia: H.C. Carey y Lea, 1822, 168 pp.).

140. *El contrato social; o Principios del derecho politico*, nueva edición, revisada y corregida (Filadelfia: M. Carey e hijos, 1821, 180 pp.; Filadelfia: H.C. Carey & I. Lea, 1822, 180 pp.).

141. *El espíritu del despotismo. Traducido del Inglés, y dedicado al Excelentísimo Señor Don Simón Bolívar, Presidente de la República de Colombia, por Eduardo Barry* ("The Spirit of Despotism. Translated from the English and dedicated to His Most Excellent D. Simón Bolívar, president of the republic of Colombia by Edward Barry" Filadelfia: Imprenta de H.C. Carey y I. Lea, 1822, 223 pp.).

142. Grases y Harkness. García de Sena admits his limited knowledge of English (42) and even apologizes for his errors in Spanish owing to the lack of access to instructive books in the United States (38).

143. William D. Robinson was the bearer of one 1815 letter that Domingo García Sena sent to his family in Venezuela (Grases y Harkness, 28).

144. Grases y Harkness tell that the Scottish-born M'Culloch retailed the histories of William Gordon and David Ramsay, as well as the travel account among the Indians by Jonathan Carver, in a book to be used by schoolchildren.

145. Simmons, Grases y Harkness assert the following: In Venezuela, in 1811, Francisco Javier Yanes wanted to declare independence on July 4 in imitation of the U.S. Declaration, and Antonio Nicolás Briceño read García de Sena's translation of the U.S. constitution aloud in the national assembly. In Buenos Aires, in 1816, an advertisement in the *Gaceta* told that David Curtis DeForest offered the book for sale, and Henry Brackenridge reported that "nearly all who can read" had read it. In Uruguay, in 1816, José Artigas openly admired it (55–56). See also León Tello (3, 1, 387).

146. Carey's translation practices differed from those of his heirs. Kaser writes " although Carey and Lea frequently hired persons to translate medical and technical works from French, they seldom did so for memoirs, biographies, recollections, and histories. They chose rather to wait until the work had been translated and published in England, so that they could reprint from a London edition. This practice they found to be considerably cheaper" (115).

147. ("Dr. Carlos Le Brun, Ciudadano de los Estados Unidos e Intérprete del Gobierno de la República de Pennsylvania; autor 'Del Beneficio de un Filósofo', 'De la Gramática Imperial Inglesa y Española', y Traductor 'del

Anti-Anglómano', de los Ensayos de Pope, sobre el Hombre', y otros libros de literatura", Filadelfia: Se encontrará de venta en casa de los Señores M. Carey e Hijo, y la de los principales libreros de los Estados Unidos, Julio 4, 1820, el 45 de la Independencia de los Estados Unidos. On the copyright page: 'Dedica, con el más alto respeto, esta obra al amante de su patria, al sabio, al virtuoso Doctor Juan G. Roscio, vice-Presidente de Venezuela, su fiel amigo y admirador; Carlos Le Brun'"). Lizardi cites Le Brun in his *Obras*, Vol. 5, 442–443. It is not clear how this Le Brun is related to Charles François Lebrun (1739–1824), member of the French Constituent Assembly, or to Jean-Baptiste Pierre LeBrun (1748-1813), husband to Elisabeth Vigee-LeBrun and an important collector of paintings for the Louvre, or if he is Charles-Antoine Pigault-Lebrun (1753–1835).

148. Le Brun must only have been a translator of this work because Clarkin says that Carey merely used as the basis "an earlier school reading book" (115), taking illustrations from earlier plates. However, Le Brun transposed the order of fables, innovated by giving the Lord's Prayer and the Creed as reading exercises, and wrote the Salve Regina in Spanish.

149. "Essai sur l'homme, traduit par Charles Le Brun" (Philadelphia: Le traducteur, 1823, 228 pp.).

150. *Retratos politicos de la revolución de España, o de los principales personages que han jugado en ella, muchos de los cuales están sacados en caricaturas por el ridículo en que ellos mismos se habían puesto, quando el retratista los iba sacando: con unas observaciones políticas al fin sobre la misma: y la resolución de la question de porqué se malogró ésta, y no la de los Estados Unidos, publicados en Castellano por Dn. Carlos Le Brun* ("Political portraits of the revolution in Spain, or of the principal personages who have participated in it, many of whom are caricatured according to the ridicule that they themselves created when the portraitist saw them: with some relative political observations: and resolution of the question of why the Spanish revolution failed and not that of the U.S., published in Spanish by . . . ") (Impreso en Filadelfia, donde se encontrará de venta en casa del editor [9], 422 pp.). *Vida de Fernando, rey de España; o Colección de anécdotas de su nacimiento y de su carrera* ("Life of Ferdinand, king of Spain; or A Collection of anecdotes of his birth and career") (Filadelfia: [I. Ashmead & Co.], 341 pp.).

151. This was a translation of Barère's *Liberté des mers, ou le gouvernement anglais dévollé*.

152. A page to this effect from *El Patriota* (December 1821) is tucked into the Sutro Library copy of *Libertad de los mares*.

153. "La Italia no extenderá a más su comercio ya tan limitado; la España no mejorará el suyo, ya tan debilitado. La Holanda será despojada de la pesca, que la hace muy poderosa. El Portugal será cultivado para mí solo. La

Dinamarca y la Suecia se limitarán a su comercio interior. El Báltico será guardado por la Rusia a mi provecho; y el pueblo Ruso no será si no mi marinero auxiliar, o mi factor comerciante . . . En la expectación de esta grande revolución que yo organizo sordamente, mis manufacturas y mis compañías de comercio me aseguran las minas del Brasil. Mis complotes me darán la entera posesión de México y Perú, de que me hacen gozar, de antemano, mis tratados y mis esquadras. Mis chucherías me aseguran los escalpelos de los salvages de la América Septentrional contra los Americanos. Mis intrigas me hacen monopolizar el comercio de los Estados Unidos y dirigir su política incierta . . ."(288–289).

154. "El gobierno Británico trafica como conquistador, navega como pirata, coloniza como déspota, trata como mercader, administra como tirano, negocia como señor" (289).

155. *El derecho del hombre, para el uso y provecho del género humano, compuesto por Tomás Paine . . . traducido del inglés por Santiago Felipe Puglia.* (Filadelfia: M. Carey e hijos, 1821). Clarkin lists 11 other works Puglia claimed to have written (238). Mier also claims to have translated Paine's work to Spanish (*Memoria*). Miliani says that Picornell also did a translation (xiii).

156. See Simmons, *Santiago F. Puglia*.

157. *El desengaño del hombre, compuesto por Santiago Felipe Puglia, Maestro de la lengua castellana en esta metrópoli. Feliz quien llega a conocer por qué el hombre afecta amor, justicia y fe. El autor.* ("Man undeceived . . . Happy is he who learns [this] because man feigns love, justice and faith. The author"). (Filadelfia: H.C. Carey y I. Lea, 1822, 257 pp.). The 1794 edition was published in Philadelphia by F. Bailey; the Biblioteca Nacional in Mexico possesses a copy of this rare edition.

158. "Reinaldo and Elaine, or the Peruvian Princess" (Valencia: Imprenta de Estevan, 1820, 225 pp.; Filadelfia: H.C. Carey & I. Lea, 132 pp.).

159. See the studies by Rich, de los Reyes, and Lara.

160. Both Shoemaker and Grases in "El círculo de Filadelfia" (280–283) erroneously attribute authorship to Barry.

161. *La vida de Jorge Washington, comandante en gefe de los egércitos de los Estados Unidos de América, en la Guerra que estableció su independencia; y su primer presidente. Escrita en inglés por David Ramsay M.D., y traducida al español por Eduardo Barry* (Filadelfia: Imprenta de R. Desilver).

162. *El solitario, o El misterioso del monte. Novela, escrita en Francés por El vizconde de Arlincourt, traducida al Inglés, y de este al Español, por Eduardo Barry* (Filadelfia: Imprenta de H.C. Carey y I. Lea, 1822, iv., [5]-201, 1 pp.). (Called in English, *The Recluse* and also *The Renegade*). Original title: *Le Solitaire* by Charls Victor Arlincourt, Vicomte d'Prevot.

163. *Jachín y Boaz; o una Llave auténtica para la puerta de Francmasonería, tanto Antigua, como moderna. Por un caballero de la Logia de Jerusalén.*

Traducida al español por Eduardo Barry (Philadelphia, 1822, 83 pp.). Original: *Jachin and Boaz; or, An authentic key to the door of free-masonry. Calculated not only for the instruction of every new-made Mason; but also for the information of all who intend to become brethren . . . Illustrated with an accurate plan of the drawing on the floor of a lodge. And interspersed with a variety of notes and remarks, necessary to explain and render the whole clear to the meanest capacity. By a gentleman belonging to the Jerusalem Lodge.* (London: W. Nicoll, 1762, 56 pp.). Shoemaker identifies the author as "R.S." In Masonic lore, Jachin are the two pillars of the temple of Solomon (Mackey).

164. *El monitor de los Masones Libres; o Ilustraciones sobre la Masonería, por Tomás Smith Webb, Gran Maestro Pasado de la Gran Logia de Rhode Island.* Traducido del Inglés al Español (Philadelphia: H.C. Carey & I. Lea, 1822, 292 pp.).

165. *La librería Masónica y general Ahiman Rezon; conteniendo una delineación de los verdaderos principios de Francmasonería, especulativa y operativa, religiosa y moral. Compilada de los escritos de los autores más aprobados, con notas y observaciones casuales.* Por Samuel Cole, P.M. De las logias de Concordia y Cassia, P.G.S. de la G.L. de Meriland. T.T.C.M.& In principio erat sermo ille, et sermo ille erat apud Deum, erat que ille sermo Deux. Evangelio de Sn. Juan. Al principio a la verdad irá con el, por caminos torcidos, y la pondrá miedo y temor, y en su disciplina le atormentará hasta tanto que se confíe de su ánimo, y le haya tentado en sus leyes; y volverá otra vez a él derechamente, y le alegrará y le revelará sus secretos. Eclesiástico. Traducida al Español por Eduardo Barry (Filadelfia: H.C. Carey y I. Lea, 1822), 2 vols.

166. *Sandoval; or, the freemason. A Spanish Tale. By the author of "Don Esteban"* (New York: E. Bliss and E. White; Philadelphia: H.C. Carey and I. Lea, Sleight & Tucker, 2 vols.). Llanos Sandoval was married to Fanny Keats.

167. *Observations on the political reforms of Colombia. By J.M. Salazar. Translated from the manuscript by Edward Barry* (Philadelphia: W. Stavely).

168. Philadelphia: H. C. Carey and I. Lea, printed by William Brown, 187 pp. At the end of the second volume of *Jicoténcal* a list of books for sale at the New York bookstore of Lanuza y Mendia mentions *Auxiliar Vocabulario de bolsillo español inglés*, por J.L. Barry, un tom. en 16o, N. York, 1825". It is not clear if Edward Barry produced this book, unrecorded in Shoemaker.

169. For Masonry in New Orleans, see Dessens, 145–146.

170. See my article in which I describe how Webb and Cole took the Englishman William Preston's manuals and "adapted" their rules to U.S. life. Then Barry, relying on Webb's and Cole's versions, adapted the manuals still further to Mexican custom. This example shows "translation" to be a suspect process.

171. "Edward Barry, gentleman" is listed in *Paxton's Annual Philadelphia Directory* for 1819; there is no listing of him for 1821 or 1822. "Edward Barry, teacher" appears in *The Philadelphia Index or Directory for 1823* (Philadelphia: Robert Desilver, 1823), and in Thomas Wilson's *The Philadelphia Directory and Stranger's Guide for 1825* (Philadelphia: John Bioren, 1825), and directories for 1828 and 1829.

172. *The Selected Papers of Charles Willson Peale and His Family*, Vol. 4 (CWP: His Last Years, 1821–1827), ed. Lillian B. Miller (New Haven: Yale UP, Smithsonian Institution, 1996, 511–516).

173. Historical Society of Pennsylvania, Tench Coxe papers.

174. I have consulted the 1821 edition. See Vol. 2, 345-347.

175. Salvucci (2005, 2006) discusses this trade and provides this information.

176. See Guimerá Ravina.

177. *Noticias secretas de América, sobre el estado naval, military, y politico de los reynos del Perú y provincias de Quito, costas de Nueva Granada y Chile: Gobierno y regimen particular de los pueblos de indios: Cruel opresion y extorsiones de sus corregidores y curas: Abusos escandalosos introducidos entre estos habitants por los misioneros: Causas de su origen y motivos de su continuación por el espacio de tres siglos. Escritas fielmente según las instrucciones del Excelentísimo Señor Marqués de la Ensenada, primer secretario de estado, y presentadas en informe secreto a S.M.C. El Señor don Fernando VI. Por don Jorge Juan, y don Antonio de Ulloa. Sacadas a la luz para el verdadero conocimiento del gobierno de los españoles en la América Meridional, por don David Barry. En dos partes* (Londres: Imprenta de R. Taylor, 1826).

178. Others preceded H.C. Carey and I. Lea in their use of traveling booksellers. Shoemaker records a 25-page *Catalogue of Latin, English, French, Spanish and Italian Books, Maps, &, for Sale by J.L. Fernagus de Gelone, agent for the U.S., Canada, New Orleans, Spanish America, and isles*, published in New York in 1816.

179. It was sold in New York by C. de Behr. The copy owned by the American Antiquarian Society is inscribed to "la Sr. S.S. McKean de Folsom, Baltimore" (Susanna Sarah McKean). It seems clear that Susanna Sarah (1805–1887) was the daughter of Sally McKean and the Marqués de Irujo, living in a Spanish-speaking community in Baltimore.

180. Kaser, 46.

181. James N. Green, 10.

182. Murphy, 72, 79.

183. See Toll.

184. Bustamante in his diary for 1822–1823 noted on February 7, 1823, a gazette report that the U.S. government had sent a squadron of ten ships,

along with an equal number of smaller vessels, to patrol waters off Cuba, Puerto Rico and the Gulf and protect U.S. shipping from pirates, 153.

185. Clarkin, 199. The Gilpin family papers, in the Historical Society of Pennsylvania, are voluminous. Among them are materials pertaining to Joel Poinsett; see *Guide to the Manuscript Collections of the HSP.*

186. HSP, Edward Carey Gardiner Collection.

187. It was reprinted a year later in London, in two volumes, by Lackington, Hughes, Harding, Mayor and Lepara. In 1824 the London printer, Rudolph Ackermann, published a Spanish translation, done by José Joaquín de Mora.

188. For a Venezuelan view of this community, see Grases's "El círculo de Filadelfia."

189. Salvucci (2006).

190. Roscio praised this example in *Triunfo*, 210.

191. Spell, *Rousseau in the Spanish World*, 282–284.

192. Grases y Harkness write that the Palmer printing company had Spanish-speaking employees (41).

193. "Rasgo imparcial: Breves Observaciones al papel que ha publicado el señor D. Tomás Romay en el Diario del Gobierno".

194. For background, see Brickhouse, Chapter 2.

195. Weekend Interview with Mario Vargas Llosa," Emily Parker, *Wall Street Journal*, June 23–24, 2007.

196. See by Brown and Brown.

197. "Apology of Bartolome de las Casas, bishop of Chiapas, by Citizen G; read at the National Institute, in 1800," published by Badouin, 1802). For background on Grégoire, see Sepinwall; Fauchon.

198. Documentation for this transmission, as well as background on editions of Las Casas's works, are to be found in Mejía Sánchez.

199. Mejía Sánchez says that the work may be related to the Italian translation of the Fifth Treatise of Las Casas's *Breve relación*, *Il supplice schiavo* (Venice, 1616, 1636 and 1657) (81) and that it was advertised for sale at Recio's bookshop in Mexico City (85). Today the Bancroft Library has a copy.

200. A copy exists in the Library of Congress.

201. The Mexican patriotism of the printer is apparent in the title: *Destrucción de las Indias, o sea su conquista publicada en Sevilla el año de 1552 por el ilustrísimo Sr. D. Fr. . . . religioso dominico, obispo que fué de Chiapa. Ahora la da a luz un ciudadano en obsequio de su nación a quien humilde la consagra* (today held in the Sutro Library).

202. "La Suprema Junta Gobernativa del reyno a la nación española".

203. "Memoria político-instructiva".

204. "El Hidalgo de Dolores".

205. "Bendición que nuestra madre la santa Iglesia da al nuevo rey o emperador en el día de su coronación".

206. "Ceremonias de la Iglesia".

207. "En honor del gran padre San Agustín".

208. "Carta escrita al padre maestro fray Bartolomé Carranza de Miranda, residente en Inglaterra con el rey Felipe II, en el año 1555, sobre la perpetuación de las encomiendas de los Indios, que intentó entonces".

209. "Respuesta de Don fray Bartolomé de Las-Casas, a la consulta que se le hizo sobre los sucesos de la conquista del Perú en 1564".

210. "Sobre la potestad soberana de los reyes para enagenar vasallos, pueblos y jurisdicciones".

211. "Memoria apologética del Señor Grégoire, antiguo obispo de Blois en que se procuró persuadir que el venerable Casas no tuvo parte en la introducción del comercio de Negros en América".

212. "Disertación del doctor Don Gregorio de Funes dean de Córdova de Tucumán en forma de carta escrita al Señor obispo Grégoire sobre el mismo asunto".

213. "Memoria del doctor Mier, natural de Mégico, confirmando la apologia del Obispo Casas, escrita por el reverendo Obispo de Blois, monseñor Henrique Grégoire, en carta escrita a las Memorias de los señores Grégoire, Mier y Funes".

214. However, it must be noted that, in 1817-1819, the Royal Academy of History in Madrid approved the issuance of Las Casas's *History of the Indies*, though it was not published there until 1875 (Hanke, 54–56).

215. Here I omit consideration of the early crypto-Jews of the southwestern United States whom Hordes considers.

216. See Diner; Karp.

217. *El Redactor Mexicano* (Sept. 30, 1814, Imprenta de D. José María de Benavente): "Pensaba escaparme/dispuesto el hatillo,/y allá en Filadelfia/huir del castigo".

218. Baltimore, too, during this period seems to have accepted a number of political refugees. However, the city, though it became a center for political and commercial adventurers, did not become the publishing center that Philadelphia was. See Griffin.

219. See Mier's *Memorias*. For background on Mier, see Brading; Rotker's edition of the *Memoirs*; and Rodríguez O.'s edition of Mier's *Obras completas*, Vol. 4 for Mier's Philadelphia-printed materials.

220. *Memorias*, Vol. 2, 140.

221. Domínguez Michael, 601–608.

222. "Manifesto the Spanish Colonel . . . makes in which he demonstrates the unjust and violent means, observed in San Agustín, Florida, when he was robbed of his governing authority, the archives of his government and other papers, after the delivery over of the province to the United States" (Filadelfia: Juan F. Hurtel, 1821).

223. These are available in Spanish in Mier's *Obras completas* Vol. 4, 211–243, along with the anonymous pamphlet that provoked Mier's second pamphlet, "Observaciones sobre la opinion del Reverendísimo Servandus A. Mier, doctor en sagrada teología, &, sobre ciertas preguntas que le propuso el Reverendo Wm. Hogan" (Filadelfia: Bernard Dornin, 1821). In these pages, Mier takes to task his English translator for changing his meaning ("Comentarios sobre la traducción de 'Una palabra sobre un folleto anónimo).

224. Shoemaker records William Hogan's publications for 1821: "An address, to the congregation of St. Mary's Church, Philadelphia" (Philadelphia, 28 pp.); "A reply to a ludicrous pamphlet . . . " (Philadelphia, 47 pp.); "Continuation of an address to the Congregation of St. Mary's Church" (Philadelphia, Feb. 2, 36 pp., reprinted 30 & 1 pp.); "Hoganism defended: or the Detector detected . . . " (Philadelphia: printed for the author, 8 pp.); "Hoganism examined according to the canons of criticism, sacred and profane; or A short letter to a late reverend pamphleteer, on the republicanism of his famous pamphlet" (Philadelphia: Bernard Dornin, 12 pp.).

225. Rich and Lara examine this exchange in "Mystery." However, what they describe as a "protracted struggle, fought in the courts as well as in the pews, over whether the Catholic laity would have the same right of control over church decisions as did most Protestant congregations" (221) is complicated by evidence of the following pamphlet: "The trial of the Rev. William Hogan, for an assault and battery on Mary Connell . . . The whole taken in short hand by Joseph A. Dowling, stenographer" (Philadelphia: R. Desilver, 1822, 8 pp.). Hogan, born in Ireland, was later named U.S. consul in Havana. Some of this exchange is examined by Warren.

226. De Bufanda.

227. Jacob in *The Origins of Freemasonry, Facts & Fictions* describes how these pocket handbooks contained lists of Lodge members for travelers.

228. See Domínguez Michael, 600–601.

229. On Torres, see Bowman. Torres was named to his post of commercial agent by Venezuela's president, Francisco Antonio Zea, and by Roscio, who by then had returned to his country. In fact, Bowman tells that Torres was an activist, soliciting help for Bolívar's war; he lobbied Presidents James Madison and James Monroe, and traded Venezuelan tobacco for U.S. gunpowder.

230. Duane's life was similar to Carey's. He was born in Newfoundland (although he presented himself as born in the United States), and was taken to Ireland at a young age. There he learned the printing trade, went to India where his newspaper writings caused him to be arrested, and then came to the U.S., where he entered the printing business of Benjamin Franklin Bache, publishing the Philadelphia journal, *Aurora*. He married Bache's widow, and took over the firm. Like Carey, he authored many political pamphlets. In

1822 he left Philadelphia, traveling in what is now Venezuela and Colombia; reportedly landing in La Guaira, it is tempting to think that he was part of Carey's "adventure" there in 1822. In 1826 he published *A Visit to Colombia in the Years ;1822–1823 by Laguaira and Caracas, over the Andes to Bogotá, and thence by the Magdalena to Cartagena* (Philadelphia: T.H. Palmer, 1826, vii, 9–632 pp.). On his life see Little. The *Aurora de Chile*, which we have seen, probably took its name from the Philadelphia paper.

231. *Annals of the Congress of the United States*, 1270–1271.

232. In fact., Irvine had published in Philadelphia in 1822, with the annotation " Printed for T.T.H.***" "Commerce of Southern America; Its Importance to Us, with Some Remarks on a Canal at Darien and other Cognate Subjects."

233. Reprinted in *El Libertador, Writings of Simón Bolívar*, 156–158. Bolívar, incensed that Irving had requested Venezuelan impartiality in its shipping trade while the United States did not observe neutrality and seemed to show partiality to Spain, rebuked the U.S. agent for denying the Spanish American colonies the supplies they needed to pursue their wars of independence. Irvine soon entered the U.S. print world. In 1824 he had published in Baltimore *Traits of colonial jurisprudence or, A peep at the trading inquisition of Caracas* (59 pp.), and became editor of the Baltimore *Whig*, the *New York Columbian*, and the *City of Washington Gazette*.

2

THE LETTERS

IN THE BUSINESS LEDGER THAT H.C. CAREY AND I. Lea kept for January 1822, through December 1823, Thomas W. Robeson's shipment is unrecorded. However, it can be guessed to have been a kind of subcontract, under the entry for Follin and Malsain, for several reasons. George Follin and Malsain (whose first name we never learn) were charged with going to Veracruz for the firm with a load of books in April 1822. Follin and Malsain carried a number of Masonic titles and when we read in several of Follin's letters to Carey and Lea in another file (May 22, 1822, from Veracruz; May 30 from Veracruz; and October 23 from Alvarado) that their cargo was refused entry by the customs inspector, we wonder if Robeson did not follow up on Follin's failed shipment as some of the titles in a list alongside Follin and Malsain's names are some of the same ones Robeson did carry in later. Follin informed Carey that he would have to ship seven cases back to Philadelphia and leave one with Mexican customs. In fact, the ledger's list, penciled in alongside the Follin and Malsain entry, reveals some doubt on the part of Carey's bookkeeper that the shipment would succeed. The penciling, as opposed to entries for the other "adventures" in the ledger (whose cargoes are unidentified and whose captains, ships, and destinations are written in ink), suggests either guardedness in revealing the Masonic titles or the fact that it was a later addition pending Robeson's success. Follin's stay in Mexico overlapped with Robeson's; and Follin's letters tell that his ship was the *Mary Washington*, one of the three ships in Robeson's fleet. Follin's letters also say that he, like Robeson, relied on Capt. Warner, U.S. agent in Cuba for transmitting bills. Follin and Malsain's consignment was valued at $6,653.25, the account running from May 24, 1822 to January 1, 1826. But Carey and Lea only received from him $150 "hard Spanish dollars."

Although the ledger does not mention Robeson, his name does appear in the Lea and Febiger File of Correspondence (December 16, 1822–June 30, 1823) as a Carey agent, responsible for the sale of books in Mexico (Lea and Febiger inherited the Carey business). Bills for book storage in New Orleans with the firm of McKean and Pennoyer reveal that Follin left some of his Mexican books with them but it is not known whether Follin or Robeson ever retrieved them. The ledger's book list follows:

46 *El Triunfo de la Libertad*
78 *Masonic Catechism*
45 *El Contracto Social*
25 *Systema Pol. Moral*
 2 *El Derecho del Hombre*
 2 *Manual de Voyageur*
37 *El Desengaño del Hombre*
65,000 Quills

These titles are respectively: Roscio's *Triumph of Liberty over Despotism*, *Masonic Catechism*, Rousseau's *Social Contract*, Puglia's *Political-Moral System*, Paine's *Rights of Man*, *A Seaman's Manual*, and Puglia's *Man Undeceived*.[1] It is not clear what the numbers alongside each title mean since they do not square with the larger quantities Robeson reports having sold; perhaps the tallies indicate the Follin and Malsain shipment was small, or they refer to boxes rather than copies of books, or they disguise the actual quantities in a kind of code.

It appears that Robeson thought it prudent to touch in at Alvarado rather than go through the more tightly controlled Veracruz as Follin had done. Judging from Robeson's instructions to Carey as to which titles to pack in the boxes, it seems that he had the upper hand in selecting from among the books returned to Philadelphia which ones he thought he could bootleg through customs and sell. Although Robeson had left Alvarado by October 23, the date of Follin's third letter, the fact that Follin had been in Alvarado in October makes it likely that the two met there after Robeson's arrival on August 15 and that Robeson took over the case that Follin left in the customs house (whose content we do not know). Robeson never mentions Follin in his letters, nor says that he assumed his cargo. However, he does note Malsain's arrival on the *Mary Washington*, a ship that apparently shuttled between Philadelphia and Mexico.

I have used the term "consignment" because the Carey and Lea ledger assigns a value to the Follin and Malsain "adventure," and I assume their outlay. However, that is a provisional term for there is no evidence as to how Carey and Lea managed that relationship—either with Follin and Malsain or with Robeson. It seems likely that the large amount represents Carey and Lea's investment in the books; payment to their agents, ships, and crews and so forth. "Consignment" would suggest that Robeson could return unsold books, and that detail is never mentioned. Because little cash was available in those years, one guesses that a credit system supported the operation, counting on future returns; that arrangement is confirmed in the letters, which we will see later. However, one notes that Robeson sold materials other than books (writing materials and pictures), some of his own products (cream of tartar), and that he scouted possibilities for future trade (other titles, minerals, and a printing press). Robeson, like Weems, appears to have been more than just an agent under instruction from Carey and Lea; instead he made use of friendships it seems he already had in Gulf ports and took the initiative in contracting with a Mexico City book dealer so as to set up a permanent import arrangement.

Robeson's letters begin in New Castle, down the Delaware River from Philadelphia, on July 17, 1822 (see Figures 2.1–2.3). His ship, the *Mexicana*, and two others, the *Highlander* and the *Mary Washington*, will sail in two hours.[2] Robeson writes:

> I had a conversation with Col. B this morning, and find he is not pleased with our communicating with Mr. Barry, concerning the shipment of books. Mr. Barry was so imprudent as to inform Col. B of what passed between us; I had to give him the assurance that Mr. Barry should not be concerned in shipping them or know anything concerning our plans. Col. B saw Mr. Meade yesterday morning and requested him to take in charge for him five trunks and two boxes.

"Mr. Barry" appears to have been the translator Edward Barry, whom we have seen; Robeson's description of him as "imprudent" suggests the youthful indiscretion noted before, and some Carey relationship with Col. B that Barry is not supposed to have known about.

"Meade" is Richard Worsam Meade, the Philadelphian mentioned earlier. Meade was familiar with Spanish life, having lived in Cádiz for ten years where he was U.S. naval agent. In addition, he appears to have operated his own business there. Meade was detained by the Spanish government in 1816, presumably for illegal activities; in 1818 the U.S. House of Representatives sought information on his detention.[3] In August 1820, he returned to Philadelphia, bringing with him an extensive library of Spanish books, as well as a collection of valuable paintings that he probably acquired when Napoleon looted the Spanish collections and churches and they were up for grab.[4] Meade, like Carey and Mier, was a member of St. Mary's parish and had entered into the Hogan debate; it has been suggested that he translated one of Mier's pamphlets. In 1822, when Mier was detained by the Mexican Inquisition, his papers and books were confiscated; found among his possessions was a dossier on Meade's imprisonment. Meade was known to be sympathetic to the independence of Spain's American colonies, and reference to him in this first letter suggests that St. Mary's introduced several of the backers.[5]

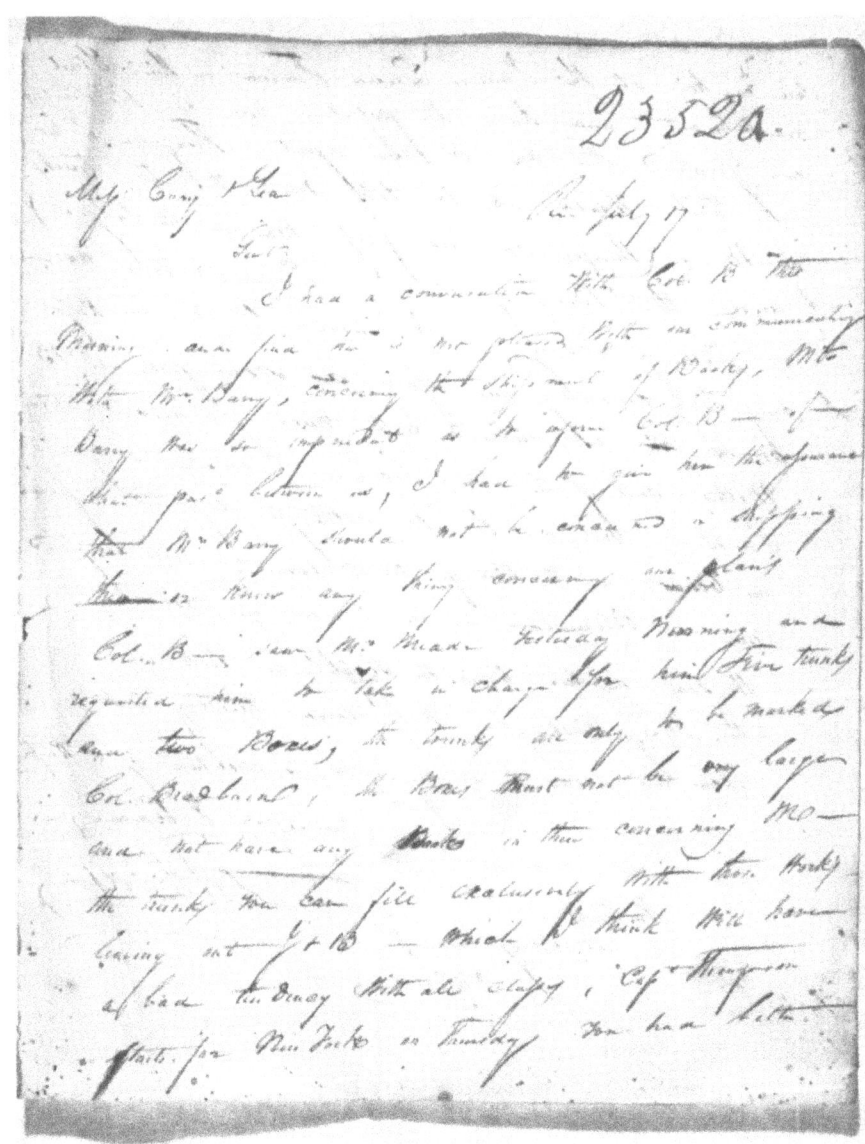

FIGURE 2.1   Page from the first letter to Carey and Lea written by Robeson.

"Col. B" is Colonel John Davis Bradburn, an officer then in Iturbide's army. Bradburn is far from an obscure figure in Mexican history books.[6] A native of Kentucky, he accompanied Mina in his invasion of Mexico in 1817. Bradburn and others had joined up with Mina in Baltimore. The expedition, consisting variously of U.S. romantics and freebooters, Spanish royalists and Napoleonic sympathizers, Spanish American revolutionaries, and adventurers

FIGURE 2.2 Letter addressed to the publishers Carey and Lea.

from all over, was financed by men in Baltimore such as Dennis Smith and Mier. The effort failed when Mina was shot in a battle at Soto-la-Marina. But the men who survived and who stayed on in Mexico after independence were hailed as heroes. Between 1830 and 1832, Bradburn figured prominently in the early history of Texas: I will discuss later his involvement in that territory, which Mexico would soon lose to the United States.

Thus Meade and Bradburn are revealed as two of the sponsors of Carey's book business. Bradburn's name, Robeson says, should appear on the five trunks and two boxes of his. The boxes "must not be very large"; the trunks "you can fill exclusively with those works leaving out J and B which I think will have a bad tendency with all classes." "J and B" probably was *Jachin and Boaz*, the Masonic manual mentioned earlier; the detail instructing Carey to put Bradburn's name on several of the boxes suggests that Bradburn's name would mislead Mexican censors into thinking that the contents were his personal belongings. Robeson also notes: "the bill of Mr. Bustamante will be paid me in Alvarado as he is out of cash."

"Mr. Bustamante" probably refers to Carlos María Bustamante, a leading Mexican republican.[7] One historian claims that Bustamante met regularly

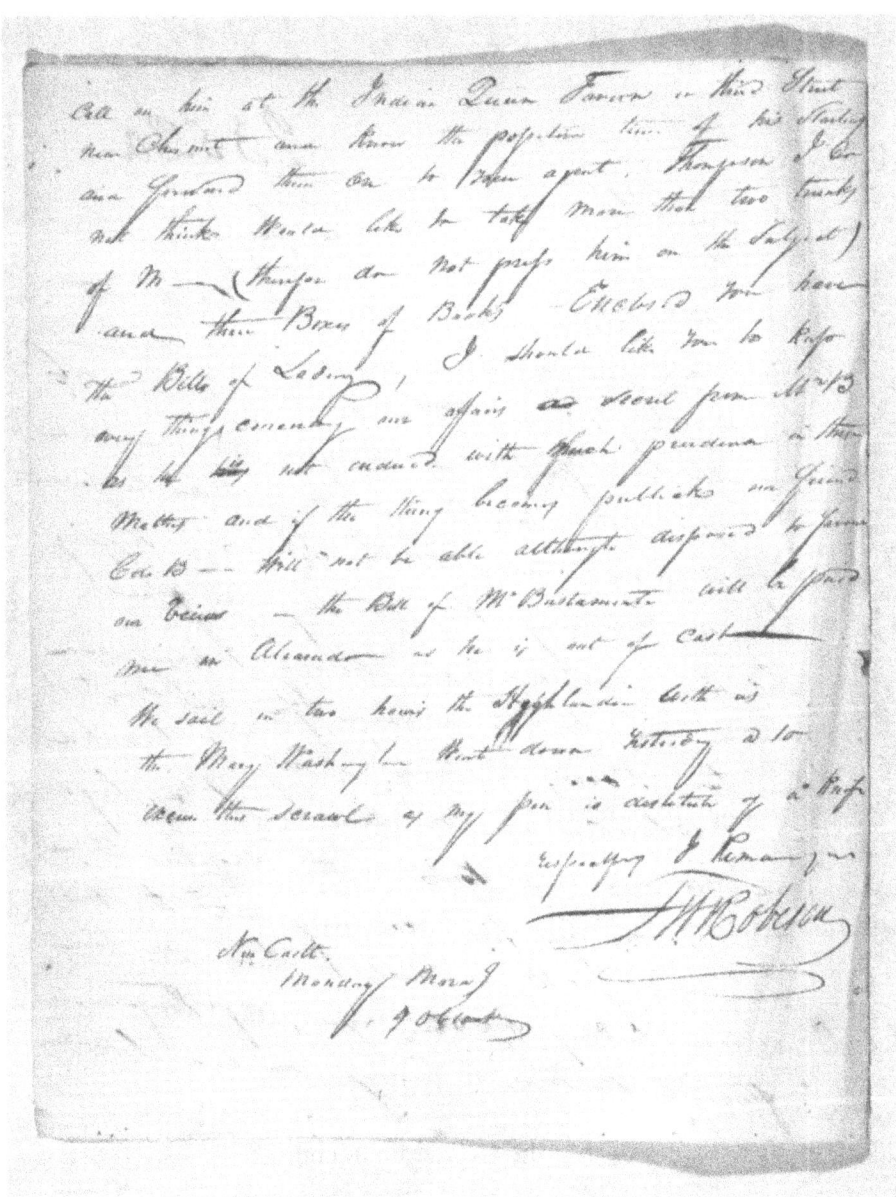

FIGURE 2.3 Page from one of Robeson's letters.

with other republicans—Miguel Ramos Arizpe, Mier, José Mariano Michelena, Carlos Fagoaga, and Vicente Rocafuerte—in the home of the Colombian representative in Mexico, Miguel Santamaría.[8] Santamaría, as Robeson tells us later, was forced to leave Mexico in November 1822; Mier did not return to Mexico City until July 1822, when he was freed from San Juan de Ulúa, the Spanish fortress and prison in the harbor of Veracruz. Rocafuerte, as we know, was in Philadelphia (but also in Cuba) between May 1821, and November 1823; however, he did make a secret trip to Veracruz in November 1822.[9] So it is not clear when the republican activity in Santamaría's house took place.

Bustamante planned to go to the United States as early as December 1816.[10] Wanting to escape royalist persecution since by that time the royalist side appeared to be winning the Mexican independence war and he had made known his insurgent alliances, he went to Veracruz. He was frustrated in this first attempt to leave, but then he sent his wife to Mexico City to try to procure resources for another attempt. She was captured and made to march back to Veracruz with a band of prisoners; this insult, says José María Miquel i Verges "increased even more Bustamante's desire to flee abroad."[11] In fact, Bustamante boarded an English ship but was captured by Spanish officials and imprisoned in San Juan de Ulúa until 1820.

Bustamante was a member of Mexico's first Congress, which was sworn in on February 14, 1822. A delegate from Oaxaca, he enjoyed considerable prestige. However, Bustamante ran afoul of Iturbide when he participated in a republican plot against him; and Iturbide had him imprisoned again, along with others of the Congress, on August 26. Bustamante did not leave prison until Iturbide fell in April 1823. Thus, although he was in jail in the months that Robeson traveled in Mexico, Robeson's letters seem to prove that Bustamante provided some of the money for the venture.

Robeson will mention "B" again in his January 17 letter, telling of the transfer of B and Mier from one prison to another managed by the Inquisition; Bustamante records the episode in his diary of 1822–1823 and the care with which Robeson mentions the detail seems to confirm the involvement of all three in the business. Bustamante's intention to relocate to the United States makes it likely that he began to plan for his move by making contacts with U.S. republicans. The fact that Mier was in and out of Philadelphia suggests that he was the link between Carey and Bustamante. In his diary, Bustamante calls Mier "bishop of Baltimore" and generally sides with him in congressional debate (although increasingly they would be at odds).

In the next letter (Alvarado, August 15), Robeson tells that the passage lasted 29 days and that they did not have 12 hours of a steady course. The morning after their arrival the ship was visited by the *alcalde* and the *comandante* "[who] was particular in his inquiries respecting our intentions of coming here, the amount and quality of cargos, the disposition of the Americans to his government, the Spanish Minister's protest relative to the recognition of American independence by our government and a thousand trifling questions which he was careful to note and which as he informed us was to be transmitted to the governor of Veracruz." Alvarado, under the jurisdiction of Veracruz, "has been a port of entry but two months, and [as] we are the first vessel arriving with a cargo, the delay here will be consequently longer than at Veracruz, in consequence of the absence of materials necessary to internal commerce." A messenger was sent to Veracruz who reported that the fort of San Juan Ulúa was still held by the Spanish and that the duty there would be 8%. Therefore the ship would stay on in Alvarado where the duty was less, and Robeson could more freely unload the cargo and secure mules for travel into the interior.

Robeson is pessimistic about disposing of any articles in Alvarado. There are no gazettes to mail back to Philadelphia and only six stores for whose whole stock "I should be sorry to give fifteen hundred dollars." The ship will be there ten days. Robeson's stay is uncertain, awaiting the arrival of Col. B. He asks Carey to write to A. Thompson at "Wilkinson," informing him of his arrival. (The detail implies that Wilkinson, whom we have seen before, knew of the business, if he was not also one of the sponsors.)

In the next letter (Alvarado, August 18), Robeson tells that his letter of the 15th was sent by skiff to Veracruz. He seems confident that from there it would have been transmitted promptly to Philadelphia. In succeeding letters we read that he sends his letters to Carey under the care of friends and trusted persons. The route is via Havana to either Philadelphia or New York. Robeson writes guardedly because he fears his letters might be read by unsympathetic eyes. Sometimes a space is left blank when a crucial piece of information, such as a name, might be given. In the custom of the day, the letters have their recipient's name and address on the back, avoiding the use of envelopes. Traces of red sealing wax tell how the contents were secured.

In this August 18 letter, Robeson reports that he spoke with Don Manuel Reyes, the administrator of the customs house for the town of Tlacotalpan, "situated on this river rather of the same name which empties itself opposite the village of Alvarado." This town, 20 miles away, "is said to contain 8 thousand inhabitants, who are so refractory, that a guard of 300 soldiers has been situated there some time to keep them in array." Hearing that Robeson had books, Reyes came on board with his son. Robeson "waited on him immediately and was received with a great deal of frankness and civility, and was pleased to find him a man of considerable literary taste." Reyes asked whether Robeson had books such as *Arte de armas*,[12] *Ruinas de Palmira*,[13] *Carta de Tallibran*,[14] novelas de Voltaire." Fearing that Reyes was testing him asking for these titles, Robeson said "no, "and then added, "I had to act with the utmost caution at the same time manifesting a considerable openness of character." Then: "I tried him by the square and compass but received no answer" (Masonic scholars have read this as a test of Masonic brotherhood). However, Robeson and Reyes soon reached a level of trust; and Reyes reported his impression of the book business in Mexico City, where he had been six weeks before. There were only five bookstores there: "not one of which had any works of merit and appeared to be the rendezvous for disputations more than a place of business." Although the following works were prohibited, they were sought after avidly, and Reyes provided their going prices:[15] *Arte de armas* (one vol. $18), *Ruinas de Palmira* (one vol. $16), *Carta de Tallibran* or *Letters of the Bishop* (one vol. $6), novellas de Voltaire (3 vols., $2 per vol.). Reyes said he was anxious to obtain an up-to-date Spanish dictionary, though Robeson told him none but "ancient" editions were available. Reyes reported that Mexicans desired paper and Robeson asked that Carey provide it in the size and quality he was using for his letter. Reyes also said that he had seen a large map of Mexico "the size of Tanner's map of North America sell in the city for $90."[16]

A postscript, dated August 23, tells that the *Highlander*, with Col. B. on board, had now arrived and that Robeson and the colonel were each contacting their "friends." However, there were new difficulties. A "Col. Cortés" accused Capt. Riley of the *Mexicana* of smuggling so officials in Veracruz placed guards on the U.S. ships to prevent their cargo from being unloaded. Because Robeson's shipment was already in a warehouse in Alvarado, it was safe. But Robeson feared the other cargos might have to be sent home. "Col. Cortés" appears to have been Eugenio Cortés, mentioned in Meade's letter to John Quincy Adams. An Iturbide agent, Cortés bought ships in the United States with which to attack the Spanish fort at San Juan de Ulúa. Among them was the schooner, the *Anáhuac*, one of the first ships of the Mexican navy. When the Mexican government failed to meet the price for the ships, Cortés was jailed but Meade paid the bond for his release. Later, the Mexican government paid the bill. If this "Col. Cortés" is indeed Eugenio Cortés, it is unclear why he was now back in Mexico and why he would have interfered with the book business that Meade supported (except that the business threatened Iturbide's hold on power).

The next letter (also dated August 23) reports that Robeson had come on to Veracruz, traveling with Col. Aldama, "the officer commanding on this station."[17] They went via Punto Altesardo [Antón Lizardo?], "distant from this 12 miles, the site of an old fort which the present Sovereign and Independent Congress has ordered to be built on a very extensive scale, making a fine harbor for the reception of vessels of commerce as well as their navy." (With San Juan de Ulúa still in Spanish hands, Mexico needed its own port.) Robeson says that the climate in the region was extremely healthy, "not a case of the yellow fever these ten days past." Before leaving Alvarado, Robeson contracted to have his cargo there loaded on mules for transport to Mexico City; he paid $24 per mule load for the 18-day trip. He was hopeful that a friend would be able to secure the transfer of the other ships' cargos to the docks. Col. B. had already left for Mexico City; because his business was urgent, "he could not wait."

Robeson then lists the duties along the route: "At Veracruz, 25%; the fort of S.J. Ulúa 18% demanded by the governor. At Alvarado this is avoided; at Jalapa 6% if the articles stop for sale, not otherwise. At Puebla 8% if entered as the former." In Mexico City the duty was 10%. Robeson says the Congress ought to abolish this latter duty. He also reports that he saw "in the hands of a French gentleman in Alvarado which I think would answer viz. *La Europa y la América* by M. De Pradt. It was published and translated in France, two small volumes in the fall of 1821."[18] He describes Veracruz:

> [I]t is a neat city, the streets paved better [than] your city, and well lighted having also a considerable guard stationed to prevent depredation. The houses are all built of stone and plastered each having a balcony and, were the inhabitants to whitewash the front and tops, the city would exhibit an appearance singularly beautiful. The streets are not as wide as yours but run parallel and more rigidly [?]. Its churches or government I have not seen as I have only been here three hours.

Robeson reports that a gentleman, just arrived from Mexico City, has told him that "there is not much business transacting, the people too much impoverished to purchase." He adds:

> the Americans and other foreigners are so jealous of each other that it is impossible to come at the truth in any particular concerning commercial pursuits. I feel ashamed of such conduct to one another in a foreign land. This to me was as visible as the sun on a clear day, in the conduct of persons who came in the three vessels from the City and were the Inquisition in full force I would as soon seek for information from that source as from those [from whom] we ought to expect it. Perhaps this jealousy may subside when we all reach Mexico.

Because his coach to Mexico City is delayed, he will stay on at the home of Col. Aldama. When he leaves, he will travel with others since "it is dangerous to travel alone."

The *Mexicana* is preparing to sail back to Philadelphia and Robeson says that its captain, Mr. Riley, has agreed that in the future his vessels would bring books or stationery, "but no other articles," at a freight of 3% on the amount of the invoice, and for bonding and forwarding 2%. Carey is not to mention to Riley "anything concerning what was in the trunks as he is too much afraid of his owner to do any business for us of that nature." Finally, Robeson requests that Carey send a "handsome plaid cloak with a crimson collar lined with green (but not baise [beige]) which is indispensable here."

In the next letter (August 26, Veracruz), Robeson names the Mexican "friend" who has carried his letters on board—"Señor Basan." Winds have prevented the ship from sailing so he can write again, this time in the care of Andrew Lockhart, merchant from New York who has just come from Mexico City and will take his letter, as well as eight copies of the Veracruz gazette, on to Havana and then to Carey's house in New York. Robeson tells that the country is extremely impoverished "by having destroyed all their sources of revenue. They have a large army, no money to pay them and are still increasing it. The inhabitants are principally in the country, having left this [the coastal area around Veracruz] in consequence of the fever. The population at present is estimated at six thousand, three of whom appear to be military." Mr. Lockhart reports that the government has just issued an order prohibiting the export of specie and cochineal but that this order may soon be rescinded since "they appear to act altogether in the dark." He tells that $50,000 left Mexico City for Veracruz but as soon as "the money departed an order was issued to stop it. In a few days it was suffered to proceed after paying a duty of 3%."

Then:

> Mr. Barry embarked from this place for England with Col. O'Reily a month ago after concluding a loan to this government of 1 million dollars. The terms are these. Mr. B. has drawn bills of $4,000 each on two houses in London to the specified amounts which agents in the different cities are endeavoring to sell but without effect. If the amount cannot be raised on this plan he is to remit the amount from England from which he is to receive ten percent. The government has advanced him 4,000 on his bills to enable him to carry his measures into execution. Col. O'Reily is entrusted in this speculation.

Confirming this loan, Lucas Alamán in his history of the period describes a loan "Diego Barry" made to Iturbide, saying that the money came from tobacco earnings (which, we have seen, William Robinson said was the product he was involved with in the Barry family business).[19] Another source reports that Diego Barry, along with Felipe O'Reilly and Tadeo Ortiz de Ayala, presented a proposal to the Mexican government in the first months of 1822 to "settle 10,000 Irish and Canary Islanders in Texas."[20] Ortiz de Ayala had been in Baltimore earlier, and it is almost certain that this "Diego" (James) is the Baltimore Barry Robinson mentioned. He both lent the Iturbide government money and advanced a colonization project.

However, why, if Diego was from Baltimore, was he departing Mexico for England? The answer seems to be that the Barry family's assets were in banks in London and that the family's members, like the Rothschilds, were spread out across the globe in the business. In her book, *La lucha de Hispanoamérica por su independencia en Inglaterra (1800–1830)*, María Teresa Berruezo León says that in 1819 a "Mr. Barry" granted a loan of 200 pounds to the Guatemalan revolutionary representing Chile in London, José Antonio Irissari. Irisarri had wanted money to pay for printing an anti-Spanish newspaper; but, because this amount was all he got, he used it to pay for the publication of one of his pamphlets (1989, 265–266). Berruezo does not otherwise identify this Barry, but his willingness to lend money to further Spanish American independence suggests that he belonged to the same Barry family that profited from American trade, lending money for political purposes and publishing.

Robeson writes: "I am anxiously waiting an opportunity for Mexico by a return coach but none occurs. Were I [to] hire a *volante* or a litter which only carries me to Jalapa, which is 90 miles from this, the expense would be more than my passage from this to Mexico in a return coach. As the quarters are comfortable, I shall detain here a few days to check an opportunity." Robeson advises Carey not to go any further in their business until Robeson can get to Mexico City, "fearing we may be too sanguine in our expectations." Lockhart has told Robeson that Mexico City's customhouse refuses "to receive any instrument of writing save that which was on Spanish paper." Carey may have to imitate that paper. Robeson then reports that he went to bookstores in Veracruz ("if such they deserve the name of as neither was larger than DeSilver's in Walnut Street and they the principal in the city"). There he inspected paper and priced books: "*Don Quixote* in 4 vols. without plates handsomely bound 12$, the same in 6 vols. small with plates and well bound, 14$."[21] However, he says it is almost impossible to ascertain the regular price because prices are not fixed. The booksellers requested that Robeson return the next day for "further conversation" and Robeson agreed to do so. A postscript (August 17) says that the ship is to sail soon and he will close to get the letter on board.

Then follows a "Bill for the contents of four boxes that I remit to ? [who is] from Mexico City, with the muleteer Mariano Candio under my consignment and that I receive in the schooner *Mexicana*, proceeding from Philadelphia, its captain Thomas Dawson as follows:[22]

II.6 y 7	44,000 plumas para escribir	82	4
	120 doz. lapis "	45	
	1 carpitita para escribir	nada	
	Considered for my own use		
8	6 doz. Tintas	2	2
	6 otras i/u Vida	1	4
5	8 pinturas	16	10
		$146	10
III. 1 1	1 Cajón con 310 libros)		
2	1 Cajón con 352 libros)		
3	1 Cajón con 361 libros) 393 pasta	110	2½
4	1 Cajón con 290 libros)		
5	1 Cajón con 8 libros)		
1	1 Cajón 050)		
2	1 Cajón 051) 725 de pasta o de cartón	99	
3	1 Cajón 067) 353 a la rústica		
	1481	$209	2½

These goods are, in order, pens, pencils, writing case, ink, paintings, books. Eight boxes—one more than the seven supposedly shipped (perhaps the eighth box was Follin's, which he left in the customshouse) and four more than the number stated in the invoice—are said to contain 1,481 books. A note on the margin explains that this is a copy of the duty serviced in Alvarado of 20% on the supposed actual value in the empire. A later reference reveals that the paintings are of George Washington. A separate sheet, serving as an envelope, reads: "Direct my goods to the care of Messrs. RILEY and SOUBERVILLE. La Vera Cruz or Alvarado." In Juan Schmaltz's report to the French king we learn that Riley and Souberville were Frenchmen, naturalized in the United States, who had a commercial office in Alvarado and who enjoyed the confidence of the Mexicans as a result of "their great exactitude, intelligence, and activity."[23]

The next letter in the file (Veracruz, August 29 at six in the morning) reports on a visit to the gazette office to get a book setting out the duties and regulations for importing into Mexico; the bookstore owner promised to send by Robeson's "dwelling" such a book, which Robeson would remit to Philadelphia with Captain Dawson. Robeson inquired in the office about the paper used for printing. He says the paper on which he was writing was from France, used for printing proclamations of the emperor, governors of provinces, and so on. A sample enclosed was used for printing the gazette on one half, and another kind of paper in the manufacture of cigars [cigarettes?]. Robeson inquired about the difference in the price of an unbound versus a bound book, "some books presented to my view on the shelf being a calendar of the Offices of Government, Army, the price $1.75 unbound and $2.50 bound, precisely the same in size as *Cornelia Bororquia* which you see at Dufiefs Book Store.[24] If none should be there Mr. Basy can inform you [of] the size. [T]he books which I see are principally bound and in two or three private libraries here they are filled with neat and elegant bindings, chiefly French authors, a considerable number of whom are prohibited. The better part of the people here are as conversant in French and Spanish and their libraries have as many French authors without translation as Spanish."

Remarking on the Spanish character when dealing with a bookseller, he says: "when you present yourself to purchase they demand 1/3 more than they intend selling at. If you wish to sell they offer you one half the value. If you wait until they wish to purchase you receive your price." He refers again to the duties for the export of spices. The governor of San Juan de Ulúa will negotiate duties because he does not want to lose revenue to Alvarado. However, all has to be done secretly. Vessels coming in to San Juan de Ulúa have to stay at a distance of 200 *varas* and then, as there is no wharf, unload their goods onto lighters. Robeson ends, saying he will leave for Jalapa in one hour in a litter.

The next letter (Mexico [City], September 2) gives no information about the five-day trip. Presumably Robeson took the same route through Jalapa, Perote, and Puebla that Joel Poinsett took a few weeks later and that required 16 days. Poinsett provides details of this trip with mule drivers over rough roads in a report to President James Monroe; he slept in inns but also in homes. However, Poinsett tells that he took time along the way to meet with important men like José Antonio Echávarri, captain general of the provinces of Puebla, Oaxaca, and Veracruz. At that dinner he says there were two Americans present, who were attached to the general's staff ("one a physician and the other a *soidistant* [French, so-called] engineer"). He describes those expatriates:

> I wish most heartily that our countrymen were not quite so adventurous, or that they would qualify themselves to fill the stations they aspire to in other countries before they leave their own. They certainly possess a facility beyond all other people of turning their hands to any thing; but they ought to be aware, that there are sciences which do require some previous education and knowledge, to enable them to understand and to practice them. (*Notes* 1824/ 1969, 26)

Robeson's September 2 letter says only that "I have handed Col. Bradburn a letter of introduction to you. He will perhaps request you to forward him some articles, amongst the rest books. I would attend to having it sent in due time. The Col. is shortly to be married to an interesting and beautiful girl, the daughter of the Marquis of Valle. The marriage banns were signed a week since. She brings a fortune of thirty thousand a year. The Col. has rendered me many important services here and your attentions will confer a favour on you."[25]

In the next letter (Mexico City, September 25), Robeson reviews the letters he has sent, fearing that they may not have reached Carey. Indeed some of the letters from now on are incomplete. Robeson repeats that he has refrained from writing "anything political or touching with freedom on my affairs." He tells that there are 20 Americans in the city, six of whom are leaving tomorrow for the United States. Bradburn, who will carry this letter from Mexico City to the coast, will stay on in Veracruz until the fall of San Juan de Ulúa; the government is preparing an immediate attack on the fortress. Robeson reports that, although he feared the goods he sent from Alvarado were "plundered by the numerous quantity of ladrones which infest the mountains," they arrived safely in the customs house of Mexico City.

Then begins a narrative that reveals lingering Church controls over Mexican readers: "I called on M. Racio (the bookseller who wishes to purchase) and presented a list of the titles and requested him to note those that were objectionable in the eyes of the archbishop." The reference is to Manuel Recio, a

Spanish book dealer though not a printer, in Mexico City at that time (Robeson will later correct his misspelling of Recio's name).

> Racio replied there was but one, *El contracto social*. I then drew up a list excluding that work and waited on the *vista* (examiner at the customshouse). I presented my list for his inspection. He cast his eyes rapidly over it and returned it with the command that I must wait on the archbishop for him to express his opinion of the works. No sooner had I left him than he communicated to a friend of mine that there [were] prohibited books amongst them. This friend sent me a note and on our meeting communicated what had [passed]. The objectionable are *Desengaño, Derecho* and *Contracto.*
>
> In consequence of this unexpected occurrence, the books will be detained for several days in the customs house while some secret measures are concerting to get them clear, which at this moment I have no doubt I shall effect.

Robeson complains that, although persons express interest in doing business with him, they are not willing to pay his price; and he repeats similar experiences of other foreign merchants in Mexico City. "Every man who vends goods here wishes 200% for his money and he certainly ought to receive a handsome percentage to pay him for the trouble he experiences here in doing business." He says he will rent a room and retail "by which I shall certainly save $800." He describes the dismal business scene:

> There is no article you can import here but that you will lose from 5 to 20% if sold wholesale. A person who arrived from Baltimore with a cargo of dry goods informed [me] that he should lose 40%, which I verily believe. Linens which cost 1$ in the U.S.—the highest price he can obtain here is 75 cents. There is a person who has opened store, from France, of a variety of articles finding it impossible to vend them in any other manner. Amongst them he has some letter paper the same as I now write on and the only person who has the article in the city.

Robeson continues on the subject of writing paper, saying that it abounds and, if Carey sends it, should be of the highest quality. He repeats the complaint that each town through which the goods pass exacts its percentage; as a result "a considerable business is done in smuggling." Congress has had a bill before it to abolish these internal duties but "since the imprisonment of 18 of their number the question has not been brought forward." Robeson has a plan to have the goods shipped to Alvarado and then apportioned to agents in Tlacotalpan, Veracruz, Jalapa, Perote, Oaxaca, Puebla, Mexico, and other places. He would then increase his business as these agents extended demand and reduce duties as his quantities became smaller along the road.

He considers whether it might be cheaper to send unbound books to Mexico, because the duties would be less. But:

> If books here are to be retailed, it is difficult to dispose of them without binding, as the purchaser has to pay an extravagant price for binding and they do not wish to see a book in their library without it. Their religious books are bound very extravagantly, with gold leaf on it in great abundance, from 6 to 8$, rich but not delicate.

> [M]ost wanted are those [books] on arts, industry and political economy, a few of the new editions of Neuman's *Dictionary* which you are about publishing,[26] also *Grammar of Spanish and English* similar to [Matthias James] O'Conway's if they can be had reasonable, a few of *Cornelia Bororquia*,[27] if to be had in paste at from 25 to 37 1/2 I think would sell, but do not attempt printing it. You would not be able to dispose of any quantity. There are no maps of Mexico, or of any province or county, to be had ... I have made particular inquiry and the amount of it is that maps are much wanted and a few would sell well of those in the atlas form or those hanging on the walls, the latter I would not advise you to prize any expense with until I had tried the smaller form.

Robeson says that Capt. Dawson brought out some of Tanner's maps of the United States and wanted to take them on to Mexico City to sell; however, it seems he had to sell them in Alvarado. Thus both Capt. Dawson and Capt. Riley appear to deal on their own.

Robeson reports that "in the Inquisition they have established a school on the Lancasterian plan which I will visit" so as to see what geography and other school books they need. Robeson's meaning seems to be that the school, based on a system of education which the Englishman Joseph Lancaster introduced in Baltimore, was located in the Inquisition building.[28] The school's innovations elicited great enthusiasm in Mexico when the editors of the Masonic newspaper, *El Sol*, founded it in 1822. It freed education from Church controls and, as Bustamante noted approvingly in his diary, it taught public service to children as they worked in hospitals, and charity to adults as they watched children marching out in uniforms the school had paid for (1896, 139). Rocafuerte, who was convinced that new school systems could change old-fashioned ways of thinking in Spanish America, sent copies of his 1823 *Lecciones para las escuelas de primeras letras, sacadas de las Sagradas Escrituras, siguiendo el texto literal de la traducción del Padre Scio, sin notas ni comentarios* to the Lancasterian school in Mexico. He reported later to the British and Foreign School Society that "[s]ome old priests opposed the introduction of these [*Lecciones*], stating that it was prohibited to read extracts from the Bible without notes."[29]

Although Robeson does not mention the school's Masonic connection (he seems only concerned with telling Carey of possibilities for selling books in quantity to dealers and institutions), one can trace his thought to his next warning that Americans must always be on their guard not to advance any sentiments concerning the government for you know not what party you are conversing with. Every American is pointed at in this city as being a Mason and at this time of the imprisonment of Congress, the Masons are caricatured and, as they are under the displeasure of the clergy they are afraid of making themselves known. The Lodges which used to meet here are closed for the present until things wear a more favorable aspect. The M– here are numerous and I am positively informed that the bishop of Puebla [Antonio Joaquín Pérez] who is at present here, is one, and he is the most bitter persecutor of the fraternity in the whole empire.

The archbishop of Mexico [Pedro José de Fonte] forbid the crowning of Iturbide [?]. But the bishop of Puebla not regarding this injunction came on and performed the ceremony.[30] The archbishop in consequence retired into the country and there lives retired, it is said he intends representing the affair to the Pope.

The next two pages in the file, written in a larger, looser handwriting, seem designed to have accompanied the earlier invoice. Robeson's signature appears at the end of what seems to be a letter, but there is no salutation and no date (although at the end he says he is leaving the next day with his friend Col Aldama for Punto Altesardo [Antón Lizardo?] to go on to Veracruz and then Mexico City. Suggesting that Reyes, customs official at Tlacotalpan, is more than a casual acquaintance and instead will be a link in future traffic, Robeson repeats the warning that "Don M. Reyes may be too sanguine a man" and that "if so, you will have to make some allowance." Robeson presents two proposals for future hauling: The first by Cap. Riley, who "has offered me freight from Philadelphia at three percent on the invoice price in the city, and two percent on the amount for bonding and forwarding," is one we have seen before. Riley will carry none on any other terms and only books or stationery. The other is Malsain's, on board the *Mary Washington*, who apparently is supercargo as he is never called captain. He "offers to bring freight for me if his vessel should be in the trade. His offer will no doubt be on more moderate terms." Robeson says he has "succeeded admirably in having [the goods in his shipment] valued very low in the customs house but this valuation is not intended to govern them hereafter unless it should be found correct as they acknowledge their ignorance of the quality and price." The duty on books with "pasted covers as *Desengaño del hombre* was valued at 37$^{1}/_{2}$; those with blue paper covers as *Spanish and English Conversations* have no duty to pay." Robeson describes how the inspectors first valued his camphor at $70 per lb. but he succeeded in having the amount lowered to $5. His 400 lbs. of cremor tartar [cream of tartar] was valued at $2,000. (An ingredient used in baking, cream of tartar was also used in galvanic tinning of metals. It probably was used for that purpose in Mexico and so its price was high.)

Robeson seems confident that the next letter (Mexico City, November 12) would arrive safely. He was sending it with the Colombian minister Miguel

Santa María, who was leaving Mexico for New York because Iturbide considered him hostile since he "associated in the meetings of those members of Congress whom the emperor has imprisoned." The emperor is "absolute and the Congress a figure of Neme [the Nemean lion that Hercules slew?] with his tail cut off." Robeson also forwarded with Santa María, "the documents relating to the affair on the part of the empire with Santa María's protest and the letters between him and the Secretary of State"; he requested that Carey preserve them.[31]

Robeson alludes to a feud between Cap. Riley and Mr. M. (one assumes Malsain), who is jealous of Riley and who wishes to destroy his reputation and take over his trade. Malsain is attempting to draw Col. Bradburn to his side but Bradburn is declining "so base a proposal"; later Robeson accuses Malsain of "commercial cupidity." Robeson notes the arrival on the ship *Anáhuac* of more goods subject to his order, though he does not say what these goods are. But the detail documents the large size of this early commercial contact with Mexico, as well as the fact that the Mexican warship served U.S. mercantile interests. If delivery can be made, Robeson says it will net 150%. The goods from the first shipment are now out of Mexico City's customshouse thanks, Robeson says, to "a number of liberal and enlightened men." Three of them are Republicans in the Congress; the other "a counselor of state for whom I have an order for sundry articles which are enclosed." This latter is Florencio Castillo, who wishes: "Two mahogany writing desks with secret drawers; 10 copies of Delolme on the constitution of the British government;[32] 2 copies in French of the constitution; 1 atlas of Baron Humboldt, French without the *Works*; 1 copy of Volney's *Works* complete; 2 doz. Silk pocket handkerchiefs of the most fashionable, many with blue ground fancy stamp varying the patterns; 2 doz. very fine holland (white); 4 doz. linen shirts handsomely ruffled."[33] If Castillo's request seems frivolous in his desire for luxurious personal items, it must also be noted that the lawmaker was acquainted with European constitutional writers and asked for them.

Robeson then says that he has:

> made sale of 600 volumes although not [at] as favorable a price as I expected. The prices of *Derecho* and *Desengaño* are diminished 15% in consequence of their imperfect translations. Recio, the purchaser as also others, say it ought to be revised or they will not meet with as ready a sale. *Contrato social* is for sale here in the French and at a cheaper rate and the well informed are all acquainted with the language. Therefore the work will not command a price proportional to its merits. *Triunfo de la libertad*, of this work there were too many for a place where priests abound in such numbers with the influence they possess. *Lazarillo* has been imported from Madrid, therefore there is no currency to this. *La Dulce*[34] and *Galatea* are more inquired after. But the sale of them will not justify a further supply. These last three I am selling at 1$

each. *Naturaleza descubierta*[35] is dull sale, having disposed of but one copy at 11$; *Vocabulario* dull sale @ 1.75, six being wanted; *Quotidiana*[36] the same @70 and 75 cents, plenty imported from Madrid. *Manuel de Voyageur* no sale.[37] *Dictionarios*,[38] both copies sold @ 14.50 ea. A further supply of 15 or 20 copies would sell. *Dictionary of Spanish and French* are enquired after. Grammars intended to facilitate the Spaniards in learning the English with the rules in Spanish—these would sell if not exceeding the number of thirty.

He then lists other articles sold: quill pens, lead pencils, ink stands, writing desks, glass, and so forth. "Ink stands of glass and copper are fabricated here at a cheap rate." He has not sold any of the pictures of George Washington. Mexicans express an interest in buying them but poverty stops them: "Even the most wealthy families feel the pressure of the times." He continues:

> I find no novels in this country as they import them and all religious works from Spain and but few have any desire of reading any other than political books, the ladies as well as the men read but little, preferring intrigue and gambling and any source of amusement to that of the cultivation of their minds. There [are], however, some exceptions, some of whom I have the pleasure of their acquaintance, whose minds are as much enlightened as any of my acquaintance in the U. States. This city, although populous, yet the composition is such a mass of ignorant superstition that a long time must elapse before they have a relish for instruction.

Robeson ends, saying he is submitting the bill to the house of Morgan Dorsey in New Orleans, with instructions to invest the amount in sugar. In this way Carey will fund his next shipment. To save duty in Alvarado, Robeson instructs Carey to mark the boxes as containing 50 books fewer than they actually have. He repeats previous orders and requests that Volney's *Works* be sent, concealed at the bottom of the boxes.

Then follows another undated invoice with the same quantities of items as the previous invoice, but arranged differently, with different values and notations. Instead of eight boxes, there are now twelve. In this bill and the previous one the captain of the *Mexicana* is said to be Thomas Dawson, not Riley:

> Bill for the contents of 12 boxes that I remit to ? from Mexico with the muleteer Mariano Candio to my consignment and I receive on the schooner *Mexicana*, proceeding from Philadelphia, its captain Dn. Tomás Dawson. As follows:[39]

N. 1	1 Cajones con 310 Libros)	Vale			
2	1 Cajones con 352 Libros)				
3	1 Cajones con 361 Libros)				
4	1 Cajones con 240 Libros) 393 Libros Pasta	440	16	110	4
5	1 Cajones con 8 Libros) Duty 25%				
6	1 Cajón con 50) 725 pasta de cartón	398	75	99	68

		1481	363 a la Rústica	
5	1 con 44.000 Plumas de escribir		82	04
6	1 con 120. doz. Lapis		45	
7	6 doz. Tinteros		2	2
8	6 otras	1	4	
	8 pinturas		16	10
			356	92

Before the table:

1 Cajón con 51)
1 Cajón con 67)

Rate the articles generally of the second quality and status. Value the articles by the quality, and the *vista* as he is called is not a judge of any of the articles he is called on to inspect. You can inform Mr. Le Brun that his work is highly spoken of. His duty is 47.25 to be deducted from the above.[40]

In the next letter (Mexico City, November 23), Robeson describes the maneuvers of the Church:

> The priests who are lending all their support to sustain on the throne his Imperial Majesty Agustín I are at the same time by intrigue and cunning endeavouring to raise themselves to the same pinnacle of power to which they were exalted previous to the demolition of the Inquisition. On last evening on a visit to some sincere republican friends I was confidentially informed that the priests had applied to the counselors of state at the last sitting for an order to prohibit the introduction of *Derecho del hombre* and *Desengaño del hombre*, alleging they contained principles foreign to their form of government and inflating the minds of the people with what they ought to know nothing of, viz. liberty. The council of state, amongst whom I have some friends, informed them that such works were useful and they could not sanction such [a] procedure. Finding their views thwarted, they had recourse to the minister of state who has always been noted for his liberal principles [who] in this case, in order to please the clergy or obey the commands of his master, stopped a letter out of the usual track. The minister, knowing some [of] my acquaintances, sent a note requesting an interview, which he obeyed. The minister requested him to state who was the importer and what were the titles of the books then circulating in the city. To this question he could receive no satisfactory answer from my friend. He then replied that he would issue an order for the search of all the libraries [bookstores] as well as my dwelling for such works. To this my friend replied that Mr. Robeson had an order from the *provisor* (the secretary of the archbishop) to draw them out of the customs house, to which he responded that if the ecclesiastical authority did not think proper to restrict the introduction of those works, the government would as they contained principles inimical to the well-being of the empire. Thus I am waiting every hour to receive an order to show the remaining books in my possession, which are such that I do not feel the least alarmed to produce.
>
> In a week or so I expect to see a secret tribunal established taking cognizance of all cases which interest the priesthood, being a revival of the Inquisition, although under another name.

Robeson closes: "This goes by a private *correo* (courier) of the government and I have perhaps said more than prudence warranted.

The next letter (Mexico City, November 1) breaks the chronology. However, I include it here, assuming that the file's order reflects when the letters were received. This letter repeats information from previous letters and tells how Robeson's letters were carried back to Carey—by what ships and by what bearers. He is always afraid his letters will "miscarry." He describes a Masonic network (or Mexicans' perception of one):

> The articles are all safe with a friend at Alvarado and under present circumstances it requires the utmost caution and circumspection in proceeding, as although the fraternity are memory here, they are afraid to be known. Every Brother as well as the Americans who are all taken as such, more especially if they dress in black, are viewed by the clergy and the great mass of populations as Jews and atheists, two classes of character which they believe would be conferring an honor on all their patron saints to eliminate. It therefore behooves the Americans to act with caution. At this moment, however, I am arranging a plan for their introduction which I have no doubt will succeed; if so, the profit will be 150%.

Robeson then complains of

> the conduct of a certain character who spoke to you relative to the introduction of certain works, the same who aspires to the appointment of consul general.... This friendly gentleman requested me to call on him, that having understood I had some prohibited works it would afford him much pleasure to assist me in drawing the same out of the customs house, that his acquaintance was such he could succeed without any risk and positively refused making any charge, alleging that it was the pact of friendship. This friendly man baffled me for two weeks and every day he had some new fangled tale relative to the intricacy of measure and the secrecy and caution to be observed. His character, however, was soon by me to be discovered. On my last visit he informed me that if he was known in this business it would be a stain on his character and he could not think of employing his ingenuity without a compensation of $200. To this I gave him to understand I would not accede and instantly left him to reflect on the truth of his friendship.
>
> This man, I assure, is despised by every American as well as the Mexicans for his uncouth and ungentlemanly manner, as also his haughty carriage. I in common with my countrymen will be surprised and mortified in having a representative of his character. Mr. W— in Mexico is perfectly an insatiate [?], being [in] his company are two royalist families who live in a state of retirement. The secretary of state, as well as some of the Senate, will be informed which I trust may arise in due time to frustrate his desires.

Robeson here describes James Wilcocks, a Philadelphian involved with mining interests in Mexico who was later named U.S. consul general.[41] Wilcocks,

Robeson reveals, had given Carey the idea of importing Philadelphia-printed books into Mexico.

Robeson then says that he sent back to Carey "a book on Spanish cookery which I wished corrected by Mr. Barry and a thousand copies printed and bound the same as *Desengaño, Derecho*." This detail is noteworthy for several reasons. Such a large printing seems strange, until we read later that cookbooks were to be packed as decoys on top of the prohibited books in the boxes for Mexico. "Corrected" suggests translation (although it is not clear from what language to what language) and signals that at this point Barry would be involved in the business. Robeson says he is providing a list of other books he wishes Carey to print and send; presumably this is the list we will see later.

Robeson reiterates the difficulty of selling *Desengaño* and *Contrato*; because they are prohibited, they "have to be sold with the greatest caution." Congress has just passed a law authorizing "the bishop or his offices to enter any house and seize prohibitary works." Thus, on the advice of friends, Robeson sold a considerable portion of his stock "although not at as good a price as I expected." The Congress has many liberal priests but also two who "spoke for some time in favor of establishing the Inquisition." "You will observe that no novels, or any religious works, ought to be sent here as they import from Spain works of these descriptions cheaper than can be had from the U. States. All works on liberal and republican principles, all that has a tendency to destroy the power of the priesthood will command a ready sale."

Robeson then says that he cannot remit to Carey the money he has received in sales because two caravans were recently robbed. In one instance it was owing to "the great number of *ladrones* who infest the highway between this and Veracruz"; $250,000 was seized, $70,000 of which was the property [of the person] who was sending the amount to Spain (in fact the whole amount was destined for Spain). In the other, the culprit was the government, which intercepted a shipment of $300,000 in Perote. "Thus you perceive the government are thieves as well as those who are brought up in that service." To avoid cash transmissions Robeson will issue a draft to buy sugar and coffee in Havana, then to be shipped to New Orleans. John Warner, the U.S. consul in Havana, will handle the transaction. Robeson will forward the bills with "Mr. Dennis A. Smith of Baltimore who leaves on the 12th for the U. States in the *John Adams* with Mr. Poinsett."[42]

This is Robeson's first reference to Joel Poinsett, who was traveling through Mexico from October to December 1822, under orders from President Monroe to report on conditions. The *John Adams* was a U.S. Navy ship. Poinsett returned to Mexico as minister from the United States from 1825 to 1829, when he was expelled for political meddling.[43]

Then follows a list of book titles and quantities sold, which fleshes out the numbers Robeson provided for customs in Alvarado and which is the most reliable document yet for telling of sales. The sizeable quantities of the first four items, sold on October 20, suggest they went quickly to a dealer. Three titles, which Robeson mentions elsewhere as part of his cargo, are missing from the list—perhaps because they remained unsold: Le Brun's translation of *Libertad de los mares, Naturaleza descubierta,* and *Vocabulario*:

Sales on Account of Messrs. Carey and Lea of Philadelphia
1822

October 20	190 Copies of *Triunfo de la Libertad* @ 2.22	$421.80
20	160 *Contrato social*)	
20	75 *Derechos del hombre*) 235 copies @ 1.87 1/4	$439.45
20	165 *Desengaño* " ") @ 1.56 1/4	$257.81 1/4
22	2 Copies Neuman's *Dictionary* 14.50 ea.	$29.00
22	6 Copies *Ejercicio Cuotidiana* @ 70 c. ea.	$4.20
23	2 *Diálogos* @ 2$ ea.	$4.00
23	2 DQ @ 1.75	$3.50
23	1 *Galatea* $1	$1.00
23	1 *La Dulce* $1	$1.00
23	3 *Lazarillo de Tormes*	$1 $3.00
26	2 boxes quills contg. 26,000 @ 14.37 1/2 per mil.	$373.75
26	3 dozen lead ink stands @ 4.50 per doz.	$13.50
26	3 dozen glass ink stands @ 2.75 per doz.	$8.25
26	40 dozen lead pencils @ 62 1/2 p. doz.	$25.00
		$1,597.26

A note:

> In consequence of the overcharge of duties at Alvarado I have made a reclamation on them for $400 and not having the matter adjusted cannot at this time favor you with a list of the duties. The duties I paid here on all my articles was 140$, 1/3 of which I paid for my medicines. The balance of the quills I expect to obtain from 150 to 175 per hundred as they are not very plenty here.

The duty on quills at Alvarado was	$1.87 1/2 (mil)"
at Mexico	1.33"
freight 7$ per box or 13,000	.54"
freight to Mexico 24$ for 20,000	.92 1/2
Cost in Philadelphia	5.00
Insurance, duty on remitting money and commissions	3.50
	13.17
Sales made	14.37
Profit per thousand	1.20

The insurance alluded to above is the 3 percent which I presume you paid on the articles to Alvarado, duty on remitting money is what you are subject to in this country to escape which you must buy bills or some article of merchandise that will pay costs, but in consequence of the depreciation of credit here no persons will take bills, and articles of merchandise that will pay are difficult to obtain. I am, however, negotiating for the purchase of some gold chains which I think will net a profit in the U. States.

In order to conduct everything to the best possible advantage I have thought it best to accept of four bills of exchange (as per copy enclosed) to the amount of eight hundred dollars which I've not the least doubt will be duly honored; if so, the saving will be from 12 to 15 per cent. The bills on Havana I have forwarded to our friend the consul, with directions as per copy of letter enclosed, those on N. Orleans I considered most safe to forward direct to you (as enclosed).

Then follows a duplicate of the above, dated November 1, 1822, Mexico City, with slight modifications. Robeson signs it and notes: "First cost" for quills means cost in Philadelphia. He concludes: "Thus you perceive notwithstanding the high prices obtained, the profit is very small, the freight is considerably higher than is customary but this you are aware of. The boxes may be increased four inches more in breadth without the freight to this place being any more."

The next item in the file appears to be a letter, although without salutation or date. I will transcribe it in its entirety since it provides a valuable narrative, unfortunately interrupted. It repeats previous material, but the repetitions underscore the author's outrage at the Mexican government's thievery:

The duty and expenses to which a merchant is subject when remitting specie from this empire is as follows:

Duty.		
	From the capital to any part of the coast	2%
	Insurance and carriage of Do.	2%
	Export duty from Veracruz	3½%
	Freight to the U. States	1½%
	Insurance 2%, if in the Winter 3%	2½%
	Merchant's commission for shipping	½%
		12%

Independent of these charges the anxiety of mind you are under until you hear of the safe arrival in their distant port is fully worth 5 percent more, for you must know there have been robberies unparalleled of private money both by the orders of the emperor and the numerous *ladrones* who infest the road from this to Veracruz, as per example,

A caravan with two hundred fifty thousand dollars left this a month since, escorted by 15 soldiers. On the road near Perote they were attacked by 30 *ladrones* (who are no other than those who desert from the army). The escort instead of repelling their assaults joined the freebooters and made a safe capture of the whole amount which was on its way to Spain, 70 thousand of which was the property of a resident merchant here. The adjacent mountains furnish for them a secure retreat.

The government has lately followed the good example set them and seized one million of dollars at Perote. The excuse was for this flagrant act that they wanted the mules to conduct the cannon, troops and provision to the siege of the castle at Veracruz. The emperor, however, informed the new elected Junto[44] on Saturday evening last in person that this necessity justified the measure and the money must be appropriated to paying the troops, conducting the siege. One hundred and fifty thousand of this being the property of Americans, it will be restored without much delay, though at some cost and trouble (so says the minister of state).

This government has a happy method of doing business. When a loan is necessary, they apportion the amount amongst the different cities. For instance, Veracruz, the amount to raise there, say $100,000; the wealthy characters are selected; a note is sent to this purport: Sir: You are requested to pay into the treasury in three days time — dollars, being your assessment or abide the consequence.

Thus you perceive there is something of the inspiration in this proceeding and you may note it down as a fact that the emperor is and will be as absolute as ever Napoleon Bonaparte was. He has imprisoned 18 of the republican party in Congress, together with 60 military officers, two months since and has as yet not granted them a trial. In this agreeably to the [?] treaty of Iguala [45]and sworn to by him on the day of coronation he has forfeited his words, twenty four hours is the utmost period allowed for imprisonment without being brought for trial and yet two months are elapsed and changes scarcely promulgated, he has went further. The Sovereign and Constituent Congress he has dissolved at his will and pleasure and methinks you enquire for what cause. I answer his wants, his inordinate desires, his every wish received a check. Congress, the liberal and republican party of Congress have always. . . .

The letter ends abruptly and two commercial documents follow. The first is a letter to Consul John Warner in Havana:

> Enclosed I hand you the first of two different bills of exchange. $100.00 drafts on Havana @ 5 days sight exchange No. 1.2.3 dated Mexico 26th October payable to the order of D. Juan Warner Consul of the United States or in his absence to his lawful attorney for value received of Dn. Tomás W. Robeson to Dña María Trinidad Torróntegui de Céspedes. Signed Manuel de Céspedes.[46]
>
> $300.000 Exchange No. 1.2.3 of date Mexico 26th October payable to the order of Don Juan Warner, cónsul of the United States or in his absence to his lawful attorney, for value received of Don Tomás W. Robeson. To Don José Nicolás Arratte de Peralta.[47] Signed José Agn. Peralta, Havana.

The second, another letter to Warner, is almost the same:

> Enclosed I hand you the first of two different bills of exchange, the 2 and 3 unpaid. A bill drawn by Manuel de Céspedes at 5 days sight his mother Doña

> María Trinidad Torróntigui [sic] de Céspedes, payable your order or in your absence to that of your attorney of the sum of $100. A second drawn by José Ag. Peralta at same sight his father Dn. José Nicholás Arrate de Peralta, payable to your order as above bill for the sum of three hundred dollars, which I trust will be duly honored. The drawers of those bills are holding commissions of Lieut., Col. in this empire, their families are represented to me to be wealthy and that previous draft of theirs has been regularly paid. On the payment or non-payment of these drafts, you will please advise me by the first opportunity directed to Alvarado or Veracruz to the House of Messrs. Riley and Souberville, if to Tampico, to Angel Benito de Ariza, merchant Pueblo Viejo.[48] If regularly paid you will please invest the same in coffee or sugar on such terms as will net a handsome profit in the United States, which I wish you to ship on account and risks of Messrs. Carey and Lea of Philadelphia, advising them in due time that should they deem it necessary, they can effect insurance. In a few days the 2nd and 3 of same terms and date will be forwarded you.

Then in a letter (Mexico, December 10) Robeson answers Carey's from October 9, reproaching him for the manner in which he sent Philadelphia gazettes. They arrived in a bundle and since Mexican customs charged by weight, the price for claiming them ($5) was too high for Robeson. So he returned them to the customs office. In the future, Carey should put the gazettes in the book boxes he is sending. Robeson says that Gen. Wilkinson received a bundle for which he had to pay $27. The reference is additional evidence that Robeson was acquainted with James Wilkinson, whom we have seen in connection with Aaron Burr's plan to set up an empire joining an independent Mexico to western U.S. lands. Wilkinson had come to Mexico in March 1822, hoping to acquire one of the Texas land grants that Stephen Austin was negotiating for colonist development; Wilkinson, we remember from Robeson's August 15 letter to Carey, was at an address in Mexico at which A. Thompson, sailing with another load of Carey books to Mexico, could be reached. Thus a network begins to be seen.

Written in the margin of this first page is a note, hardly readable, which refers to Robeson's fear, expressed earlier, of a house search:

> The affair is all settled and nothing done. It originated from the circumstance of an Englishman here being offended at the works of Le Brun and [who] informed the minister of state that such a publication circulating through the empire was calculated to embitter the mind of the people against his government and requesting the minister to grant an order to that effect, to which he assented; but did not carry it into effect. I have drawn them from circulation and the matter is at rest. The *Liberty of the Seas* is not relished here and am afraid I shall not be able to obtain more than 3$ if that for them. Political works at this time is what is principally sought after, more especially those which point out the rights and liberties of man.

Robeson also reproaches Carey for having written a letter with so little news; scarcely half the page was filled with writing. He reminds Carey of how far away from the United States he is, and he traces the customary mail schedule: "It is very rare we can obtain a letter from Veracruz by post short of 18 to 25 days, thus as the post arrives but once a week it consumed nearly two months in receiving a reply to a communication, which circumstance renders this city disgusting to every American for in the absence of news they are fomenting lies." He complains of "being in a country where the too free utterance of speech has assigned to some a convent for a habitation. It naturally incited in us foreigners a timidity in expressing our frustrations on paper."

He continues:

> [T]his much I must say for the man who at present sways the scepter over the empire, that he is the only one in it capable of governing a race of people so base, superstitious, ignorant, and idle as they are. Every American is soon convinced that this people are unworthy of a government like ours. A republic for this people would not stand 12 months, anarchy, confusion, and civil war with all its horrors would spread death and desolation over this empire until its population would be reduced one half. It therefore is my belief and in this I am not alone, that reason and sound policy ought to govern, that this people ought not to receive these blessings until they know how to appreciate them.
>
> The cry of a republic was heard two months ago by a body of people of the interior provinces headed by the governor of the province, named [Francisco] García [from Zacatecas]. The plan, however, not being sufficiently matured, did not succeed. García then threw himself on the leniency of the emperor who thinking it most safe to confine him until his empire was firmly established, cast him into prison at Puebla where he remains.
>
> On the 1 September another defection occurred. Genl. [Antonio López de Santa Anna] Santana who, at the head of some brave troops (at that time a colonel) stormed and carried Veracruz a year ago, was on the first arrested by order of the emperor and ordered to this place to stand trial for a plan laid to destroy the Cap. General of V. Cruz at this late attack between them and the fort. He, feeling considerably alarmed for the result, begged the emperor for a day or two to arrange his business and he with his guard of honor would follow the emperor to Puebla from Jalapa. No sooner had His Imperial Majesty started for Puebla than Santana ordered his guard of honor for Veracruz and in 6 or 8 hours followed them. Having arrived there, he visited the barracks, secured the fidelity of the regiment he commanded, altered [?] the flag partially, and raised the cry of a republic. He has had possession of it from the second and today's gazette, by express from Puebla under date the 9th, says he has formed an alliance with the castle of S. Juan de Ulúa. This though impolitic measure was a *dernier resort*. He has by this alliance enlisted the feelings of empire against him as it proved that this burst of republican feeling which he shouted was not real, that it was all one to him [as] to whether they were governed by a European prince or a president, that he was willing to sacrifice the public interest and the welfare of the country to gratify his own glory. That not succeeding in destroying [José Antonio de] Echávarri, the Captain General expected from such an event to fill the same stations as also reap the advantages which were to ensue from the engagement. On that night with

the fort, he was stimulated with a blind ambition which has led him to this base act for which the emperor has denounced him as a traitor, and will no doubt inflict the punishments he merits.

Your charge relative to the minerals I had not neglected. I have some specimens of silver ore with a variety of others which were presented to me, and in a few days I expect to set out for the mines 60 miles from this with some friends to collect a quantity. Specimens can be purchased here but the price is high. Mr. Poinsett when here purchased some and informed me that they charged him extravagantly.

The pages of this letter are not in order but next appears to be the "list of books written for in my letter of the 14th":

100 copies *Letters of Eloisa y Abelardo*,[49] some bound in a handsome style, the balance the same as *La Dulce*, varying the stamp and color of the leather on the books as some prefer red, others green and blue.

50 copies J. Rousseau, if not in Spanish, send 10 in French

50 Voltaire, without the poem *Henriad*,[50] in French or Spanish

50 sets of every modern work of the arts, industry and political economy

20 sets on surgery and physick printed since the year 1820. This latter I presume you have not and the small demand for the article would not compensate you to translate any of our American works.

1,000 copies printed in octavo in the Castilian language of the *Catechismo* which is at the end of the *Ruinas* de Palmyra, bearing the name of the natural and physical principles of morals taken from the *Constitution of Man and the Universe*
Note these must be in paste but cut smooth round.

All of these enumerated above are prohibited and must be sent as described below. The following works if translated in the Castilian would I think sell well. Of this I leave to your better judgment. Political as well as works of merit are eagerly inquired after, more especially the works of Voltaire, Rousseau. . . .

Book No. 1 (1 vol.) Delolme on the British Constitution. This work is inquired after by several members of Congress, and an order is enclosed for two copies of the same for a counselor of state in the French. I think there is no doubt you will find it translated in the Castilian. It is his wish, nevertheless, to have it in the French. I cannot say to you that the sale of this work would be very extensive and unless you can find part of the edition in other parts I would not urge you to put it to press. Yet I presume I could sell 150 copies.

Book No. 2 (1 vol.) *The Federalist* written by Hamilton, Madison and others. The edition of this would be an experiment like the former.

Book No. 3 (1 vol.) 1st Declaration of the Independence of the United States

2nd Constitution of the U. States
3rd Washington's Farewell Address
4th Declaration of the Rights of the Several States
5th Constitution of Buenos Ayres
6th Constitution of Colombia
7th Constitution of Chile and Peru

All that I can say in favor of this work is that a Declaration of the Rights of the Several States, namely (say 4) (these are all sold and I cannot find a copy) has been published here and sold well. This government, having formed no constitution as yet and the emperor having dissolved Congress by a public order, for their incapacity and dilatory proceedings and out of this body chose 56 thorough-going imperialists which are to act as an Intermediate Junto during the time necessary employed in forming a new Congress, which if formed will take 6 to 9 months.

These proceedings are, to be sure, rather against republican[s] but [I] assure you there are more liberal men here than you have any idea of. But the situation of the time renders it necessary for every man to speak with caution if his sentiment does not agree with the ruling party.

Book No. 4 (1 vol.) 1,000 copies of the works on the *Art of Cooking*, as forwarded you by Col. Bradburn, well corrected and bound the same as *Derecho, Desengaño*. 40 sets of every modern work on the arts, industry, and political economy, if not voluminous.

Here follows a list of prohibited works which must be introduced cautiously:

Book No. 5 (1 vol.) 1,000 copies of the *Catecismo*, in octavo, which is at the end of the *Ruins of Palmyra*, bearing the name of the natural and physical principles of morals taken from the *Constitution of Man and the Universe*. These must be in paste, cut smooth all round and introduced as I shall hereafter point out.

These books with those on cookery I wish forwarded in boxes 4 inches more in width than those first sent, with three layers of the prohibited books in the bottom and three of those on cookery and then those others on the top. Disguise the prohibited in the invoice by the name of novels. Have the bottom piece well secured by two hoops to prevent its being opened when it arrives in Alvarado, and the top lightly secured by a small hoop.

I also wish you to place at the bottom of each 50 sets of the *Monitor*, *Catechismo* and *Library*. There is no danger here and I do not apprehend any in Alvarado. Be particular, in noting in your invoice to Alvarado, the inspection of the vista, which box is *"a la rústica"*, *"pasta"*, and *"pasta de carton"*, or how many there are in the box of each description. *"Libros pasta"* is books bound the same as *Derecho*, Contrato; '*libros pasta de cartón*' is books bound although not in calf; '*libros a la rústica*' is those with paper covers.

> Send none unbound (with the exception of the *Catechismo* at the end of *Ruins of Palmyra*) as I know how to manage the duties; send me (if a new edition), 100 copies of *Derecho*, 50 of *Desengaño*, 50 of *Triunfo de la Libertad*. Scatter on the top of each box 5 of *Exercicio*, *La Dulce* and *Galatea* and insert them and some innocent novels' names as composing the whole in the invoice you send to Alvarado, which you will direct to Messrs. Riley and Souberville, Alvarado. Send nothing to Veracruz as they are rather too prying into matters for me. The boxes may be increased from 2 to 3 inches more in breadth but no more in length. You will send in one of the boxes a catalogue of all the books you have as also a catalogue of all the books for sale in the United States, that the booksellers may select such works as they think will answer the market.

Robeson then adds: "Since writing the above, a friend stepped in and informed me that those works of Voltaire and Rousseau were very costly and from the situation of the country, he did not think they would command a brisk sale. Independent of this the risk is to be considered. I therefore for the present wish you not to forward them until you receive another communication from me." He advises Carey to fill the secret drawers of the writing desks with pen knives. Although some of the writing desks will be of a high quality and will command high prices in Mexico, the invoice should indicate that all are of low quality. The shipment should be addressed to J.D. Bradburn in Alvarado. Manuel Recio, "introduced to me by my friend Basan," now appears to be Robeson's source for information about the book market in Mexico; and Robeson orders special writing paper for him. Common paper is plentiful in Mexico but Recio wishes some with gilt edges. Books should either be bound in paste or in calf. "[T]he book binders here never bind in board; the price if they did would be the same as in calf." The prohibited books, which mainly are in paste, should be introduced "clandestinely"; shipment should be made "as soon as possible."

Robeson and Recio have come to an agreement on a new edition of the *New Mode of Cooking*, which Robeson requests that Carey prepare, bound as cheaply as possible. Recio will have ¼ of the project and has expressed a wish to acquire the copyright. However, Robeson says, "the book is not very well written, the writer having blended certain letters together which insures a correct pronunciation but is badly spelt so that I think you will have to employ Mr. Barry to revise it. But the compensation ought to be trifling, as the labor is not much."

He continues:

> Señor Recio has requested me to inform the American printer that the escolastic nature of Mexico is going to prohibit the editions of the New Testament

for not having the notes which Father [Felipe] Scío [de San Miguel] put in his translation and if they print a new one, they must be careful to embody the notes or have it excluded. These notes of the Padre I will endeavour to obtain and note his explanations of the Scripture.

This exchange between Robeson and Recio, relative to Carey's printing of the Catholic Bible for export to Mexico, points to several considerations: The Mexican clergy, like Catholic authorities in the United States, were wary of Bible reading that was not guided by commentary.[51] Carey's reputation as a major printer of the Bible is implied; in 1790 he printed 471 copies of the Catholic Douay Bible and in the early 1800s he continued to print both Catholic and Protestant editions. But when the American Bible Society was founded in 1816, their many advantages such as new technology in the use of stereotyping (introduced into the United States in 1812) and distribution networks undercut his position.[52] Thus Carey may have seen Catholic Mexico as an alternative to his frustrated Bible publishing in the United States. Felipe Scío's translation of the New Testament from Latin into Spanish had just appeared in editions in New York (1819) and London (1821).[53]

However, complicating Carey's plans for printing the translation for export to Spanish America was the relationship Rocafuerte was beginning with the American Bible Society. When Rocafuerte arrived in the United States in 1821, he was introduced to Rev. Dr. James Milnor, rector of St. George's Episcopal Church in New York and secretary of the Society. In 1823 Rocafuerte addressed the Society and soon afterwards the Society voted to send Bibles to Spanish America.[54] We have seen that Rocafuerte based his 1823 schoolbook, destined for Spanish America, on Padre Scío's Bible translation (copies of which he sent to the Lancasterian School in Mexico). Thus, these imports likely also deterred Carey from acting on Robeson's recommendation to print Scío's work for the Mexican market.

Dated January 17, 1823, a two-page list sets out the reduction in duties Robeson was able to secure on 12 boxes shipped to Alvarado. I will not reproduce this list, except to note that Robeson says that the adjustment was made because of "the great error they [the customs officials] committed in valuing the price of the books instead of the leather with which it was bound."

In the next letter (Mexico, November 28, again breaking the chronology), Robeson writes:

> I have this moment seen the express sent on by Mr. Riley to his partner in this place with the information of the arrival of the *Mexicana* as also stating the loss of the *Dido*, wrecked between Veracruz and Alvarado. I waited immediately on Mr. Souberville and learned that the *Mexicana* has had a passage of 15 days with a full cargo. He informed me that no mention is made in Mr. Riley's letter of any article being on board for me, which surprises me no

little; this, however, in the hurry of sending off the express may be been overlooked. A week, however, may determine.

I enclose to you the 2nd of exchange at sight (the first remitted by Mr. Poinsett in the *John Adams*, dated 23 November, for four hundred dollars, drawn by Wm. McQueen on his father Rob. McQueen (steam engineer of New York), payable to your order, which I trust will arrive safe to hand and meet due honor.

I also enclose the precise amount of duty which you will perceive varies essentially from those heretofore remitted to you. Through the friendship of Mr. Riley I have obtained a reduction which satisfies me that justice has been duly administered.[55] In every article you will perceive a very material reduction—twenty cents on each book full bound and ten on the others, the difference of which between this and the former charges arises from this circumstance (the former *vista* laid the duty on the supposed price of the book, the latter on the value of the leather with which the book is bound)—which is, in fact, the true mode of proceeding for, in the other case, the paper, printing, with everything else connected, is made chargeable.

Robeson closes, saying that he had sent a letter dated the 26th with a friend (Poinsett) via Tampico to forward "by the first opportunity."

The next letter (Mexico, December 20, 1822) describes historic developments:

The revolution which Santana has set in motion with [Guadalupe] Victoria you no doubt have heard as this reaches you by way of New Orleans. It is impossible for the wisest analyst to tell what will be the result. Too many revolutionary chieftains remain on hand who are opposed to the present form of proceeding to insure a solid government for some time. This revolution promises much evil. The troops who are on what is termed the republican side amounted to the number of 4,000 and are strongly posted in Veracruz and Puente del Rey. The imperial troops are so few and so scattered over this immense empire that but few can be spared to march against them, and the imperial gazette of the 20th quotes a letter from the commanding general at Jalapa who notices the lamentable circumstance of the troops wanting shoes, and in consequence cannot march. The dilatory proceedings of every department of this government is much to be regretted, not only in this case but every other. I mentioned in my former letter that Santana had formed an alliance with the Castle [San Juan de Ulúa], but in this I erred having taken it from a government paper which you know even in the U.S. can lie when necessary.... Martial law is about being [passed?] here and every tongue is mute, save those on the side of the emperor. No news is, therefore, to be heard. A few weeks must, I think, determine the point between the contending parties, the result of which I cannot hazard an opinion.

Robeson acknowledges receipt of a letter from Carey and advises that, given uncertain events, Carey should hold off sending the books Robeson requested.

The last item in the file (Mexico, January 17–26, 1823) was appended to the letter to have been sent to Tampico; because Poinsett could find no vessels there, leaving for New York, it was returned to Mexico City.[56] Robeson reports:

> On the first of this month the celebrated Padre Mier, one of the late Congress whom the emperor imprisoned, made his escape from the convent of Santo Domingo (through the agency of a priest) at 4 o'clock in the afternoon. He took refuge in the house of some ladies who had promised to protect him, but as the emperor was somewhat exasperated that he should have effected his escape, dispatched troops in every direction in pursuit. The ladies became fearful that some accident might befall them, gave information to the proper authorities, and the Rev. Padre was removed with Bustamante and [Anaya?] to the Inquisition, which at present is a rendezvous for the soldiers.[57]
>
> 7th. Last evening [Vicente] Guerrero and [Nicolás] Bravo with officers and soldiers amounting to 150 made their escape. It appears that the emperor had ordered the arrest and imprisonment of the former. The officer who was charged with the execution of it, being the friend of G., apprised him of the circumstance early in the evening, which afforded him sufficient time to concoct a plan of operation with Bravo, and both were off by dusk. The officer at 12 at night repaired to the house of G. and demanded entrance. His guard refused. The officer wishing to give him as much time as possible repaired to the barracks for 100 soldiers to force his way. On presenting so great a force, the general guard withdrew and a search was made but to no purpose as the bird had flown. A runner was immediately dispatched to the emperor, who ordered a troop of horse of 120 men in pursuit, who the next day came up and joined his party. Finding matters growing worse and the government exhibiting a sad picture of maladministration, poverty, ruin and disgrace, the emperor as a *dernier resort*, to replenish his exhausted treasury, summoned a council of 300 friars at the convent of San Francisco. He then exposed to them his sad situation. Deserted, he said, by G. and Bravo, with a view of waging war against him, he was unable from the present state of the treasury to levy troops and stop their career and therefore felt himself compelled to ask of those whom he knew had it in their power to assist him in this case of emergency. He observed to them that the Church was embellished with a large amount of silver plate which would be of essential service to him and which would eventually be refunded them.
>
> Their leader informed His Majesty that it was very true there was a considerable quantity of plate, but that it was not at their disposal. What he saw, they observed, was the bequest of persons deceased to their patron saints, and donations made to the Church, of which they were no more than trust for their security. But notwithstanding they had an administrator who had the sole power of disposing of the trust, and as he was on the eve of departure for Spain, they would in that case be necessitated to appoint another and would, therefore, by permission of His Majesty name him as *administrador*. Thus the poor friars do not give the plate, but the *administrador* takes it and he alone is responsible. The emperor has, therefore, as the responsible person taken a considerable quantity to the mint to be coined; and the supposed amount he will be able to obtain from all the churches is one million.

This morning in consequence of a decree of Congress for the replenishing of the treasury an issue of 4 million of paper money made its appearance, but its unseemly appearance and the facility it offered to counterfeit brought it instantly 15% below par, 1/3 is made a legal tender and in the payment of duties you are obliged to give 1/3 paper. This very plan is devised to bolster the credit but of no avail as this people has been too long accustomed to the precious metals to deem paper of any value.

Jan. 20. For these two weeks past, there has been a total silence which augurs no good for the government and although I had full belief that things would be brought to a close, in this I am sorry to say we remain in the same or rather a worse situation. The people are poor as well as the government and therefore during the present distress have but little to advance beyond their necessary wants.

25. A *bando* [edict] was published a few days ago laying a tax of 40% on household property and 150% on each male member of the family, which I assure you is not relished by the Mexicans.

26. The extraordinary has just been issued from the government press, giving the details of a battle of the imperial troops against Guerrero, 30 leagues distant from this. The forces opposed were 600 strong each. The imperial leader Gen. [Epitacio] Sánchez has been slain, the number of soldiers who fell in battle are not stated but [I] presume from reports it must have been a considerable portion on each side. Guerrero and Sánchez, it is stated, were opposing breast to breast for some time. At length the latter threw his lance at the former and unhorsed him, the former at that instant seizing his pistol shot his opponent in the head, which terminated his career in a few minutes. Guerrero is also stated to be mortally wounded, but this is contradicted by a handbill a few hours after. His Imperial Majesty has settled on the widow of Sánchez two thousand dollars per annum and taken under his sovereign protection their only son. Yesterday was the *Jura* or oath that was taken by [the] municipality to protect on the throne His Imperial Majesty, Don Agustín Primero, equal to that of any European monarch. The church and streets leading to the palace were crowded with people to witness the sumptuous display and the evening was ushered in [by] the cannon, rocketry and a brilliant illumination. Thus you see everything is set in motion to please the fancy of those poor creatures, and blind them to the fate that awaits them. Passing through the streets the same evening, voices frequently vociferated "Death to the Republicans." In front of the palace were a great number of mottoes, one of which struck me forcibly. It was this: "Here are no unthankful. Here are no republicans. But faithful, united Mexicans." There were more of the same import and others composed of such a mass of flattery as to sicken a republican like me. Great preparations [sic] is making for the Christmas holidays and [I] presume this will be nothing but feasting and rejoicing for these three weeks.[58]

The colossal statue of Charly [the Spanish king, Carlos IV] which you will see described by Humboldt in the publick square is rather too offensive to the eyes of some persons, and is at present removing to the Alameda to remain in obscurity. The place it occupied was nearly two acres which is to be fitted up for the *plaza de toros*, or a place to fight bulls. This and cock fighting being their principal amusement, Sunday and feast days are those devoted to it. Ten of the former and fifty of the latter are slain on each of those days, the continuance of this barbarous amusement is the best evidence I can give you of the cast of these people.

Gen. W. is still with us, he has some Mina claims[59] and is endeavouring to obtain a grant of land in Texas, neither of which he has accomplished and is only waiting a safe passport for the U. States. His health is not improved and from present appearance do not think him long for this world. He is making collections for publishing a work on this empire on his return. [Indeed, Wilkinson died in Poinsett's house in Mexico City on December 28, 1825.][60]

No strangers are arriving in this city; at present there is not more than 10 Americans, and the principal part of those are making arrangements to start.

A *bando* has just been published declaring war against Spain. As yet I have not seen it but am told it is severe against the Spaniards here.

The works you mentioned would, I've no doubt, do well here but not in large quantities. If *Derecho* is reprinted you may send three hundred copies, *Desengaño* one hundred and fifty, *Triunfo de la libertad* a few, say fifty, and no novels, *Dictionary de Newman* say fifty copies with those I have before enumerated.

The file of Robeson letters ends here, the reader left with the impression that Robeson's last communiqués only record scattered facts and, although they ask for future shipments, reveal confusion. Iturbide abdicated on March 19, 1823, but up until that date his opponents feared that he would rally supporters and reestablish control. Bustamante reports in his diary on March 4 that boxes of books, telling of his life and "miracles," printed in Philadelphia, were awaiting distribution in Alvarado (1896, 283). He names no publisher but says they are good editions, selling for 25 *pesos duros*.

****

The Lea and Febiger File of Correspondence (Incoming) includes three letters from George Follin to Carey and Lea. The first (May 24, 1822, Veracruz) notes his arrival on the 27th (of April ?) and tells that the shipment of books, sent on the schooner *Mary Washington* "consigned" to him, has been landed but is not yet in his possession.

> Owing to [the] great number of Masonic books there [are] in your invoice, the collector of the customs did not think proper that they should be dispatched until he had received order from Government. Therefore, I have taken all the necessary measures to have them restituted, but the *Intendente* is of [the] opinion that I shall be compelled to reship the M.B. [Masonic books] to the U.S. as soon as they shall be in my possession. I shall endeavor to sell them for your account and will advise you by every opportunity of what I have done for your account.

In the second letter (May 30, 1822) Follin writes:

The *Mary Washington* being detained for a few days, I have time to inform you that I have just received order to reship seven cases of your books, one case still remaining in the custom house subject to the decision of the government. What it will be I cannot tell. The worse it can be (as I am told) will be the order to reship them in all cases. I beg you to believe that I will do all in my power for the best of your interest. It is truly unfortunate that you assorted your cases with so many Masonic books. The only object of all this detention I have more to do to get these books to sell all my cargo. Enclosed you have bill of lading for the seven cases; they are shipped on board the *Mary Washington* after Warner for your account and risks.

In the third letter (October 23, 1822, Alvarado) Follin writes:

Enclosed you have bill of lading for one hundred and fifty hard Spanish dollars, shipped on board of the schooner *Mary Washington* and Capt. Warner being on account of the sales effected for your account of the shipment you had made by me by the said schooner to Vera Cruz, of which shipment I returned you all the books except one small case. I should have been glad to have heard that they had all come to hand. As soon as your sales are closed, I shall send you the balance with your account of sales.[61]

The hundred and fifty dollars shipped for your account and risk is placed to your debit as follows:

Dollars as per bill of lading..............................$150
Export duty 3^{1}/2%..$5.25
Commission of remittance 2^{1}/2%.....................$3.75
To your debit $159.00

The Lea and Febiger File of Correspondence (December 16, 1822, to June 20, 1823, Outgoing) provides a sequel to Follin's story. The File includes the following: Six letters from Carey and Lea to Thomas W. Robeson (April 1, April 14, May 20, May 21, and two letters on May 31); two letters to Messrs. Morgan and Dorsey (Feb. 7 and March 27); one letter to Messrs. Follin and Malsan [sic] (April 16); and one letter to Allen Thompson (May 15). The Lea and Febiger ledger for 1824–1825 shows that the account of Follin and Malsain (Veracruz) was not closed until January 1826 when William McKean paid $635 on the total amount, $6063.55. On this page, is penciled a list of books similar to the titles on the list in the 1822 entry. McKean and James Pennoyer, whose firm had offices in Natchez and New Orleans, were apparently middlemen who exchanged cash and commodities for Carey and Morgan Dorsey. Both men worked for Carey and Lea; in 1822 Pennoyer wrote from Quebec to Carey and Lea of his difficulties in selling an atlas there (Kaser 1957, 30).

First, Carey and Lea's letters to Robeson, which indicate how Robeson's letters were read and clarify the relationship between the Philadelphia book dealers and their agent: Carey and Lea seem only concerned with the cash flow. As long as Robeson sold books, the dealers appear not to have cared about how the books might have been advancing republican or Masonic causes. The letters reveal that the business continued for several months after Robeson's letters stopped.

Although the first letter from Carey and Lea to Robeson is dated April 1, the February 7 letter that Carey and Lea sent to Morgan Dorsey describes ongoing correspondence with Robeson: "By a letter just received from Mr. T.W. Robeson, Mexico, we learn that he has remitted to you a bill for $400 with instructions to invest the proceeds in sugar and remit to us. If not already done we should much prefer that you should purchase with a bill on this place in New York and remit it per mail."

In this April 1 letter of Carey and Lea to Robeson, the business owners seem both willing to proceed with shipments and reluctant to continue:

> We have received your letter per *Mexicana* and now forward you five boxes by same vessel, invoice of which is enclosed. We have enclosed to Riley and Souberville invoice and bill of lading, amount $921.37, binding described as you wished and packed as requested. No objectionable books mentioned in this invoice. With this we forward you a letter which should have gone by Capt. Thompson but by some error his duplicate note only was sent you which we hope you have collected. One of the drafts on New Orleans was paid and we have received the sugar—the other protested and we presume received to you. We hear nothing yet from Mr. Warner.
>
> You will observe that we send you such books only that we have on hand. While the country is in such an unsettled state we deem it better to risk such things only as have no market here. Under these impressions we neither manufacture or purchase for this shipment which, should it arrive safely with you, we think will do well.
>
> Many of the books ordered by you cannot be had here. Others are at such prices as could not be obtained in Mexico. Nothing could be sent but what we make.
>
> Unless things materially change for the better, we would advise the closing of the business and your return. It will have had a firm trial.
>
> The draft on New York has been paid.
>
> We refer you to newspapers in one of the boxes for news of the day. We send you many letters for your friends with this.

Carey and Lea's letter of April 1, 1823, to Riley and Souberville confirms this shipment of five boxes to Robeson: "Herewith we hand you invoice and bill of lading for five cases of books for Mr. Robeson. We presume he has given you instructions to enter and forward to Mexico any articles that may be shipped to him."

In their April 14 letter to Robeson, the dealers sound worried:

> Your several letters of 22 and 23 February [missing from the file] are just received. We are happy to learn that there is a probability of your business

taking a more favourable turn. The slowness of sales and great difficulty and danger of remitting has been seriously inconvenient to us. We hope, however, the future will be more productive of success but at the same time we do not feel much disposed to incur new expenditures with a prospect of returns which are so slow and dangerous. If the property with you and now on the way to you was sold at the prices per your account of sales it would produce about $10,000 in the gross. As yet we have not received $600, although a large portion of the articles have been shipped 9 mos.

This has arisen out of circumstances which could not be foreseen by anyone and we would not wish to be understood to attach the least blame to you. Far from it, we think you have acted with every caution having our interest constantly in view.

Under those circumstances we think it better to avoid for the present making any shipment that would require an additional involvement of capital. Your orders, therefore, for type, presses, etc., which would amount to something like $6,000–$7,000 and which would have to be paid for at once, we will be compelled to decline at all events for the present. Future letters from you may induce us to change our minds.

We shall not for the present put any new Spanish works to press but will continue to send you such as we have already made. With this we send you duplicate invoice of books sent per *Mexicana* a few days since [missing from the file].

It will depend somewhat on your next letter if we shall send the boxes to Jalapa as you request. We shall send them all to Alvarado to the care of Riley and Souberville to whom you can give the necessary instructions; in case we should forward them we shall mention to them which boxes are for certain cities. We presume you are acquainted with the failure of the drafts on Havana and one on New Orleans. We sincerely hope you may be able to make the drawers refund.

It would be very advantageous to this undertaking to keep us in funds as far as in your power. When we receive large remittances we shall feel more free to make new investments.

We shall be glad if you would give us a regular account of sales from the commencement of your business to the time you write us in answer to this. Then continue your account up to the period of each letter. By this means we shall see exactly how the various works sell and act accordingly.

We have not heard of the life of the Emperor having been published here.

Many of the works you order are not to be had here, either in Spanish, French or English. Others are to be had at very extravagant prices and would not do to send at all.

We should be glad to have prices for Masonic books. You have not given us an idea of how they will sell nor have you said one word about the aprons, etc.[62] Have you not yet sold any Masonry works? They ought to bring a very high price.

Carey and Lea's May 20 letter to Robeson sounds a double message. On the one hand the tone is desperate but, on the other, the Philadelphians seem to cautiously hold out hope for continuing relations:

We have received your letter of 7th March [missing from the file] within a few days and regret much that you give us no information respecting your proceeding or success. On this subject we are exceedingly anxious. We fear the business is likely to turn out an unprofitable one. We now find ourselves at the end of 10 months in funds for the amount only of about $200, after deducting the necessary cash advances for your equipment, etc.

We have totally declined having anything more to do with Spanish books unless a very considerable change takes place. In the present situation of the business we find ourselves much disappointed and shall not engage any further capital which promises so protracted a return. Should we, however, receive more favourable accounts from you, we shall make further shipments of the books on hand and should we be satisfied of certain and more speedy returns, we might again be induced to reinvest all or part of such return. At present this unproductive amount is too large.

We sincerely wish a change of government may make a change in your business. Masonic and other liberal books must now be free and we presume would sell well. On the late shipments we have given a good supply of these.

We repeat our ideas expressed in a former letter that we think it would be much better to make an entire close of the business and return with as little delay as possible unless a very material change takes place in your sales...

We would send you some newspapers but that the charge is so great as stated by you for postage to Mexico. We shall always with pleasure supply you when sending any books as requested. In the last boxes sent you we put a large parcel.

The May 21 letter to Robeson is short, enclosing two accounts against Gen. Pignatelli, who is arriving in Mexico, for $29.05.[63]

The first of the two May 31 letters is directed to Robeson in Mexico. It refers to letters received from Robeson dated April 14, 16, and 17 [not in the file]. Even though Robeson has reported in them that his prospects are "brightening," Carey and Lea reiterate the necessity of closing the business and the desirability of bringing payment for the sale of the books in specie or "undoubted bills" rather than in produce. They say they have received only $200 from New Orleans and that one of the drafts was protested; from Havana they have received nothing. The second letter is directed to Robeson in Havana and repeats directions to bring the profits from sales back in specie, saying that "segars," brought in payment for debts from Cuba, had to be sold in Philadelphia below cost.

The May 15 letter from Carey and Lea to Allen Thompson provides a crisp ending to the paper trail, and again demonstrates a relationship between Thompson and Robeson: "Enclosed we have the pleasure to hand you two letters just received from Mr. Robeson. Having paid 67 cents postage on those two letters and at several different times about as much, we now charge you with $1.33."

NOTES

1. The Masonic catechism is probably Volney's, but also any of the manuals by Webb, Cole, Castillo, or Cerneau. The *Manual de Voyageur* may be Barère de Vieuzac's *Liberty of the Seas*.

2. For Philadelphia's ship trade in this period see Ritter; J. Jackson; Scharf and Westcott. The ships Robeson mentions are not included in their lists. However, the firm of Manuel Eyre and Samuel M. Massey includes Veracruz and Alvarado as ports of call for their ships and that company's ledger in the HSP's collection provides two important facts—they did packet business to Charleston between 1803–1805 for the company of Robeson and Paul, and the *Highlander* is listed as one of their ships for the years 1804–1805. Davis describes a ship, the *Mexicana*, which had been the Spanish ship, the *Santa Rita*, and, seized by pirates in 1815, was renamed. It became again the *Nonesuch* as pirates sought "to cover her tracks" (2005, 237). It is not clear if this is Robeson's ship.

3. "U.S. Message from the President of the U.S., transmitting, pursuant to the resolution of the House of Representatives of 23 Dec. last, information relative to the detention in confinement of R.W. Meade Jan. 30, 1818" (Washington, D.C.: E. de Krafft, 1818).

4. See Tinterow and Lacambre 2003, *Manet/Velázquez: The French Taste for Spanish Painting*.

5. In contacting Philadelphian diocesan offices, I was told that St. Mary's early records were consumed by fire.

6. See Alamán, Stanley C. Green, Morton, Reséndez. On Bradburn, see Henson.

7. See the prologue to *Bosquejo ligerísimo* by Labastida Muñoz.

8. Labastida Muñoz (40). Although Santamaría was Colombian representative in Mexico, he was Mexican, born in Veracruz. He was, like Rocafuerte, an Ecuadorian who later represented Mexico, a non-native who served Colombia in an overseas commercial and diplomatic post.

9. Rodríguez O., *The Emergence of Spanish America*, Chapt. 3.

10. Miquel i Verges.

11. "avivó más en Bustamante el deseo de huir al extranjero" (Miquel i Verges 1980, 100).

12. The handwriting for this title is nuclear. It could also refer to *Arte de amar*, in which case it might be Ovid's work in the edition *L'art d'aimer* (London, 1740) by François Etienne Gouge de Dessières, listed as prohibited by the Spanish Inquisition in 1761 in Defourneaux.

13. Robeson could have supplied the title, as we have seen, with Carey's 1821 edition, or one published in Madrid in 1821 by Rosa, or by still another

published in Bordeaux by P. Beaume ("nueva traduccion por don Josef Marchena, aumentada con una noticia sobre la vida y los escritos de Volney").

14. This appears to have been a letter that Charles Maurice de Talleyrand-Périgord wrote to Pope Pius VII, published in Paris in Spanish translation in 1821 and 1822, and in Madrid in 1822, "Carta escrita al Papa Pío Séptimo."

15. The prices are likely quoted in hard Spanish dollars. Follin refers to this currency, and it is known that these circulated in the United States. Invoices and balance sheets in the Carey and Lea ledgers speak of "dollars."

16. Henry Schwenk Tanner was a Philadelphia engraver and printer.

17. It is not clear who this might have been—either Mariano or José María.

18. Undoubtedly, this was Dominique George Fréderic de Rious de Prolhiac de Fourt de Pradt's *L'Europe et l'Amérique, depuis le Congrès d'Aix-la-Chapelle* (Paris: Chez Bechet; Rouen: Imprimerie de Denuzon, 1821, 2 vols.).

19. This business is not documented in any of the other sources I consulted, which cite loans from the British house of Barclay, Herring. See Webster, Tenenbaum, Platt, Kaufmann, Dawson, Baur, Rodríguez O. "Mexico's First Foreign Loans."

20. Benson, "Territorial Integrity in Mexican Politics."

21. The four-volume edition of *El ingenioso hidalgo Don Quijote de la Mancha* may be the 1810 edition (León: Tournachon-Molin), the 1814 edition (London: J. & T. Clarke, expensas de Lackington, Allen et al.), or the 1815 edition (Burdeos: P. Beaume). The six-volume set may be the "nueva edición arreglada a la tercera de la Real Academia Española. Con estampas" (Leipsique: Sommer, 1818).

22. "Factura del Contenido de 4 Cajones que remito a ? de Mejico con el arriero Mariano Candio a mi consignación y recibo en la Goleta *Mexicana* precedente de Filadelfia su Capn. Tomás Dawson". This conflicts with Robeson's earlier statement that the *Mexicana*'s captain was Riley. In a listing of ships entering and leaving Mexico, printed in the Mexico City newspaper *Aguila Mexicana* (August 1, 1823), the *Mexicana*, whose captain was "Daioson" (a phonetic spelling of "Dawson"), left Veracruz for Philadelphia with a cargo of fruit.

23. "su mucha exactitud, inteligencia y actividad" (*Juan Schmaltz y su misión* 1957, 10).

24. See Stern.

25. Ladd documents Bradburn's marriage to Josefa, descendant of the seventeenth-century Conde del Valle de Orizaba (225).

26. A. Small and H.C. Carey and I. Lea published Henry Neuman's *A New Dictionary of the Spanish and English Languages* in 1823.

27. *Cornelia Bororquia, o La víctima de la Inquisición* is a title mentioned several times in Robeson's letters. See my discussion of the book later.

28. Joseph Lancaster, "The Lancasterian System of Education" (Baltimore: Published for the author and sold only at the Lancasterian Institute, 1821, 34 & 1 pp.). For a description of this innovation in Mexico, see Stanley C. Green, Tanck Estrada.

29. Quoted by Rodríguez O., *The Emergence of Spanish America*, 66.

30. Anna describes the ceremony (80-81). Alamán (*Historia*, Vol. 5, 257–261) gives an account of one of Pérez's pro-Iturbide speeches and tells that Fonte left Mexico for Cuba (600).

31. This material is not in the file.

32. Jean-Louis Delolme (1741–1806), a Swiss jurist, who wrote the *Constitution de l'Angleterre* (Amsterdam, 1771). A modern edition exists, edited by David Lieberman (Indianapolis: Liberty Fund, 2007).

33. The *Catálogo de la Colección Lafragua de la Biblioteca Nacional de México, 1821–1853* lists a publication in which "Castillo" appears as a signatory, along with eight others: "Sin poner la inquisición la religión se sostiene" (México: Imprenta Imperial, Sept. 26, 1822, 6 pp.).

34. It is likely that this title is *La dulce venganza* (Sweet Vengeance), written by Céspedes y Monroy and published in the 1800 Madrid collection, referred to previously. However, I can find no evidence of this novel's U.S. publication. Two other unlikely possibilities: *La dulce y santa muerte, obra que escribió en francés Juan Crasset y traduxo Basilio de Sotomayor* (Sevilla: Imprenta de D. Manuel Nicolás Vázquez, 1779); *La Dulciada, poema épico en siete cantos* (Madrid: Imprenta de la Calle de la Greda, 1807).

35. This appears to be Nicolas Gouin Dufief's *Nature displayed in her mode of teaching language to man being a ... Method of acquiring languages with unparalleled rapidity, deduced from the analysis of the human mind; adapted to the French; to which is prefixed, a development of the author's plan of tuition.* Ed. 4 improved and enl. (Philadelphia: The Author, 1820, four vols. in two). Spanish version: *La naturaleza descubierta en su modo de enseñar las lenguas a los hombres: o nuevo e infalible método para adquirir una lengua dentro de muy breve tiempo ... adaptado a los españoles y a la inglesa por Don Manuel de Torres y L. Hargous* (Filadelfia: T. y J. Palmer, 1811, 2 vols.).

36. Probably Barry's 1822 *Elements of Spanish and English Conversation* (with dialogues).

37. There were many such navigational titles as this in print in English in those years; I have found no listing of this French title.

38. Newman's dictionaries were not published until 1823, so it is not clear what this entry refers to.

39. "Factura del contenido de 12 cajones que remito a ? de Mejico con el arriero Mariano Candio a mi consignacion y recibo en la goleta *Mexicana*, precedente de Filadelfia, su Cap. Dn. Tomás Dawson. A saber".

40. This deduction suggests that Le Brun sent his book on consignment and paid his costs.

41. For a view of Wilcocks, see Stanley Green (130); for a Mexican view, see Carreño, Vol. 1, Ch. 12.

42. Smith was the principal financial backer of Mina's invasion of Mexico in 1817. In the Gilpin papers of the HSP, in a letter dated April 22, 1824, in which Smith asks for compensation for his part in the Mina expedition, Mier is mentioned and called "Padre Meyers."

43. See Rippy. The reasons for Poinsett's villainization are complex. The old-Spanish elite who formed the Scottish Masonic Lodge accused Poinsett of bringing the York Lodge to Mexico and said his home was a center for liberal plotting. However, Poinsett in two letters (July 4 and July 8, 1827) to Henry Clay said that the Scottish Masons were jealous of the U.S. peace and prosperity that he represented and felt he threatened Spain's influence in Mexico. Poinsett also told Clay that he had only secured charters for five already existing York Lodges from the Grand Lodge of New York. See Bosch García (1983), Gaxiola, Fuentes Mares.

44. This Spanish word, in its masculine form, appears to have been in common usage in the United States; it appears in *The Federalist Papers* with pejorative meaning. Shoemaker records the publication in 1812 of "The Essex Junto and the British Spy; or Treason detected" (Salem, MA, 36 pp.).

45. The Plan of Iguala was Mexico's declaration of independence.

46. Alamán mentions Céspedes as a Mexican general (Vol. 4, 270–271).

47. Alamán mentions a Jose María Arrieta, "natural de La Habana y coronel que había sido del cura Hidalgo" (native of Havana and colonel under the priest Hidalgo) in connection with a military skirmish between insurgent and royalist forces in Mexico in 1814 (Vol. 4, 207). Arrieta was exiled and presumably returned to Cuba. Shoemaker lists for 1820 a brief for the case of "Caricaburu, Arieta & Company, merchants of the Havanna." The company's ship had in its cargo 152 Negro slaves.

48. Davis identifies Ariza as a New Orleans merchant, active in 1815 in the Picornell plot against Spain. Ariza was in frequent touch with Cuba.

49. An early imprint in English appeared in Philadelphia in 1775: *Letters of Abelard and Heloise, To which is prefix'd a particular account of their lives, amours and misfortunes, by the late John Hughs, Esq. To which is now first added the poem of Eloisa to Abelard, by Mr. Pope* (printed for Samuel Delap). I can find no U.S. imprint of this work in Spanish until 1824, although even here it is not clear whether the work was really printed in the United States or merely sold here: *Cartas de Heloysa y Abelardo, en prosa y en verso, con la vida de estos desafortunados amantes, nueva impresión* (Burdeos: L. Joven y Sobrino; New York: R. Lockwood & Son, 179 pp.). In 1826 it was published

as *Correspondencia de Abelardo y Eloísa. Puesta en español por M. de B.* (Filadelfia: 159 pp.). However, a translation of this sensational novel appeared in Spain in two editions in the last years of the eighteenth century: *Cartas de Abelardo y Heloísa, en verso castellano. Las da a luz Don Francisco de Toxar* (Salamanca: Toxar, 1796, 1797). It is significant that they appeared outside Madrid.

50. This caution is significant. "La Henriade," Voltaire's epic poem, describes the massacre of the French Huguenots on St. Bartholomew's Day in 1685. Robeson (or his Mexican handlers) probably wanted to avoid offering this example of religious intolerance and state-inflicted bloodshed to Mexican readers. "La Enriada" had just been published in a verse translation by Pedro Bazán de Mendoza in Madrid in 1821.

51. See Gutjahr, 126–136.

52. Gutjahr, 29–32.

53. *El Nuevo Testamento de Nuestro Señor Jesu Cristo, traducido de la Biblia Vulgata en español por Felipe Scío de San Miguel* (New York: Edición esterotipa por Eliu White a costa de la Sociedad Americana de la Biblia, 1819, 376 pp.); *La Biblia o El Antiguo y Nuevo Testamentos traducidos al Español de la Vulgata Latina por el Rmo. P. Phelipe Scío de San Miguel, de las Escuelas Pías, Obispo electo de Segovia* (Londres: B. Bensley, 1821), translated by José Blanco White and Andrés Bello.

54. This description is drawn from Rodríguez O., *The Emergence of Spanish America* (50–66), who also reports that Rocafuerte carried with him when he went from Baltimore to Cuba in 1821 copies of his pro-republican *Ideas necesarias*, which were in turn taken to Mexico for distribution.

55. Three letters by T. Reilly, identified as U.S. vice consul at Veracruz, are included in Manning (Vol. 3, 1618–1619). These letters, dated October 2–3, 4, and 13, 1823, are directed respectively to John Quincy Adams, Commodore David Porter (commanding U.S. squadron at Thompson's Island [Key West]), and Adams

56. Rippy: "[Poinsett] reached the port of Tampico on December 15, where he was dismayed to find that the *John Adams*, which he had left at Vera Cruz, had not yet arrived. Once more he was in the sickly lowlands, and people were dying daily of yellow and biblious fevers. . . . He had to remain two more days in this pestilential town before he could find his vessel. The coast was dangerous, the season was boisterous, and the atmosphere was thick with fog. Finally, having been assured that the *John Adams* was somewhere in the region, he paid a pilot $150 to take him out in a 'sixteen-oared' boat in search of the corvette. Finding it at last, he climbed aboard, and was soon on his way to Cuba" (98).

57. Bustamante's diary entry for January 1, confirms this arrest and mentions the deputy Juan Pablo Anaya, along with 50 other men.

58. The Jura was celebrated on January 24, 1823, so the reference to the Christmas holidays seems to refer to ongoing festivities after January 6, the Feast of the Epiphany.

59. "Mina claims" apparently refers to payment for services rendered in Mina's invasion of Mexico in 1817.

60. See Dunkerley, who claims Wilkinson was on a "mission to collect debts owed to the USA by Mexico" (282). Wilkinson's niece married James Long, a filibusterer who led a group into Mexico with the intent of making an independent republic. Long was captured and shot; his men were freed by Poinsett (Rives, I, 126–127).

61. Follin's language is telegraphic, with many run-on sentences.

62. Aprons are part of Masonic garb.

63. In the Lea and Febiger papers in the HSP, a letter from Pignatelli Cerribora, dated June 26, 1822, Philadelphia, requests books written in French.

3

MEXICO

IN A PAMPHLET PRINTED IN MEXICO CITY and dated October 3, 1822, a writer who signed himself P.F.S. claimed to have just received a copy of a printed work from Philadelphia.[1] He considered its anonymous attack on Iturbide libelous, but he had it reprinted together with his rebuttal (the pamphlet is formatted as if P.F.S. were writing a letter to a friend). He wanted, he said, to publicize the attack because the foreign publication unjustly indicted a fellow Mexican and was proof that outsiders were plotting Iturbide's fall. The libeler, who claimed to be a Spaniard active in the Spanish Cortes, which were meeting again in Madrid in 1820–1821, accused Iturbide of stealing 6,000 pesos, likening the crime to Spain's illegal seizure of the Americas in the sixteenth century. That example of massive state land-grabbing was apparently so prevalent in men's minds that someone—whether a Philadelphian or someone someplace else who used a Philadelphia printer—thought it could serve to disgrace Iturbide. As we have seen, publication in London, Philadelphia, and Mexico of Las Casas's indictment of Spain's conquest in the Americas helped Spanish American revolutionaries to justify their early-nineteenth-century overthrow of Spanish rule. In a reference that is obscure, the pro-Iturbide P.F.S. said that an American in London, José Isidro Irana y Torre, could teach this libeler some lessons and went on to say that a letter by Irana was for sale in a Mexican bookstore for three *reales*.[2]

This October 3 pamphlet is significant to our story of U.S.–Mexico relations for several reasons. The date suggests Robeson was its bearer. Along with his books, he probably transmitted other materials—here, a Philadelphia-printed pamphlet dealing with Mexican politics.[3] In Robeson's August 29 letter to Carey, he says that he was leaving the coast for Jalapa; the first letter he sent from Mexico City is dated September 2, though it seems unlikely he traveled so quickly. One could surmise, then, that P.F.S.'s dating of his pamphlet reveals his effort to demonstrate, if not his source for the Philadelphia item, his quick response. The format of the pamphlet—first the Philadelphian's words, then the Mexican's (referring also to an American in London)—suggests an international exchange among men in those three areas. The U.S. pamphlet told P.F.S. that Spain might try to retake Mexico and he cautions that the country must not be divided, that *criollos* should not set themselves off from the indigenous population. Indeed, in an interesting case of rewriting definitions of native peoples, he says that all Mexicans who want independence can be called indigenous.

A pamphlet in the Abadiano collection of the Sutro Library in San Francisco, a treasure trove of materials originally from the warehouse of Alejandro Valdés, a Mexican printer and bookseller in the first decades of the nineteenth century, which I have used extensively in this study, also shows linkages around the Atlantic perimeter. In "Carta escrita a un Americano sobre la forma de gobierno que para hacer practicable la constitución y las leyes, conviene establecer en Nueva España atendida su actual situación," we see a pamphlet in the form of a "letter," printed in San Sebastián in northern Spain in 1821.[4] The anonymous writer, ostensibly a Spaniard in Madrid but probably Juan Antonio Llorente in Paris, used the fiction of a letter to write to "Rafaelito," a family member in Mexico. Even if government ties between the two areas were at the point of breaking (the letter is dated June 6, 1821, before Iturbide marched into Mexico City to declare independence on September 27), the two correspondents, the writer argues, still belong to the same family and should work at their level to help one another. Together they can realize a practical politics that governments, following theories, cannot. The Spaniard says that Mexico's plan to follow the model of Brazil and invite the Spanish king to rule from there is ill advised. "Letters," quietly addressed to friends and hopefully slipped in under the radar screen of censors, created an unofficial network, as opposed to the treatises or political pronouncements that circulated openly and self-importantly. Letters circulated in the hands of whatever ideologue or merchant might carry them. But, of course, the letter format was only a subterfuge because print carried the words beyond two sets of eyes.

The Carey/Robeson letters fall into the same category as the two pamphlets. Although the former are true letters and exist in manuscript rather than in print form, they are simultaneously private and public, functioning interpersonally but with a sense that writer and reader had larger identities and a relationship beyond family ties or friendship.[5] Robeson's letters detail the day-by-day progress of their mutual business, against the background of historical figures and events. However, what at one level could be uninteresting information about sales sets out two important facts relative to U.S.–Mexican relations in the first decades of the nineteenth century—facts that astound when compared with the feeble estimates of books coming into Mexico in dribbles and drabs that previous evidence has indicated. The letters tell the dimensions of the trade and the nature of the books Robeson carried to Mexico.

Robeson's itemizing of 1,481 books, and Carey and Lea's statement in their April 14 letter to Robeson that their investment amounted to $10,000 gross, reveal that the operation was major and expectations high. The scale went beyond the small amounts normally associated with smuggling or individual secretiveness; instead the large operation was obviously designed to function in a semiopen, semilegal way. It was not carried out according to a hurried plan but with men in place to facilitate the business. It went beyond the evidence of the exchange of letters we have seen because Carey and Lea refer to a later shipment they sent at Robeson's request. If the players anticipated minor difficulties, they could not have foreseen Iturbide's overthrow, thus dooming the business. Revolution was a thing of the past in the United States and so perhaps the participants were lulled into thinking that the gamble would pay off.

Second, the three titles Robeson referred to most frequently were Paine's *Rights of Man*, Rousseau's *Social Contract*, and Puglia's *Man Undeceived*. These suggest, first and foremost, the desire of U.S. republicans to support Mexican liberals engaged in a campaign against Iturbide's imperial rule. Fearing that some member of a European royal family might come to Mexico as Iturbide had at first proposed, and outraged over Iturbide's aspirations for his own hereditary dynasty, Mexican liberals were anxious to have literature that might help them to assemble intellectual arguments into a respectable philosophy and convert their opposition. Wanting to argue for a government that did not depend on one man, they sought evidence of constitutional models from France, England, the United States, Colombia, and Chile. Desperate to separate ecclesiastical and civil powers, liberals were searching to end the influence of the Inquisition and introduce modern notions such as a free press and civil tolerance (if not of other faiths, then of factions created by war).

Mexican liberals would have known of Paine's and Rousseau's books; these authors had an international reputation and importing their books would have made it seem that Robeson's Mexican backers were in touch with the latest intellectual trends. In fact, *Social Contract* had been published in a Mexican edition in 1822 without its title or author attribution. The editor and publisher, Francisco Severo Maldonado, had cautiously put the text out as *El Fanal del imperio mexicano o Miscelánea política extractada y redactada de las mejores fuentes, por el autor del Pacto Social para inteligencia de esta obra*,[6] printing it as though it were the continuation of an essay by another author. He left parts out, particularly those regarding religion. Maldonado had planned a series of ten or twelve books on the topic of social organization but soon abandoned the plan. Whether Maldonado's printing reduced demand for Robeson's importation of Rousseau, or increased it by stimulating interest, is not clear.

It must be noted, however, that *Social Contract* did not always have then the revolutionary meaning associated with the book today. Different authors used the text for different purposes. For example, in an 1808 pamphlet printed in Mallorca, "Los derechos de la soberanía nacional contra el despotismo y la hipocresía,"[7] a conservative Spaniard used the concept of "sovereignty" to argue against the invasion of José Bonaparte and for the intrinsic right of the Spanish "nation" to delegate governance to the persons or bodies it preferred (i.e., the various juntas scattered throughout Spain, each of which claimed legitimacy in ruling locally until the king could return). Although the writer refrained from talking about "the people," his logic reflects Rousseau's notion of a social contract.

Reasons for the relatively poor sale of Paine's *Derechos del hombre* can only be conjectured; only 75 copies sold despite Bustamante's report in his diary that everyone was reading it. Perhaps by 1822 the interest Spanish Americans had initially shown in Paine's 1791–1792 work had abated in Mexico. Paine's defiant publication of men's rights, as well as the French bill of rights of the citizenry—which early on had attracted supporters in the Caribbean and formed the intellectual bases for the revolts of Juan Antonio Picornell and Pedro Gual (1797), Francisco Miranda and Simón Bolívar (1811–1812)—were no longer pertinent in a country that was even contemplating monarchy.[8] The portrayal of revolution in France might have been too incendiary in a country that had just passed through its own revolution and now wanted peace. English interests in Mexico might have suppressed circulation of the anti-English work (Robeson reports that English complaints ended the sale of Barère de Vieuzac's *Liberté des mers ou le gouvernement anglais devollé.*) Paine's ridicule of the aristocracy as "a seraglio of males, who neither collect the honey nor form the hive, but exist only for lazy enjoyment"[9] might have offended a still-aristocratic society. However, paradoxically contradicting this initial poor sale is Robeson's request in his last letter that Carey send 300 copies of Paine's work.

Desengaño, Santiago Puglia's diatribe (published in Philadelphia in 1794 and reprinted by Carey in 1822), was well known in Mexico. The Mexican Inquisition had banned it in 1794, posting a proclamation throughout its jurisdictions in Mexico, Guatemala, Nicaragua, and the Philippines that the work was injurious to public morality.[10] Persons owning copies were threatened with excommunication and fines, and even those persons with a license to read prohibited works were forbidden to read it. However, the public listing only advertised the work. The inquisitors centered their denunciation on the person of Puglia. He wrote badly in the Spanish language, which was not his own. A failed businessman ("mercader quebrado"), he had become a pedantic writer who dared to take on material as sublime as politics and public law. He was ignorant of sacred and profane literatures. Most grievously, he attacked the monarch, anointed by God. From his corner of the world he had sounded a call to rebellion, imitating French revolutionaries. The inquisitors said they thought their copy of *Desengaño* was the only one in Mexico but, in case there were others, they were issuing this prohibition to safeguard "pious America." In fact, 300 copies entered Mexico via New Orleans (Rydjord 1972,128). Thus, liberals might have remembered this work and caused them to request it from the Philadelphia sources that had originally printed it.

Puglia himself underscored the revolutionary character of *Desengaño* in another work, *The Federal Politician*, published in English in Philadelphia in 1795. There he said that the object of *Desengaño* was "to rouse, as if it were from a lethargy, an oppressed people, and encourage them to assume their national dignity, by their exertions to shake off the galling yoke of Despotism.... [T]he doctrine, that might be useful to the Spaniards, Italians, Germans, or other vassals, would be ill-adapted to the citizens of America." The European-born Puglia was sensitive to American oppression in the form of colonialism and to Americans' need to be "undeceived."

Even a cookbook in the shipment suggests politics. Because we do not have a copy of the book Robeson sent back to Carey for translation, we do not know what cuisine was represented. It surely was a decoy to divert censors but its contents may also have had political meaning. French haute cuisine would have been replacing old-fashioned Spanish food preparation and Mexican cooking in the kitchens of some in the elite. Thus, what seems to be an unimportant detail may have broader implications for modernization and liberalization.[11] We remember that some of France's cooks were responsible for revolutionary activities in the Americas. For example, Henri Christophe, one of the principals of the Haitian revolution of 1802–1803, had been a cook on the island; and, in Mexico, the Frenchman, Juan Laussel, one of the first persons to have been found by the Inquisition to have been a Mason, was a cook for the Conde de Revillagigedo when this viceroy came to Mexico in 1789.[12] Working in the intimacy of the houses of liberals, these men brought to their employers not only knowledge of new foods, table refinements, and etiquette, but also of new political notions. The cookbooks Robeson sought to import, then, probably were not how-to books for ordinary housewives but instructions to republican households.

JUAN GERMAN ROSCIO

Despite Robeson's repeated mention of works by Paine, Rousseau, and Puglia, another title stands out as his bestseller. His accounting tells that he sold 190 copies of *Triunfo de la libertad* (see Figure 3.1), 160 of *Contrato social*, and 75 of *Derechos del hombre*. (These figures are extraordinary, given the spending

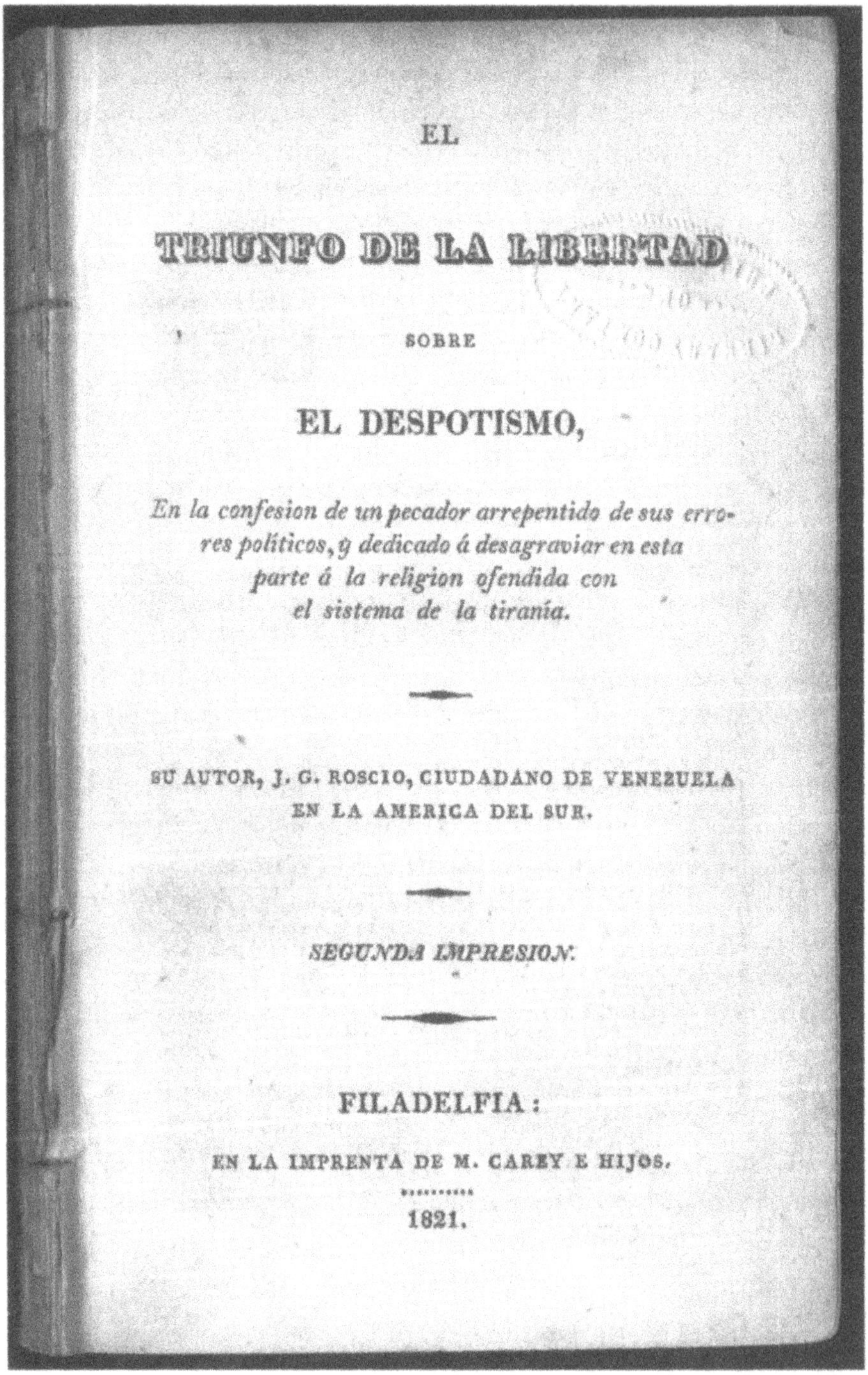
EL

TRIUNFO DE LA LIBERTAD

SOBRE

EL DESPOTISMO,

En la confesion de un pecador arrepentido de sus errores políticos, y dedicado á desagraviar en esta parte á la religion ofendida con el sistema de la tiranía.

SU AUTOR, J. G. ROSCIO, CIUDADANO DE VENEZUELA EN LA AMERICA DEL SUR.

SEGUNDA IMPRESION.

FILADELFIA:

EN LA IMPRENTA DE M. CAREY E HIJOS.

1821.

FIGURE 3.1 Title page of *Triunfo de la Libertad.*

capabilities and literacy levels of Mexicans.) *Triunfo*'s sales, despite Robeson's warning that too many priests in Mexico probably meant that he could not dispose of it, pose the question of why that work especially resonated with Mexicans. Roscio's text was quickly reprinted—in 1824 in Mexico City by Martín Rivera in an abbreviated edition of 120 pages, and in 1828 in Oaxaca in a complete edition of 291 pages by the Imprenta de York (a Masonic print house) under the direction of Juan Oledo. *Triunfo* has been said to have influenced the thinking of Benito Juárez later in the century, yet historians have been puzzled by how Juárez in Oaxaca knew of it.[13] Thus, Robeson's letters, which tell how the work entered Mexico, reaching readers not only in the capital but also in towns along the route from Veracruz, help explain its circulation. Contrasting with Mexico's enthusiasm for Roscio is Venezuela's lack of interest in one of its own authors. Domingo Miliani remarks on the strangeness of the fact that the work was not published in Caracas and says that copies of the Philadelphia edition were burned there in an auto-da-fe (1996, xxv). Yet he does not theorize as to why Venezuelans rejected the book yet accepted Roscio as their vice-president.

One explanation for Mexicans' purchase of *Triunfo* is the fact that Mexicans were familiar with Roscio's authorship of Venezuela's declaration of independence in 1811, and his arguments for American rights in the face of the Spanish king's abdication. Mexicans, writing a constitution at the Congress of Chilpancingo in 1813, had consulted Roscio's writings.[14] Roscio, though relatively unknown in the United States, had a ready public in Mexico.

A second explanation derives from reading the text of *Triunfo*. There one finds that Roscio, with doctorates in civil and canon law from the University of Caracas, understood the uniqueness of Spanish America's independence movement. Educated in Latin and the classics so that he applied to be professor of Latin at the university (he also knew English and French), he appreciated the role of language in trapping colonials and maintaining their servitude (for "language," read ideology conveyed through figures of speech that channeled thought). His book took the ideas of Paine and Rousseau on the rights of man and the social contract, the French statement of the rights of man and the citizen; but then it adapted them to the Spanish American world. "Rights," "citizen," society," "government," "universal right of conscience"—all of the terms used by Paine and Rousseau had different valences for Spanish Americans. Their experience with Spanish colonial rule had conditioned them to paternalism; and they were too close to the Spanish Inquisition, in many cases, to stand back from it to analyze its controls. That "mule animal," or cross between church and state, as Paine called the Inquisition,[15] required thoughtful criticism in Spanish America, instead of the mere ridicule that Anglo Americans gave it.

Roscio's book was a major intellectual undertaking in the tumultuous years after the Congress of Vienna. Throughout Europe monarchies were reestablishing claims, threatening new republics. In England abolitionists were rewriting natural law so as to challenge ancient arguments that some men were born with rights to enslave inferiors, yet many persisted in that belief. In new nations where constitutions were being written and rationalist Enlightenment philosophies had created skeptics and agnostics, confusion reigned. Men somehow had to justify the recent terror, fratricide, and tyrannicide that had won them independence. Civil codes seemed to be the only solution to ending a social construct based on divine sanction.

Roscio, responding to Spanish American needs, aimed especially at separating religious faith from political manipulation and clerical abuse so as to allow the new nations to go forward. Many, in instituting reform, did not want to leave their faith behind. Roscio's insistence, then, on remembering an historically pure Christianity as a means of understanding how church and state had erroneously been joined was pertinent in Mexico where priests, Miguel Hidalgo and José María Morelos, had led revolt. Unlike the independence movements in South America, Mexican insurgents were largely religious and their Indian combatants deeply pious. Thus, when the viceregal government called on the Church to excommunicate Hidalgo and Morelos, the faithful questioned the legitimacy of the government's resort to a Church penalty for a political crime. They asked themselves whether traditional ecclesiastical immunities were still valid protections for the priests (and whether their own excommunication, when they still retained their religious faith, was not unjustified). Mexicans wanted to know how their new nation might affirm its piety and retain its religious identity when modernization in more advanced countries pointed to a society where tolerance of various faiths in fact meant secularism.

Roscio was similar in his concerns to two other Spaniards of his generation—José Blanco White and Juan Antonio Llorente. In 1811 Roscio had exchanged correspondence with Blanco White, a former Catholic priest then in London who was writing a newspaper for distribution in Spanish America. Llorente, also a Catholic priest who had been forced into exile in Paris, had been a secretary to the Spanish Inquisition. From that perspective he saw the inner workings of the Inquisition and the complications religion posed for political liberation. We will see both men later. Yet Roscio's essay is more personal and philosophical than Blanco's and Llorente's mostly legal and political works.

Roscio's life experience, which he recorded in his book, was typical of that of many Americans. He had originally been a loyalist, supportive of the divine right of kings and defender of Spanish claims in the Americas. But a series of events caused him to open his eyes to the hypocrisies of the powerful and realize how he had been betrayed by Church and monarchical teachings that belief in one automatically meant subordination to the other. In fact, the Spanish monarch Carlos III had seemed to attack religion when he expelled the Jesuit order from the empire in 1767; the same king had undercut monarchism when he supported British colonists in their independence war. In 1808 at the *motín* in Aranjuez, partisans of Fernando had proclaimed his right to rule even before his father, Carlos IV, had abdicated; religious leaders rallied to the son's cause in that coup. In a seeming contradiction, the doctrine of the sovereignty of the people, which the Mexican insurgents had used to defend their rebellion in 1810, was seen to condemn them; yet at almost the same time the doctrine was invoked by the Spanish constitutionalists working in Cádiz. The Pope stood by, seemingly in support of Napoleon when this usurper crowned himself; but in 1817 when Roscio was writing *Triunfo*, Europe's monarchs, with everyone's consent, exiled Napoleon to an island. These inconsistencies radicalized Roscio and turned him into a preacher for American independence.[16]

Roscio wrote *Triunfo* while imprisoned in a Spanish jail in Ceuta (north Africa). When he escaped via Gibraltar, he went first to New Orleans where he unsuccessfully tried to have the book published. He then went on to Philadelphia where it came out in two editions—in 1817, when he paid to have the book published by Thomas H. Palmer, and in 1821 when M. Carey and Sons reprinted it posthumously. In 1821, as we have seen, Carey also published a second edition of Roscio's translation of the *Homilía del Cardenal Chiaramonte, Obispo de Imola, actualmente sumo Pontífice Pío VII, dirigida al pueblo de su Diócesis en República Cisalpina, el día del nacimiento de J.C. año de 1797. Traducida del francés al español por un Ciudadano de Venezuela en la América del Sur, que la publica rebatiendo con ella un papel del mismo Papa a favor de Fernando VII, contra los insurgentes de las llamadas Colonias españolas*. The homily in which the Pope chastised American revolutionaries for disobedience to the Spanish king had been published first in a bilingual Spanish–English edition in 1817.[17] Roscio reproduced the Pope's text but then, in a lengthy second part, challenged his authority to meddle in American politics. The "homily" in the form of spiritual advice (by the same Pope who had crowned Napoleon and signed a concordat with him) had angered many Americans and contributed to their estrangement from the Church, if not from their faith. It was so controversial that it was reprinted in Mexico in 1823[18]; in that edition the translator says that he knew of Roscio's 1817 translation but that he had not seen it and instead followed Bishop Grégoire's 1814 French version.

The subject of religion, then—faith but also Church politics—can be seen to have been at the heart of Roscio's analysis of Spanish colonialism. His Catholic American perspective was an aid to ending its powerful aura. Spain held its territories because theologians had been able to convince the population that God had ordained the Spanish king and thus loyalty to one meant loyalty to the other. Conscience, a powerful force, held men rather than any fear of punishment. Therefore, the psychology that colonialism produced in its subjects—blind obedience, ignorance, apathy, an inclination to fantasy and exaggerated prejudice, anger at anyone who tried to free them from their servitude—concerned Roscio. He also was interested in the moral rationale of those Catholic insurrectionists who had dared to take up arms—first against José Bonaparte and then against Fernando VII when he returned to Spain in 1814 and imposed his despotic rule. Roscio considered the crimes of regicide and tyrannicide sympathetically (yet he worried about fratricide). He questioned what right Pope Alexander VI had to grant to Spain and Portugal in the late fifteenth and early sixteenth centuries lands already in the possession of American monarchs (Roscio noted approvingly that William Penn had paid Indians in Pennsylvania for their land despite the fact that his king had delegated to him the authority to seize it [1817/1996, 201–210]). Roscio's work, then, in contrast to those of Rousseau and Paine, was topically and rhetorically more suited to Catholic America.

Roscio's work—a confession of prior sins—was a genre his Catholic readers would have been familiar with as a result of their reading of the confessions of St. Augustine. Roscio's sins in this combination of spiritual autobiography and historico-legal treatise were his support of the Spanish monarch on occasions when he opposed Venezuelan reformers; in 1797 he helped to frustrate the plot of Juan Bautista Mariano Picornell y Gomila and he said he was still a royalist as late as 1809.[19] However, he awoke to his error and was spiritually reborn when he became aware that God had given the faculty of reason to each human being, thus empowering him to perceive governmental wrongs as separate from religious faith. Indeed this is the enlightenment Roscio's book describes. Rather than the enlightenment based on science and modernization, which secular philosophers in Europe were formulating, Roscio's is predicated on this recognition of God's goodness. The sovereignty that each man possesses by virtue of his reasoning capacity permits him to enter into a social contract for the common good; however, his reason also authorizes him to break this contract if a tyrant abuses it. Roscio's arguments, designed to refute theologians who had used quotes from Scripture to substantiate God's seeming selection of one man or one family to rule over others, are drawn from those theologians' same sources.

Roscio returns to the Bible, drawing analogies between the colonial status of Judea under Rome and present-day American rebellion. He restates the Biblical teaching that the faithful should render under Caesar what is Caesar's (traditionally used to teach colonial obedience) to mean that the coin, on which Caesar's head appears, is owed to Rome, a temporal power. But man's soul belongs to God and thus a church has no right to impose earthly charges on the faithful. Roscio situates the phrase in the historical context of the confusion Christ's first Jewish converts faced; recently won to freedom from sinful passion, superstition, and bloody sacrifice, they misunderstood "liberty" and needed to be reminded of their civil obligations (1817/1996, 103–104). Similarly, Roscio describes the defiance of tyranny of the Maccabees and of Moses; the republican spirit of Sparta and early Rome, which allowed the Jewish tribes to seek alliances with them; Jesus' refusal to be drawn into political compromise; and so on. He deconstructs the familiar sayings of Peter and Paul, which had been used to teach meekness and passivity, for fulfilling one's obligation to the state, and for the Pope's authority, by showing the context in which these writers wrote. He thus alters the lessons of earlier theologians and represents them not only as misreadings, but rather as deliberate falsifications. This linguistic and textual strategy to bring about decolonization would have been especially suited to those among the Spanish American elite, whose religious training, socialization, and schooling had been based on historical knowledge, recourse to authority, and techniques of legal disputation that looked to language usage.

Roscio defines natural man in a manner similar to, yet different from, philosophers like Rousseau. "Nature" for Roscio implies God's gift of innate reason to man. "Art" is the overlay that society places on this natural capacity, thwarting its exercise. For Roscio art particularly was the twisted rhetoric that theologians, beginning in the feudal Middle Ages, used to subject men to tyrants. Like other Americans of his generation who felt that European intellectual abstractions ignored the specifics of their experience, Roscio distrusted pure theory. Instead, "nature," he believed, required that Americans read the book of the world around them, and reread the Biblical texts on which the "mercenaries of tyranny" based their arguments so as to discern how theoretical language disguised their self-serving dictates. Reading for oneself had previously been the work of gentiles; now it meant overcoming the ignorance that feudal education mistakenly held out as faith so as to discover the true spiritual message of Jesus. "Reading" meant going back to the Bible's original language, avoiding the restatements and dogmatic interpretations of others.

Roscio's book is not an angry, propagandistic attack on Spain, the monarchy, or Spain's conquest of the Americas. Its tone is generally even and its arguments intellectually complex and subtle. At one point, however, in considering the metaphor of the king as father and the figure of the mother as "la madre patria," his tone sharpens as he presses questions of a king's right to conquer, force in the context of the metaphor of "two swords," and property rights. He says that with the notion of the divine right of kings, "art" intervened to supersede the rights of a natural mother and nature was falsely allegorized so that she as "semillero" (seed-bearer) was made to serve "la mania colonial" (the colonizing mania, [1817/1996, 220]). This passage is one of the few in the book in which his American anger seems to get the better of him and he shows his exasperation with Spanish colonialism. Similarly, he criticizes recent events. He condemns the Spanish constitution of 1812 for saying that Spain never had a despot king (1817/1996, 215). He rages against the bishop of Ceuta, Esteban Gómez, who in 1815 in a solemn church ceremony, approved of the execution of the Spanish patriot, Juan Díaz Porlier. And he indignantly tells of a letter designed to get the Portuguese princess, at that moment in Brazil, to marry Fernando so as to help stabilize the Spanish monarchy.

Triunfo shows that Spanish Americans could not enter a modern world without first taking leave of the past. They were tied to their Spanishness and, although books by authors from the United States, England, and France were helpful, their independent, liberal future depended on the critical perspective of fellow Americans, which might help them to disengage from their old thinking. Thus the record of Mexican sales of Roscio's book, as well as Robeson's reporting that Mexicans were interested in the constitutional formulations of other American nations, is a valuable insight into that country's decolonizing process.

Carlos Maria Bustamante mentions *Triunfo* in the diary he kept from December 6, 1822, through 1823. On February 18 he rebukes the bishop of Oaxaca for not having read Roscio but instead the "libracos" (lousy books) of other religious writers who counseled obedience to political authority. Urging a counterrevolution against Iturbide, he expounds on the misuse of religious literature and invokes Roscio's reexamination of the apostles' lives and words to show how Roscio argued for that original sense of a spiritual kingdom. This diary, in which Bustamante also mentions Paine, Pradt, Rocafuerte, and the British constitution, provides a record of his reading that suggests not only the liberalism many Mexicans might have expressed but, more to the point, Bustamante's familiarity with the contents of Robeson's shipment. He records on December 16, 1822, that Paine's *Derechos del hombre* was in everyone's hands. Bustamante wrote this diary for publication, and thus it contributed to the mythologizing of Philadelphia among Mexicans. On December 16, after the elaborate ceremony the night before in which Iturbide's newborn son was anointed, he wrote: "Dichosas márgenes del Delaware donde no se representan [estas escenas]!"[20] And on March 23, 1823, he described with envy the "Congreso de Filadelfia," which simultaneously declared independence from England and joined the various American colonies in a federalist union that was the basis for national growth (in the name of federalism regionalist factions were at that moment tearing Mexico apart).

LITERARY STYLE

Because Roscio's book was so important in Mexico, I want to elaborate on its tone and the kind of reading it presupposed. In avoiding satire's obfuscation and learned professions' pomposity, its unadorned style stepped beyond what literature in the colonial period habitually exhibited; it clearly set out the author's thinking, reaching out to readers rather than tormenting them with obscurity. Although we do not have much information as to how Mexicans received the new foreign authors, we can read in the rhetorical level of *Triunfo* the new demands Roscio was making. Carey probably saw, not only in the book's discussion of religion and politics but also in its no-nonsense language, its pertinence for Mexico. A Catholic, he probably understood more than Robeson, whose religion is unknown and who uniformly advised that all works condemnatory of the priesthood would be unwelcome in Mexico,[21] that Mexicans needed a lay person with the experience of American disillusionment to somehow reconcile revolutionary political action with the faith they had been taught.[22] (Here I do not mean to suggest that Carey read Spanish; I assume that he took advice from Catholic Spanish speakers.)

Pablo González Casanova in his book on the Inquisition in eighteenth-century Mexico has observed how in the second half of the century inquisitors had trouble interpreting the satire of the emerging literature.[23] They were forced into the role of literary critics, gauging to what extent the sacred cows of religion and monarchy were being secularized and debased by the many print, manuscript, and oral forms of poetry, theater, critical exegesis, imaginative fantasy, essays, and so forth. During moments of suppression but also during times of relative press freedom, they pondered questions such as an author's literal or metaphorical expression, how near common people could and should enter into contact with the sacred in viewing religious theater, if a society should continue to permit long-admired and satisfying popular poetry if its theology was wrong, how legitimate the new secular genres were that were replacing the old religious categories, and so on. They had to read carefully through the satirical play so as to come down with an official verdict as to the work's theological purity; indeed, after the Inquisition was ended in Mexico, some lay readers lamented this loss of validation and assurance of moral certainty because they now had to decide that for themselves.

During the colonial period satire in written form was an elitist form of expression directed at an in-group of readers who understood its allusions. Allegory, fables, fictions, words with double meaning disguised what colonials could not express openly. Wit and erudite display softened cruelty. Then, after independence, if writers from elite advantage wanted to communicate with a broader readership, they had to be clearer and inclusive in their use of language;

less well-educated writers, who lacked knowledge of Greek and Latin, philosophy and the classics, but who were entering the print world, were ignorant of such references and might have taken irony literally. Neither group wanted to alienate persons needed for political coalitions. Loosening governmental restrictions, as we will see, were beginning to permit directness, which in turn permitted a growing sense of Mexican community as men were joined and local concerns were confronted. Tough issues demanded that writers abandon ambiguity. They had to abandon selfish displays of virtuosity and narrow class statement in the interests of solving problems. They had to sort through language that clouded thinking so as to find preciseness.

Satire reflected cynicism, which inquisitors judged to be unhealthy in a society of believers; the contagion was dangerous if the satirist spread it very far. Although they refused permissions for the printing of suspect items and ordered dangerous materials destroyed, they could not stop the mind-set once it had begun to take hold. They realized that mockery of worship and decency in both written and oral forms was prevalent in the caricatures of hated officials, in popular catechetical parodies, and in the lascivious sexuality of folk dances. If satire once had been contained, now toward the end of the empire, it required more regulation. Roscio, as we saw, pointed out the apathy and passivity colonialism produced in its subjects; and readers of his books would have concluded from his avoidance of cynicism and cruelty that these were other negative psychological consequences of colonialism.

Satire had the value of stepping away from official literature and looking at it critically. Yet it had the disadvantage of reducing debate to ridicule and destroying one's opponent. Thus, writers who wished to engage in thoughtful discussion of new issues of politics, economics, theology, and science, had to find a different social vocabulary, a new level of verbal exchange. They might have been cynics relative to some beliefs but their political advocacy meant that they were not total nihilists.

Throughout the colonial period Spain's hold on Mexico through Inquisition inspections was tight. Civil and ecclesiastical authorities had pretty much restricted Mexican creativity to the affirmations of loyalty and adulation demanded of colonial subjects; oaths, poems in praise of a distant king, wordy sermons were permitted yet they said nothing new or personal.[24] Thus satire was colonialism's only outlet for sincere self-expression. However, in many ways, satire was bound to the dominant discourse in needing to counter and subvert that discourse. Therefore, new nationals had to invent still another form of expression, one that broke away from those two forms of colonial consciousness.[25] José Joaquín Fernández de Lizardi realized that fact when he wrote that under colonialism only praise and satire were permitted to function as modes of public communication. He, therefore, in 1816 envisioned what is considered to be Spanish America's first novel as a third kind of discourse.[26] He used the genre for purposes of self-expression and criticism; the novel's serious and humorous elements, the play of fiction and documentation, both opened up and hid truth.

Questions of tone and literary exposition were common in both the United States and Mexico at that decolonizing moment. Rather than just topics of concern only to authors, they exposed to the general populace the ways in which language had formed their colonial minds and how much they needed to critically examine such language so that they might think anew. For example, in the United States in 1808 Bertrand Guerin had published in Baltimore "Satire against Satire" (printed by John W. Butler, 25 pp.); and in 1814 in New York an anonymous writer had printed "False Stories Corrected. Learn to unlearn what you have learned amiss" (48 pp.).

Rousseau's *Social Contract*, Paine's *Rights of Man*, and Roscio's *Triunfo de la Libertad*, then, contributed not only their decolonizing ideas but also their sober, straightforward literary style to the detachment from imperial rule that Mexicans required in their first years of nationhood. Their books—though Paine's contained a great deal of satire—were examples to Mexicans of secular literature, which, because their authors did not have to be afraid of censure, were free of irony and subterfuge. Their books were not broad attacks but nuanced criticisms and reasoned considerations of formerly held beliefs. They attempted to engage readers at levels other than malicious humor.

It must be noted, however, that these books were not Mexicans' only source of rhetorical directness. Late in the eighteenth century and in the first decade of the nineteenth, Spain alternately permitted, and then shut off, publication of philosophical inquiries and reporting of scientific advances. During those moments, when Spanish leaders like the Conde de Aranda, Manuel Godoy, and Gaspar Melchor de Jovellanos exerted their liberal influence in Madrid, Mexico got directly from Spain works by those authors, as well as by Enlightenment writers in France, Italy, Germany, and England. The Mexican newspapers reprinted selections from the Madrid paper, *Semanario Patriótico*, which ran several months in 1808 under Manuel Quintana, from *El Espectador Sevillano*, which ran from 1809 to 1810 under Alberto Lista, and then from the various Cádiz papers once French troops pushed Spanish resistance to that southern city.[27] Spanish translations, journalism and the prose of emerging disciplines, which were entering Mexico, then, also provided models of clear style.[28]

"Style" concerns literary critics who by that measure situate writers on a continuum ranging from plain to elegant. Yet it is obvious that in Mexico in the late eighteenth and early nineteenth centuries, style involved more than just an individual writer's preference or a community's taste. Choice of style—

whether opaque or clear, high-handed or democratic—pointed to surrounding constraints and freedoms. In many ways the inquisitors were right to understand that the ideas propounded by the new books, but also their style, undermined belief. They were right to especially distrust foreign books.

Mario Vargas Llosa, the contemporary Peruvian novelist mentioned before, makes an interesting observation on censors' reading acuities. He says that today "in undeveloped countries censorship doesn't reach that point of subtlety [in scrutinizing literature such as novels for hidden meaning], as it did in Spain for example. Because in undeveloped countries, the dictators are, well, functioning illiterates that don't think that literature can be dangerous."[29] In measuring today's dictators against Spanish inquisitors or Francisco Franco's censors, Vargas Llosa not only damns Latin American stupidity but also acknowledges that, historically in Spain and Latin America, the game of writing required then, and requires now, guessing at the education or watchfulness of the censorial bureaucracy.

COMMERCE

The books chosen for the Robeson shipment reflect the importance that Carey and his generation attached to economics. Carey's personal social philosophy with respect to the United States—his attitudes toward banking and credit, protective tariffs for the new manufacturing economy, charities for the poor, and so on—points to his understanding of the power of business to shape a new nation.[30] He subscribed to an Enlightenment explanation of morality, not according to the Church's teachings of an individual's choice between good and evil but according to society's structures. If a society was stable because its economy did not depend on one product and it provided full employment to all its citizens, if trade with other regions could be relied on to supply diverse needs, it usually was peaceful and personal virtues could be cultivated.

Economic theories of the period (those of the Abbé Guillaume-Thomas Raynal,[31] Adam Smith,[32] Dominique De Pradt,[33] Jean-Baptiste Say[34]), were showing the deleterious effects European colonialism had had on world trade, and the liberating power of capitalism and free commerce to create different forms of wealth in the newly free American societies. If Carey believed in tariffs for U.S. goods and thus protection for that developing market, in what seems to be a theoretical contradiction he also saw the value of promoting the export of U.S. goods to other markets in the Americas, and of advocating maritime freedoms so as to ensure that trade.

However, the question of free trade versus protectionism was far from settled in his mind and it apparently worried him. In a pamphlet Carey wrote in 1822, "Desultory Facts, and Observations, Illustrative of the Past and Present

Situation and Future Prospects of the United States," he stated that the U.S. free trade policy differed from the restrictive policies of all other nations. There he reviewed the tariff protections of other countries (including Mexico); he complained that specie was leaving the United States as imports exceeded exports; and he argued that because U.S. exports (cotton, tobacco) were not finding buyers internationally, domestic markets had to be increased to consume them. He said that "two systems so diametrically opposite as theirs and ours, cannot both be right" and that "sober-sided men who have a deep stake in the welfare of the United States" should reexamine U.S. trade policies (1822, vi). This pamphlet explains several aspects of Robeson's letters: It suggests why books, a new source of income derived from expanded print production and foreign markets, could stir optimism among planners in the United States; it reveals why Robeson persisted in providing information about Mexican duties (both externally and internally); it helps to clarify why, absent an international banking system and in the face of dangerous robberies, businessmen avoided cash transactions and instead relied on letters of credit and commodity exchanges.

Other titles on Carey's trade list—Paine's *Derechos del hombre* and Barère de Vieuzac's *Libertad de los mares*—demonstrate a faith that commercial freedoms could end old despotisms and permit the growth of new nations. Before American nations had yet formed in the shape and size we know today, their sovereignty, rather than being based on the fixity of territoriality or politics, appears to have rested on their economic nature, on their ability to trade freely. Decolonization required detachment from old ideas of colonial dependencies based on exploitation and so-called protectionism; instead it assumed development of new sources of wealth so as to compete freely and maturely in international markets. One became "a commercial nation," ranking with others who had achieved that status. In the case of British America, this process took the form of converting an agricultural to a manufacturing economy, of coining money, of inventing banking and insurance industries, of mobilizing a fleet of ships so as to make the seas safe. In the case of Spanish America, it took the form of moving from an economy based on the extraction of minerals and forest products; on the monopolistic trade, which in the case of Mexico the ports of Veracruz and Acapulco permitted; on unpaid slave and Indian labor; to a future in which agriculture and domestic industry (such as Puebla's textile production) could thrive.

The faith in business that U.S. republicans had seems to have been widespread. Poinsett, in his *Notes on Mexico Made in the Autumn of 1822*, which Carey and Lea published in 1824, affirms this faith. This report, which parallels Robeson's letters, shows that Poinsett traveled with the eye of Humboldt, viewing Mexico's geography, population, its cities' civilizing advances, and its countryside's diversity, for purposes of semiscientific documentation. Into it he inserted historical information, culled from Clavijero but also from Spanish-language colonial administrators such as Cardinal Francisco Antonio Lorenzana, which the Spanish-speaking Poinsett realized would not have been available to U.S. readers. But Poinsett also traveled with the consciousness of a businessman, assessing what Mexico would provide for itself in the way of agricultural and manufacturing products and what it might import. He contradicts Humboldt's statement that "Mexicans will one day undersell us in bread corn, in the West Indies and other markets" (1824/1969, 95), saying that transportation from the interior to the coast is too difficult. Instead he thinks that U.S. agriculture will "be able to undersell the Mexicans in their own markets" (1824/1969, 96), providing goods especially along the Gulf coast. He notes, as Robeson did, the duties to be paid along the Mexican roads; and his list of articles that may be imported free of duty includes "all unbound books but, prohibiting the importation of all such as are contrary to good morals, and to the catholic religion" (1824/1969, 103). On his way home Poinsett visited Cuba and concluded:

> Cuba is not only the key of the Gulf of Mexico, but of all the maritime frontier south of Savannah, and some of our highest interests, political and commercial, are involved in its fate. We ought to be satisfied, that it should remain dependent on Spain; or in good time, be entirely independent of every foreign nation. In the first case, we shall enjoy the commercial advantages which we do at present, and which our proximity and mutual wants naturally secure to us. In the latter case, the same causes will continue to operate, and we must remain closely united by a common interest. The independence of Cuba would not increase those advantages, but might produce others that would be common to all commercial nations. (1824/1969, 220–221)

Throughout his report Poinsett speaks of "the great commercial nations of the world" (especially 223), which will together end the piracy that Spain protects in the Caribbean. "Commerce" appears to be the access to this new-world brotherhood, the common denominator in this new definition of nationhood. Nations are no longer equivalent to their monarchs, to their state religions, or even to their trading companies (as in the cases of England and Holland).

Poinsett never mentions Robeson. However, other familiar names appear in his report. Poinsett lodges in Mexico City with Wilkinson. He has an interview with Iturbide ("who is making great exertions to negotiate loans in England") and says, "an agent has lately gone to London" (this may have been James Barry). He visits Herrera (Iturbide's secretary of state), meets with Santamaría (who apparently has not yet left Mexico), and refers to Padre Mier. He describes the palace of the Marqués del Valle, the "government house built by Cortés opposite the residence of the Mexican monarch." In an "Historical

Sketch," appended to the *Notes*, which brings the account up to April 1823, when Iturbide fell, Poinsett mentions Bradburn as having accompanied the Mina expedition but does not tell of Bradburn's marriage into the Valle family. In that appendix he also mentions two loans to Mexico from Londoners: Twenty million dollars from the house of Barclay, Herring, Richardson & Co., and one million and a half dollars from the house of Robert Staples & Co. "who have a partner in Mexico" (1824/1969, 288).

Mexican historians today generally vilify Poinsett, noting the coincidence of Poinsett's meeting with Santa Anna in Veracruz on his arrival (against Iturbide's orders) and Santa Anna's so-called republican proclamation against Iturbide on December 3; they resent Poinsett's intervention to obtain the liberty of 39 men, imprisoned in Mexico, on charges they had conspired against the Mexican government in Texas (half were U.S. citizens).[35] However, the U.S. reader of Poinsett's *Notes* more forgivingly understands a trip to assess Mexico's economy, as well as to determine whether the United States should recognize an imperial government that so many Mexicans condemned and thus lend it "moral strength." Poinsett tries to unravel the European politics that put Iturbide in power and argues that the European support the United States received in its independence war was justifiable but that Mexico's was not (here Poinsett fails to acknowledge that Baltimore and New Orleans' money backed Mina's invasion of Mexico). He sketches commerce, manufactures, and revenue after the civil war that had devastated much of Mexico, and recognizes the capacity for industry in the tropical America that the European naturalists, Cornelius de Pauw and the Comte de Buffon, had recently said only produced indolence. He enthusiastically describes the agricultural and mineral wealth in Mexico. However, he gloomily forecasts that the United States will not be able to supply Mexicans with manufactured goods because "[t]he mass of the people here will not for many years consume foreign manufactures. Their dress is simple and they are accustomed to wear cloth made in the country, and in many instances to manufacture it themselves" (1824/1969, 140).

We read of a corresponding Mexican faith in commerce in a document that Poinsett appends to his report—an address by Iturbide to the Mexican Congress. Inter-American commerce will help ensure European recognition of American independence and thus stave off European meddling. A future based on American cooperation can be bright:

> The whole of Europe will not consent, unless obliged to do so by force, that this continent should have governments independent of them. Europe is aware, that the Americans, organized into constituted societies, will become the depositaries of knowledge, of power, of commerce and industry; and that at the end of five years, she will be with respect to us, what the Greeks and Romans were with respect to her, after the death of Alexander and the destruction of the eastern and western empires. (1824/1969, 290–291)

Today U.S. and Mexican historians often view the Monroe Doctrine, which Poinsett's report contributed to, as a U.S. imposition on the rest of the Western Hemisphere. Both sets of historians see Iturbide critically, despite the fact that he negotiated Mexico's independence from Spain and took steps to try to protect it from reinvasion; he is not viewed as his country's liberator in the same way that Simón Bolívar is.

However, in retrieving primary material from the period, one learns of a need for something like the Monroe Doctrine. Leaders in both the United States and Mexico realized the importance of proclaiming a strong, united Western Hemisphere so as to resist European encroachments, and to ensure free trade in American waters as well as American equality with other "commercial nations." Still another appendix to Poinsett's summary of his trip, a report by Mexico's Secretary of State of Foreign Affairs to the country's Constituent Congress (November 8, 1823) expresses this desire for hemispheric solidarity in the face of, particularly, British and French takeovers: "If our political and commercial relations bring us in contact with the nations of Europe, some of which are our neighbors by means of their establishment on our continent and on the adjacent isles, more powerful motives unite us with the states lately formed in America" (1824/1969, 314).

Realizing the desirability of a close relationship with the United States, Iturbide chose Manuel Zozaya as diplomatic envoy to the United States in March 1822. Zozaya did not arrive in Baltimore until December and his reception was spoiled by anti-Iturbidists in the United States such as Rocafuerte. Zozaya provides a less optimistic view of the future of U.S.–Mexican relations in the letter he wrote back to Iturbide from Washington on December 26, 1822:

> The pride of these republicans does not allow them to see us as equals but as inferiors; their conceit extends in my judgment to their believing that their capital will be the capital of all the Americas; down-deep they love our money, not us, nor are they capable of entering into an alliance or trade except for their own convenience, not recognizing reciprocity.[36]

On March 7, 1822, Monroe had recognized the independence of Mexico, as well as that of several other Spanish American countries. However, after several nominations and then resignations, no minister was sent from the United States to Mexico until Poinsett accepted the post in 1825.

"Commerce" concerned still another traveler to Mexico—this time a Frenchman who was reporting on trade opportunities in Mexico for the French king. Juan Schmaltz was reconnoitering in Mexico between January and November 1823, for purposes of drawing that country into the French commercial orbit.[37] He returned to France via New Orleans and thus had an opportunity to witness from that city Mexico's trade routes out of Tampico, a port that was growing in importance as Veracruz lost traffic because of high duties and the brigandage along its outlying roads. Tampico was furnishing Mexico's northern cities and towns with the goods that viceregal centralist policies had previously funneled through Mexico City. Although Schmaltz's report only hints at the reasons for beginning trade between the United States and Mexico, it valuably contains observations on commerce. The report demonstrates the competition among European nations for domination of the markets in the recently freed American lands. It compares French economic policies with those of England, Germany, and the United States. Schmaltz says that presently the United States is Spain's only competitor in Mexico, providing that country with most of its needs. However, U.S. shipping is mostly contraband traffic (its merchant Navy numbers almost 10,000, in contrast to France's 1,000). Because the United States is still a small country and manufactures very little, it trades mostly in European goods. Then Schmaltz provides an important detail, which illuminates Robeson's situation: "Americans [U.S. businessmen] have opened [in Mexico City] shops entrusted to commissioned agents who add their 5% and who, because of constant replenishments, manage a goodly amount of merchandise" (1957, 17).

Schmaltz says that England's system, alternatively, considers commerce on a grand scale and does not engage individuals. England concentrates its business in large commercial associations. These decide what a market requires and then determine which factories will produce for that distant market in England's expanding empire. Capital is thus allocated efficiently. Useless rivalries are eliminated. Quality is maintained. Schmaltz reports that England was already moving into Peru, Chile, and Colombia and was rapidly entering Mexico to take control of her mines. Germany, too, he said, had an interest in Mexico's mining. France, lamentably, was missing an important economic opportunity. France's woolen goods were entering Mexico, imported by U.S. businessmen through Tampico. But the quality was inconsistent so that Mexicans were growing dissatisfied with French woolens, as well as wines.

Schmaltz's report documents not only France's economic interest in Mexico but also the interests of the Bourbon monarchy in controlling that American market—if not for Spain and its Bourbon king, then for France. His report reminds us that France (and metonymically French books, which are often thought of solely as revolutionary, antireligious tracts) was in its return to monarchism a source of conservative thought. However, "commerce" was apparently forcing monarchists like Schmaltz to recognize new truths. For example, in a comment that substitutes new psychological expectations of human behavior for old Christian beliefs, Schmaltz acknowledges "the interest of individuals is always the measure of commerce among peoples." He predicts that, after a time, Mexicans, because of a latent sympathy for Latin culture, will prefer to buy from the French, who were their "oppressors" during the Napoleonic occupation of Spain, rather than from the English, who seemingly were their "protectors." Schmaltz's report, written from a European point of view, enlarges the view of commerce that Robeson's and Poinsett's American analyses provide.

FREEMASONRY

Carey and other U.S. publishers had early on profited from printing Masonic materials (minutes, speeches, rulebooks, songbooks, etc.) in English for English-speaking Lodges in New England, along the Atlantic coast, and into inland areas that were developing (in Pennsylvania, Kentucky, etc.). Then, as territories and trade opportunities opened up, they began to think they could also print Masonic materials in Spanish for Lodges in New Orleans, the Caribbean, and Mexico. Philadelphia seems to have been known for multilanguage Masonic printing at an early date—an early Inquisition report from Manila tells that a Philadelphia-printed item, *Recueil Précieux de la Maçonnerie* (1787) was seized in the effects of a French doctor who left Marseilles in 1788, bound for Mauritius and then the Philippines.[38] And, proving that beyond printing for export, book dealers in the city catered to Philadelphia readers by offering news of continental Masonry is Carey's advertisement in 1815 that he had for sale the Barcelona and Sevilla-printed *Compendio de la vida y hechos de Joseph Balsamo llamado Conde Calliostro, Que se ha sacado del proceso formado contra él en Roma el año de 1790 y que puede servir de regla para conocer la índole de la secta de los francmasones*.[39] This work by Giovanni Barberi apparently entered Philadelphia with other Spanish-language books Carey imported from Spain and either sold or reprinted.

Philadelphia was an early center of Lodge activity, and the city became even more important as it became a nerve center for Lodges in distant French- and Spanish-speaking areas. Beginning in 1818 records of the Philadelphia Lodge report requests for patents by a French-speaking Lodge in New Orleans, and by Spanish-speaking Lodges in several cities and towns in Cuba (Havana, Regla, and Santiago). These Lodges were under the jurisdiction of the Philadelphia Lodge (though later some were under New York's and South Carolina's); and their minutes in French and Spanish were forwarded back to Philadelphia for approval.[40]

Philadelphia's printers added to the city's importance as a Masonic center as they retailed Masonry for those distant areas (however, it must be noted that New York, too, was a Masonic publishing center). In 1818 the Philadelphia printer, Thomas H. Palmer, printed the 30-page *Reflexiones imparciales sobre la franc-masonería* (authored by "C.N."). In 1820 an unknown printer in an unknown place printed *Estatutos generales de la masoneria escocesa*. In New York, in 1822, an unnamed printer printed J.G. Castillo's *Espíritu de los estatutos y reglamentos de la orden francmasónica, y diccionario de todos los términos y expresiones, que están en uso, para los trabajos de las logias*.[41] In New York, in that same year, J. Kingsland & Co. printed Joseph Cerneau's *Senda de las luces Masónicas*;[42] and Joseph Desnoues printed *Monitor, o Guía de los Francmasones utilísimo . . . escrito en inglés por un Francmasón y traducido al Castellano*.[43] Cerneau, who was said to have been initiated into a Lodge in Santo Domingo by the Jew Esteban Morín, stirred division among Masons in New York when he sold Masonic memberships and symbols; he fled in 1831 with the money.[44] In 1826 the New York printer, S. Marks, published Cerneau's 389-page work, *Manual masónico, conteniendo los estatutos y reglamentos generales de la Orden Fran-Masónica: seguidos de algunas piezas de arquitectura, &*. And in 1827, an unnamed printer in Boston put out William Morgan's 95-page *Ilustraciones de masonería*.

For a few years, however, Carey led in Spanish-language Masonic publishing. In 1822, as we have seen, the firm published three book-length instructional items: *La librería Masónica y general Ahiman Rezon*,[45] *Jachin y Boaz; o una llave auténtica para la puerta de framasonería*, and *El Monitor de los Masones libres* (see Figure 3.2). These were expensive editions with plates; *La librería masónica Ahiman Rezon* has a fine engraving of Solomon's temple; the twentieth-century *Enciclopedia de México* reproduces in its article on Masonry the frontispiece from *Jachin y Boaz*, together with two of its elaborate illustrations of symbols; and *El Monitor* has a frontispiece that Carey lifted from *The True Masonic Chart*, printed in New Haven in 1819 (Carey eliminated aristocratic references from this attempt to standardize Masonic symbols and had the caption translated to Spanish—The Master's Carpet became "*La alfombra del maestro*").[46] Edward Barry translated all three from English to Spanish, staying true to, but also deviating from, the original texts—as indeed the U.S. authors had done in their borrowing from English sources. *Librería Masónica* was written by Samuel Cole from Maryland *Jachin y Boaz* by "R.S."; and *El Monitor* by the Rhode Islander Thomas Smith Webb. Cole based his work on the history by the English historian, William Preston, *Illustrations of Masonry*, as well as on the London-printed *Ahiman Rezon* by the Irishman Laurence Dermott, and on several other unidentified sources. Webb also based his book on Preston's *Illustrations of Masonry*; and studies of his translation have shown how Webb omitted parts he judged inapplicable to U.S. society. Thus, British Masonry, filtered through U.S. authors in "selective Anglicization," went on to Mexico in translations and taught Masons there lessons in social organization, obedience, and charity, which had their origins in northern Europe.[47]

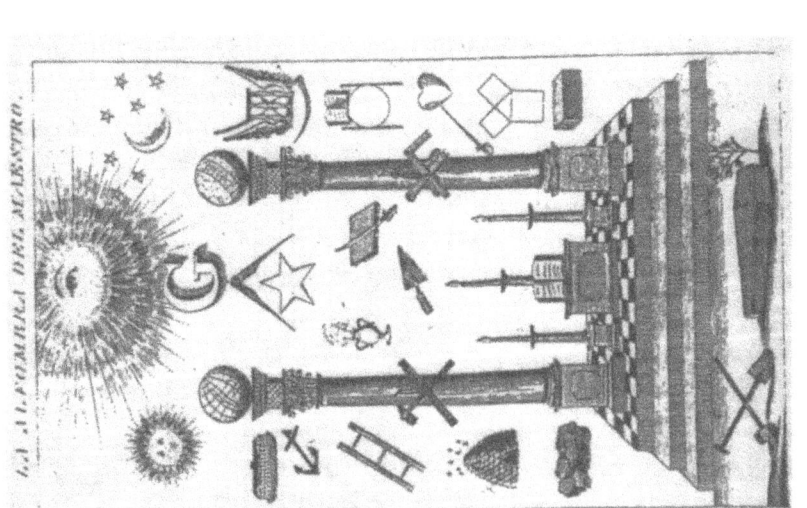

FIGURE 3.2 Frontispiece and title page of *El Monitor de los Masones Libres*.
Courtesy of The Masonic Library and Museum of Pennsylvania, Philadelphia, PA.

Philadelphia's extensive printing of Masonry's history, rules, and philosophy contrasts with Mexico's first exposure when Spanish military men, troop leaders who had been inducted into Lodges in Cádiz and who had come to Mexico to quell the 1810 uprising, brought news of the movement.[48] Their word-of-mouth enthusiasms, together with the short pamphlets that came out of Cádiz into Mexico in periods of relative press freedom, impressionistically defined Masonry as a kind of elite brotherhood rather than a formal code. Spanish Masonry was mainly influenced by France, where Stuart claims to the English crown were fostered throughout the eighteenth century; French as well as Italian Masonry was thought to be a gathering of aristocrats with its origins in chivalry and the Crusades. England, Ireland, and Germany, however, tended to view Masonry as a union of craftsmen with common origins. Mexico's first Lodges were Scottish-rite Lodges; later York Lodges under U.S. auspices arrived.

The Scottish and York branches of Masonry brought to Mexico, then, some of the class divisions that separated European Masons. However, both branches taught an international consciousness. As Andrew Michael Ramsay (1668–1743), a Scot who converted to Catholicism and spent most of his life working for the Stuart cause in France, wrote: "Le monde entier on'est qu'une grand république dont chaque nation est une famille et chaque particulier un enfant."[49] Volney wrote in his *Catéchisme* that Nature was the same among all men. God rules the universe and, regardless of country or religion ("pays ni de secte"), He imposes the same moral laws by virtue of each man's capacity for reason (1821/1934, 97). Here, although acknowledging cultural diversity, Volney affirms Nature's universality. Although Volney has not been proven as having been a Mason,[50] his works were distributed among the same readers as Masonic books in the late eighteenth and early nineteenth centuries. *Catéchisme*'s emphasis on domestic and social virtues in the name of social usefulness, its criticism of cupidity and luxury, blind filial obedience and monkish celibacy, were appealing to many. "Patrie" was "la communauté de citoyens, qui, réunis par des sentiments fraternels et de besoins réciproques font de leurs forces respectives une force commune."[51] In *Ruines*, as we have seen, Volney also put forward a philosophy of history based on an empire's morality. Therefore, apart from any divine plan or any one monarch's battle successes, a society's collective goodness explained its rise or fall. Because a society was defined by its pieces, individuals—as well as colonies—counted in on a nation/state's destiny in on a way they had not before.

Carey's first shipment to Mexico, entrusted to Follin and Malsain, appears to have been composed mainly of the Masonic books he had in his warehouse. All facts point to the conclusion that Carey, frustrated in that first attempt, engaged Robeson in a second try at entering Mexico with more acceptable materials. Once in Mexico Robeson requested for later shipment from among the Masonic titles only Volney's *Catéchisme du citoyen français* (1793), which he several times instructed was printed at the end of Volney's *Ruines; ou Meditations sur les revolutions des empires*.[52] In 1821 Carey, in a joint venture with publishers in New York and Boston, had printed James Philip Puglia's Spanish translation of *Sistema politico-moral*—the second part of which was Volney's *Catequismo del Ciudadano Francés*. We have seen that *Sistema politico-moral* and a *Masonic Catechism* (either *Librería Masónica* or *El Monitor*) were shipped in Follin and Malsain's cargo. It is not clear whether Robeson wanted Puglia's translation or was specifying another edition, because he repeated his instruction several times. Neither is it clear whether Robeson calculated that that text would be saleable in Mexico, having observed Masonic activity there, or whether Mexicans told him so. Throughout the spring of 1823, after Iturbide's fall, Carey and Lea insisted in their letters to Robeson that they thought Masonic items should sell well.

In 1822, Iturbide's government was indecisive in its control of Masonry. Members of the country's Scottish Lodges, with Spanish affiliations, remained loyalists though they also saw in Masonry an opportunity for reform. Thus a mixture of Spanish allegiance and liberalism lingered in Mexican thinking during the first years of Iturbide's rule, allowing some confusion and openness in discussion of the movement. Among the printed materials for that year in the holdings of the Sutro Mexican collection there is a history of Masonry, printed in Cádiz;[53] a sympathetic discussion of why Masons were persecuted by various papal Bulls;[54] and a long treatise that attempted to explain Masonic society and adjust it to Christian principle and Spanish constitutionalism.[55] A broadside was posted on the cathedral on January 30, written by a woman defending Masons.[56] However, the mood was also changing as reactionary clergy were asserting control and opponents to Iturbide's authoritarianism like Antonio López de Santa Anna and Guadalupe Victoria were using the secrecy of the Lodges to foment criticism.[57] Mier, a Lodge member from his Cádiz days, returned to Mexico in July 1822; but he was soon jailed along with other members of the Congress. In 1822 Lizardi was excommunicated for having written what many viewed as a defense of Masonry. One of Iturbide's original claims to legitimacy had been his protection of "religion" in Mexico; and, as his hold on government began to loosen, he prosecuted Masonry so as to win the support of the clergy and the pious.

To explain the interest of Mexican Catholics in Masonry in those years (indeed some priests were Masons) it must be emphasized that Masonry was not the anti-Catholic or anti-Jewish movement it is perceived to be today. Instead it seems to have been a kind of belief-structure that transcended sectarianism and affirmed brotherhood. Masonry reached back to antiquity for symbolism suggesting universal principles. It emphasized its contribution to civilization's progress in telling that, because it had preached philanthropy over the years, man had been brought out of his original selfish, brutish state. In exploring human nature beyond religious definitions, it was sometimes accused of humanism. Masonry retained notions of the divine so that it was neither totally secular nor antireligious. Like Deism and philosophies of natural religion of the period, or the distrust of dogmatism that Volney expresses in the following quote from *Ruins*, Masonry moved beyond the view that one church possessed truth to instead encourage men's ethical conduct in the face of uncertainty:

> By means of the contrasted opinions I have scattered through [the *Ruins*] it breathes that spirit of doubt and uncertainty which appears to me the best suited to the weakness of the human mind, and the most adapted to its improvement, inasmuch as it always leaves a door open to new truths; while the spirit of dogmatism and immovable belief, limiting our progress to a first received opinion, binds us at hazard, and without resource, to the yoke of error or falsehood, and occasions the most serious mischiefs to society.[58]

In 1822, when Robeson and Poinsett arrived in Mexico, there was an appetite for Masonic literature among already-existing Scottish-rite Lodges in the capital and in Veracruz. Then, between 1822 and 1824, as new Scottish and then York-rite Lodges were established in Puebla, Tabasco, Campeche, and Papaloapan at the port of Alvarado (where Eugenio Cortés was a member), the United States moved in to exert influence as these Lodges sought their patents from Lodges in the United States and asked for instructional materials.[59] An example of U.S. oversight, together with British influence, is a letter exchange between a New York Lodge and an English Lodge over the years 1820–1822. Brother Joseph De Glock D'Obernay had been sent by England to New Spain (Mexico) to install the Royal Arch Degree there. But he had acted improperly. Therefore, New York, where he presented himself, was told to confiscate his diploma.[60] In 1825, when more U.S.-backed York Lodges were founded in Mexico, the character of Mexican Masonry changed. An anti-Spanish, democratic Masonry developed, attracting upwardly mobile men from the army and business; in their ranks republicanism grew. *Ahiman Rezon* emphasized that preferments in the Lodges were based on "real Worth and personal Merit only, not upon Seniority" (30).

George Fisher provides an important view of Mexican Masonry in the years (1825–1830) when Joel Poinsett served as U.S. plenipotentiary there.[61] Fisher had been a member of a Philadelphia Lodge from 1820 through December 9, 1822, when he gave up his membership and went to Mexico. Later he would go on to Panama, Galveston, Matamoros, Houston, and finally California where he participated in Masonic activities into the 1840s. From his standpoint,

Mexican Masonry was elitist, far from the preachments of "democracy" that might have existed in the United States; "la plebe" (or as he called it "the rabble") did not belong but instead Mexican Masonry, whether Scottish or York, was confined to the "higher ranks of society" ("Desaguiliers" 1858, 5). Its members, among whom were Bradburn, Bravo, José Ignacio Esteva, "several Senators, members of Congress, and other distinguished men of rank in the nation" met with their families every Thursday evening in Poinsett's mansion "for social entertainment, cultivating the friendship and thus calling to their aid the knowledge of the American Minister, of the art of self-government by the people, or the *modus operandi* to carry on a Republican Federal Government" (5–6). In the promenading, dancing, card-playing, and dining, but also in the "social assemblies" in which men conversed "upon political, legislative, ecclesiastical, commercial, judicial, and other topics of the day, according to the taste and inclination of the several parties present," Mexicans learned republican lessons in a protected place. "[T]he bonds of friendship between him [Poinsett] and his government, and of his guests and their government, were drawn closer and closer" (6). Fisher claims that Poinsett, though he secured authorization for the establishment of the democratic York Lodge in Mexico, never was affiliated with any of the Mexican Lodges. In late 1826 there were 25 Lodges in the country, but "they soon became dormant." Fisher continues:

> The Mexicans did not realize the Spirit of Masonry; although they were captivated with the forms, ceremonies, the ritual, the imposing and costly paraphernalia of the Lodges (that of the Grand Lodge is said to have cost over $3,000), and the Grand Lodge bore much similarity with the Roman Catholic Church, especially that of the Grand Royal Arch Chapter of Mexico, typifying the Pontifical and the Levitical orders of Priesthood; but these curiosities soon became an every day occurrence, and hence obsolete; same as the religious festivities in Spanish America. The mysterious part of Masonry, however, was the cohesive element, for the time being, as it was regarded a quasi "*Carbonarian*" institution for the propagation of democratic republican principles of government in secret, and thus, thwarting the machinations of the opponents of the new system of Government in Mexico, instigated by the votaries of European influence. These causes, however, finally brought Masonry into disrepute, and by an act of the Congress, all secret associations were declared dangerous for the public safety and proscribed. (1858, 8)

Thus Masonry's collision with Catholicism in Mexico was at once an affirmation and repudiation of cultish externals. On the one hand Masonry appealed to Mexicans because it was an alternative to the Catholicism associated with the country's colonial past, labeled "fanaticism" by forward-looking Mexicans in the post-independence period. On the other, Masonry's rituals and the secrecy they afforded, as Fisher documents, created safeguards for new political alliances.[62] Its spirit of tolerance and charity echoed some aspects of Catholic teaching yet fit their liberal agenda. However, the "Masonic" literature selected for shipment to Mexico points not just to Masonry per se but to a different language in use in Europe and the United States, which could be used to implement reforms. Masonic books furnished a discourse frame for the republicanism that Mexicans had begun to consider and wanted to articulate for themselves. The legal language of other countries' constitutions provided a model for new public relationships. But the vocabulary of Masonry, with its concepts of universal family structures, equality, fraternity, and philanthropy, apart from the domain of any institutional church, taught lessons for new private behavior.

Masonry, however, was not the only modernizing language available to Mexicans then. Rocafuerte's *Ideas necesarias a todo pueblo americano independiente, que quiera ser libre*, a compilation of selections from Paine's *Common Sense*, a speech by John Quincy Adams, the U.S. Articles of Confederation, and the Constitution of the United States, made available another discourse source. In the prologue of that work, Rocafuerte says he wants his book, written in Philadelphia "asylum for the oppressed, center of enlightenment, bastion of liberty,"[63] to benefit compatriots in Ecuador. He quotes from the U.S. Declaration of Independence: "All men are created equal; they are endowed by their Creator with certain unalienable rights; that among these are life, liberty, and the pursuit of happiness."[64] In this handbook, Rocafuerte makes specific the importance of commerce to the future of republicanism and its pursuit of freedom:

> The mercantile spirit is an enemy of privilege, of monopoly, of royal trading companies and of monarchism. Commerce is the inseparable companion of liberty and of national wealth; it can only exist under the auspices of liberal governments as is demonstrated by the mercantile history of Holland, of the Hanseatic cities, of the United States, of England, and of the republics of Genoa and Venice. ("Prólogo," 1821, 1–18)[65]

The United States was a model for many Spanish Americans. The country's system of government and its "mercantile spirit," which, after centuries of colonial monopolistic rule Spanish Americans had to learn, were thought to be exportable. Later, in 1826, the Cuban Félix Varela also translated and had published, for the use of Spanish Americans confronted with new relationships often requiring argument and negotiation, Thomas Jefferson's *Manual de práctica parlamentaria, para el uso del senado de los Estados Unidos*.[66]

Whether Carey was a Mason and this motive was behind the Mexican book shipment is a possibility that scholars have considered.[67] Suggesting that he was a Mason is a record in the archives of Lodge No. 2 in Philadelphia (April 13, 1829) that "ten dollars was given to Mr. M. Carey, chairman of the

Committee, to give to the Public Committee for the relief of the poor."[68] In his work on behalf of Catholics and the Church in the United States, he seems to have been a committed Catholic. Therefore, it does not seem likely that he would have wanted his print business to undermine the Catholic Church in Mexico, or that he thought that Masonry threatened Catholic faith. Indeed Robeson tells that Carey was interested in selling a Catholic New Testament in Mexico. However, in 1821 Carey did publish the anti-Catholic *Italy* by Lady Morgan, and William Clarkin remarks, "It is a wonder that Carey was enabled by his conscience to publish—or to join in publishing—a work which was so hostile to his religion as this" (220).

ROBESON AND VERACRUZ

Among the impressions produced by the bookrunner's letters is the personality of the writer, Thomas W. Robeson. Robeson and Paul was a Philadelphia company that dealt in iron, lumber, and general merchandise in the period from 1807 to 1813; the company also engaged in the hauling and transportation business (as far south as Charleston and as far into the Atlantic as Madeira).[69] It is not clear whether Thomas W. Robeson belonged to this family and got his training in that business (however, as we have seen, he was not a Philadelphian). Two letters, dated 1815, in the files of E.I. du Pont de Nemours Co., which manufactured gunpowder, tell that he dealt with that company; one letter mentions that he was staying with A. Thompson.[70] In 1825 he was recommended to be consul in Havana, though he did not receive the appointment; in that documentation he is said to be from Delaware.[71] In contrast, George Follin was named vice-consul of Mexico for the port of Philadelphia in 1834.[72]

Robeson's letters to Carey show him to have been an educated man, familiar with the classics and with some knowledge of French. His failure to remark on his time on the water suggests that he was not a seaman. As Carey's agent, he was primarily a representative of that book business, yet he also attended to profits from his own "medicines" (camphor and cream of tartar). Thus he seems to have had latitude to deal on his own.[73] His eyes were open to new ventures, suggesting importation into Mexico of furniture (a growing Philadelphia industry as the city's cabinetmakers flourished) and "pictures" of George Washington. The Spanish term "pinturas" in one invoice indicates that these were not the ordinary prints the U.S. printshops were producing, but paintings. Philadelphia painters were multiplying the image of the first president in copies for the domestic market, and here we learn that these paintings were also marketed abroad.[74]

In his first letter, Robeson instructed Carey to contact Capt. Thompson at the Indian Queen Tavern "on Third Street near Chestnut" so as to find out his departure time for New York. Thompson would take "two trunks of M— ... and three boxes of books." It seems that the two men were leaving for Mexico at approximately the same time, that Robeson coordinated the shipments, and that Thompson was carrying the Masonic materials. (Because Carey's files are silent on Thompson's trip or the books he was responsible for, I am guessing that the two divided the Follin shipment between them and that they entered Mexico at different ports.) In his August 15 letter, Robeson requested that Carey write to A. Thompson in care of Wilkinson, notifying him of Robeson's arrival in Mexico, thus suggesting that Thompson might have awaited him in the capital. Proof of their joint venture is Carey's May 15 letter to Thompson in which the firm requested payment for postage on Robeson's letter. Because we have no other information about Thompson's—or Wilkinson'—involvement, our picture of the scheme remains incomplete. However, significantly, Thompson is called "captain," whereas Robeson seems to have been just a passenger, or perhaps supercargo, on a ship on which Capt. Riley assumed seaboard duties.

Robeson's dealings appear to have been based on prior contacts and familiarity with Caribbean ports and the Mexican Gulf coast. Yet his letters offer no clues as to who his "friends" in Alvarado were, who "Sr. Basan"—who carried his letters back to Carey—was, or who "Col. Aldama" was in whose "dwelling" Robeson stayed while in Veracruz. Esteva, Grand Master of the York Lodge when Poinsett returned to Mexico in 1825, had been a bookseller in Veracruz before he came on to Mexico City; he would have been in Veracruz when Robeson touched in there so that his role in Robeson's book business is almost certain.[75] Esteva's political leadership in post-independence Mexico suggests the importance of both his personal influence and that of the book business and Masonry on Mexico's development. However, Robeson never mentions Esteva and he discreetly refrains from naming other contacts.

Veracruz was accustomed to the comings and goings of ships and traders; its population was made up of Mexicans, transplanted Spaniards, and persons of other nationalities like the Frenchman Souberville. Foreign ideas poured readily into this cosmopolitan mix in the waning years of the Spanish empire and the first decades after independence.[76] Veracruz understood rather more than other parts of Mexico that Spain's erratic policies of alternatively opening and closing the borders of its empire, particularly with respect to the flow of books and ideas, were a measure of change. Thus the port saw not just illegal activity but also, during periods of relative freedom, open exchange with non-Spaniards. In 1796, 41 Frenchmen had been deported out of Mexico via Veracruz because the Spanish government feared their possible Napoleonic sympathies.[77] Yet only a year earlier, Madrid had authorized the port's participation in international affairs when it recognized Veracruz as a consulate (despite the fact that the merchants wanted instead an independent guild). The concession provided the legal justification for maintaining an agent in Spain, Pedro de Mantilla, to whom in 1801 the Veracruz merchants directed their request for a library, composed of the latest works of political economy. The list that Mantilla prepared for them the following year is only that—there is no indication that the merchants got those books. Nevertheless, the list is revealing for its awareness of new ideas in agriculture, taxation, law, foreign exchange, and so on. Heavy in Spanish names such as Capmany, the list also includes works by Adam Smith, Necker, Grotius, Filangieri, Montesquieu, Pufendorf, and journals such as *Bibliothèque de l'homme publique*.[78] Like Cádiz, Veracruz was open to the sea, and so its location but also its merchant character caused it to have a more liberal and up-to-date identity than the interior.[79] Veracruz had two print shops in those years; however, they were largely restricted to printing a daily paper, shipping reports for the consulate, and government materials (although, as Spanish control was shaken in 1820 as a result of Rafael de Riego's military revolt against Fernando VII, the shops did reprint news of the revolt and the Spanish king's appeal to his overseas subjects to remain loyal).[80] Alvarado got its first printing press in 1825, probably because the Spanish fort, San Juan de Ulúa in Veracruz's harbor, was under attack then and a local organ for printing commercial news was needed.[81]

However, Robeson's network extended beyond "friends" in Veracruz and the Gulf coast to the American consul in Cuba (which was still in Spanish hands), investors in Cuba and the United States, and sugar traders and banks in New Orleans. He made use of casual travelers who would carry his letters (Poinsett, Dennis Smith, and Santamaría). Nowhere do we read whether Robeson spoke Spanish or whether his knowledge of French consisted of more than an ability to drop phrases; we do not know how he communicated with Mexicans. His letter-writing abilities, compared with those of Follin, are superior;[82] and he also sounds more assertive. Although he clearly was a republican, his letters do not show that he saw his books as any other than merchandise. He seems ignorant of the present state of Spanish letters in that he thought there was a Mexican market for sixteenth- and seventeenth-century Spanish novels. However, when we read that these novels and books of cookery were to be spread over the Masonic books to be shipped, we understand that the novels might not have been packed to be read but as decoys. That tactic, plus Robeson's instruction to undercount the contents of the boxes on the bills of lading so as to reduce duties paid, and to place the barrel hoops in such a way that only one end might be opened, suggest, if not deceptive practices then recognition of the clandestine nature of their venture. Robeson tells of the help of "enlightened and liberal" Mexicans in getting his goods out of the customshouse in Mexico City; it is not clear if he rewarded them. However, he does become indignant when a fellow American approaches him, demanding pay-off.

Robeson was only one of many U.S. opportunists who came to Mexico in 1822. William Parrott, a dentist, came but soon abandoned the idea of practicing and "acquired a fortune as an importer, broker, and moneylender." In the mid-1830s Parrott became U.S. consul and villain in the eyes of Carlos María Bustamante, who attacked Parrott's manipulations in his paper, *El Mosquito Mexicano.*[83]

It is not known whether Robeson was experienced in the book business, whether he was a Mason, or indeed what motive involved him in the trade. In his first letter, written while his ship was downriver from Philadelphia in New Castle, we learn that he was still deciding what books would be sent in the boxes Carey was only then packing for him. He tells Carey—as though he controlled the shipment—that he considered including *Jachin y Boaz* but that he kept the Masonic title out because he judged it unacceptable to Mexican customs. He warns the book dealer that he "must not have any books in [the trunks to be sent in care of Bradburn] concerning M—"; one assumes that he meant "Masonry." However, once Robeson got to Mexico and Mexicans requested works like *Ruinas de Palmira* and *Cornelia Bororquia o La víctima de la Inquisición*, he appears to have been willing to run the risks of importing such titles and requested them for future shipments. Although not, strictly speaking, Masonic books, the latter two were lumped into that category by traditional Catholics.

We have seen Volney's *Ruinas. Cornelia Bororquia* was an epistolary novel whose circulation the Mexican Inquisition had prohibited in 1803[84] and again in 1817. Inquisition prohibitions, in fact, advertised the book; and thus Mexicans learned of its importance in Europe, where by 1819 it had gone into a fifth edition. Mexicans also learned from the Inquisition's ban that others had dared to criticize the Holy Office, suggesting that they might do the same. Like other anti-Inquisition literature of the period such as Ann Radcliffe's novel, *The Italian, or the Confessional of the Black Penitents* (1797), *Cornelia Bororquia* portrayed unfavorably this relic from an earlier, intolerant Europe.[85] Attributed to Luis Gutiérrez, a Spaniard in exile in Bayonne, *Cornelia Bororquia* was published anonymously in Paris in 1801. Robeson says that Dufief sold it in his Philadelphia bookstore, presumably one of the many editions in Spanish, printed in France and in Spain. This novel, then, which anteceded the debate over the Inquisition at the Cortes de Cádiz and the publication of the history of the Inquisition by Juan Antonio Llorente in 1818,[86] would have been a sensitive importation—perhaps more dangerous because its love story, in which a villainous inquisitor betrays his religious vows and ruins young lives by lecherously seducing a young bride, would have attracted a wider readership than a dry indictment of the Inquisition.

Cornelia Bororquia introduces the question of other novels or novelesque works that Robeson carried to Mexico—*Don Quijote*, *Lazarillo*, *La Galatea*, and a work identified only as *La Dulce*. *Cornelia Bororquia* (though not part of Robeson's first shipment) causes us to examine Carey's assumption that Mexicans might want fiction. Such innocent-looking titles could have been a calculation to divert censors, but it is also possible that Carey and Robeson wondered whether Mexicans were beginning to acquire a taste for the genre, popular in Europe, and could be counted on to be buyers. *Don Quijote*, *Lazarillo*, and *La Galatea* would have been familiar to Mexicans as classics from Spain's Golden Age; thus they seemed like sure sales. But *La Dulce* seems to have been a gamble.

I suspect that *La Dulce* was Pablo de Olavide's *La dulce venganza*, part of a collection titled *Lecturas útiles y entretenidas* published in Madrid in 1800, and again in 1816.[87] We know that Carey sold foreign books in his shop so it is reasonable to think that Robeson got this title from Carey's stock. Carey was so impressed by Olavide's fiction that in 1811 he printed three Olavide novels. However, *La dulce venganza* could have been thought to be most suitable for Mexican readers for several reasons: It was not on the Inquisition list of banned books so it could avoid censorship; its storyline conformed to eighteenth-century didactic standards. And it dramatized problems that the new commercial world posed.[88] A young man from a trading house in Sevilla wants to marry. He rejects the custom of looking for a bride who will bring a large dowry to secure the house, not because he loves a plain girl but because he theorizes that a woman of wealth brings habits of luxury. He prefers a wife who will dress modestly and shun society. The story goes on to tell of those new bases for marriage and family, but also the risks of Spanish businessmen who trade with Mexico (kidnapped by Dutch pirates, the hero is taken to Ceylon and then to the Philippines). Commerce and international dangers threatened the happiness and economic lives of Spain's young men. *La dulce venganza*, then, puts forward less of a resolved than a problematized morality.

Olavide's brand of realism has been overlooked by literary scholars. In addition to drawing contemporary characters and situations, Olavide has the novel's tradition of deconstructing previous narrative in mind when he says in a long prologue to the collection of ten novelettes that, just as Cervantes set out to destroy a harmful literary mode with his novel so, too, he wants to replace the immoral stories and plays that presently entertain the young with instructive examples of morality. He says that by the late eighteenth century the form Spaniards had invented was perverted by French immorality and that a Spaniard needed to restore the genre to its original function of monitoring literature's potential for harm. In his international vision (remembering that Olavide was born a Peruvian, went to Spain and then on to Paris), and his sense of the novel's Spanish origins with its meta-fictional capacity for demolishing fantasy and teaching truth, Olavide gives evidence of a profound understanding of novel-writing.

However, Robeson sold only one copy of *La dulce venganza*, and only a few of *Lazarillo*, so he and Carey apparently guessed wrong in thinking that Mexicans might want the genre. Perhaps more appealing would have been the Spanish translation of *Pablo y Virginia*, which Carey published in 1808, or Chateaubriand's *Atala*, which Mier claimed to have translated in Paris in 1801.[89] Mexicans did have an appetite for novels, however, because Robeson reports that Mexicans preferred to get their novels from Spain. They were ready to get political books from the United States, but they still felt themselves to be part of that European belle-lettristic tradition. The new novel, as opposed to Golden Age production, was thought of as either French or English; but even these often-sentimental stories were channeled through Spain, carrying that approbation. French novels were translated and printed in Spain, and imported openly into Mexico in the late eighteenth and early nineteenth centuries (with the exception of forbidden works like *Cornelia Bororquia*, which were smuggled in). Translations of English novels by Defoe, Fielding, Swift, and Richardson, printed in Spain, were permitted for reading in Mexico; Mrs. Radcliffe's Gothic novels, though apparently not read there, were known. Although the Spanish translation of *Waverley* was read in Mexico, as we have seen, other works by Scott, and Southey's Romantic evocations, were either not available in Mexico or not relished by Mexicans. Consequently, imaginative and linguistically artful books remained Spain's prerogative, and the United States would supply Mexico only with political and how-to books (scientific and legal texts but also dictionaries and grammars).

Robeson's pleas for good-quality paper suggest its scarcity in Mexico.[90] Spanish paper mills, largely in the Cataluña area, had supplied Mexico throughout the colonial years, and the recent war would have ended that source. Even toward the end of colonial rule, however, administrators worried about paper shortages in the colonies, to some extent because this official commodity was being ill used. For example, in an edict dated December 10, 1799, the viceroy in Mexico City prohibited "the extraction of papers, documents and books from archives and libraries, and their sale to Biscuit-makers, Rocket-makers, Apothecaries, Shopkeepers, and the like, for consumption in their trades."[91] A similar scarcity apparently existed in Santo Domingo where it was reported that, in 1807, food was found wrapped in pages taken from the *Social Contract*, the *Rights of Man*, and writings by Thomas Paine and Viscardo.[92] In a largely illiterate world, paper had other uses.

Robeson was not the first to bring U.S.-printed materials into Mexico. Earlier, the *Diario de México* announced two book-length, anti-French items that the *Diario* said had come from the United States. Attributed to "Stewarton" (probably the English writer Lewis Goldsmith), they were "The revolutionary Plutarch, containing the biographical, historical and secret memoirs of the Buonaparte family" (printed in Baltimore in 1806 by G. Keatinge and L. Frailey and advertised in the *Diario* on August 15, 1809); and "Historia secreta de la corte y gabinete de St. Cloud, distribuida en cartas escritas en París el año de 1805 a un lord de Inglaterra" (published in Mexico in 1808 by the Imprenta de Arizpe whose editor said that it was a reprint of a New York item, translated into Spanish there by "un español americano"). "Historia" was cited seven times in the *Diario* over the course of 1808 and 1809 as its chapters came out in installments.[93] Apparently, Napoleonic hatreds licensed entry into Mexico of these U.S. imports. In its August 17, 1808 issue, the *Diario* reported that when a French ship arrived in Veracruz from Guadaloupe, bringing news that Napoleon had named his brother José king of Spain, Fernando loyalists in Veracruz burned the "seditious papers." On November 1, 1808, the *Diario* relayed news of José's defeat in Pamplona; a ship out of Philadelphia had brought the report to Havana from San Sebastián (Spain)—thus documenting a Philadelphia ship's travels in Spanish territories. We see, then, that Robeson was not the dangerous innovator he might seem to have been; others had brought books (and news) from the United States into Mexico before him.

Yet how Mexicans might have remembered this cooperation and aided Robeson almost twenty years later is a question for which we seem to have no good answers. Robeson obviously had planning and financial help from Bradburn, and probably also Bustamante, Mier, and Wilkinson. However, Bradburn is mentioned most frequently. Bradburn's move to Mexico, his marriage to a titled Mexican woman, his career as a Mexican military officer can be understood either as enthusiasm for the ideals of the new Mexican nation or opportunism. Bradburn's frequent travels—from Mexico to the United States and then within Mexico from the capital to Veracruz to receive consignments—tell of his intrigues. Iturbide had taken Bradburn into his army and arranged for his marriage. He was a link to the Mexican Eugenio Cortés who, we have seen, worked in the United States to further Iturbide interests. Lucas Alamán, a contemporary observer, credits Bradburn with securing U.S. recognition for Mexico's independence under Iturbide.[94] Yet Robeson's republican books, which Bradburn helped to bring into Mexico, contributed to the failure of Iturbide's imperial government. After Iturbide fell, Bradburn survived the infighting; and in 1829, another Mexican president, Vicente Guerrero, under whom Bradburn had fought in the independence war, granted him exclusive rights for fifteen years to introduce steamboats onto the Río Grande. Manuel de Mier y Terán, in charge of the project to colonize Texas, wrote that in view of the "continual proofs that [Bradburn] gave of [his] zeal for the welfare of the Mexican Republic," Bradburn had been chosen to establish the garrison Anáhuac at the head of Galveston Bay.[95]

Thus Bradburn's role in the Robeson book business raises questions. Was he a true republican or an opportunistic double agent, seemingly loyal to Mexico but really furthering U.S. designs on Mexican territory? Did Bradburn meet with Stephen Austin when Austin arrived in Mexico City on April 19, 1822, staying for a year so as to secure support for his colonizing schemes in Texas? (They probably did meet since the two were in Mexico City in those months.) Does the fact that Bradburn was a Mason implicate him in Poinsett's activities in Mexico? Was Poinsett's trip to Mexico in 1822, as Francisco Javier Gaxiola believes,[96] more than simple observation and instead a spy's assessment of the success of schemes by which the United States might annex Texas and then Mexico? (Gaxiola is perhaps partially right since Austin and Poinsett did indeed collaborate, to the extent that we know, when both worked to secure the release of the 39 Texas conspirators.) Does Robeson's connection with Wilkinson, famous for shifting loyalties and for collaborating with Philip Nolan "the man without a country," suggest a larger plan than bookselling? These are questions for which, as yet, we have no conclusive answers.

BOOK CULTURE IN MEXICO

We turn now to another set of impressions, left by Robeson's letters, relative to the cultural climate in Mexico. We have seen that Robeson emphasized the warm reception Reyes gave him when he arrived in Alvarado; the apparent absence of yellow fever in Veracruz, which favored future visits; the interest of Mexicans already familiar with "works of merit," that is, the writings of Rousseau and Voltaire, who would buy these works if they were provided; as well as the cooperation of "enlightened and liberal" men in important positions in Mexico. Robeson praised the beauty and order of the streets in Veracruz; he expressed surprise at the excellence of the private libraries in Mexico and the high degree of culture possessed by many in the population. Contrasting with these favorable views, however, is his criticism. He said that Mexico's superstitious population was undeserving of a republican form of government, the common people were easily impressed with ostentation, and that Mexico City bookstores did little business and were no more than places for disputation and frivolity.

This last, denigrating observation misreads Mexicans' taste for oral argument. What Robeson saw as scorn for reading would have been instead an explosion of contradictory opinion after several years of frustrated silence. Late in the eighteenth century and in the first decades of the nineteenth, newspaper and pamphlet activity had introduced to Mexicans the possibility that ideas could be freely admitted and exchanged. Periodical literature, at first largely scientific in nature, supplemented the official gazette. The Mexican economy relied heavily on mining, and news of scientific advances abroad was eagerly sought. Mexicans read in journals like José Antonio Alzate y Ramírez's two papers — *Diario literario de México* (1768–1772) and *Gacetas de literatura de México* (1788–1795) — discussion of scientists like Benjamin Franklin.[97] Through such reading they learned that chemists, mining engineers, geographers, astronomers, and so on, could challenge received knowledge and even disagree among themselves. They also learned they could enter this debate by sending in their own letters. Then, in the first decades of the nineteenth century, Mexican print shops widened this opportunity for discourse by addressing contemporary social issues in newspapers and pamphlets. The most prominent of these papers, competing with the official gazette, was the *Diario de México*, published in Mexico City between 1805 and 1817; one of its editors was Carlos María Bustamante.[98] The *Diario* reported useful announcements and reprinted materials from Cádiz, London, Havana, the Bahamas, and Buenos Aires. Beginning in January 10, 1806, it reprinted excerpts from Humboldt's *Ensayo político sobre el reino de la Nueva España*, thus allowing Mexicans to see themselves as others saw them.[99] It is important to note that the editors also invited Mexicans to send in essays. One topic that elicited much attention was the country's language; men and women were exercised as to whether Castilian usage should still prevail or whether de facto Mexican speech should determine new rules. The debate over what language the inscription on the new mining building should be written in — whether Latin, Castilian or even Indian tongues — thus revealed conflicted self-identity and a growing awareness that Mexico differed from Spain in many ways besides language usage.

Nevertheless, in the war years (1810–1821), Spanish authorities clamped down on Mexico's press. Newspapers continued, but under censorship; and orality handled the contradictions that earlier print exchanges had allowed to surface. When the author we have seen before, José Joaquín Fernández de Lizardi, published Mexico's first novel, *El Periquillo Sarniento* in 1816, the fiction, with its adversarial dialogues over daily topics, was in many ways an attempt to continue the newspapers' and pamphlets' free debate. The novel's voicing was a means of preserving this climate of independent thought. The form, traditionally associated with pretended characters and entertainment, was a ploy to attract censors away from its more serious purpose of expressing critical argument.[100]

An 1820 pamphlet, written by Manuel Recio,[101] our book dealer in Mexico, records a real-life exchange in which he documents how Spanish government officials were, at that late stage in the war, still intervening to stifle Mexican demand for contemporary literature:

> This October 31, in the afternoon, a person unknown to me came into my shop where I deal in books, engravings and other papers. He never even greeted me, like most well-bred people do, but instead spit out the question: "Do you have the pamphlet called 'The First Part of Infractors of the Law Ought to be Punished'"? "Yes," I said, and presented him with it. Then he asked, "Do you have more copies?" I looked in all the boxes and corners and presented him with others. The third time he asked if I had more. "How many do you want?" I asked. He answered, "All, as many as you have." I looked and all those I found amounted to no more than 29. That's when he took from his breast an official document, signed by Juan Josef Flores Alatorre [the head of censorship], authorizing collection of all copies because the work had just been banned.

Under the pretext of criticizing the boorishness of the censor's delegate, then, Recio reveals the government's control of the press (despite supposed constitutional freedoms) and the criminalization of authors, printers, and book dealers.

The pamphlet's look into Recio's bookstore, and Robeson's letters, tell how important bookstores were to developments in Mexican culture in those years. Like coffee houses, bookstores were becoming the new venues for meeting and conversation in which ideas were increasingly being appropriated by classes competing with the old aristocracy. An elite still met in private homes but the new political and commercial wealth required its own, more public and accessible gathering spaces. Bookstores were such places, and their owners were apparently the new *salonnières*. Book dealers such as Recio not only sold the political and entertaining materials on which conversation was based but they also must have provided fuel for the discussion as they relayed stories of their contacts with censors and foreigners. Robeson's assessment, then, that Mexican men and women read little and instead indulged more in "disputation" and "intrigue," tells rather of the obstructions to book ownership that censorship threw up and the fact that face-to-face speech substituted for reading. Oral exchanges meant that Mexicans were still thinking and freely contradicting one another. Debate, carried on where books and other paper-formatted items were sold, could not fail to be influenced by that medium; personal testimony must have denounced the complications surrounding publication of those materials. Indeed, Lizardi provides evidence of these book-based gatherings; he said that while he was excommunicated sympathizers came to his *alacena* (bookstall) on Santo Domingo plaza to support him with their presence and talk.[102]

In 1820, the last year of the independence war, Mexico's print world was in the process of change. Although the Inquisition was ended, an "ecclesiastical tribunal" monitored book consumption and speech for a few more years. In 1823 the Congress required that the Inquisition turn over its book holdings—one assumes all the books reviewers had read—to the government to form the basis of a new national library.[103] In 1820 Mexico City had seven presses (Robeson's informant reports five bookstores); and Oaxaca, Guadalajara, Puebla, Mérida, and Veracruz had their own presses.[104] By 1822 Iturbide's government was permitting the advertisement of many imported books; for example, the May 1 edition of the newspaper, *Noticioso General*, printed an announcement that Manuel Recio's bookstore had 101 items for sale (reprinted here as Appendix B). Most entries consist of one title, although "missals" and "breviaries" suggest multiple titles. Many on the list are religious books or titles such as schoolbooks from the classical and Spanish traditions, books relating to chemistry, physics, medicine, geography, military arts, and so on. Some are novels such as *Pablo y Virginia*. Yet there are also controversial works such as Montesquieu's *Espíritu de las leyes* and Benjamin Constant's *Curso de política constitucional*.[105]

In June 1822, *Noticioso General* advertised for sale the second edition of Mier's *Memoria*, which, we have seen, was first printed in Philadelphia in 1821; thus we know that that book traveled quickly to Mexico and, despite its politics, was allowed to be reprinted. On June 15 the Mexico City newspaper, *Sabatina Universal*, published a refutation of Mier's arguments in a defense of Iturbide. *Noticioso General*, which noted the dispute in its pages, thus further publicized Mier's work. Rocafuerte's *Ideas necesarias a todo pueblo americano independiente*, printed in Philadelphia in 1822, was reprinted in Puebla in 1823.[106] Both reprints, as well as Severo Maldonado's disguised reprinting of *Social Contract*, which we have seen, suggest some degree of press freedom.

Poinsett provides a valuable view of the range of Mexico's print sources, the population's literacy level and appetite for printed material in his report of November 1822:

> Most of the people in the cities can read and write. . . . I have frequently remarked men, clothed in the garb of extreme poverty, reading the Gazettes in the streets; of these there are three published every other day in the week, which are sold for twelve and a half cents a piece, and pamphlets and loose sheets are hawked about and sold at a reasonable rate. There are several booksellers' shops, which are but scantily supplied with books. The booksellers have hitherto laboured under all the disadvantages of the prohibitory system of the catholic church, but are now endeavouring to furnish themselves with the best modern works. The few books to be found in the shops are extravagantly dear. There are several valuable private libraries, and many Creole gentlemen, who have visited Europe, have a taste both for literature and the fine arts. This is certainly more rare among those who have never been out of their

own country. The means of education were more limited; and under the colonial system, liberal studies were discouraged. The latin language, law, theology and philosophy, were taught in the colleges, and only so much of the latter as the clergy thought might be taught with safety. To give you some idea of the influence of this class in the city of Mexico, I will merely observe, that there are five hundred and fifty secular, and sixteen hundred and forty-six regular clergy. (1824/1969, 83–84)

Poinsett's assessment of Mexico's bookstores and education system suggests that Robeson's observation that Mexico City bookstores did little business may, to some extent, be accurate—but it does not mean that Mexicans were not readers or that they were unthinking chatterers. If bookstores were places for "disputation," it was probably because lingering regulation, and prohibitive pricing, caused books to be out of reach for the average Mexican. Poinsett also recalled the title of one Iturbide-related political pamphlet that he heard a crier hawk on the streets (1824/1969, 195).[107] Cheaper periodicals helped fill that intellectual and artistic need, and orality (bookstore debate and street cries) satisfied the minimal requirements of many. Yet "disputation," in addition to reflecting the economic and political exigencies of independence, meant that Mexicans were necessarily thrashing out new ideas (such as federalism vs. centralism and religious pluralism) before they wrote down on paper their first constitution in 1824.

It is useful to explore at this point the notion of "press freedom" as it existed in Mexico then. In 1822–1823 the Mexican press was not free in the way we mean it today. Iturbide's government, through ecclesiastical interventions, still controlled the domestic presses and tried to prohibit importation of materials it considered seditious and dangerous to morality. Lucas Alamán indicates that the government blamed its problems on the Masonic intrigue and republican conspiracy that books imported from France introduced. Masons and republicans, rather than revolutionaries, were convenient villains because Mexicans had just challenged authority by revolution themselves. Translated in France by Spaniards who had followed José Bonaparte out of Spain in 1813 and who were paid by book dealers there, the French-authored books set a bad example. Translations "[of] all the works most pernicious for politics, religion, and morals" were dangerous because of their content, but their language—"bad Spanish"—was also thought to have undermined Mexican loyalty and morality.[108] The translators, exiled Spaniards (Frenchified Spaniards or *afrancesados* in Alamán's terminology), then, whether they worked in France or Philadelphia, were accused of disrupting Mexico's peace.

France had a long history of threatening stability in Spain and Spanish America. Spanish troublemakers like José Marchena (1768–1821) had sought refuge from the Spanish Inquisition by crossing the Pyrenees and from there spreading news of France's revolution by translating into Spanish the works of Montesquieu, Rousseau, Molière, De Pradt, Volney, Voltaire, Depuis, and Benoit.[109] Spain's border with France then facilitated entry of their translations back into Spain, and from French seaports the works went to Spanish America. Between 1820 when Rafael de Riego's liberalism momentarily triumphed in Spain, and 1823 when Fernando VII executed him and took back power (to the relief of many European monarchs), new controversial works and re-editions of French works proliferated. For example, Carey reprinted *Social Contract* in 1821 and 1822; though supposedly drawn from a new translation by José Collado, Jefferson Rea Spell suspects that it was really Marchena's with a few corrections.[110] Marchena also translated and had published the fourteenth-century work by the Aragonese inquisitor, Nicolau Eymeric—*Manual de inquisidores*. This handbook, which came out in editions in 1819 (Montpellier and Avignon), in 1821 (Montpellier), and in 1822 (Madrid), had an explosive effect in Spain and its colonies. From the point of view of an Inquisition insider, it detailed how inquisitors could spot Jews, Moslems, and other heretics who claimed to be Christian; it provided scripts for interrogation; it talked about torture. Lodged in France, Marchena, and José Antonio Llorente whom we will see later who wrote a history of the Inquisition with materials he took with him into exile there, released pent-up hatreds when Spaniards saw in print what they had formerly suspected.[111] Thus, conservatives like Alamán—and later Marcelino Menéndez Pelayo—attributed the break up of the Spanish empire and the "loss of America"[112] to France, whose revolutionary example, coddling of Spanish critics, and press activity sowed discord in areas that, they felt, had previously been content under traditional Catholicism and monarchy.

A parenthesis: "Translation" did not mean then what it suggests today—a faithful and full rendering of the original text in another language. Instead it usually meant that the translator paraphrased the author's ideas and, especially, omitted troublesome passages. Marcelin Defourneaux in his study of the Spanish Inquisition in the eighteenth century tells how Raynal's *Histoire philosophique et politique des établissements et du commerce des Européens dans les deux Indes* (1770), prohibited in Spain because of its criticism of Spanish colonialism, was cleaned up by its Spanish translator so as to be acceptable. Eduardo Malo de Luque, duque de Almodóvar, eliminated the offensive parts and published the book anonymously. Later, in the first decades of the nineteenth century, translators, less concerned with the Inquisition looking over their shoulder and more worried that the books they were translating could deepen the hatreds that wars had produced, self-censored and left out sensitive passages.[113] It is no wonder, then, that Mexicans preferred to read books like *Social Contract* in their original language, and that they kept those books away from Inquisition eyes in private libraries. However, Mexicans were less well prepared to read books in English and so they did require translations of those books.

Lizardi's career offers an example of the mixed press freedom that existed in Mexico in 1822. On February 22, 1822, an ecclesiastical panel excommunicated Lizardi for a pamphlet he wrote that seemed to approve of Masonry. The pamphlet had circulated for a while but then the authorities, reading it again and understanding another message, clamped down. Their ban lasted until December 1823 and severely isolated Lizardi and his wife. During that time priests discouraged print shops from publishing his works and hassled persons buying the output from Lizardi's press. The excommunication of the popular writer raised all sorts of questions for the new nation—most important of which was the Church's continuing intervention in civil matters. Many Mexicans had not forgiven the Church for siding with Spanish administrators and imposing a religious penalty, excommunication, on the insurgent priests, Miguel Hidalgo and José María Morelos, in 1810. Many believed that religious authorities should not intervene in political affairs and that the press should be totally free; others held that civil authorities should license and monitor what people wrote and said; still others thought that it was only the clergy who were responsible for determining morality and civilized custom. Recio befriended Lizardi during his excommunication; Lizardi wrote that Recio was someone who would answer for him and that his bookstore was a drop-place for receiving messages.[114]

Lizardi is a major writer in Mexican, as well as Spanish American, literature. He, together with Mier, Bustamante, and Alamán, represent Mexico's contribution to a distinctive literary corpus that was forming then. Consequently, foreign writers whom Lizardi refers to as a frame for his Mexican story in his novels, pamphlets, and newspapers are a major source for our knowledge of that generation's intellectual roots. By 1825 Lizardi felt comfortable identifying some of these writers. In that year he quoted Thomas Paine in the context of a constitution as a first step toward reform,[115] and identified "Mr. Lebrun" as "a foreign producer of paper."[116] In 1826 he mentioned Roscio and his *Triunfo de la libertad*, and on December 16 wrote, "We take from the newspapers coming from Philadelphia the following posted circular...." Lizardi's list, then, points to materials in Robeson's shipment, and to Mexico's continuing receipt, later in the decade, of printed items from Philadelphia.

Press freedom had been a basic principle of the Spanish constitution, promulgated in Cádiz in 1812.[117] Men there, who have been called liberals, had argued for that enlightened ideal, which would put an end to the Inquisition, an eyesore to the rest of Europe. Increasingly, throughout the eighteenth century, the Inquisition had become a force in league with the state for censoring books and sinful priests, rather than pursuing heretics, idolaters, or blasphemers as in previous centuries. Pragmatically, the Cádiz liberals recognized that a free press (one that allowed their viewpoint, different from the official press) could be a counterweight to Napoleonic despotism, the only means by which that small elite (composed of lawyers, clergy, but importantly, many Cádiz merchants) could communicate with, and urge resistance from, the larger Spanish population; "the people," backward in their religiosity and stubbornly loyal to the Spanish king, were useful to that elite in driving out the French.[118] However, the constitution's compromise language, which was finally arrived at (though it outlawed the Inquisition), still allowed bishops to keep out of the empire any books or writings contrary to Catholicism. It said that writers and printers did not need prior licenses to put their work out, but that they were still subject to having it censored afterward according to a criterion of religious orthodoxy. Juridically, the constitution attempted to return to the thirteenth-century legal code, the *Partidas*, when the bishops and the people supposedly coexisted happily, without interference by the Church bureaucracy, which the king had appointed (the Cortes were attempting to institute reforms by reducing the power of the king and bulking up their own parliamentary role).[119] Later, in 1820, a commission to review the constitution separated freedom of the press from freedom of speech and, although it preserved the former, recommended restrictions on speech and association. Secret societies had formed by then whose orality was seen to be seditious; and speech, which at first had been thought of as enlightening the common people, now was understood to be dangerous. Such speech aimed at commoners was said to be unnecessary since it would produce a nation of philosophers rather than workers.[120] That Spanish legislators were beginning to qualify freedom of expression by 1820 shows some experience with the effects of the constitution in the Peninsula and throughout the empire; and this appreciation of distinctions between print and speech would have extended to Mexico, by then well on its way to independence.

However, even in their debates in the Cortes in 1810–1812, liberals were cautious about both press freedom and free trade. Many of the city's merchants, reading of Adam Smith's "invisible hand" regulating supply and demand, were convinced by that market theory, supposed to establish a healthy competitive equilibrium.[121] Theoretically, elimination of controls sounded attractive, proving that the country was leaving behind its restrictive past and becoming more like Enlightenment Europe. On the other hand, they recognized that trade freedoms would hurt their business, which had always been protected by monopolies and tariffs. Throughout most of the eighteenth century Cádiz had been the designated port for sending and receiving goods to and from the American colonies; the convoy ships docked there and foreign merchants clustered there in trading houses with their warehouses and banks. If other

Spanish ports were permitted to compete with Cádiz (as they were campaigning for), and American ports were free to deal directly with other nations, with other cities in Spain, and with one another, Cádiz would lose revenue. Cádiz businessmen especially wanted protections from British encroachment. They took under advisement the cautions of Veracruz consuls that Spanish trade had to be protected from foreigners.

In the first decade of the nineteenth century Mexico was beginning its own trade with Havana, Jamaica, and the United States. For example, in 1810 goods in the amount of 20,000 pesos were sent from Veracruz to Philadelphia.[122] Earlier, Mexican silver had gone through Philadelphia illegally, bypassing Spanish minting and banking fees on its way to Paris.[123] In addition to Spain's official ports in Mexico, Veracruz on the Gulf and Acapulco on the Pacific, others were opening up legally and illegally in that first decade. Tampico and the Yucatán were increasingly doing business and the Spanish consul in Veracruz reported that as early as 1813 Alvarado was robbing it of tariffs.[124] Thus, liberals in both Spain and Mexico went back and forth in their thinking about freedom—whether as competitive trade or as the play of the press. Mier was one of the most vocal critics of the Cortes' language of free trade, seeing it as illusory, an unequal pact by which elitist commercial interests in Cádiz only pretended to recognize the American colonies, and made up their losses by imposing heavy taxes on American shipping, thus forcing Americans into contraband activity.[125] Yet, regarding freedoms of speech, association, and the press, Mier argued that, although silence might be preferable to noise, it was the product of conformity to tyranny and that, in a country settling on its future, loud dispute was preferable.[126]

Economics, understood at that time as political economy, was the context for much modernizing thought. Men like Foronda, who had translated Bielfeld's *Institutions Politiques*[127] and whose travels outside Spain had familiarized him with other countries' developments, and Jovellanos, who had participated in the reformist government of Manuel de Godoy and whose essays had proposed solutions to some of Spain's problems such as underused lands, made it seem as though more government control was the solution; schemes to colonize remote areas, policing, campaigns to improve public hygiene—all seemed to be ways in which central administration could improve the empire. Yet businessmen led a powerful faction that was beginning to think the opposite, that fewer government controls advantaged society (or at least their interests). Businessmen were the new travelers, experiencing new social arrangements. They were learning firsthand that the decline of Spain's naval power meant that the old monopolies they had depended on no longer existed; their kinsmen in far-flung offices of trading companies provided reassurances that trade exchanges were lucrative and expansion was necessary despite risks that they themselves would have to assume. They were the new moralists in advocating the self's search for earthly happiness and desire for profit, thus replacing the lessons of abnegation and charity that the Church had taught.

Within the context of this free-trade debate, then, liberals ("liberal," usually used to characterize the Cádiz constitutionalists, is perhaps too all-encompassing, and therefore misleading, a term) were divided as to whether public discourse should be controlled. The Crown itself, at various moments in the eighteenth and early nineteenth centuries, had encouraged the press, protecting it through generous licenses. It viewed the press as an educational instrument, necessary to the enlightening and civilizing mission of a modern state and potentially contributory to a modern work force. Especially after the Jesuits were expelled from Spain and the empire in 1767, education began to be thought of more democratically. Prime minister under Carlos III, the Count of Campomanes was responsible for founding Economic Societies of Friends of the Country (Sociedades Económicas de Amigos del País) throughout Spain's territories. In these gatherings (between 1770 and 1820 some 70 were created on the Iberian Peninsula), men discussed new domestic and foreign books.[128] French and English translations were allowed; the Bible was read in its vernacular form; scientific advancements were reported in new newspapers. Campomanes's own essays, "Discurso sobre el fomento de la industria popular" (Discourse on the Development of Popular Industry, 1774, of which 30,000 copies were sold) and "Discurso sobre la educación popular de los artesanos" (Discourse on the Popular Education of Artisans, 1775, 4,000 copies) posited an even larger role for the press. His essays opened up economic issues, which previously had been restricted to official eyes, not only to guild members and government inspectors of prices and goods for whom he was writing, but to other readers, too—among them, lesser nobles who had stayed away from vile money-making and who might now be made to be productive if business was seen to be a decent occupation. Directing attention to the training of workers, the essays implied that more books on political economy, and more technical books on arithmetic and drawing for master craftsmen and their apprentices, would be appearing. "Education," then, was not basic literacy as Campomanes said most Spanish workers knew how to read and write, but encouragement of the labor force to greater productivity.[129]

However, by 1811, when the Cortes de Cádiz wrote "press freedom" into their constitution and thus took responsibility for public opinion and public morality, Spain was at war. Fighting the French in the Iberian Peninsula and rebels in the American colonies, the Spanish leaders who filled in for the absent Fernando in quasi-governments were faced with uncertainty. If they could not agree among themselves whether to affirm the older monarchism or side with José Bonaparte, who seemed to be introducing the reforms liberals wanted, how could they let the country sink into what seemed to be a disordered free-for-all, or assume the role of the hated Inquisition and dictate belief? The Mexican viceroy exemplifies this confusion. When news of the constitution's "press freedom" reached him, he did not implement the decree immediately. When he did, he realized after only two months that he had set off an explosion of contradictions and he revoked the freedom. During those two months, the *Diario de México* printed the text of the Spanish constitution, thus publicizing freedom of the press and abolition of the Inquisition. The paper printed Spanish translations of the U.S. Constitution, the Bill of Rights, and—from Argentina, the "Manifiesto del govierno de Buenos Aires."[130] New newspapers appeared; Lizardi began publishing then his *El Pensador Mexicano* and Bustamante his *El Juguetillo*. The viceroy's curious solution after those two months was to end freedoms for the domestic press but to continue to permit entry into Mexico of foreign-produced news.

Indeed the viceroy, Francisco Xavier Venegas, had much to worry about. Immediately after the insurgency had begun in 1810, rebels started their own presses in the countryside (called *tierradentro*, the hinterland). Just as in Cádiz where liberals used press freedom as a tactic to publish alternative newspapers and win supporters, the Mexican rebels used their presses to publicize their criticism and agenda. If they could not rouse the illiterate peasantry, they could communicate their complaints of "bad government" to an educated elite in remote agricultural and mining regions, and transmit news of uprisings throughout Mexico and in other parts of Spanish America. That readership, often connected to Peninsular families, played an important pivotal role in swinging the war toward remaining loyal and staying in the empire or declaring independence. Late in the fighting, Lizardi was editor of Iturbide's press, a portable operation that traveled with that army in the provinces.

Mexican newspapers and documents issued during the final months of 1810 show other threats to the viceroy's authority; official pronouncements but also the reporting press that traded news items with the rebel presses show that the viceregal government was unsure of its control.[131] On September 15 Miguel Hidalgo rallied his Indian parishioners to revolt against the government, invoking the Virgen de Guadalupe, who was believed to have appeared on Mexican soil and who had become a symbol of national pride. To counter Hidalgo's call Venegas summoned the help of the Spanish Virgen de los Remedios, making her a general in the Royalist army.[132] Thus Hidalgo and Venegas confused the spiritual and the profane in pitting the two Virgenes against one another. As we have seen, Venegas had persuaded the archbishop to excommunicate the priest on the charge of apostasy.[133] In return, Hidalgo issued a manifesto on December 15 in which he challenged the logic of the penalty.[134] Why had the Inquisition, "a tribunal so respectable and whose institute is the most holy been dragged by love of civil society to prostitute its honor and reputation" in such a manner?[135] How could the Inquisition charge him with following "the perverse dogmas of Luther" and denying the authenticity of Scripture, since "if Luther deduced his errors from the books that he believed were inspired by God, how could he who denied this inspiration sustain his own dogmas, deduced from the same books that he thought to be fables"?[136] Among the many new and troubling questions, then, that Hidalgo's queries introduced, were the difference between religious transgression and civil disobedience—and suspicions that an individual might test his reasoning capacity against an authoritative text as he read for himself. Literate peoples increasingly were concerned with their liability before the Inquisition as they dared to read sacred literature that previously had been forbidden to them as well as new secular books. Thus books and new techniques of reading played an important part in Hidalgo's crime. Apostasy, likened to Protestantism with its unauthorized reading, was apparently the most awful example of disobedience Venegas and ecclesiastical authorities could come up with to accuse the priest.

Venegas would also have been threatened by the Mexican *junta*, or rump government, that had formed, understanding that it had deposed the previous viceroy and therefore had the potential to challenge him.[137] He would have been worried by news of insurrection in Venezuela,[138] and by reports of Napoleon's effort to subvert Spanish control in the Americas.[139] He would have been confused, seeing that some of the anti-Napoleonic literature, published in Cádiz and reprinted in Mexico, was being drawn from English sources[140]—a power that he had previously feared but now had to believe was the Spanish king's ally in driving Napoleon out of Spain.

Although news of independence wars in South America mainly came on to Mexico via Cádiz, recently founded newspapers in those other colonies were finding their own inter-American routes into Mexico. Those papers established their own anti-colonial rationale for freedom of the press, different from that of the Cádiz merchants. We have seen already the *Aurora de Chile*, published there in 1812–1813 by three U.S. printers.[141] Its name suggests its inspiration in the successful republican paper of the same name, begun in Philadelphia by Benjamin Franklin Bache and continued under William J. Duane. In a long article, dated 17 September 1812, the *Aurora* printed the report of Hidalgo's death, which, the paper said, had come in from San Blas on Mexico's west coast; if traffic went out of Mexico to Chile via this route, it is to be supposed that news also came in this way.[142] The *Aurora* pointed out to its readers that freedom of the press was a corrective to years of colonialism in which colonials had been taught to be silent; the press was the means by which they would learn political lessons and graduate to an appreciation of their natural rights as free men. Thus "freedom of the press" in the Americas was a different construct from its European version. Indeed, Mier in the *Memoria político-instructiva*, which he wrote for fellow Mexicans in 1821, warned that England's so-called "freedom of speech and the press" was only concerned with libel and that he had had to anglicize the history of Mexico's revolution, which he wrote there in 1813; "to anglicize" meant that he had to suppress some facts and hide his authorship behind a pseudonym (1987, 50).

Under Spanish rule until 1821 Mexico relied mostly on Cádiz newspapers and pamphlets for its political and military news from Europe. Spanish resistance had retreated to that southern port after Napoleon invaded Spain in 1808, and a junta (an assembly that claimed to be a governing regency) had established itself there after having first gone to Aranjuez, then to Sevilla. Finally the junta ended up in León and Cádiz—both on an island in the bay of Cádiz.[143] There fifty-six newspapers were published between 1810 and 1814,[144] and access to sea routes facilitated distribution in Europe and Spanish America. Stereotype printing had been introduced into Spain in 1801 when the Spanish Academy convinced the king to send a representative to Paris to study the operation and bring it home. The new technology was used in 1804 in Madrid to publish a Spanish classic, designed to flatter the monarchy's history.[145] Yet it would be a while before that innovation reached Cádiz so as to permit, in greater and cheaper print runs, the publishing of materials that criticized the monarchy.

Up until 1810 when the Cortes opened, the only newspaper in Cádiz was a mercantile sheet announcing ship comings and goings. Manuel de Godoy, the prime minister, had imposed censorship on Spanish printers in the early years of the century, thereby frustrating new endeavors. However, after 1808 when the French invaded, periphery printers realized their opportunity and at once began to publish newspapers and pamphlets devoted to the war and politics.[146] One paper from the south, which went beyond reporting news to consider questions of social organization in extended essays, exemplifies that coverage: *El Robespierre Español, Amigo de las leyes; o Questiones atrevidas sobre la España* was published in León from March 1811, until some time in 1812.[147] The paper considered issues such as whether a country's monarchy could exist without a noble class, whether it was right to confiscate the goods of that class and the clergy, and whether the people (who essentially were Spain's protectors in the Peninsular War) did not now deserve to be rewarded by the Crown through some conferral of privilege just as the nobility had been in the late Middle Ages and throughout the sixteenth, seventeenth, and eighteenth centuries when Spain extended its empire in the Americas, Europe, and the Mediterranean. Proof that *El Robespierre Español* was influential and reached Mexico is a Mexican 1815 Inquisition decree, prohibiting its circulation and ordering collection of any copies.[148] A rejoinder to one of its numbers, printed in Cádiz, is to be found in the Sutro Library, also attesting to its arrival in Mexico and to its ability to stir debate.[149] Another of the editor's journals, published in London between 1824–1825, *El Español Constitucional*, though archived in few places, is held in Mexico City—also confirming Mexican reception.[150]

When Cádiz was liberated from the French and the Cortes convened there, its presses exploded with the output of writers whose liberalism, as we have seen, was a mixture of elite commercial interests and authentic desire for reform. Yet it must be stressed that not all the Cádiz writers were liberals. Some were Catholic apologists who feared change. Some were earnest respondents to the unsettling new ideas; others rehearsed old grievances. For example, in 1811, "J.A.C." answered his friend's "Disertación histórico-político-legal que trata de la sucesión a la corona de España,"[151] saying that when the last Hapsburg king died in 1700 and Spain's government was replaced by a Bourbon line, old Spanish practices ended as French and Italian advisers arrived. Their new legal codes and secret accords were drawing Spain into unwanted European alliances and ruining an empire that the Hapsburgs had happily administered. The juntas that were formed throughout the empire in 1808, each claiming regency, also produced confusion among the Cortes's delegates. What set of laws should they base constitutional reforms on? Highlighted in this 1811 pamphlet are two concerns, important to the development of a writing society: (1) whether oral and manuscript precedents could be taken into account, alongside printed materials, as a basis for consensus and (2) how a new genre, the political pamphlet, should be treated. In the pamphlet the still-respectful discourse of conversation was progressively sharpening as the pamphlet writer recognized the satiric and comic tone of fellow observers at the Cortes. The pamphlet, in its personal address, shows itself to be evolving from the private letter into a statement launched impersonally to an unknown readership. "J.A.C." says that he is responding both to his friend's printed pamphlet and to its manuscript's marginal notes. When he then, however, confesses that he does not know the author at all, we understand that the fiction of "a friend" is a holdover from previous modes of oral exchange, an uncertain rhetorical strategy that politics was newly forced into so as to engage an opponent.

Throughout 1813 the Mexican presses anxiously followed Cortes debate because their freedoms hung on the constitution.[152] Delegates to the Cortes defended their work in articles that quickly reached Mexico and were reprinted.[153] Three conservative writers were Francisco Alvarado who used the pseudonym "The Rancid Philosopher" (El filósofo rancio); Pedro Cevallos, Godoy's prime minister, whose shifty-sounding pamphlet title "Peculiar Politics of Buonaparte with respect to the Catholic religion; methods that can be used to extinguish it, and subjugate Spaniards by seduction, since he can no longer dominate them by force" demonstrates some of Cevallos's political manipulation of religion after the French had occupied Spain; and José Ignacio Gómez who counseled confessing the Catholic faith and denouncing sins against it. These conservatives worried that French thought and domestic liberalism meant the end of Catholic faith; their views were widely reprinted in Mexico in 1812–1814, and throughout the 1820s.[154] Such was the flow from Cádiz into Mexico that in 1812 a Mexico City printer reprinted a satire, "Diarrea de las imprentas."[155]

Presses in other Spanish ports besides Cádiz (La Coruña, San Sebastián, Palma de Mallorca, and the Canaries) sent materials to Mexico. So did Bordeaux and London.[156] The Caribbean was a launching site for military plots against the Venezuelan mainland, as well as for print assaults on Spanish rule, which traveled throughout Spanish America. Simón Bolívar published important manifestoes from Cartagena (1812), Jamaica (1815), and Angostura (1819). The Spanish translation of "The Rights of Man and the Citizen" came out of the Caribbean.[157] In 1821 Roscio had published in Maracaibo his "Political-religious Catechism Opposing the Royal Catechism of Fernando VII."[158]

On April 19, 1810, Roscio wrote from Caracas to Andrés Bello, a fellow Venezuelan on his way to London:

> Bring, although it may only be a compendium, [a copy] of the present English legislation, and some grammar and English–Spanish dictionary; also any other small, important books. Remember that London was the place where Padre Viscardo wrote his *Letters* and where he got hold of the apology for Rousseau's *Social Contract*.[159]

Roscio's request underscores the importance of person-to-person transmission of books; it shows the close ties that South Americans were developing with England (contrasting with antipathies toward England that lingered in the United States as a result of recent wars and sympathies for Ireland, which Irish immigrants to the United States had promoted). It also illustrates London's influence on Spanish America in sending printed materials there, in English and in Spanish. An important newspaper, *El Español*, was edited in London between 1810 and 1814 by the émigré Spaniard, José María Blanco White; the paper circulated widely in Spanish America and both Roscio and Mier acknowledged its influence on their thought.[160] In Caracas in 1811, the British-owned *Gaceta de Caracas* reprinted the essay "Freedom of Religion" (Libertad de cultos) by "William Burke," a friend of Miranda's in London who is sometimes thought to have been James Mill.[161] This argument for religious tolerance caused an uproar among Catholic readers there, who viewed such a principle as anathema. However, Roscio defended Burke in a follow-up essay "The Catholics of Ireland" (Los católicos de Irlanda). Catholic Ireland, where that faith was persecuted in a Protestant empire, may have made Spanish Americans think twice about mandating one religion and constitutionally outlawing other forms of belief.[162]

By 1822, private presses in Mexico City had begun to lure Mexicans away from reliance on Cádiz output and Mexico's official gazette. Despite conservatives' wish that a Church-controlled panel still rule on what could be said publicly, or published, post-independence political and business interests, which were no longer uniform, paid printers to publish their diverse views. Divisions often took the form of hostile personal attacks, thus giving ammunition to the conservatives that the partisanship the war had produced was worsening. Passions, which religion had been thought to control, were seen as being inflamed by press freedoms. "Low scribblers" (bajos escritores) were reprimanded for their grubby issues. In 1820 the printer Alejandro Valdés published an explanation of why, despite the Spanish constitution's ruling on a free press,[163] he had refrained from printing a certain paper.[164] Although Mexicans in their first constitution in 1824 ended up by proclaiming Catholicism to be the country's official religion, many writers in the years leading up to this decision openly expressed heterodoxy. They wished to detach from Spain's dogmatism and end the Inquisition, to modernize by instituting secular social institutions, to compromise pragmatically with non-Catholic countries in trade and treaties, and to tolerate alternative beliefs such as Masonry (if not Protestantism and agnosticism).

THE PHILADELPHIA/MEXICO TRADE: A SUMMARY

Robeson's letters help to throw light on this brief period after independence when Mexico initially opened up to outside influences. The fact that the U.S. book agent was able to enter the country at all, the evidence he provides of Mexican backers and buyers, his revelation that Recio bought openly from foreigners who brought him books and was ready to begin a long-term relationship with the Philadelphia booksellers, his request that Carey send him type and presses for sale to domestic presses—all provides proof of Mexico's move toward establishing there the freedoms that enlightened governments elsewhere enjoyed. Mexicans' interest in developing a domestic print industry reveals not only some printers' realization that money could be made by producing for that market but also a larger understanding that their product was necessary for the ruling class's political education in modernity and compromise. Mexicans' awareness of constitutional models, not only from the United States but also from Colombia, Buenos Aires, Peru, and Chile, shows an eagerness to engage with other nations. The hemispheric consciousness that both the United States and Mexico evinced then relates to Simón Bolívar's dream of a union extending from North America through the Isthmus of Panama to South America.

My guess as to what impelled Carey to undertake the Mexican venture has less to do with Masonry and more to do with the opinions of the original owner of the firm. Of all the factors behind the business, I believe Mathew Carey's personal philosophy—the result of being an Irish immigrant and enthusiastic patriot in his adopted nation, an active Catholic, businessman, and cultural arbiter in the United States as a purveyor of books—was the most important in conceiving of the expedition to Mexico, and then in choosing the merchandise for the shipment. Although by 1822 he was no longer head of the company that bore his name (after 1817 he seldom came to the shop), he remained a vigorous voice in community and national affairs; and it is to be supposed that his beliefs affected the company's choice of what works to print and sell. In 1821 the company published second editions of two of Roscio's Spanish-language works.

Carey, as we learned, had left Ireland because the first pamphlet he wrote there, "The Urgent Necessity of an Immediate Repeal of the Whole Penal Code," offended both the English Protestants who governed and Irish Catholics who wished for peaceful reform. He was further radicalized in France. In 1818 he began to gather materials in preparation for writing a history of Ireland. Carey's experience with religious tensions in Ireland, his Catholicism unburdened of the Church's past and clericalism and instead free to exercise liberties of conscience in the religiously tolerant United States, made him appreciate the special needs of Mexican Catholics. He must have understood that Roscio's reexamination of the language of Biblical texts, his definition of a religious population's psychological profile, would be especially useful to Catholic readers. While Paine and Rousseau complained of religion's historical support of monarchy and the desirability of the separation of church and state, Roscio was far less certain about what a new state should look like. In its reflections on decolonization his book was politically unprogramed.

Carey's faith, but also his ideas about economic life, inspired his own employ of the printed word. He used his business to promote the social and moral causes in which he believed, apparently feeling that print connected him, not to strangers, but to fellow minds. James N. Green has written of him:

> Throughout his life, when faced with a special problem or injustice, Mathew Carey's immediate reaction was to appeal to the public—by writing a letter to an editor, by publishing a pamphlet, by calling a public meeting, by forming a society. In 1792, moved by the wretchedness of many recent immigrants,

> he called a meeting of influential Irishmen at a coffee house and got them to incorporate as the Hibernian Society for the Relief of Emigrants from Ireland with a constitution he had prepared in advance. In the same way he formed a Sunday School Society in 1796—one of the first in the country—which he served as an officer for decades.... [F]rom 1819 until 1835 Carey published a pamphlet or wrote a letter to an editor about once a week. (1985, 29–30)

In the 35 years or so between Carey's arrival in the United States and the start of his Mexican book business, Carey's youthful revolutionary spirit apparently abated. After independence, the new nation was facing other problems; and economic concerns dominated his public addresses and essays. Although the national climate was different, he still believed that print could elevate a people, that discussion of common topics across a society's subgroups could unite those groups and resolve larger problems. Several Carey "addresses" to various constituencies illustrate this personal optimism. For example, in 1801 he wrote to printers and booksellers throughout the United States: "The patriotic spirit of fostering domestic arts"; in 1819 he addressed several missives to the Philadelphia Society for the Promotion of National Industry; in 1822 he addressed the citizens of the United States on the tendency of our system of intercourse with foreign nations; in 1829 he addressed the liberal and humane, "A few observations on the state of charitable institutions of this city"; in 1831 he addressed the wealthy of the land, ladies as well as gentlemen, "On the character, conduct, situation, and prospects of those whose sole dependence for subsistence is on the labour of their hands." Nevertheless, he confided to his diary on December 15, 1822, that he detected a public spirit "in which prevail the most sluggish apathy and the most sordid meanness."[165] In 1824 he wrote that he was withdrawing from discussion of the tariff question, because he was receiving no support from the persons protections would benefit, and would henceforth devote his leisure hours to literary pursuits.[166]

Rather than attacks on a European despot and incitements to violence, U.S. society—and Mexico's at that post-independence moment—needed public discourse that addressed political and economic concerns, literature that encouraged peace and conciliation yet, at the same time, disrupted unthinking reading habits. Both needed reflections on their respective colonial histories and where republicanism—an untried form of government—might take them. The titles in the cargo to Mexico, touching on a range of political and legal topics but also containing books of language study that would enable communication among countries in the Americas, represent the effort by one nation to assess another nation's needs and desires in an effort to send appropriate reading material. The book trade between the two American societies reveals the faith that both postcolonial worlds shared in the possibility that books might ameliorate conditions and show the way toward a better future.

NOTES

1. "Respuesta a las imposturas de un folletista español. O sea Tapaboca al Libelista autor del anónimo publicado en Filadelfia intitulado: Manifiesto a los hombres de la injusticia que llama justicia el Dr. Manuel de la Bárcena. Carta a un amigo". P.F.S. (México: Imprenta de Doña Herculana del Villar y Socios, 24 pp.). Bárcena, archdeacon of the catedral of Valladolid de Michoacán (Morelia), had just published a pamphlet in favor of the independence of New Spain, "Manifiesto al mundo la justicia y la necesidad de la independencia de la Nueva España" (Puebla y México: Oficina de D. Mariano Ontiveros, 1821). Thus the pamphlet by P.F.S., though supposedly based on Philadelphia politics, is directed at politics in Mexico City.

2. José Isidro Irana y Torre (really Inana y Torre) was a pseudonym for Antonio José Ramón de Irisarri. The "letter" in question is probably Irisarri's "Carta de un americano a un diputado de las Cortes Extraodinarias de España" (Londres: Imprenta de Nichols, 1821). We have seen Irisarri's letter already in connection with the London Barry's loan to this Guatemalan revolutionary.

3. This pamphlet does not appear in U.S. print lists of the period.

4. "Letter written to an American regarding the form of government it is advisable to establish in New Spain, given its current condition, that may make practicable the constitution and its laws" (Imprenta de Baroja, 16 pp.). Juan Antonio Llorente was probably the author, writing from Paris. See my article, "Llorente's Readers in the Americas."

5. See L. Jackson for a discussion of letters as important to a growing economy in the United States.

6. "Lantern for the Mexican Empire or Political Miscellany Extracted and Edited from the Best Sources, by the Author of the Social Pact for the Intelligence of This Work" (México: Nueva Imprenta de L.L.H.H. Moran, 2 vols.). For a description of *El Fanal* see Spell, *Rousseau in the Spanish World* (250–251). Spell says that Maldonado used the 1820 Madrid edition printed by Repullés.

7. "The Rights of National Sovereignty Against Despotism and Hipocrisy" (Palma: Imprenta Real, 1810, 3 & 28 pp.). Quoted in García Malo (27–28).

8. See Grases's edition of *Derechos del hombre y del ciudadano*.

9. "The Rights of Man." Edited by Foot and Kramnick, 322.

10. "Nos los Inquisidores Apóstolicos, contra la Herética pravedad, y Apostasía, en la Ciudad de México, Estados, y provincias de esta Nueva-España, Guatemala, Nicaragua, Islas Philipinas, y su Distrito, & . . . Sabed: que con asombro, y grave dolor de nuestro corazón, hemos leído y examinado . . . un libro en octavo, intitulado: Desengaño del hombre, impreso en Filadelfia en este presente año, su autor d. Santiago Felipe Puglia" (México: Herederos de Don Felipe de Zúñiga y Ontiveros, 1794). I consulted a film copy of the

original in the Medina collection (Santiago de Chile) at the John Carter Brown Library.

11. See, for example, Wheaton.

12. His case is documented in *Los precursores ideológicos de la Guerra de Independencia (La masonería en México, Siglo XVIII)*.

13. Miliani, xxxvi–xxxix.

14. See Calvillo's introduction to Mier's *Cartas de un Americano*, 32, 45–46.

15. *Rights of Man/Common Sense*, intro. Foot (57).

16. For a Spanish-language study of Roscio, see Ugalde.

17. "Homily of Cardinal Chiaramonte, Bishop of Imola, Today His Holy Father Pius VII, Directed to the People of His Diocesis in the Cisalpine Republic, Christmas, 1797. Translated from the French to Spanish by a Citizen of Venezuela in South America, who publishes it refuting a paper of the same Pope in behalf of Frenando VII, against the insurgents of the so-called American colonies" (Filadelfia: J. F. Hurtel).

18. Printed by Alejandro Valdés.

19. Picornell organized an incursion against Spanish rule in Venezuela, but his worst crime was translating the French Declaration of the Rights of Man, with his commentary, and having it published in Caracas in 1811 (from which it was reprinted throughout northern South America despite its prohibition). Picornell twice sought refuge in Philadelphia—in 1805 and 1812.

20. "Happy the shores of the Delaware where [these scenes] are not enacted."

21. Fischer describes a Quaker Robeson family settling in Burlington, West Jersey (1989, 463). Thomas Robeson was not a Philadelphian since he writes to Carey about Philadelphia as "your city."

22. Pasley describes Carey as essentially refraining from politics in his printing. Pasley contrasts Carey with the political William Duane. However, Carey's willingness to publish the second edition of Roscio's book in 1821, and his choice of books for shipment to Mexico in 1822, suggests a political consciousness forced some of his business decisions.

23. *La literatura perseguida por la Inquisición*; see particularly the chapter, "La sátira popular."

24. The best coverage is by Pérez Marchand. Torres Puga is also excellent.

25. My thinking here borrows from Michel Pêcheux's work as elaborated by Macdonell.

26. See my introduction, "Satire and Decolonization" to Frye's translation, *The Mangy Parrot*.

27. See Guerra, particularly Chapt. 7, "La pedagogía política de la prensa revolucionaria española".

28. Still another source of rhetorical innovation, important in Mexico, was the translation to Spanish of Hugo Blair's *Rhetoric*, done by José Luis Munárriz

and published in Madrid in four-volume editions in 1798 and 1804. See my article "Mexican Readings of Hugh Blair's *Rhetoric*."

29. "Weekend Interview with Mario Vargas Llosa," Emily Parker, *Wall Street Journal*, (June 23–24, 2007).

30. See Rowe.

31. His *Histoire philosophique et politique du commerce et des établissements des Européens dans les Deux-Indes* was published in 1770. The Duque de Almodóvar, Eduardo Malo de Luque, translated it into Spanish in 1784–1790 (Madrid); J. O. Justamond translated it into English in 1798 (London). For a discussion of Raynal, see Benot.

32. *Wealth of Nations* (1776) was quickly translated into French and published in numerous editions. It appeared in Spanish in the following editions: *Compendio de la obra inglesa intitulada Riqueza de las naciones hecho por el Marqués de Condorcet y traducido al Castellano con varias adiciones del original por don Carlos Martínez de Irujo* (Madrid: Imprenta Real, 1792, 302 pp.) (reed.Madrid: Imprenta Real, 1803; Palma: M. Domingo, 1814); *Investigación de la naturaleza y causas de la riqueza de las naciones, obra escrita en inglés por Adam Smith, la traduce al castellano el Lic. D. Josef Alonso Ortiz con varias notas e ilustraciones relativas a España* (Valladolid: Oficina de la Viuda e Hijos de Santander, 1794, reed. 1805–1806, 2ª ed. muy corregida y mejorada, 4 vols.); *La riqueza de las naciones nuevamente explicada con la doctrina de su mismo investigador*, Ramón Lázaro de Dou y de Bassóls (Cervera: Imprenta de la Pont. y Real Universidad, 1817, 2 vols.)

33. His *De las colonias y de la revolución actual de la América* was published in Paris in 1817. For discusión of De Pradt's impact on Spanish America, see Jiménez Codinach; Aguirre Elorriaga. Carey published English translations of De Pradt's works in 1816 and 1820.

34. Carey published Say's *Catechism of Political Economy; or Familiar conversations on the manner in which wealth is produced, distributed and consumed in society* in 1817, 144 pp. Say's *De la Inglaterra y de los ingleses, Por... autor del tratado de economía política. Traducido del francés al castellano por D.P.M.O.* was published by the Imprenta de Collado in 1817 (92 pp.); a copy exists in the Abadiano collection of the Sutro Library.

35. A list of their names is to be found in an 1822 letter to Poinsett from Lorenzo Christie in the Poinsett papers of the HSP. Their appeal to Poinsett was handled through "Judge Austin."

36. "La soberbia de estos republicanos no les permite vernos como iguales sino como inferiores; su envanecimiento se extiende en mi juicio a creer que su Capital lo será de todas las Américas; aman entrañablemente a nuestro dinero, no a nosotros, ni son capaces de entrar en convenio de alianza o comercio sino por su propia conveniencia, desconociendo la recíproca" *La diplomacía mexicana* (103).

37. Torre Villar consulted Schmaltz's report in the National Archives in Paris and reproduces it in his *Juan Schmaltz y su misión en México* (1957). Monroy Castillo calls this Frenchman who passed himself off as a Spaniard "Julián Schmaltz" and says that he was arrested and expelled from Mexico as a spy (269, 326).

38. Reported by Rangel in *Los precursores ideológicos de la Guerra de Independencia, La masonería en México. Siglo XVIII.* Tomo 1, vii.

39. "Compendium of the life and deeds of Joseph Balsamo, called Count Calliostro, that has been taken from the suit launched against him in Rome in 1790 and that can serve as a guide to know about the Freemasonic sect" (Barcelona: Viuda Piferrer, 1790; Sevilla: Imprenta de Vázquez e Hidalgo, 1791).

40. *Reprint of the Minutes of the Grand Lodge of Free and Accepted Masons of Pennsylvania* Vol. 4 (1817–1822). See also Denslow; Huss; Bullock, as excellent as his book is, does not deal with the role of U.S. Masonry in developing Lodges in Spanish America.

41. "Spirit of the statutes and regulations of the Masonic Order, and Dictionary of all the terms and expressions in use, for the work of the Lodges." It appears that Castillo was the translator, not the author.

42. "Path of Masonic Lights."

43. "Monitor, or Very Useful Guide to Freemasons . . . Written in English by a Mason and translated to Spanish," 272 pp.

44. Menéndez y Pelayo (900).

45. Original title: *Freemason's Library and general Ahiman rezon: containing a delineation of the true principles of freemasonry, speculative and operative, religious and moral, compiled from the writings of the most approved authors with notes and occasional remarks* (Baltimore: Benjamin Edes, 1817, xi, 332, 92 pp.). Laurence Dermott's *Ahiman Rezon* was published in London in 1756 by James Bedford. Full title: *Ahiman Rezon: or, A Help to a Brother; Showing the Excellency of Secrecy, And the first Cause or Motive, of the Institution of Free-Masonry; the Principles of the Craft, and the Benefits arising from a strict Observance thereof; What Sort of Men ought to be initiated into the Mystery, And what Sort of Masons are fit to govern Lodges, With their Behaviour in and out of the Lodge. Likewise the Prayers used in the Jewish and Christian Lodges. The Ancient Manner of Constituting new Lodges, with all the Charges, &. Also the Old and New Regulations. The Manner of Chusing and Installing Grand-Master and Officers, and other useful Particulars too numerous here to mention. To which is added, The greatest Collection of Masons Songs ever presented to public View, with many entertaining Prologues and Epilogues; Together with Solomon's Temple an Oratorio, As it was performed for the Benefit of Free-Masons.* I have consulted the French/English edition prepared by Georges Lamoine (Toulouse: SNES, 1997).

46. This engraving was done by Amos Doolittle from Jeremy Cross's *The True Masonic Chart* (no publisher). For comparison, the engraving from the English-language version is available in Bullock (1996, 248). I owe thanks to Glenys Waldman from Philadelhia's Grand Lodge library for this complete citation.

47. For a full discussion, see my article "Spanish-Language Masonic Books Printed in the Early U.S."

48. For background see Mateos; Stanley C. Green; Zalce y Rodríguez; Solís Vicarte; Rojas (Chapter 3), also the proceedings of symposia on Spanish and American Masonry issued almost yearly, edited by J.A. Ferrer Benimeli. For a critical view, see Cuevas.

49. "The entire world is only a large republic where each nation is a family and each individual a child."

50. See Volney (1821/1934, 11–12).

51. "The fatherland ... is the community of citizens who, joined by fraternal sentiments and reciprocal needs make of their respective strengths a common strength" (159–160).

52. *Catéchisme* is fascinating for many reasons, one of which is Volney's consideration of women's supposed inferior nature is an explanation of why continence is more of a virtue for them than for men (129–130).

53. "Discurso Masónico en que se da una idea sucinta del origen, progresos y estado actual de la masonería en Europa" (no author, Cádiz: Betancourt, 1822, 8 pp.). "Masonic Discourse in which one finds a succint idea of the origin, progress, and up-to-date status of Masonry in Europe." This "Discurso" was reprinted in Mexico in 1822 by the Oficina de Betancourt.

54. "Examen crítico de las causas de la persecución que han experimentado los francmasones, y explicación de las Bulas de los Sumos Pontífices Clemente XII, y Benedicto XIV" (no author, México: Reimpreso en la Oficina de D.J.M.B. y Socios, 34 pp.) "Critical Examination of the Causes for the Persecution that Masons have Suffered, and an Explanation of the Bulls of the Holy Fathers Clement XII and Benedicto XIV."

55. "Ilustración sobre la sociedad de los Fracmasones ... El Argos investigador, y defensor acérrimo del principio fundamental de la Constitución de la Monarquía Española, que es la religión de Jesucristo, cuya base es lo moral ... " (México: Reimpreso en la oficina de D. Mariano Ontiveros, 81 pp.). "Clarification on the Society of Masons ... The Investigating Argos, and staunch defender of the fundamental principle of the Constitution of the Spanish Monarchy, that is the religion of Jesus Christ whose basis is morality."

56. M.S. (unidentified), "Defensa de los llamados francmasones. Pasquín que amaneció en las paredes de la Catedral el día 30 de enero de este año, glosado por una Señora patriota en breves momentos y con un numen natural"

(México: Imprenta de D.J. M. Benavente y Socios, 2 pp.). "Defense of so-called Freemasons. Broadside that appeared at dawn on the walls of the Cathedral the 30th of January of this year, glossed by a patriotic woman in a few moments and with natural ability."

57. Benson, "The Plan of Casa Mata" (45–56).

58. "Letter to Dr. Priestly [sic], printed in the *Anti-Jacobin Review* (March, April, 1799), reprinted in the 1835 edition of *Ruins* (215).

59. Philadelphia records for March 1, 1824, indicate "A petition was received and read from a Number of Ancient York Master Masons, praying for a Warrant to hold a Lodge in Alvarado in the Republic of Mexico, to be called 'Hermanos legitomor [sic] de la luz del Papaloapan', and that Brother Francisco de Paula López, might be the first Master, Brother José María Guisosota, the first Senior Warden, and Brother José Lucas de Aguibra, the first Junior Warden of the same. Which Petition being in due form and recommended agreeably to the Rules and Regulations of the Grand Lodge it was on motion made and Seconded." (Vol. 5 [1822–1827], 231).

60. McClenachan, Vol. 3, 328ff.

61. "Desaguiliers." "Fisher" was not his real name; the Hungarian immigrant took the name when he arrived in the United States. For further information, see *Freemasonry in Pennsylvania; 1727–1907*; *Proceedings of the Grand Lodge of Texas*. On Fisher see Parmenter, Fisher and Mallette; Morton; Reséndez.

62. For a similar view of Masonry in Europe, see Jacob's *Living the Enlightenment*.

63. "asilo de los oprimidos, centro de las luces, baluarte de la libertad."

64. "Todos los hombres han nacido iguales. Dios les ha concedido derechos imprescriptibles inagenables, y éstos son: el derecho de vida, el derecho de libertad, y el derecho de promover su felicidad".

65. "El espíritu mercantil es enemigo de privilegios, de monopolios, de compañías reales y de realismo. El comercio es el compañero inseparable de la libertad y de la riqueza nacional; sólo puede existir bajo los auspicios de los gobiernos liberales, como lo comprueba la historia mercantil de la Holanda, de las ciudades Anseáticas, de los Estados-Unidos, de la Inglaterra, y de las repúblicas de Genova y Venecia".

66. "Manual of Parliamentary Practic for the Use of the Senate of the U.S." (New York: Henrique Newton, 177 pp.).

67. Rich, Lara, "Mystery."

68. *Freemasonry in Pennsylvania*, Vol. 3, 209. Bullock cites this same source to maintain that Carey was not a Mason due to the fact that he is called "Mr." rather than "Brother" (375).

69. The HSP owns their letterbook for this period; it also owns the Paul family papers, which tell that the family had properties in Philadelphia and

Belvidere, NJ. We have seen that Abraham Paul, printer in New York published Rocafuerte's *Ensayo politico*, and, by an unknown author, *Cartilla para los gefes y los pueblos en América* in 1823. Jeremiah Paul, described as "author, bookseller, writing master, artist, schoolmaster and storekeeper" in Philadelphia between 1791 and 1819, is listed in Brown and Brown.

70. Archives of du Pont in their Hagley Museum were consulted online (Series A, Box 12). Marjorie McNinch, curator, kindly supplied me with copies of Robeson's letters.

71. *The Papers of Henry Clay* [microform], (National Archives and Records Service, Washington, D.C., 1957), Vol. 4, p. 331 (consulted online).

72. *The American Almanac and Repository of Useful Knowledge for the year . . . : comprising a calendar for the year; astronomical information; miscellaneous directions, hints, and remarks; and statistical and other particulars respecting foreign countries and the United States.* (Boston: Gray and Bowen, 1836), Vol. 7, p. 100 (consulted online).

73. Issues of the *Aurora* from 1815 advertise Paul Co. for chemical supplies and home medicines.

74. Alamán in his *Historia de México* (Vol. 5, 630) tells that Wilkinson gave a full-length portrait of Washington to the then president of Mexico, Guadalupe Victoria, and it was installed in Mexico's Congreso hall.

75. Bustamante tells in his diary on January 5, 1823, that Esteva had just come on to Mexico City from Veracruz.

76. Some insight into its historical record of cosmopolitanism, particularly in the eighteenth century, is the *Catálogo de libros de los siglos XV al XVIII del Archivo y Biblioteca históricos de la ciudad de Veracruz*, ed. Minerva Escamilla Gómez, Gema Lozano y Natal Isabel Múñoz Herranz (Veracruz: Archivo y Biblioteca Históricos de la ciudad de Veracruz, 1991). There are many political and economic continental imprints, but also manuscripts—one assumes collected from the city and environs. For example, there is a translation of the Koran from the Arabic, done by an Englishman in Turkey and printed in Amsterdam and Leipzig in 1775. There are no U.S. imprints.

77. Fisher (357).

78. Leonard and Smith (84–102).

79. In fact, on a visit to Veracruz in 1992, I got my copy of Mateos's *Historia* in a Lodge there.

80. See Medina's *La imprenta en Oaxaca, Guadalajara, Veracruz, Mérida y varios lugares*); also del Palacio Montiel.

81. Indeed *El Mercurio* fulfilled that role in Alvarado.

82. The awkwardness of Follin's writing suggests that he may not have been a native English speaker; syntax suggests he might have been French-speaking.

83. Brack, Chapt. 6, 89–95.

84. Medina in *Historia del Tribunal del Santo Oficio* provides the text of this edict (446–448).

85. For a discussion of the Inquisition in art and literature during the eighteenth and nineteenth centuries, see Peters, particularly Chapts. 6–7. On *Bororquia* see Dufour's edition; on Gutiérrez see Fraser (328–330).

86. Llorente's *Histoire critique de l'Inquisition d'Espagne* was published in Paris. Mier probably brought back to Mexico in 1822 news of Llorente's history, if not also a copy.

87. The 1800 edition was published by Joseph Doblado-Dávilla, and Olavide signed his name "Mariano Céspedes y Monroy." The 1816 edition was published by the Oficina de Dávila, and Olavide signed his name "Atanasio Céspedes y Monroy."

88. The Biblioteca Nacional in Mexico owns a copy of this work, suggesting its importation.

89. *Atala, o Los amores de dos salvajes en el desierto* (Paris: s.e., xxiv–188 pp.).

90. For background, see Lenz.

91. "Biscocheros, Coheteros, Boticarios, Tenderos y otros, para el fin de consumirlos en los usos de sus oficios". An original exists in the Bancroft Library (Berkeley) and an English translation in the Clark Library (UCLA). Susanne Tatin, librarian at the Clark, tells me that the translation was done by Lesley Byrd Simpson in 1961 as a keepsake for the members of the Roxburghe Club.

92. Dauxion de Lavaysse as quoted in Francisco A. Encina, "The Limited Influence of the French Revolution," in Humphreys and Lynch, 106–110.

93. "Secret History of the Court and Cabinet of St. Cloud, distributed in letters written in Paris in 1805 to an English Lord." The New York edition was probably the fourth American edition, printed in 1807 by Brisban and Branna, No., City-Hotel, Broadway.

94. *Historia de México* (Vol. 5, 583–584).

95. Morton (141–146, 150–157). See also Henson.

96. Particularly Chapt. 2.

97. The *Indice de las Gacetas de literatura de México* lists 22 articles in which Franklin is mentioned. One tells of his insistence on experience and observation, and another on his innovations in printing.

98. See Wold; Delgado Carranco.

99. In 1820 the publisher, M. de Zúñiga y Ontiveros, published a 16-page summary of Chapter 4 of Humboldt's *Political Essay*—"Población de N.E. por el baron Humboldt. Censo general hecho en 1793. Progresos de la población en los diez años siguientes. Proporción entre nacidos y muertos".

100. See my *Lizardi and the Birth of the Novel in Spanish America*.

101. "Mañas viejas. Tarde se olvidan" (México: Imprenta e Ontiveros. Se vende en la librería de Recio, portal de Agustinos, letra "B", 4 pp.). (Old habits are not soon forgotten.)

102. This plaza is even important today as a site where literates and illiterates meet, where spoken words are committed to paper and go to the hands of others. Kalman studies the letter-writers who do a good business communicating the thoughts of illiterate Mexicans to friends and relatives.

103. Bustamante (595).

104. See the eight volumes of Medina's *La imprenta en México*, also Ziga y Espinosa.

105. By 1827, a newspaper ad in *El Sol* (February 26) listed 200 items for sale by the bookstore, Seguín y Rubio. Featuring the store's selection of books in French, English, Italian, Greek and Latin, the list includes *Cornelia Bororquia* and Ovid's *Arte de amar*.

106. Benson, *La diputación provincial* (115–117).

107. "Iturbide caza Garzas sin disparar el fusil" (Iturbide hunts Garzas [herons, but in this case the name of a revolutionary general that Iturbide disarmed] without firing a gun.)

108. "en pésimo castellano, todas las obras más perniciosas para la política, la religión y las costumbres" (Vol. 5, 645–646).

109. Charles François Dupuis wrote *Compendio del origen de todos los cultos* (Barcelona: 1820); A.V. Benoit, *La libertad religiosa* (Montpellier: Picot, 1820). On Marchena see McKenna; Menéndez y Pelayo (234–253); Fuentes.

110. *Rousseau in the Spanish World* (207).

111. Llorente's works contributed to debate at the Cortes de Cádiz, which put an end to the Inquisition as part of the 1812 constitution. For background see Menéndez Pelayo. For Mexican attitudes see Medina, *Historia del Tribunal del Santo Oficio*, and my "Mexican Attitudes toward the Inquisition."

112. The phrase is Menéndez y Pelayo's.

113. For example, the Spanish expatriate José Joaquín de Mora, who translated William Davis Robinson's *Memoir of the Mexican Revolution* into Spanish in 1824, said that he omitted material that would induce new hatreds (quoted in Llorens, 162–163).

114. "responderá de los míos". See respectively "El Pensador llama a juicio a sus necios enemigos" (México: Oficina de don José María Ramos Palomera, 1822) and "Desvergüenzas y excomuniones no destruyen las sólidas razones" (Puebla: Imprenta Liberal de Moreno Hermanos, 1822).

115. "Conversaciones del Payo y el Sacristán", *Obras* (Vol. 5, 41–424).

116. "Conversaciones del Payo y el Sacristán", *Obras* (Vol. 5, 443).

117. For the proceedings, see *Actas de las Cortes de Cádiz*; also Solís.

118. See Barragán Barragán. Gómez Imaz corroborates this view of the Cádiz deputies to the Cortes. He quotes the testimony of Antonio Alcalá Galiano, one of the deputies, that the liberal elite did not have the backing of the populace, which was still monarchist in supporting Fernando and only wanted to throw out of Spain the "intruso" king, José Bonaparte. On "popular resistance," see also Fraser.

119. Fontana (96–97).

120. Fontana (144–150).

121. David Throsby, in a review essay in the March 23, 2007, *TLS* (5425, 23), "Hands Off," on Nelson's *Economics for business*, and Foley's *Adam's Fallacy*, helpfully discusses the primacy of this concept in Smith's work. In the Spanish and Mexican worlds, Smith's economic theories appear to have been understood in terms of freedoms from the controls of Spanish monopolies and "self-interest" as a profit motive as "self-love," which confused these traditional societies.

122. Quirós in "Memoria de Instituto. Ideas políticas económicas de gobierno" in *Memorias políticas y económicas* (291).

123. Stein and Stein.

124. Quirós, "Memoria de Instituto" (306–307).

125. See his *Memoria* (97–102). One of Mier's main concerns was the hypocrisy surrounding Spain's lucrative slave trade, which flourished around Cuban waters, despite international agreements prohibiting the contraband.

126. *Memoria* (68ff).

127. Published in Leyden in 1767–1772.

128. See Shafer. For a specific example in Mexico, see the *Memorias* of Quirós.

129. *Discurso sobre la educación popular*, ed. F. Aguilar Piñal (Madrid: Editora Nacional, 1978), 117. On Campomanes, see MacKay.

130. Neal; Wold; Delgado Carranco "Las primeras discusiones en torno a la libertad de imprenta".

131. I have drawn this discussion from the *Catalogue of Mexican Pamphlets in the Sutro Collection*.

132. "México a su Generala María Santísima de los Remedios en la procesion solemne del día 21 de Febrero con que concluyó el novenario de acción de gracias por la prosperidad de las armas del Rey contra los rebeldes" (México: Imp. de Arizpe, 8 pp. in verse).

133. See the pamphlet by Fermín de Reygadas "Discurso contra el fanatismo y la impostura de los rebeldes de Nueva España dedicado a todos los hombres de bien" (México: Imp. en casa de Arizpe, 1811, 35 pp.).

134. "Manifiesto que el Sr. Don Miguel Hidalgo y Costilla, generalissimo de las armas americanas y electo por la mayor parte de los pueblos del reino

para defender sus derechos y los de sus conciudadanos, hace al pueblo, contestando el edicto anterior, 15 de diciembre de 1810", reprinted in *Visiones de la Guerra de Independencia* (49–52).

135. "... un Tribunal tan respetable, y cuyo instituto es el más santo, se dejase arrastrar del amor del paisanaje, hasta prostituir su honor y su reputación".

136. "... los perversos dogmas de Lutero. Si Lucero deduce sus errores de los libros que cree inspirados por Dios, ¿cómo el que niega esta inspiración, sostendrá los suyos, deducidos de los mismos libros que tiene por fabulosos?"

137. Francisco Manuel Sánchez de Tagle and Mariano Elizaga, "El 16 de Septiembre de 1810. Himno cívico para toda orquesta o forte-piano, dedicado a la junta patriótica de México por los ciudadanos... que se publica por acuerdo de la misma junta" (México: Imp. del Aguila, 4 pp.).

138. "Apéndice a las reflexiones histórico-críticas sobre la insurrección de Caracas" (Cádiz: Imp. de Carreño, 42 pp.).

139. "Manifiesto contra las instrucciones comunicadas por el emperador de los franceses a sus emisarios destinados a intentar la subversion de las Américas" (México: Reimp. en casa de Arizpe, 1811, 16 pp.).

140. "El Plutarco de la revolución francesa. Obra traducida del inglés. Tomo I" (México: Reimp. en casa de Arizpe, 1811, 44 págs). "El Plutarco de la revolución francesa. Obra traducida del inglés. Cuadernos primero, segundo y tercero" (México: Reimp. en casa de Arizpe, 1811, 107 pp.). We have seen these titles before, probably by the English writer Lewis Goldsmith ("Stewarton").

141. Samuel Burr Johnston (his name suggests some involvement with Aaron Burr's conspiracy) left New York with William H. Burbridge and Simon Garrison on July 22, 1811. The three were typographers, contracted for by the Swede in Chile, Mateo Arnaldo Hoevel, to travel with a press destined for the independent government there and to work for a year, running it. Burbridge was killed shortly after their arrival at a Fourth of July celebration at the American consulate in Santiago (where Poinsett was consul). The celebration got out of hand and, as he was being escorted out, Burbridge was shot by a guard. It is unclear how much involvement they had with the press. Johnston said he spoke only "broken Spanish"; and in his book about the experience he said nothing about the press but instead spoke as an adventurer and observer of political events. Camilo Henríquez apparently functioned as the editor; and a translator, Samuel B. Benítez from London, was paid to translate the news and dispatches, which the *Aurora* published from foreign papers.

142. In this unsigned article Hidalgo is described as a traitor to his nation, anxious to realize his own gain from revolution. However, the Chilean author

says that his death ironically has made the Mexican revolutionary movement stronger ("The majority of the nation is republican" "La maza de la nación es republicana").

143. This Cádiz body called itself the "Junta Suprema" but others throughout Spain and the Americas (as we have seen) claimed legitimacy, too. Goya painted the Philippine junta.

144. See Gómez Imaz; González Palencia; Riaño de la Iglesia.

145. In the introduction to *Jornada de Carlos V a Tunez por el Doctor Gonzalo de Illescas, edición esterotípica* (Madrid: RAE, 1804), the editors explain stereotyping's arrival in Spain.

146. Solís (319–347).

147. "The Spanish Robespierre, Friend of Law, or Daring Questions about Spain" (reprinted in an edition by Alfredo González Hermoso (Besançon: Annales Littéraires de l'Université de Besançon, 1991).

148. The decree is reprinted in Torres Puga. Suggesting that *El Robespierre Español* arrived in Cuba is an 1821 imprint from "El Sábelotodo" o "El Robespierre habanero," reprinted in Sevilla Soler (136).

149. "Respuesta que por su parte da el Duque de ... al Núm. VI. del Robespierre" by Mariano Téllez-Girón y Beaufort Osuna (Cádiz: Imp. de Niel, hijo, 1811, 80 pp.).

150. The editor was Pedro Pascasio Fernández Sardino.

151. "Carta crítica sobre la Disertación histórico-político-legal que trata de la sucesión a la corona de España" (Cádiz: Oficina de la Viuda de Comes, 32 pp.). "Critical Letter relative to the Historical-Political-Legal Dissertation that Deals with the Succession to the Throne of Spain."

152. For example: by Doctor Antonio José Ruíz de Padrón, "Dictamen del ... que se leyó en la sesión pública de 18 de enero (1813) sobre el tribunal de la Inquisición" , Impreso en Cádiz y reimpreso en México en la Oficina de Jáuregui, 1813, 38 pp.

153. See the *Catalogue of Mexican Pamphlets in the Sutro Collection*.

154. "Política peculiar de Buonaparte en quanto a la religion católica; medios de que se vale para extinguirla, y subyugar los españoles por la seducción, ya que no puede dominarlos por la fuerza". Cevallos was first secretary under Carlos IV, cousin-in-law to Manuel Godoy. Liberal delegates to the Cortes, too, like Antonio Puigblanch, had their works reprinted in Mexico—thus provoking reaction from Mexican conservatives. "El filósofo rancio", eight "Cartas", all printed in Cádiz—most from the Imprenta de la Junta de Provincia, 1813, ranging from 33 to 44 pp.); Pedro Cevallos, "Politica peculiar ... " (México: reimp, en casa de Arizpe, 1812, 52 pp.); and José Ignacio Gómez, "Confesar la religión católica y denunciar los pecados contra la fe son las obligaciones del Buen cristiano. Sermon moral que en el día 21

de Marzo del presente año de 1813 ... en la santa iglesia catedral de Cádiz y ante su ilustrisimo cabildo dixo Don ... cura propio del sagrario de dicha Santa Iglesia ... (Cádiz: Imp. de Carreño, 26 pp. 1 p.). [See my "Actitudes en México hacia la Inquisición."]

155. "Diarrea de las imprentas. Memoria sobre la epidemia de este nombre que reyna actualmente en Cádiz. Se describe su origen, sus síntomas, su índole perniciosa, su terminación, y su curación. Escribíala en obsequio de la patria afligida el Doctor Pedro Recio de Tirte Afuera" (México: Reimpresa en Casa de Arizpe).

156. "Resumen imparcial de los sucesos militares más notables acaecidos en España y Portugal desde 1807 hasta fines de Mayo de 1811, publicado en Londres y traducido al Castellano en Mexico año de 1812". (México: En la Imprenta de Arizpe, 1812, 47 pp.).

157. For discussion of the various translators of *Rights*, see the edition by Grases.

158. "Catecismo religioso politico contra el real catecismo de Fernando VII". This work appears to be a version of the pamphlet *Homilía del Cardenal Chiaramonte*, which Carey published in that year.

159. "Traiga aunque sea un compendio de la actual legislación inglesa y alguna gramática y diccionario anglo-hispano; ítem algunos libritos de importancia. Acuérdese Ud. de que Londres fue el lugar donde escribió el Padre Viscardo su *Legado* y donde obtuvo la apología del *Contrato Social* de Rousseau", Grases Vol. 3, 5.

160. Mier, *Cartas de un americano*.

161. Racine, 284.

162. De Onís, 65–66.

163. The "Reglamento de libertad de imprenta," passed by the Cortes de Cádiz, was reprinted in Mexico in 1820 by the Oficina de D. Juan Bautista de Arizpe, 8 pp. It is available in full in the *Catalogue of Mexican Pamphlets in the Sutro Collection*.

164. "La prensa libre" (México: Imp. de Alejandro Valdés, 4 pp.).

165. Available in the Rare Book Room of the University of Pennsylvania Library (Philadelphia).

166. "Sir, Having on mature consideration, resolved to withdraw from the discussion of the tariff question." For a longer description, see Clarkin, 260.

CONCLUSION

THE ROBESON/CAREY CORRESPONDENCE CONTRIBUTES TO that cultural cluster for which "the book" is a shorthand for authorial creativity, secularization, freedom of the press, class consciousness, literacy, taste, intellectual preference, education, and so on. "The book" can also be framed in economic terms, and so the processes of its production and consumption (printing, translating, distributing, purchasing) make it important in analyzing a country's transition from patronage to a market economy, from colonial dependency on the mother country and isolation from all other influences to self-sufficiency. But "the book" as go-between in which one culture represents itself to another is yet one more of its functions. The material object and text may appear to be in a position of dominance and superiority as they travel, bearing a message of priority and newness. The world that they enter is usually a composite, however, whose readers' reactions range from interest to indifference, from wild acclaim to hostile rejection as old attitudes persist, so that the importation is a mixture of cultural takeover and failure. Old books, in Mexico's case, still linked the country to several global, seemingly universal, traditions so that opening up to another could seem to have been threatening and unnecessary.

In connecting Philadelphia's Spanish-language printing to readers in Mexico, the Robeson/Carey correspondence argues for a kind of cultural transfer unlike the unbalanced, disruptive ones we customarily think of; this one, based on shared postcolonial Americanness and, therefore, some feelings of equality between donor and recipient, suggests some smooth passage. The correspondence, detailing a business based on personal contacts, common interests, and easy land and maritime access, tells that, in those first years after their respective independence movements, mutualities and geographical proximity brought peoples together who previously had not had much to say to one another, communicating only through parents. The letters show that both countries recognized that their insertion into international affairs would begin, first of all, with each securing relations with the other neighbor. The United States was interested in developing trade with Mexico (if takeover still lingered on the U.S. agenda, it had to be disguised once Mexico asserted national status); and Mexico realized that alliance with the United States, which was declaring jealousies in protecting the hemisphere from European encroachments, would be advantageous. Because, in 1822, Mexico was further along in its national life than South America, where independence wars still raged, it could expect to benefit from importing the governmental theories and models that Anglo America offered. Yet Mexico, as we have seen, had chosen an emperor as its first ruler after independence. The country, one of Spain's two administrative capitals in the colonial years, still had a number of conservative members who favored that form of government. Consequently, republican-minded Mexicans understood that those persons especially required books describing other political options if their minds were going to change. Roscio's book in Robeson's cargo especially evinces that concern; and Robeson's sales tally registers, in fact, Mexican appreciation of that essay. That list, and in what quantities those titles went into that bank of readers, is our most valuable record to date of inter-American intellectual transfer.

——— UNITED STATES/ENGLAND/FRANCE ———

Mexico's experience of state-building has often been subsumed into generalizations about Spanish American nationalism. These have emphasized the impact of the Venezuelans Francisco Miranda and Simón Bolívar and their British influences in, first of all, declaring independence and then drawing up appropriate forms of government (Berruezo León 1989; Roldán Vera 2003; Belaunde 1938/1978). The Venezuelans enjoyed friendships with philosophers and politicians in England and the continent. They left Europe as Anglophiles, and died, leaving behind stories of military heroics and a paper trail of such dimension that historians could document their lives and novelists could base "foundational fictions"[1] on their personalities. In contrast, the leaders of independence in Mexico—Miguel Hidalgo and José María Morelos—did not travel outside Mexico and were killed off early in the war. The few summaries of their thought, which were printed, were limited to Mexico; although Morelos's antislavery ideas were remarkable for their time, their philosophies were not considered to be useful for later development or applicable outside of Mexico. Thus they are national heroes but footnotes to histories elsewhere. Mier, who was an enthusiast of England while he was in London, became a critic when he arrived in the United States and found a more appealing government. Iturbide, who took Mexico to independence, is too controversial a figure to be acclaimed as the personification of any national or hemispheric liberating spirit.

Jeremy Bentham thought of immigrating to Mexico in 1808, but then turned his attention to Venezuela because of his friendship with Miranda. Bentham figured that Mexico was set on its course but that he could help those still-forming South Americans in drafting their constitutions.[2] The Peninsular War, in which the British had fought alongside Spanish troops in driving out the French, had brought important Spaniards to London in a first wave of immigration. José Blanco White left Spain then; and his newspaper, *El Español*, published in London between 1810 and 1814, as we have seen, influenced Spanish American thinkers like Andrés Bello and Mier. White's fast friendship with Lord and Lady Holland, who had lived in Madrid and were enthusiasts of Spain, provided a circle for these visiting and resident Spanish speakers to meet one another and to involve important Englishmen (e.g., Bentham, James Mill, Robert Southey) in their plans for independence.[3] British newspapers such as *The Westminster Review* and *The Edinburgh Review*, as well as the Spanish-language *Biblioteca Americana* and *Repertorio Americano*, published the writings of these South Americans. England's press had for decades reached the country's island possessions in the Caribbean, to be taken then to the South American mainland. After 1823, when a second wave of liberal Spaniards fleeing Fernando's oppression arrived in England and protested that they were better translators than those the U.S. printers had hired, Londoners largely took over what trade the United States had begun to establish with Spanish America.[4]

In 1824, when the South American wars were concluded, London printers especially moved into that territory. Rudolph Ackermann, who led in Spanish-language publishing, established bookstores in Peru and Argentina and sent there the translations, textbooks, and newspapers that émigré Spaniards were producing for him. By 1826 Ackermann had a bookstore in Mexico City (run by his son Jorge and Juan Henrique Dick), stepping into the Mexican market that U.S printers were leaving. Between 1823 and 1825 Ackermann published Blanco White's journal, *Variedades, o Mensagero de Londres: periódico trimestre*. Between 1823 and 1828 he published a series of readers on basic topics like arithmetic and agriculture, which were distributed throughout Spanish America (the readers were called catechisms for their often-used question-and-answer format, designed for memorization).[5] The extent and innovations of Ackermann's export is seen in a list of books for sale, appended to a collection of readings he published in 1826, *Curiosidades para los estudiosos*, compiled by F.A. Fernel (included here as Appendix C). In *Curiosidades* and in the other titles, one reads concerns for science, explaining, for example, how new laws of optics and physics could do away with popular myths of enchanted castles. English-centered views of European history tell why England's wars with France had lasted so long, perpetuating rivalries. Still another section reports that recent auction sales in London were making collection of rare books like Boccaccio's *Decameron* a new aristocratic activity. Ackermann's name is on a Mexican journal, *Museo universal de ciencias y arte*, printed with aquatint plates in both London and Mexico between 1825 and 1826.[6] Yet Ackermann was not the only London printer to be interested in publishing for Spanish America; *Ocios de españoles emigrados* (Leisure Pastimes of Emigré Spaniards), though its title would seem to have excluded Spanish Americans, was exported to Spanish America. That journal's circulation run was upped to 1,000 when Rocafuerte came to London and guaranteed it 200 Mexican subscribers in 1824.[7] British capital, larger than what the United States had to offer then, was attracted to Mexico, moving in to sell goods, to make loans, but also to invest in the country's resources, particularly its mining wealth.[8]

Britain had the advantage over the United States of early on having begun to court Spanish American revolutionaries. In 1781 the Peruvian Jesuit, Juan Pablo Viscardo, directed a report to the English consul in Livorno, suggesting invasion of Buenos Aires as the best entry into the South American continent. In 1797, Viscardo's letter, *Carta a los españoles americanos*, which we have seen was printed in London and promoted by Miranda, was widely circulated.[9]

However, British authors and publishers had shown an interest in Spanish America decades before. In 1776 Adam Smith's *Inquiry into the Wealth of Nations* compared British and Spanish colonialisms. In 1777 William Robertson had published his *History of America*; of the four volumes the first three and most of the fourth deal with Spanish America and the system of government there—only at the very end does Robertson introduce the histories of Virginia and New England.[10] In the preface he says, "the principles and maxims of the Spaniards in planting colonies, which have been adopted in some measure by every nation ... will serve as a proper introduction to the history of all the European establishments in America" (vi).

Robertson included in his history a long "Catalogue of Spanish Books and Manuscripts" (reproduced as Appendix D) and here I call attention to that innovation. What Robertson calls a "Catalogue" is what we would call today a bibliography; in the preface he describes the difficulty he had getting hold of these primary materials and lengthily contrasts the secrecy with which the Spanish king kept them in the archive at Simancas with the willingness of Austria, Russia, Portugal, France, and the United States to make them available. The "Catalogue," then, not only serves the modern author to justify the truth of his history and tell of his labor, but also serves the publisher in advertising sources he might print later. This list of 288 chronicles of conquest and exploration, missionary reports, scientific studies, and literary works (in Spanish, Portuguese, French, Italian, English, and Latin), draws together a body of materials that must have been one of the first looks Spanish Americans had into their history. Although labeled "Spanish Books and Manuscripts," the list is only pertinent to Latin America (Mexico, Central America, the Caribbean, all of South America, but also the Philippines). Some of the items are manuscripts; some are rare imprints from Madrid and other towns in Spain, Mexico, Peru, and the Philippines; some were published in London, Leyden, Amsterdam, Antwerp, Paris, Cologne, Rome, Florence, Venice, and Lisbon. Robertson does not say so but the number of works on the list, relative to Jesuit history, suggest that Jesuits who had fled to Italy after their expulsion from Spanish America in 1767 might have sold off archives there they took with them, supplying him with his documentation.

Significantly, England, a competitor and frequent enemy of Spain in those years, provided Americans with this full account of their colonial history. Although Madrid publishers in the late eighteenth century were beginning to publish (and republish) works by Spanish colonial writers (often court-approved chroniclers), London was in a better position then to gather materials from other European book repositories besides Madrid, a tactic that made Spanish Americans aware of the many non-Spanish influences on their history. The Catalogue thus helped to shake notions of exclusively Spanish development in the colonies and loosen dependency on Madrid; it taught Spanish Americans that their history was separate from Spain's. Perhaps it took England's Protestant perspective to make obvious how powerfully the Vatican had intervened in Spanish history—a fact that was underscored in the list's merger of ecclesiastical and secular materials.

In February 1823, on the heels of Robeson's foray into Mexico, the Englishman William Bullock entered Mexico with the idea of bringing back to England artifacts for a museum. Bullock secured permission to work in the country from Antonio Santa Anna and indeed transported home molds of important archaeological finds (the Aztec calendar stone, which had recently been unearthed), copies of codices, but also actual antique items. He opened his exhibit of materials "collected on the spot in 1823, by the assistance of the Mexican Government" in London the following year. Charles Willson Peale had similarly founded a natural history museum in Philadelphia in 1784, sending his sons out on expeditions into U.S. territories in the first decades of the nineteenth century to gather curious specimens of Indian relics and native animals such as bison and a mastodon. Robeson apparently was not charged with bringing back Mexican materials for Peale's collection. However, Bullock's expedition shows that, in the cultural as well as in the political and economic spheres, England was moving to edge out the United States for preeminence in Mexico.[11]

In 1822, as the United States started to move into Mexico, England was terrified that Mexico and the other Spanish American nations that were forming would concede commercial privileges to that country which had officially recognized their independence. In a London-printed proclamation, housed in the Abadiano collection of the Sutro Library (attesting to its receipt in Mexico), James Henderson addressed South Americans and Mexicans, and pleaded with them not to go ahead with such concessions. Henderson reported on a dinner meeting, held on July 10, 1822, in the main room of the hall of the city of London to honor Francisco Antonio Zea, plenipotentiary of the republic of Colombia. Henderson acknowledged that England had been slow to recognize the newly independent countries but said that its delay was explained by its "principles of integrity and national honor." The Mexican reader of Henderson's pamphlet might have understood two messages: That South Americans, still in the throes of their revolutionary wars, were being courted, but that Mexico, where U.S. commerce had already advanced, was England's real fear. However, English merchants were also concerned about French entry into Spanish America; Ackermann, for example, wrote in a preface to an 1826 work that he knew that everything he had put out in Spanish was being printed in France, to be sold at a lower price. He said he had been assured by the congresses of the newly formed Spanish American republics that they would respect literary property and warned that he had circulated his catalogue to their customs agents so as to prevent entry of illegal French editions.[12]

Mirroring Ackermann's criticism of France is a French view of the British publishing industry. In *Quince días en Londres, o sea corto viage de un francés a Inglaterra a fines de 1815* (translated into Spanish from the French and published in Mexico in 1826) an unidentified author tells how a French visitor to London was approached in a bookshop by its owner, who wanted him to translate into French and have published in Paris a German work.[13] The Frenchman would buy the rights to do so from the Englishman and then recover his costs by sale of the book, which had already been plagiarized without attribution in France. The Frenchman refused the offer but the incident is an excuse for him to comment at length, half-disparagingly but half-admiringly, on the English commercial genius for speculation. He does not take the moral high ground; instead he announces that plagiarism is a small crime in France and that few would buy the book. Mexicans would have learned several lessons from their reading: Although previous books had alerted them to the problem, they would have been warned in the translator's preface how transfers from one language to another were subject to one man's judgment; in the narrative they would have witnessed how different European nations viewed intellectual property rights; and they would have seen how books were increasingly the basis for an international business.

France's Spanish-language publishing industry, then, competed with England on the continent but also in Spanish America. Paris, as we have seen, but also Bayonne, Bordeaux, Avignon, and Montpellier, were publishing centers where liberal Spaniards sought refuge and employment after Fernando returned to Spain in 1814. The political essays and translations of au courant political materials they wrote and had printed there were intended for readers in Spain but also for the Spanish American market. Often labeled "liberals," these émigrés ranged from disenchanted royalists who wanted reforms but retained many conservative notions, to outright revolutionaries.

Juan Antonio Llorente (see Figure 4.1), whom we have seen, is foremost among those Spaniards in France who significantly influenced Spanish America then.[14] Llorente is key to understanding that source, different from the generally less-politicized Spanish émigrés in London. Writing in Spanish (though sometimes in French), Llorente had greater access to Spanish America than English political theorists like Bentham, whose works written in English required translation if they were to be imported into Spanish America. Clergyman, canon lawyer, historian, and secretary to the Inquisition in Spain, he had been gathering materials to write that institution's history, so as to make recommendations for its continuance. When José Bonaparte took over in Spain, Bonaparte asked him to proceed with his work, though for different reasons; Bonaparte needed evidence of the Spanish monarchy's collusion with the Church so as to justify abolishing the Inquisition. In 1792 Llorente had published *Leyes del Fuero Juzgo, o Recopilación de las leyes de los Wisi-Godos españoles, titulada primeramente "Liber judicum."*[15] In 1808 he published praise of Bonaparte for having brought a national code of law to Spain, replacing provincial codes. In 1812 he read a report to the Academia de la Historia (Madrid) on the Inquisition's history and national opinion of that institution. In 1813, when Bonaparte's forces were expelled from Spain, Llorente, because he had collaborated with the enemy, was also forced to leave for France where he spent the rest of his life (though he died in Madrid in 1823, a few months after amnesty permitted his return). Llorente published his *Histoire de l'Inquisition d'Espagne* in Paris in 1818—a masterful work that was immediately translated and circulated throughout Europe and the Americas. It appeared in the United States in English translations in two editions in 1826—in Philadelphia, printed by T.B. Peterson,[16] and in New York, printed by G.C. Morgan.[17]

In addition to his Inquisition history, which arrived in Mexico in French and Spanish editions, Llorente is notable in Mexico for essays in which he considered problems Mexico and the other new American nations faced as they rejected Spanish rule and prepared for self-government. In Paris he was surrounded by Napoleonic debate over legal codes; later, once the monarchy was restored and France returned to close relations with the papacy, cancelling out liberal reform, Llorente wrote five essays that either were reprinted in Mexico, or whose publication in Paris, London, and in the seaports of Bordeaux

FIGURE 4.1 Portrait of Juan Antonio Llorente.

and San Sebastián (Spain), suggest their export to the Americas. Thus they tell not only of Llorente's influence in the Americas but also the importance of French printing and distribution networks there.

The first, probably written in 1814—*Aforismos politicos escritos en una de las lenguas del norte de la Europa por un filósofo y traducidos al español por don Juan Antonio Llorente*—appeared originally in Madrid in 1821; it was reprinted in Mexico City and Guadalajara in 1822.[18] In that work, in which Llorente hid behind the claim that he was the translator, he began his concern for how religion might survive in the civil societies new nations were forming, free from European powers (Spain and Rome). Although he does not mention Mexico, the fact that it was quickly reprinted there suggests that Mexicans noted the pertinence of his recommendations.[19]

In the second, *Discursos sobre una constitución religiosa, considerada como parte de la civil nacional. Su autor un Americano* (Paris, Imprenta de Stahl, 1819), Llorente also concealed his identity, calling himself an "American."[20] In the 16-page introduction to the 187-page work, he addressed Americans, sympathizing with the fact that, as nations with a Catholic inheritance writing new constitutions, they were confronted with what seemed to be a relic from the colonial past—religious faith but also financial obligations to Rome and obedience to the Pope. Llorente proceeded like an historian, reviewing Europe's printing history to see whether that Protestant innovation had hurt faith. He said print was "a divine gift" because it allowed the common man direct access to the Bible, thereby deepening his faith. However, print showed him, as he read for himself, how the Roman Curia had misrepresented the early Church's teachings and misused "religion" in controlling Catholic populations; Jesuits in particular had furthered political schemes. Yet Llorente argued that, even if the Church had been wrong, religion should not be abandoned; it had the benefits of being a moral force and bringing unity to a nation. A country's educated elite might have been exposed to doubt and alternative beliefs through Enlightenment reading; but that elite should recognize that the masses were steadfast in their beliefs, and there were advantages to building on that base. Rather than separating church and state as the United States had done in its constitution, or tolerating the practice of all faiths, Catholic societies should preserve faithful custom and official orthodoxy. It was essential that Catholics not leave behind prescriptions for fasting, abstinence from meat, clerical celibacy, attendance at Mass, marriage prohibitions, and so on, so that they began to resemble individualistic Protestants and thus lose their identity and social cohesiveness.

Discursos is a longer work than the related 162-page *Projet d'une constitution religieuse, considerée commo faisant partie de la constitution civile d'une nation libre indépendante, écrite par un Américain. Publié avec une préface, par don*

Jean-Antoine Llorente (Paris: L.E. Herhan, 1820).[21] The latter was republished in London in 1823 by C. Wood as *Proyecto de una constitución religiosa: considerada como parte de la constitución civil de una nación libre e independiente*, In the introduction the author credits *Discursos* with the reprint. The London edition I consulted in the Sutro Library (San Francisco) is small sized and unbound, suggesting its portability and cheapness.

The fourth essay, 256 pages long—*Apología católica del proyecto de constitución religiosa, escrito por un Americano*—was published in Spanish by two printers in Paris in 1821, and also in San Sebastián in that same year.[22] In 1821 the San Sebastián printer, Baroja, also published the fifth essay as a 16-page pamphlet; it, too, deals with the topic of official religion. We have seen this work before—*Carta escrita a un Americano sobre la forma de gobierno que para hace practicable la constitución y las leyes, conviene establecer en Nueva España atendida su actual situación*.[23] Dated June 6, 1821, it notes that Iturbide had just launched his *grito de independencia* (shout of independence, thus substituting Iturbide for Miguel Hidalgo, who began Mexico's revolt in 1810 with a famous cry), and Llorente expressed the hope that Iturbide would not soon be shot like other American heroes. In 1821 Llorente is still arguing for a Mexican monarchy so as to avoid the election turmoil that periodically plagued the United States.

In 1826 two other Llorente works (the first of which had been published in Madrid in 1810) were reprinted in Mexico—*Disertación sobre el poder que los reyes españoles ejercieron hasta el siglo duodecimo*[24] and *Pequeño catecismo sobre la materia de concordatos*.[25] In 1826–1827 Fernández de Lizardi reprinted Llorente's *Retrato político de los papas* in his journal, *Correo semanario de México*.[26] In 1827 Llorente's *Colección diplomática de varios papeles antiguos y modernos sobre dispensas matrimoniales y otros puntos de disciplina eclesiástica* (published first in Madrid in 1809) was also reprinted in Mexico.[27] We have already seen that Llorente's gathering of Las Casas's works, which he had published in Paris in French and in Spanish, and in Brussels in French, had a great effect on American politics in 1822. Llorente, a Spanish Catholic with French intellectual and publishing connections, is significant for channeling European thinking into Mexico in the 1820s.

The sea itself, however, offered printers freedom from national censorship and access to distribution routes. In 1813 an anti-Inquisition speech to the Spanish Cortes by Antonio José Ruíz de Padrón was printed in English by a press on board His Majesty's ship, *Caledonia*.[28] This 96-page speech, which gives as its place of publication "the Mediterranean" off Toulon, is held in the Library of Congress, thus suggesting its dissemination in the United States. No translator is listed for it.

By the late 1820s, then, England and France (but also increasingly domestic printers) were taking over the publishing business in Mexico that U.S. printers were abandoning. Robeson's foray had proven that the risks involved in selling books abroad were great and profits slim. The United States itself was growing, and so the country's printers turned attention to that safe market; the few Spanish titles that we see, put out by printers other than Carey and Lea, seem destined for internal consumption. In 1825 Olavide's *La paisana virtuosa* was reprinted in Philadelphia; in 1828 three of Olavide's novels were printed in New York by Lanuza, Mendia without Olavide's name but attributed vaguely to the author of *El Evangelio en triunfo*, the anti-Inquisition work for which he was known in Europe. In 1829 works by recent Spanish writers, José Cadalso and Gaspar Melchor de Jovellanos—*Noches lúgubres* and *Delincuente honrado*—were published in New York, also by Lanuza, Mendia. (Cayetano Lanuza, the New York publisher and bookseller, had come to the United States in 1825, taking over much Spanish-language printing. A Spanish medical doctor who had had a publishing and translating career in Madrid before going on to France in 1823, Lanuza seems to have been responsible for bringing Olavide manuscripts to the United States.)[29]

U.S. printers' retreat to internal markets can also be explained by the fact that they did not yet have the international network of banks that England did. As we have seen, Robeson was having trouble bringing his money home. Yet even Ackermann repented of his initial enthusiasm for supplying books to Spanish Americans; a Madrid journal in 1838 tells that an Ackermann agent in Mexico suffered great losses when he failed to sell his books. The reporter says that, because the independence wars were merely military shifts, only a few military men were buying the new books; most Mexicans stuck to their reading of old catechisms and classical authors.[30]

However, the Carey/Robeson letters valuably document what previous histories have elided: that is, that in the first phase of Mexico's development the U.S. book business aided in making the United States that country's most important external influence. For a brief moment after Mexican independence at least one Philadelphia printer that we now know of supplied the country with the books useful to its decolonization and governance. In the period between 1821 and 1824 (when Mexico wrote its first constitution), U.S. merchants like Robeson, adventurers like John Bradburn and Stephen Austin, and emissaries like Joel Poinsett, entered the country, bringing with them cultural materials and social innovations. They met with Mexican officials but also businessmen like Recio, and conversations were often begun around the topic of trade.

The letters demonstrate a desire, at the personal level, to establish a relationship of parity between the two nations. If, previously, contacts with foreigners had been unequal, the result of conquest and exploitation, now money exchanges between American sellers and buyers seemed to suggest equality.

Books were a common denominator for the tradesmen. Although books conserved some aura of elite knowledge, one that older generations had revered, they also represented a new, democratic commodity, which anybody might print and sell and anyone who could afford it could buy.

ADDITIONAL U.S. INFLUENCE

We have seen the results of that U.S. influence on Mexico in the writings of Lizardi and Bustamante, in the quick reprinting in Mexico of Mier's *Memoria* and Roscio's *Triunfo*, and in the 1822 pamphlet written by P.F.S., inspired by a Philadelphia "libel." But there are other proofs of U.S. influence. In Mexico City in 1821 José María Luis Mora began to publish a newspaper, *Semanario Político y Literario*, in which he reprinted the U.S. Declaration of Independence, the Articles of Confederation, two speeches by Washington, and the Constitution.[31] Mora, a member of the Scottish Lodge, was reputed to have had "the best library in Mexico" (Hale 1968, 73). In the spring of 1822, two other newspapers appeared that drew material from sources in the United States: *El Sol*[32] and *El hombre libre*.[33] The Masonic-inspired *El Sol* would have a long life. In the May 8 issue the editors focused on the language of a speech by a U.S. president, which proclaimed his country's neutrality in Spain's war with its American colonies; the editorial focus on language was an excuse to criticize the translator (and thereby indict English foreign policy). In pulling apart the translation from English to Spanish, which had appeared in a "gacetero imperial" (one supposes an English paper where the original also appeared),[34] the editors attacked the change in meaning that twisted the U.S. president's words so that recognition of the de facto independence of Mexico and Buenos Aires was lost and the president's "good disposition" toward Spain and Mexico was eliminated. The editors said that England, rather than tarnishing the image of the United States, whose political wisdom Mexicans envied, should laud it. *El hombre libre*, though it did not specifically dwell on the United States, showed the influence of that country in its long essays on the duties of citizens, obligations of society, the economy of liberty, enlightenment of the people, and common detestation in the Americas of monarchy.

In the spring of 1823 *El Federalista* began publication.[35] Its name suggests its slant. Its editors argued that because of the great extent of the Mexican territory a federal union was preferable, and they quoted Volney, Montesquieu, Rousseau, and Destutt de Tracy, as well as the letters of M.A. Jay [John Jay?] and David Bailie Warden's *Déscription statistique, historique et politique des Etats-Unis*,[36] in describing the benefits of federalism. Essays told how well the system was adapted to U.S. territories, larger than all of Europe, and thus a useful model for Mexico in administering vastness and diversity. Travelers reported on theater in the United States and enthusiastically commented that the U.S. population's pride in itself was based not on past accomplishments but on expectations for its future. *Aguila Mexicana*,[37] begun in April 1823, although it started by promising news from Europe (principally Paris, London, and Madrid) and Lima, later, in 1825, relied heavily on the news it got from the United States—for example, in letters from individuals in Philadelphia and articles from the Baltimore *Daily Advertiser* and from the New Orleans *L'Argus*, which relayed antimonarchical and republican opinion. In August 1823, "El Tapatío" (from the region of Guadalajara) argued in *Aguila's* pages that liberal ideas were born in Anglo America as a result of its revolt against Britain, and that from there federalist beliefs (which assured liberty) went to France; the writer also took Bustamante to task for his centralist preferences. In *Aguila's* printing of speeches in the Mexican Congress, remittances from correspondents throughout the provinces, and reports of ship traffic in and out of Mexican ports, press freedom became more apparent. In an article in 1824, announcing the opening of an "Instituto de literatura y comercio," the paper listed the newspapers the Instituto subscribed to for its members—from England and the continent but also from New Orleans, Washington, Philadelphia, New York, Richmond, and Boston. In *Aguila's* advertisements we learn of the proliferation of bookstores and availability of books.

In October 1823, *Miscelánea de literatura, ciencias y artes* began to publish.[38] Its first issue contained material from the *Federalist Papers* (authored by Alexander Hamilton, James Madison, and John Jay, and translated into Spanish by Manuel Larrainzar). In 1828 four pamphlets, printed by different Mexico City printers, responded to an essay in a Philadelphia literary review, *Revista trimestre de Filadelfia*.[39] The first is the 32-page translation from the December 1827 issue: "México como nación independiente: descripción de su estado moral, politico, intelectual & y esperanzas de su condición futura";[40] the second, a 16-page response, "Contestación al artículo infamatorio contra la República Mexicana";[41] the third, a 31-page essay, "Contestación," written by J.G., a native of Tenerife in the Canaries but published in Mexico by his friend, J.D.M.;[42] the fourth, a four-page essay by J.V.L. "Ideas interesantes en favor de la república Mexicana, contra el artículo publicado en la revista trimestre de Filadelfia."[43]

José María Heredia, the Cuban we have seen who, after two years in the United States, immigrated to Mexico in 1825, testifies to the closeness between the United States and Mexico in those years. On arriving in Mexico, Heredia published a comparison of George Washington, Simón Bolívar, and Napoleon in journals that were published in Mexico and Cuba. His conclusion—that Washington's role in winning independence and then leading a civil society to ordered development surpassed the military heroism of Bolívar and Napoleon—helped establish the preeminence of the United States in Mexico and the Caribbean.[44] Indeed, Washington was an icon in Mexico. He was hailed as an American hero who had ended European tyranny in the hemisphere militarily but who, as a civilian, had instructed his country in peace. The translator of a funeral oration for Washington, published in Mexico City in 1823 and advertised for sale in Recio's bookstore, said that the Mexican generals who had just liberated their country could use Washington as a model.[45] Washington was virtuous; in another pamphlet, published in Mexico in 1822, he was compared admiringly with William Penn. These men, "neighbors to the north," pointed the way for Mexicans out of the darkness of ignorance and oppression to constitutional liberty.[46]

A few of the books in the Robeson shipment were written by Europeans (for example, Rousseau's *Social Contract*). However, most of Robeson's books had their origins in the United States, a former English colony, thus reproducing rejection of English imperial rule and the U.S. republican model. Often representing the thinking of émigrés who had lodged in the United States after unhappy experiences in Europe (Paine, Puglia, Roscio, Mier), these books (*Derechos del hombre, Desengaño del hombre, Triunfo de la libertad,* and *Memoria politico-instructiva*) frequently contained pro-U.S. sentiment and anti-European (and anti-English) feelings. Barère de Vieuzac was anti-English; thus Mexicans read in his *Libertad de los mares* that prejudice. Foronda's pamphlets, apparently exported out of Philadelphia to Mexico in shipments earlier than Robeson's, also favored the United States. Indeed, Foronda's roots in Vizcaya, rather than Castile, suggest that that region's independent traditions (which John Adams recognized, praising it as a modern, democratic republic)[47] helped him to criticize Madrid's imperial policies even though he was Spain's chief consul in the United States. Educated in France and Italy, rather than England, Foronda assumed the viewpoint of peripheral peoples, whether learned in the Basque country or acquired in the United States.

The republicanism of these U.S.-produced books, however, was not programmatic or all of one kind. Although a main thread connecting them was rejection of tyranny, they still revealed bones of contention such as centralism versus federalism, and trade protections versus a free market.[48] Political and often disputatious, if they were philosophical in their exposition, the books in the Mexican cargo generally (with the exception of Rousseau's *Social Contract*) did not go back to the humanism or the republicanism of Greece and Rome for the historical grounding that Mexicans would have looked for. They were often raging in their antimonarchism and utilitarian in their focus on contemporary politics and commercial advantage. Reading them more carefully, Mexicans were put off by their violent attacks and commercial arguments, considering them base and their practitioners selfish.

Robeson's books lacked the classical aesthetic dimension that republican works had brought to the United States and that would establish the symbolism of its Federalist furniture, architecture, sculpture, dress, and so on. Considered revolutionary in the United States because the French taste broke with English custom and was associated with Napoleonic reforms, classicism in Mexico was instead regal, associated with the Bourbon regime of the late-colonial period. This aesthetic classicism, called "neoclassicism" in eighteenth-century Mexico to distinguish it from the Latin education and philosophical humanism that persisted in the schools and intellectual circles throughout the colonial period, had come in in 1785 when the Academia de San Carlos was established there by order of viceregal authorities.[49] Imposed by the Bourbons in an effort to counter older Hapsburg ways and that family's Baroque preferences, neoclassicism in Mexico was contaminated by its colonial importation. The aesthetic was not revolutionary in Mexico, and the new political books from the United States, devoid of aesthetic statement in their republicanism, did not much alter that perception.

Aesthetic taste, however, affected South America in English guise. Romantic currents took greater hold there than in Mexico.[50] When Bello returned from England to Venezuela in 1829, and then went on to Chile, he brought with him reports of Wordsworth and the other Romantics.[51] In contrast, Mexican travelers abroad then, like Manuel Gorostiza, did not spend much time in London but for the most part were in Madrid, Paris, the Low Countries, and even the United States.[52] Spain judged Romanticism revolutionary, and kept the fashion out until 1833; France, having experienced revolution, preferred Rococo taste and Neoclassicism throughout the first decades of the nineteenth century. What Romanticism entered Mexico, then, seems to have come via a literary journal, *El Iris*, published there in 1826. Its editors were Heredia and two Italians—Florencio Galli and Claudio Linati. Heredia brought to Mexico the Romanticism he had learned in the United States. For example, he set a tone for poetry when he criticized a young Mexican who had sent him some of his poems, calling him "a school-boy poet" (Heredia used the English phrase) and deriding him for his excessive passion.[53] The Italians, republicans who had fled monarchist Italy, brought a revolutionary politics rather than an aesthetic consciousness that might have affected literature and the visual arts.[54]

Mexicans did not always see nearness to the United States as benign. Especially in northern areas many feared aspects of U.S. culture. In an undated pamphlet (probably written about the time of Hidalgo's declaration of war in 1810), a writer from Durango held up the devastation Napoleon caused in Europe and said: "Turn your eyes to Pennsylvania and you will see those Anglo-Americans, subject to a scandalous toleration. Do you want to lose our Catholic religion?"[55] In another pamphlet dated 1820 a Mexican warned a friend: "Don't settle in Texas because it will soon become a theater of war, occupied by the U.S. . . . The U.S. has just acquired Louisiana."[56]

Cubans in the United States, like Félix Varela, added to this cautionary view of the United States. Although Cuban fears of annexation by sugar-producing, slave-holding interests in the southern United States would not be widely voiced until later, one reads criticism of a mercantile U.S. mentality that had spread to Cuba in articles in Varela's newspaper *El Habanero*, published in Philadelphia in 1824 for export to Cuba (and probably Mexico).[57] Varela praises the freedoms of the country from which he writes; he admires Washington. But in the first numbers he warns of its politics that do not rise above money-related concerns. In Cuba, where U.S. interests predominate, "all matters of state are conducted on the docks and in the warehouses" (1997, 16); in Cuba "there is no love for Spain, for Colombia, or for Mexico—only for sacks of sugar and coffee" (1997, 18). Varela saw that Cuba would be the battlefield where Spain would fight to protect her possessions and England and France would come, supposedly to help a fellow king but really to press their own interests. He feared interventions by Mexico and Colombia (Colombia was having ships built in Philadelphia). Realistically, he conceded that the United States could be a friend to help Cuba gain independence from Spain. But now it harbored Spanish spies and plotters, and Philadelphia bankers like Stephen Girard were meddling in Spanish America's affairs by lending money to French agents to prevent Cuban independence (Varela 1997, 133).

Nevertheless, the friendships and business relationships described in Robeson's letters suggest an initial closeness between U.S. citizens and Mexicans. Robeson's description of the accessibility of the port of Alvarado, and Schmaltz's of the growing role of the northern port of Tampico, tell of increasing contact (by sea and by land) between the two countries; their testimony also recognizes, beyond personal networks and despite disagreements, the advantages of cross-border cooperation. One historian has claimed that the Mexican constitution of 1824 was based on a translation of the U.S. constitution that Stephen Austin made, handing it to Jose Miguel Ramos Arizpe who headed the commission that wrote that constitution.[58] However, Mexicans had seen and experimented with constitutional language before. American delegates to the Spanish Cortes de Cádiz in 1810–1812 had helped to write that constitution; and in 1813 insurgents had written a constitution at the Congress of Chilpancingo. Mexicans had had advice from legalists like Llorente. So attribution of indebtedness to a U.S. model may be only partially correct, if not wrong.[59]

Although the United States and England struggled for diplomatic and commercial hegemony in Mexico throughout the 1820s, Joel Poinsett and others initially pulled Mexico into the U.S. orbit. Yet Poinsett wrote to Monroe from Mexico that although "the people everywhere are more attached to us, . . . [t]here exists with all the governments of Spanish America, a great desire to conciliate Great Britain," fearing Britain's power and "aware that their commercial interests require the support of a great manufacturing and commercial people" (1824/1969, 69). As the decade wore on, then, U.S. influence lessened, yielding to English advances. Vicente Rocafuerte, who once had been a strong voice in Mexico, advocating ties with the United States, became less important after leaving Mexico. After a stay in England, he reverted to his South American identity when he returned home to Ecuador. Correspondence from Rocafuerte to Humboldt in 1824 reveals that by then Rocafuerte admired Bolívar and was absorbed with British and Ecuadorian politics.[60] Some Mexicans like Lucas Alamán, director of the London-based United Mining Association, retained connections with British investment. Yet, despite England's increasing access in Mexico, Mexicans generally realized that their future lay with close association with the United States.

BOOKS AS COMMODITIES

The fact that Mexico was so near to the United States makes the cultural influence of the United States on Mexico practically inevitable; it is almost as if the Robeson/Carey letters (or others like them), which might prove the transfer of large quantities of books, had to exist somewhere. For years historians repeated the cliché that Enlightenment ideas and books were instrumental in bringing about Spanish America's independence. Yet they had little hard evidence to substantiate that hypothesis of a bookish framework for political action. They vaguely said that Spanish Americans traveling abroad brought back in their baggage clandestine books; that ideas entered by way of "Spanish disseminators"[61] intermediaries like translators who brokered foreign thinking; or that mysteriously, "Rousseau's thinking . . . filtered through the cracks that the Inquisition doesn't watch."[62]

These explanations do not account for the large number of books that apparently entered those controlled colonial societies, or the unexpurgated versions that Mexicans and others seem to have read. Another reason may be posited, then, based on the letters Robeson wrote back to Carey: That is, that commercial interests structured a trade that worked somewhere between legitimate routings and once-in-a-while illicit entries by individuals. Although Robeson reports on close calls with customs officials, censors, and jealous Mexicans, the letters, taken up with routine marketing questions, seem to suggest that Carey and Robeson were accustomed to handling merchandise that, though suspect at first, could later surface with the approval of a new government and be the basis for regular trade. Books for them were commodities, and ideas only paper fantasies for trading in a shop. It is even possible that Carey's selection of Roscio's Catholic book for the shipment, rather than a thoughtful, sympathetic choice, was only a businessman's calculation that such a book would be welcome in Mexico. Instead of being Masonic or republican missionaries, Carey and Robeson, in one light, were salesmen who sent books that would pass censors and draw customers. Instead of selling one book here and another there, Robeson quickly tapped into the Mexican market by approaching a Mexico City bookseller and inviting him to buy quantities of his shipment. Looking to enlarge the size of his business, Robeson noted the lack of basic supplies in Mexico (paper, quill pens, etc.) and, in addition to new book titles, proposed the future importation of other goods (even a printing press).

It is difficult to be precise about this kind of trade on the basis of one bookseller's "adventure" into Mexico. Was it a haphazard experiment, a single circumstance, as this one set of letters records? Or are the letters symptomatic of a larger scheme, which the shipping arrangements, brokerage houses in Veracruz and New Orleans, and contacts in Havana that Robeson describes, would seem to indicate? Is "contraband," implicit in Robeson's semiclandestine operation, a term that requires a better definition than historians have usually accorded it? As late as 1810, José María Quirós, the Spanish consul in Veracruz, prepared a *Guía de negociantes. Compendio de la legislación mercantil de España e Indias*,[63] in which he attempted to draw together and update contractual expectations for trade between Spain and the colonies, rules of the sea, and so forth. In that year, at least on paper, Spain controlled Mexican trade.[64]

On December 15, 1821, in an independent Mexico, commercial interests pushed forward a taxation policy whereby the country admitted freely all printed books (so long as they were not injurious to religion and good manners [*buenas costumbres*]). Also permitted were loose engravings; models to teach painting, sculpture, and architecture; scientific instruments; machines useful for agriculture, mining and the arts, and so on. Paper of all kinds, wines, and spices were taxed; tobacco, arms, and luxury goods such as lace were prohibited. The new government seemed to want to distance itself from old colonial restrictions by proclaiming new freedoms, though it tried to limit traffic to the established ports for purposes of gaining revenue and protecting monopolies such as tobacco.[65] Then, in an agreement between Mexico and the United States, signed July 10, 1826, in the language of friendship, mutual respect for one another's ships, diplomatic and commercial representation, reciprocal assurances of trading possibilities, and so on, one reads of "contraband."[66] Contraband is defined mainly as armaments of various types; books or printed matter are not mentioned. That several articles of this later agreement describe how contraband might be seized suggests some attempt at regularizing the traffic that, in fact, was occurring in the Caribbean and the Gulf of Mexico. Ships continued to bring slaves to Cuba despite English efforts to stop the trade. International proclamations of freedom of the seas even after the U.S.

war of independence had not prevented England from seizing men from U.S. ships, claiming they were still British. Piracy and privateering still existed. Contraband, therefore, can be considered to have been a category that legal systems in those years were in the process of defining.

In questioning why men risked sending books that the buyers' society might condemn and call contraband, it is misleading to impute one society's motives for valuing book ownership and reading to another. The printing and distribution of books that Protestant America viewed as the edification of a population, necessary to a democracy, Catholic America tended to understand as increasing the availability to an elite of luxury goods.[67] Books, like the decorative objects from Europe and Asia that filled Mexican homes, were often a kind of furniture, acquired so as to signal high status. It is true that some Mexicans read the new books and reflected on their ideas; these thoughtful men recognized that Mexican minds could only be changed if others got over their phobias and read these books. They assumed that enlightenment would be conducted at the level of the elite class, convincing old-guard monarchists of the benefits of republicanism; they never considered that their mission might extend to indoctrination of Indian-speaking peoples and other castes in the work force—most of Mexico's population. Civilizing them, as Spanish priests in the colonial period had been thought to do, was one thing; but the independent state could not yet think of teaching them to read, much less to read and understand the new books.

Others in the literate class, however, because of old colonial habits of seeking permission to read books, never read the new books. They only bought and displayed them to show their acquisitive power or signal their alliance with a certain faction.[68] Certainly, the books imported by Robeson were never intended for readers beyond the wealthy class. The *Manual de Voyageur*, which Robeson included in his shipment, apparently did not sell in Mexico because attitudes toward seafaring were disparaging there. Unlike these manuals' popularity in the United States among a growing merchant class, this kind of book lay outside the range of experiences Mexicans had historically been permitted to engage in; during the years of colonial rule, Spain reserved its sea trade for itself or contracted with other European nations to transport the colonies' goods.

In the decades after independence Mexican printers grew to be more like their North American counterparts, trying to gauge Mexican taste and cater to it. In so doing they became commercial entities, subject to the rise and fall of market forces. Colonial distinctions between Catholic and Protestant societies, with their respective expectations for the function of a book, did not matter as much. Instead, as literature became secular and took on the character of entertainment in addition to the instruction of former times, readers' needs and whims determined sales. Foreign goods were attractive so domestic printers competed with them, often reprinting foreign news and serializing their novels. They derived revenue from the new partisan politics and the need for new national histories in the schools.

Heredia, the Cuban émigré to Mexico who spent time in the United States from 1823 to 1825, demonstrates in his career the changing fortunes of Mexican publishers. When he first came to Mexico his translation of *Waverley* and editorial participation in the literary journal *El Iris*, but also publication of his own poetry, won him fame. Later, in 1831–1832, he published a translation of *Elements of General History* by the Scot Alexander Fraser Tytler (Lord Woodhouselee)—a book that he said he got in the United States. His stay there had taught him some English, and his several translations from English to Spanish point to Mexico's new intellectual needs and borrowings. Heredia translated material from the New Orleans newspaper, *La Abeja*, for the Mexico City paper, *El Sol*. In 1833 he founded his own literary magazine, *La Minerva*, in Toluca. In those pages he documented how Mexico was changing, explaining the rationale for the magazine. In France, Germany, and the United States, he said, literary and scientific journals "extend the taste for reading, spread useful knowledge, and encourage the progress of civilization." In the present day men have neither the money to acquire large, private libraries, nor the time to read books in their entirety. Thus, Mexican journal editors (and their translators) would select from among the foreign papers the most useful portions for their readers. Because the Mexican public generally did not know foreign languages, or have the money to buy those foreign papers, journal editors would take it upon themselves to represent that literature; they would become the new diffusers of civilization and up-to-date information. Books would be replaced by periodical media and novels would often be serialized and sold as pulp fiction.[69] Thus one reads of Mexicans' thirst still for foreign news but also the fact that in the 1830s Mexico's readership was changing. Mexicans were buying newspapers and literary digests instead of books, and Spanish Americans themselves were beginning to write for their fellows. Heredia's words tell us, then, that Mexican printers were taking over the market that Carey and other U.S. printers had addressed earlier.

We have seen that Philadelphia printers were hurt by aggressive London printers. Alcalá Galiano boasted that émigré Spaniards in London handled the language more satisfactorily than U.S. translators (implying that Peninsular Spaniards were linguistically superior to the Spanish Americans, Frenchmen, Italians, and Irish Americans that Philadelphia employed—although Alcalá Galiano fails to comment on his translators' knowledge of English). We have seen that Spanish censors criticized Puglia's use of the Spanish language and Robeson reported that Mexicans did not like Le Brun's translation of *Libertad de los mares.* However, apart from jealousies over language ownership, another factor might have complicated the translation business in the United States and England, causing Mexican authors and printers to win out over foreigners. Foronda's cavalier statements about the rhythms of English, although he apparently did not possess a good knowledge of the language, reveal not only overconfidence but also an Enlightenment assumption that, because all men were equal and laws governing them could be considered to be universal, local differences did not matter very much. Bentham appears to have thought the same. When he wrote to Lord Holland in Madrid, requesting a safe pass for travel to Mexico, he did not appear to be concerned with not knowing Spanish. Even as late as 1824, when he learned that his *Codification Proposal* had been so badly translated by a Spanish priest that readers in Buenos Aires had thought it "unintelligible,"[70] Bentham seems to have minimized the importance of linguistic difference. However, Spanish Americans were learning to dislike and distrust the translations that printers in the United States and England were sending them and instead were making claims on their own language's credibility and their own authors.

AMERICAN READERS

American readers, to some extent, resembled their European counterparts who, in the years when religion threw up obstacles to book production, had to search for liberal printers. Philadelphia's servicing of Mexico suggests the way in which Dutch, Flemish, Italian, and English printers handled the demands of readers in Counterreformation Europe, and Swiss printers those of prerevolutionary France; readers in controlled societies got elsewhere the works their printers were forbidden to publish.[71] Yet there were differences in the flow of books in the Americas. Distances were greater; and seas often separated printers from readers, thus requiring the intervention of many more petty players in the distribution drama. Translators, peddlers, trading houses, consuls, ship captains, customs inspectors, and muleteers determined the spread of the books—as well as the printers, government licensors, and censors, whose roles we usually recognize. By the early 1800s, religion, though still a reason to screen books in Mexico, had yielded to political considerations. The French Revolution and its bloody aftermath alarmed and gripped readers in both Americas, terrifying them but also showing how popular violence could succeed in overthrowing hated governments. In Spanish America, where Madrid still exerted control, books describing those events were considered seditious and thus proscribed. However, local authorities, monitoring port traffic and anxious to have a cut from any business, often facilitated their entry. When a national government was formed, "sedition" persisted as a criterion for monitoring domestic production and particularly scrutinizing foreign print.

Yet readers in the Americas differed from Europe's for another reason. Colonialisms had trained their subjects to respect as superior to their own fashionings the "civilization" of their mother countries so that American demand for books printed outside their borders reflects psychological insecurities and inferiorities that European readers, with longer and more established literary and intellectual traditions, may not have felt. Therefore, in the first decade after independence from Spain, Mexicans would still have been conditioned to look beyond themselves for guidance. Once Spain was discredited as a source of direction and refusing to acknowledge the value of their own, slowly emerging culture, Mexicans looked to other European countries and the United States for models of modernity. Even Carey's book list for the U.S. population reflects a similar colonial mind-set; although Carey printed the works of some domestic authors, he and his readers seemed to prefer works originating in Europe and titles produced by European émigrés to the United States.

Mexico's colonial past provides yet another explanation for the young nation's fever for foreign goods. Racial differences in Mexico marked cultural and social strata. A growing *criollo* class, composed of European-blooded but American-born Mexicans, was beginning to assert its voice. In the middle between a ruling Spanish-born elite and a large Indian and mixed-race mass, *criollos* were the Americans whose confused identity had triggered the Mexican independence war.[72] Disenfranchised under Spanish rule because Peninsular Spaniards were preferred for positions of power, they felt inferior and orphaned by their Spanish parent; in expressing their resentment, they often compared their situation to that of a younger brother whose father had bestowed all his gifts on the older son. Yet *criollos* enjoyed status in the colony because their whiteness and Spanish education set them off from the larger Indian population—with whom, however, they shared being "American." *Criollos'* recognition of Mexico's needs (as opposed to servicing the metropolis) had made them understand the necessity of separation from Spain, and thus they were among the instigators of the independence revolt and leaders in the new national government. Many of Robeson's book buyers, therefore, would have been *criollos* because, literate and Spanish-speaking, they could appreciate that only non-Spanish literatures could offer them ideas for their future. Having rejected Spanishness, they now sought some new identity that the United States, England, France, and Italy might provide. They affirmed Americanness as they saw similarities between their history and British America's, and they began to listen to, and revalue, the indigenous voices around them.[73] Thus that *criollo* psychology—unsettled and searching for a *raison d'etre*—is apparent in the Mexican appetite for Robeson's foreign books.

The character of Mexican readers is also explained when one notes differences between marketing in Anglo-America and Spanish America. If Carey used agents like Weems in the United States to circulate books on the frontier and practical texts like atlases, elementary-school books, and medical how-to handbooks, and simple biographies of national heroes were the most that could be sold, Robeson's markets in Mexico were in the cities, among sophisticated readers, already familiar with most of the titles he was selling. Well educated, they did not need to be persuaded of the value of books to their lives. Robeson's requests for future shipments tell that their interests lay in politics and the sciences, but he stressed that the latter be understood in terms of practical applications rather than theoretical formulations. Works on surgery were called for but demand would be small for a few. Thus, the Mexican book market was limited to an elite that did not require vulgarized knowledge but instead new thinking. Mexican scientists—particularly in mining technology but also in natural history, astronomy, archaeology, and so on—had been in touch with trends in Europe for decades; indeed they had contributed to development in Europe.

It is interesting to compare Robeson's and Ackermann's assessments of the books required for the Mexican market. Robeson aimed for an elite readership, predicting books for the adult customers Recio had already and perhaps attracting new ones. To a great extent, because he was in the field, he listened to Mexicans who told him of books they had heard about and saw French titles he thought Carey could provide. Ackermann, in London with his covey of Spaniards ready to write basic educational texts, envisioned a readership at the level of juveniles and nonspecialists. He obviously had more capital behind him and was prepared to move into the Spanish American markets in ways that Carey was not. However, neither seemed interested in providing Spanish Americans with translations in which language itself would have been of paramount concern and skill in rendering the original artistry would have been necessary—for example, English poetry.

Mexico's opening up to foreign books recalls how print advanced Luther's Reformation in the sixteenth century. In both cases the growing printing business, as well as expanding literacy, allowed a larger portion of the population than an intellectual and professional elite to consider ideas unmediated by institutional overseers. However, in Spanish America, rather than the growth of a middle class, this expansion took the form of more diversity in the books educated men had access to, more women's literacy at the upper levels of society, and greater consumption by both sexes of the new secular literature. Newspaper editors and pamphleteers used the vernacular for common readers' understanding. If Luther's sermons, translations, pronouncements, hymnals, and so on, raised religious awareness, now utopianists, legislators, economists, moralists—even satirists and novelists—raised political awareness. Old texts were freshly examined and new ones proffered new topics. Like Protestant vernacular translations of the Bible that demanded critical attitudes toward authority, the new literature demanded new modes of reading. Colonial governance had taught the rote, mechanical learning of catechisms and unquestioning recitation of loyalty oaths; now independence required new approaches toward print. Articles in the *Diario de México* tell that Mexicans realized this need, counseling a critical method of reading—one with frequent interruptions so that the reader could back off from the text and restate mentally in his own words what he had read.[74] Thus the books Robeson carried to Mexico, with their challenges to traditional thought, aided in developing this independent mind-set.

The fact that Robeson's books had been printed in Philadelphia, passed Mexican censors surreptitiously, and often entered bookstores or homes undercover would have contributed to the care with which Mexicans picked up the books and turned their pages. Depending on their closeness to the old Spanish ways, they might have frozen, terrified with their audacity in confronting new words, or raced enthusiastically along with the writers. One imagines that those readers silently compared the books with others colonialism had permitted so that criticism—of previous Spanish administration, of precedent and faithful belief, even of social usage such as language—was a natural consequence of that new reading experience.

Robeson gave a face to the myth of Philadelphia, growing in the Mexican imagination.[75] In the 1820s "Philadelphia" stood for successful revolution and separation from a European power, a peaceful post-independence government, and international dealings that might bring a young republic respect. Mier, who had spent time there, returning to Mexico in 1822, contributed to the mythification. A pamphlet, published in Mexico City in 1822, describes that North American model (which had as its center Philadelphia and Pennsylvania); in the preface to a reprinting of the constitutions of Virginia, Maryland, Delaware, Pennsylvania, North Carolina, and Massachusetts, the Mexican author writes:

> Mexicans... In this constitutional era, in the modern age of the common man, America gloriously occupies the vanguard. Our neighbors to the north, inhabitants of the hemisphere, who were enlightened by the virtues of Penn and the memorable victories of Washington, are the first who announced to the world the principles of true liberty. Among all the known nations: [they revealed] the criminal and execrable hands of ambition and the despotism [which], protected by perfidy and error, worked to throw a dense veil over the majestic panorama of the rights of man, traced by the brush of Nature.[76]

Memory of Philadelphia, if not the mythic ideal, can be seen to have survived in Mexico into the twentieth century, influencing a Mexican reader turned writer. In 1933 Martín Luis Guzmán, evoked Philadelphia in his short fiction, *Philadelphia, Haven for Conspirators*.[77] In that story, set in the period from 1809 to 1814, the Spanish hero goes to the United States as business agent and spy for the Regency, which assumed governance while Fernando VII was jailed in France. He carries letters of introduction from Ricardo Meade, consul for the United States in Cádiz. In Philadelphia he meets Luis de Onís, José Alvarez de Toledo, Miguel Cabral de Noroña (the latter two of whom are villainized), and, finally, "an Italian interpreter" who may have been James Philip Puglia.[78] Guzmán calls Philadelphia and Baltimore centers of Napoleonic intrigue, fomenting Spanish American insurrection. Philadelphia's Masonic temple is described ambiguously, suggesting that even in the twentieth century Mexicans could not agree as to whether the movement deserved criticism or admiration: "The Great Masonic Lodge [was] a kind of temple where men, who were called unbelievers, met for purposes a little strange and mysterious."[79]

Guzmán returned again to that early-nineteenth-century moment in Mexico's history in a longer work, *Javier Mina, Héroe de España y México*, not published until 1990 and reissued in 2001 as part of the series, "The Great Novels of Mexican History." There he repeated his description of Philadelphia as a hotbed of revolutionaries where Mina rallied support for his invasion of Mexico: "In the United States there enlisted under his ensigns some North American officials, some of other nationalities who had served in Europe in the French or English armies, and a multitude of enthusiasts and adventurers of those who, in that period, abounded in Philadelphia and Baltimore."[80]

Guzmán thus recalls Philadelphia's importance in Mexican affairs in the early nineteenth century and portrays, as principal actors in his stories, some of the characters in the book world we have seen. His fiction is more than nostalgia, however, because in evoking the myth of that U.S. city, he draws attention to the complexity of U.S.–Mexico relations in Mexico's collective memory. On the one hand, the United States has been a staging ground for influences, which, over the years, have benefited Mexico; on the other hand, many Mexicans have seen those intrusions as harmful. Yet Guzmán's stories also tell of more than just ambivalent attitudes toward the United States. They reflect Mexico's concern with all foreigners, whether in Mexico's midst or in the form of international relations. Early in the 1820s Mexico welcomed U.S. and English diplomatic recognition and investment; the country accepted enthusiastically traders from all nations, Cuban immigrants, and Italian revolutionaries. Later on in the decade, however, this policy became suspect and the country became isolationist. In 1826 John Jordan had a warning printed in Philadelphia: in *Dangers of foreigners and foreign commerce in the Mexican States: Useful information to all travelers in that country, and especially to the merchants of the United States; and equally important to the cabinets of Washington, London, and to the congress of Tacubaya,* Jordan said that a young Italian had been killed in Mexico, foreigners were being expelled, and that, for the future, commercial treaties with Mexico required assurances of rights. In 1828–1829 Spaniards who remained in Mexico were deported out of fear they were a fifth column that might enable a Spanish reconquest. Throughout the nineteenth and twentieth centuries, Mexico's history can be seen to have continued this alternating embrace of foreignness and retreat into extreme nationalism.

As early as 1823 Carlos María Bustamante, who probably participated in the Robeson book business, was calling the new foreign traders venial because they wanted cash for their goods; he wished for the good old days when Cádiz merchants waited a year to be paid. He particularly rebuked U.S. tradesmen, saying that they showed bad faith in their dealings. One sold an inferior felt hat, claiming that it was beaver. Bustamante hoped that Wilcocks, the U.S. consul, would clamp down on his countrymen (1896, 393, 480). Bustamante, an early admirer of the United States, soon became a critic.

COMMERCE AND BOOKS: POSTCOLONIALISMS

The Carey/Robeson letters display that generation's faith, prevalent in both the United States and Mexico, that a new kind of commerce would help to sever ties with old colonial powers and aid in building a new nation. New commerce was thought to replace the older inequalities of coerced monopolies, reliance on specie as the only form of wealth, treaties negotiated between kings. Isaac Kramnick in his study of *The Federalist Papers* says that it was "commerce" that drove the former U.S. colonies, divided among themselves in jealousies over their states' rights, to call the first Continental Congress and then surrender their individual liberties to a constitutional union (1788/1987, 28–29). Commerce in that historical context meant the advantages that a larger state could command. It meant the abolition of internal taxes and duties for greater efficiency. It meant an expansionary economy that could look to compete on the seas with the sea-faring nations of England and Holland. It meant a militia and navy that could defend the new nation's territorial borders against European invasion and piracy. It meant new reliance on credit and the emergence of banking and insurance industries. Free of monetary implications, the term described a new psychology of healthy interpersonal social exchange. In Spanish America, as Rocafuerte argued, its spirit spelled new beginnings, particularly as regards personal freedoms. Individuals could speak, speculate, and invest without the restraints of the Inquisition, metropolitan laws, and taxes. Rocafuerte's attitude is remarkable since it must be remembered that money derived from trade in the Catholic world carried some stigma of Jewishness that old-style, titled aristocrats, whose wealth was in land, repudiated.[81]

In the context of decolonization, commerce allowed young nations to rethink dependency and to undertake, as equals, diplomacy and trade with the world's mature powers they had been cut off from. Commerce allowed for distribution of wealth so that the extremes of wealth and poverty, which had characterized colonial exploitative conditions, were averted. Businessmen, operating independently from the diplomacy of European powers, which often delayed recognition of the new American states as kings honored the rights of fellow monarchs over their former colonies and debated how the balance of power would be tipped if they broke ranks, tacitly conferred recognition on the new states as they traded with partners there; thus commerce went ahead of kings and governments in setting up international relationships. Businessmen—and particularly American businessmen whose populations had declared their independence from European controls—were in the forefront of the age's enlightenment and progress. In the allegorical symbolism of the period's painting, sculpture, and so on, "commerce," along with "agriculture" and "industry," were enthusiastically represented as sources of national wealth. Commerce was thought to provide nations with a rationale for sending missions to undeveloped markets. If religion was discredited as a reason to extend faith and Western civilization, in the nineteenth century commerce (with its arguments of mutual advantage) justified the opening up of countries like China and Japan. National interests were understood to balance one another as new trading relationships were assumed to be equal. Enlightenment universals such as human commonalities and worldly happiness pushed businessmen into new regions.

In 1838, James Fenimore Cooper would write critically of commerce, of its lust for immediate material gain. He said that " a community governed by men in trade, or which is materially influenced by men in trade, is governed without principles, every thing being made to yield to the passing interests of the hour, those interests being too engrossing to admit of neglect, or postponement." An agriculturalist could recoup his losses but if a merchant lost his "adventures," he was lost.[82] Cooper's use of the term "adventure" recalls the description of Robeson's shipment in Carey's business ledger. However, in the 1820s, Americans still believed in commerce's redemptive value.

Commerce had its effect on books; it turned them into commodities.[83] Books were counters businesses used to build their volume, an export product a nation used to advertise its civilized status. Books ceased to be sacred objects, the ownership of which marked membership in a privileged class; instead, in greater numbers and in more humble editions, they left the hands of their authors and their patrons to become the property of dealers, circulating wherever buyers required. In an age when intellectual property rights did not much matter, books could cheaply and easily be manufactured; requiring little raw material in their production, they contributed income to a country's economy without straining its natural resources. Valued for their utility to a class in search of answers to social questions but also for their amusing function, books became, in the eyes of businessmen, so many units to be traded.

David Hackett Fischer has shown the error of describing U.S. culture as uniformly Protestant, where democratic attitudes toward literacy and book ownership could be thought to have determined all regional populations.[84] By contrast Mexico's culture was pretty much "Catholic," in spite of outlying pockets of native-language peoples whose worship was syncretic and, as oral, independent of a book economy. Mexico, where the colonial Inquisition had controlled the spread of books, ownership and literacy were limited to an elite, and books played more of a professionalizing role, the sudden appearance of new reading material in that newly free culture would have elicited a mixed reaction. The merchants behind the book business would have represented influences that were admired but also feared. Interaction with a foreign trader, where the Mexican's money conferred equality on him as he purchased the book, taught him assertiveness and self-confidence even as it opened up to him a world of different thought. Although Rousseau and Paine forced him to think outside the mental limits to which he was accustomed, Roscio's essay was a bridge text that allowed him to stay within his Catholic world even as the author questioned its suppositions; as the Mexican bought and read Roscio's work, he was in a comfortable frame at the same time that he was being forced out of it. Volney's *Catechism* and Foronda's pamphlets also allowed him to stay within the familiarity of ethics and reasonable questioning of monarchism, unlike the angry denunciations of Paine. This Mexican was thus forced by both his acquisition of the book and then his reading to realign his loyalties, and even to question whether his psychological balance could depend on "loyalty" any longer.

In countries opening up to pluralism, books replaced the hostilities of former days and were the new tools of dispute with which one faction could struggle against another. If circumstances did not permit production of the antagonistic literature in the countries themselves, dissidents imported them. In Mexico, then, increasing literacy was not the only reason behind the need for more, up-to-date reading material. Because the elite classes were now divided among themselves, the new books were sought by one group to try to influence the other. Indeed, as the Carey/Robeson letters show, the business of the importation helped to draw the battle lines as liberals confronted the traditionalists—yet also to neutralize factionalism as disputes were verbalized and removed to the safe place of congresses for peaceful negotiation.

Mexico could not afford outright war. Consequently, books had to mediate hatreds and help to deter bloodletting, drawing at least the elite classes together in a common national bloc. If previously government officials had feared books as corrosive of authority and divisive, after independence the time taken to read them was thought to be a unifying force and a substitute for violence. Reading, strolls along the *alameda* with fashionably dressed women, opera—all these were activities that Mexicans understood as replacements for war. "Leisure," a new concept that was different from old-time spiritual renewal that the individual practiced alone, did not have a time-wasting, frivolous connotation in that culture at that moment; instead, in both its personal and social forms, it was thought to occupy men pacifically, in ways that were beneficial to society.[85]

Thus, in a postcolonial paradigm, the reading of appropriate books could be thought to cement social relations. Reading drew men together as they cast about to replace an old patrimony. It stirred the literate elite, making them suspicious of colonial habits of thought they had gotten used to. However, the stirring was not meant to arouse anger or rebellion any longer; instead it was discomforting in a way that was meant to unite the Mexican elite. The newly produced literature employed forms—novels, short fiction, journalism, literary digests, philosophical essays, and Masonic manuals—that engaged a greater number of readers than the older literary genres. It was not soporific or designedly light-hearted. Instead, it was intended to make former abstrusities accessible, to bring new nationals together in common forays of discovery and delight, to harmonize in a country torn by civil war.

The power that books had to intervene in war and make peace is apparent in the close of one of the novels by Pablo de Olavide that Carey reprinted in 1811 from the 1800 Madrid edition. That novel, *El desafío*,[86] did not go into the Robeson shipment to Mexico, although, as I have argued, I believe that Robeson took there another novel from the collection, *La dulce venganza*. To show the faith in the printed word that books from that period inspired, that men might be undeceived as to what war was, I end this study of the print worlds of the United States and Mexico, in their respective moments of decolonization and national development, with words from *El desafío*'s "Apostrophe to War." Olavide is assailing the Napoleonic conflicts that were sweeping Europe, and his focus demonstrates how much the period's literature reflected social change. Political essays and economic treatises—but also the new imaginative literature—responded to conditions by staying close to contemporary pressures and trying to match print to them. War's ugly realities challenged neoclassical rules, which counseled avoidance of such realism. This author's impassioned plea, then, is evidence that at least one Spanish novelist was not thinking of the novel as artistry, as a money-making scheme to attract female readers or a means to teach morality to a new bourgeois society; instead his fiction was intended to be a countervailing force against new, deceptive forms of idealism.[87]

Alongside the poetry of Goethe's *Faust*, which this period also saw, this prose piece may seem minor. Yet it represents an effort to take diversionary literature in the direction of immediacy and honesty. The fact that it was chosen for republication in Philadelphia, and then for possible circulation in Mexico, suggests that its brand of fiction was more acceptable to those formerly colonial readerships than the Romantic stories other European writers were producing, which many times avoided the present by escaping to the past, borrowing plots from other countries, or recounting emotional tragedies of love and loss. The age did not produce an antiwar novel as great as Beethoven's musical indictment of war and tyranny in "Fidelio" (1805). However, Olavide's eruption shows that novelists thought that the genre could be politicized and used to bring to readers its consequences. Reading Olavide's criticism and imagining through his words war's horrible cost in lives, men might learn to avoid that solution to their conflict and thus resolve differences amicably. In that Napoleonic period in Europe and the post-independence years when that novel was read in Mexico, the old debate as to whether arms or letters best occupied men, was far from a rhetorical game; extreme partisanship, which continued after the war, made letters (i.e., reading) a preferable alternative to soldiering:

> Monster War! Your head is adorned with thirty diadems; you dominate Europe with a clutch of scepters in your hands; you are surrounded with palms of glory. Around you are pronounced the grand-sounding words—"valor", "fortitude", and "patriotism". You only walk accompanied by loud music; you offer to astonished eyes the pomp of tents, feathered cockades, fluttering banners, and the glowing faces of the choicest of the human race. I see the splendor of arms, the even and rapid trot of your neighing horses whose impatient hooves carve out the earth. I see uniforms emblazoned with gold ornament that gleams in the rays of the sun. I look at handsome men and the laurels they receive. . . . But if I lift a little the gorgeous curtain that covers you, what do I see? Wounds, blood, horrible gashes in the flesh, mutilated bodies, pieces of men, convulsions of rage . . . human butchery: and afterwards, the tears of wives, mothers, children, friends. . . . What does your horrible Colossus that tramples the entire world matter to me? I only see at your side the exterminating knife that destroys the innermost hearts of nations. I accuse you in the name of humanity, I cite you before its tribunal, I break with your manifestoes, I attribute your origins to centuries of ferocity in which nothing distinguished man from the brute. . . . The morality of nations has been created to make fearful the authority of weapons, to dissipate the atmosphere that surrounds thrones, to vilify the ambitious persons [who hide] beneath their crowns, to make odious the usurpers, conquerors and kings, hungry for riches as despicable as they are detestable, and to educate man and open the eyes of the universe to this destructive power that ruins man's real power, sets him

against his fellow man, and contradicts the plan that Nature has formulated for peace and happiness.[88]

William St. Clair does not mention postcolonialisms in his recent review of volumes of *The Edinburgh History of the Book in Scotland*. Yet in that excellent critique of national book histories he shows how Scottish bibliographers and literary historians have thrown "a possessive plaid round anything or anyone with a Scottish connection" yet have avoided the question of imports into Scotland. He says that book history must be more than cataloging of national printers' output and listings restricted to the national language; he argues for consideration of Scots' consumption of translations of foreign books and more careful concern for readership.[89]

Thus, the Carey/Robeson letters help to supply a lack that St. Clair noticed. If book history reaches to consider all book feeds into a country's mentality, it can more adequately explain a population's knowledge frame. In the late eighteenth, early nineteenth century, when colonial empires were broken apart and men of means reached across borders for resources to help them set up new systems, when men looked to reading as a replacement for warfare, when nationalisms were in the process of formation, books were in demand and traveled. Their translated character, which seemed to smooth over differences and assure acceptance into a world of free intellectual inquiry that mature nations appeared to recognize, contrasted with the restrictiveness of past colonialisms; translations seemed to promise openness and peaceful compromise. Today nationalisms, constructed according to officially proclaimed national languages as "imagined communities," have foreclosed the dreams of those postcolonials. Yet a vision of postcolonial United States and Mexico, multilingual societies with not-yet-firm patriotisms, suggests what that shared world might have been.

——— NOTES ———

1. The phrase derives from Doris Sommer's *Foundational Fictions* (Berkeley: University of California Press, 1991). On Bolívar see Conway.

2. See Williford. This interpretation continues: see John Elliott's review of John Lynch's biography of Bolívar (New Haven: Yale University Press, 2006), published in *The New York Review of Books* (July 13, 2006), 34–36.

3. Selected writings of Bolívar, Bello, and Mier are available in English in editions in the Oxford University Press Library of Latin America. See also Murphy as well as Cussen on their participation in London life.

4. See Lloréns, and by the contemporary Antonio Alcalá Galiano. This latter work, edited by Lloréns, is a translation of essays Alcalá Galiano wrote

in English in 1834 for the London review, *The Athenaeum*. The most complete scholarship is the work of Berruezo León.

5. Berruezo León, 582–590.

6. See Prideaux. On Ackermann, see the several works by Roldán Vera. It is a surprise to learn that Lizardi claimed in a letter to a Mexico City newspaper, *Aguila Mexicana* (May 22, 1826) that Ackermann had contracted to publish the *Periquillo* in London. "The engravings will be very fine and colored, and the board binding very curious." Lizardi says it is too costly to publish in Mexico and that he has no patron to underwrite expenses (*Obras*, Vol. 4, 305–306). An 1826 list of books Ackermann published in Spanish does not mention this publication and it seems no such London edition exists.

7. *Pastimes for Emigré Spaniards* was printed by A. Macintosh and sold in the bookshops of Dulau y Cia., Treuttel y Wurtz, and Rooney e Hijo (Berruezo León, 522–524). Rodríguez O. in *The Emergence of Spanish America* says that Rocafuerte founded a translation society in London, commissioning Spanish émigrés to translate new works. These books of theology, science, and so on, were kept out of Spain but did go to Spanish America. Rocafuerte was also active in the importation of Bibles into Mexico (Chapters 10–11).

8. Miranda attributes England's interest in Mexico then to the influence of Humboldt, popular in England then, on Mexicans like Lucas Alamán (188ff). However, England's interest in Mexico was long-standing. Jiménez Codinach details the early desire of British merchants in Cádiz (such as the sherry house of Duff Gordon) to enter Mexican markets and the Pacific. By the end of the independence war she sees two commercial factions competing for control there: The investors allied with Britain (Alamán, Thomas Murphy, J. Mariano Michelena, Francisco Borja Migone, the Fagoaga brothers and Rocafuerte) and U.S. investors (Wilkinson, Dennis A. Smith, John Mason). The latter curried favor with Guadalupe Victoria and Vicente Guerrero (Jiminez Codinach 1991, 354).

9. See Stolley.

10. The 1777 edition was published in London by W. Strahan and in Edinburgh by T. Cadwell and J. Balfour.

11. See Arteta; Aguirre; Costeloe.

12. Note to *Curiosidades para los estudiosos* (Fernel 1826).

13. "Two Weeks in London, or Rather a Short Trip by a Frenchman to England at the End of 1815" (México: Oficina del Aguila, dirigida por José Ximeno, 205 pp.).

14. I have found Llorente publications in the Bibliothèque National (Paris). On Llorente see Dufour and the bibliographical essay by Emil van der Vekene in Llorente's *Noticia biográfica (Autobiográfica)*. See also my articles: "Llorente's Readers in the Americas," "Lo práctico por lo teórico: Lecciones de Paris

para los americanos en transición," and "Translation and National Politics: *Gil Blas* and the Picaresque."

15. "Laws of the Fuero Juzgo (a Spanish legal code of autonomous privileges), or Gathering of the Laws of the Spanish Visigoths, titled originally 'Liber judicum'"

16. *A History of the Inquisition of Spain, from the time of its establishment to the reign of Fernando VII, composed from the original documents of the Archives of the supreme council and from those of subordinate tribunals of the Holy Office. Abridged and translated from the original works of Juan Antonio Llorente*, 583 pp.

17. *History of the Spanish Inquisition, abridged from the original work of M. Llorente, late secretary of that institution, by Leonard Gallois [pseudonym of Llorente], translated by an American*, 271, 2 pp.

18. *Political aphorisms written in one of the languages of the north of Europe by a philosopher, translated into Spanish by* . . . Llorente says the work will soon be published in Lisbon. The anonymous work begins: "Los pueblos no son para los reyes, y sí los reyes para los pueblos" (Peoples are not created for the [purposes of] kings, but instead kings are [created for the purposes of] peoples.)

19. Although the writer claims that the work appeared first in Madrid, I can find no record of this. In 1821 Mexican printers reprinted materials from the University of Caen ("Declaración de la Universidad sobre el juramento cívico, y breve de N.SS. Padre el Señor Pío VI), and from a Bordeaux newspaper, the *Diario de Burdeos*.

20. *Discourses relative to a religious constitution, considered as part of the nacional civil [code]. Its author an American.* The National Union Catalogue and that of the British Museum say "the American" is Llorente.

21. *Project for a religious constitution, considered as forming part of the civil constitution of a free independent nation, written by an American. Published with a preface by* . . .

22. "Catholic Apology for the Project of a Religious Constitution, Written by An American." This is an extensive work, 256 pages long.

23. "Letter written to an American on the Form of Government that May Be Advisable to Establish in New Spain, Given Its Present Situation, so as to Make Practicable Its Constitution and Laws."

24. "Dissertation on the power that the Spanish kings exercised up until the twelfth century."

25. "Short catechism on the topic of concordats, written in French by . . . and translated by José Mariano Ramírez."

26. "Political portrait of the Popes, published originally in Paris and Rouen in 1822 by Bechet father and son, as *Portrait politique des papes, considérés*

comme princes temporels et comme chefs de l'église, depuis l'établissement du Saint-Siège a Rome, jusqu'en 1822.

27. "Diplomatic collection of various ancient and modern papers relative to marriage dispensations and other points of ecclesiastical discipline."

28. "The Speech of Doctor D. Antonio Joseph Ruíz de Padrón, deputy to the Cortes, from the Canary Islands, spoken in the sitting of January 18th, 1813, relative to the Inquisition. Bread and bulls: an apologetical oration on the flourishing state of Spain in the reign of King Charles IV, delivered in the Plaza de Toros, Madrid, by Gaspar de Jovellanos."

29. Núñez lists many of the New York-printed works that Lanuza translated, such as Voltaire's *Diccionario Filosófico* (1825); and books sold by Lanuza such as *Cuentos y sátiras de Voltaire* (translated by M. Domínguez, 1815), Goldsmith's *El Vicario de Wakefield* (translated by M. Domínguez, 1825), and *Jicoténcal* (1826). Reyna describes Lanuza's involvement with Recio in a project in 1827. Reyna also describes a publishing contract in the 1840s between Atkins S. Wright, who had been an agent in a mining company in Taxco and who would go to Philadelphia to establish a press, and two book dealers in Mexico, who had just immigrated there from Europe—Juan Jacobo Kienart and Juan Federico Werche.

30. Jacinto de Salas y Quiroga, "Estado politico y comercial de la República Peruana", in *Revista de Madrid* 1 (1838), 225, reprinted in Lloréns, 156. (Salas is describing Mexico despite the title of his report.)

31. The paper was published by the Imprenta de Ontiveros; subscriptions were available at Manuel Recio's bookstore, Portal de los Agustinos, at the rate of 6 pesos for each four-month period in the capital and 8 pesos in the provinces, free of delivery. See Hale, 194, and Chapter 6 "Liberalism and the North American Model."

32. Published first by Tomás Lorrain and later by Martín Rivera.

33. Called "periódico politico" (a political paper), it was published by D.J.M. Benavente y Socios.

34. However, in the same issue a clip from the "Gaceta de Nueva York, 19 de marzo" reports on how offended the Spanish minister to the United States. was by the U.S. president's message to Congress. This offense is contradicted by a person visiting in Mexico who said the minister was not at all offended.

35. Published by Martín Rivera, Calle de los Donceles, in Mexico City.

36. Warden's "Statistical, political, and historical account of the United States of North America; from the period of their first colonization to the present day" was published in 1819 in Edinburgh by A. Constable & Co., and in Philadelphia by T. Wardle (3 vols.). The French translation was published in Paris in 1820 in five volumes.

37. Called "periódico cuotidiano, politico y literario" (a daily political and literary paper), it was published by the Imprenta del Aguila, under the direction of José Ximeno.

38. "Miscellany of Literature, the Sciences and Arts."

39. "Trimester Review from Philadelphia" (unknown to cataloguers).

40. "Mexico as an independent nation: description of its moral, political, intellectual state and hopes for its future condition" (Imprenta a cargo de José Márquez).

41. "Answer to the defamatory article against the Mexican republic: published in the *Revista trimestre de Filadelfia*, C.C. Sebring."

42. "Contestación al papel titulado: Revista Trimestre de Diciembre de 1827. Impreso en Filadelfia. En su artículo, México como nación independiente" (Imprenta del Aguila dirigida por José Ximeno). "Answer to the paper titled "Revista Trimestre from December, 1827, printed in Philadelphia, in its article, Mexico as an independent nation."

43. (Por un Mejicano. Tlalpam: Imp. del Gobierno, a cargo de Juan Matute y González). "Interesting ideas in favor of the Mexican republic, against the article published in the Revista Trimestre out of Philadelphia."

44. These essays are reprinted in García Garófalo Mesa (657–660).

45. "Oración fúnebre al ciudadano Jorge Washington. Pronunciada el 1° de Enero de 1800 en una Sociedad Francesa en Filadelfia. Traducido del Francés al Castellano por G.J." (Imprenta del Supremo Gobierno, 21 pp.). "Funeral oration for the citizen George Washington. Delivered the first of January, 1800 before the French Society in Philadelphia. Translated from the French to Spanish by G.J."

46. "Declaraciones de los derechos del hombre en sociedad" (México: Oficina de D. José María Ramos Palomera, 31 pp.). "Declarations of the rights of man in society." The four-page introduction is by Francisco Molinos, and the text includes statements on the rights of man in the constitutions of Virginia, Maryland, Delaware, Pennsylvania, North Carolina, and Massachusetts.

47. "A Defense of the Constitutions of Government of the United States of America" (quoted in McCullough 2001, 376). U.S. interest in Basque government is further shown by the publication in New York in 1824 of *The first seventeen chapters of the ordinances of the illustrious university, house of trade of the most noble and most loyal town of Bilbao — approved and confirmed by the king our lord Don Philip V, in the year 1737* (J. Seymour, xxvii, 181 pp.). In 1829 the Boston printer Isaac R. Butts printed Juan Bautista de Erri's *The Alphabet of the Primitive Language of Spain, and A Philosophical Examination of the Antiquity and Civilization of the Basque People*, translated by George W. Erving, 89 pp.

48. See, for example, the introduction by E. Thornton Miller to John Taylor's *Tyranny Unmasked* (Indianapolis: Liberty Fund, [1822] 1992).

49. For background see Báez Macías on Jerónimo Antonio Gil, and *Guía del Archivo de la Antigua Academia de San Carlos*. Gil was the founder of the Academia. For the visual arts (coin and metal design, architecture and sculpture), see the *Catálogo comentado del acervo del Museo Nacional de Arte and Clasicismo en México*. For academic classicism from a Mexican viewpoint, see *Las academias de arte*.

50. A valuable source for knowing about England's influence on Argentina in the 1820s through its book trade is Parada.

51. Velleman inventories Bello's personal collection of books, which later formed the basis of Chile's national library. Most English-language books (by Goldsmith, Wordsworth, Smollett, Southey) were obtained in London. Only a few U.S.-printed books, such as *Principios elementales de física experimental y aplicada*, published in 1860 in New York by D. Appleton and authored by a Chilean in the United States, Pedro Pablo Ortiz, are in the collection. Pointing to a lack of trade between the newly freed Spanish American colonies, no contemporary Mexican authors (such as Fernández de Lizardi, Gorostiza, Alamán, Bustamante) are in the collection.

52. See De María y Campos. Gorostiza, born in Veracruz, was in Spain from the age of four in 1793 until 1822. He fought in the Spanish army against Napoleon and was beginning a political and writing career as a dramatist in Madrid when he left. Although he was in London for some period, he left frequently for long stretches on diplomatic assignments to the continent. Gorostiza rather seems to have followed in the literary traditions he learned in Spain. He returned to Mexico in 1833 when he was named to create a National Library. In 1837 he was in Philadelphia on a diplomatic mission where he had published an archive relative to Texas. Tomás Murphy, a naturalized citizen with no literary bent, was Mexico's representative in Paris. De María y Campos's book is marvelous in its coverage of how the American diplomats fought in London and Paris to protect their new nations' interests from Spanish, British, French and Vatican forces.

53. *El Iris*, (II, 82–85). Heredia lived in Mexico, secure financially partly as a result of stocks he held in a New York bank (García Garófalo Mesa, 606).

54. The republicanism that the editors of *El Iris* tried to teach in Mexico was confusing. They understood that modern dress symbolized political change; and their lithographs of women with new hats, plunging necklines and shapely costumes were ostensibly designed to show a departure from old Spanish ways. Yet later editorial comment, based on Mexican reaction, reveals that Mexicans only understood these pictures as prescriptions for style and missed their political meaning. When the editors then explained that the

women were advertisements for modernity when they strolled along the *alameda* and thus brought the message of their bodies to social classes who had never seen them before, or had seen them veiled, the leap from that to understanding democracy was great. See my article "Formación cultural."

55. L.F.E. (pseudonym "El Durangueño") "Centinela contra los seductores" (México: No. A, No. 2, 4 pp. each). "Warning against seducers."

56. "Pretensiones de los anglo-americanos" (México: Oficina de D. Alejandro Valdés, 7 pp.). "Pretensions of Anglo-Americans."

57. Printed by Stavely and Bringhurst.

58. Belaúnde, 29; confirmed by Robertson, 64.

59. See Benson, *Mexico and the Spanish Cortes*; Rodríguez O. "The Constitution of 1824."

60. Von Humboldt, *Cartas americanas*.

61. "divulgadores españoles" José Luis Romero, as quoted by Miliani, xii.

62. "[e]l pensamiento de Rousseau se filtra por las rendijas que la Inquisición no vigila", Miliani xi.

63. "Guide for Businessmen. Compendium of the Mercantile Legislation for Spain and the Indies."

64. A useful document for understanding the restrictions Spain placed on her colonies in the last years of empire is the *Reglamento para el comercio libre, 1778* (Madrid: Imprenta de Pedro Marín)—what Spain exported, imported from her colonies, what commodities she permitted to be imported and the taxes imposed. For example, plain Spanish paper entered freely but decorative paper, and paper from Genoa and other "dominions," was taxed. Thus "free trade" was beginning to open Spain and her colonies up to some outside contact (particularly the importation of luxury goods such as cloths from Holland and Flanders), but the language of "libertades" and "gracias" still suggests tight controls.

65. See Loera. Though a commemorative volume, the book has scholarly interest.

66. See Bosch García, *Problemas diplomáticos*, "Apéndice documental," 273–282.

67. See my discussion of the *Diario de México* in *Lizardi and the Birth of the Novel in Spanish America*.

68. A description of readers in South America is to be found in the introduction by Humphreys and Lynch to their *The Origins of the Latin American Revolutions*. Those readers were "a minority within an upper-class minority, lost among the intellectually inert mass of Creoles. The fact of possessing or reading a book did not mean that the reader accepted or was influenced by its ideas. He might read it to condemn it, or merely out of intellectual curiosity, anxious to know what was happening in the outside world and resentful of any attempt to keep him in ignorance" (1965, 12).

69. García Garófalo Mesa (437–440).

70. Williford (20-21).

71. See Darnton's several works.

72. Villoro makes this point.

73. See my "Defining the 'Colonial Reader'"; also on the appearance of indigenous peoples in nineteenth-century constitutions and literary works, Alcides Reissner.

74. See Chapter 1 of my *Lizardi and the Birth of the Novel in Spanish America*.

75. Myth is at the heart of Schumacher's collection of essays on Mexico–U.S. relations.

76. "Declaraciones de los derechos del hombre en sociedad" (México: Oficina de D. José María Ramos Palomera, 31 pp., four-page introduction by Francisco Molinos). "Mexicanos.... En la era constitucional, en la edad moderna de los pueblos, América ocupa gloriosamente la vanguardia: nuestros vecinos del Norte, los habitantes del hemisferio, ilustrado por las virtudes de Penn, y las victorias memorables de Wasington [sic], son los primeros que anunciaron al mundo los principios de la verdadera libertad, entre todas las naciones conocidas: las manos criminales y execrables de la ambición y el despotismo protegidas por la perfidia y el error trabajaron de consuno para echar un denso velo sobre el cuadro magestuoso de los derechos del hombre trazado por el pincel de la naturaleza".

77. *Filadelfia, Paraíso de conspiradores y otras historias noveladas*.

78. Guzmán lived in Spain from 1925 to 1936, where, it is assumed, he used diplomatic correspondence from the Spanish archives as a basis for his fiction.

79. "la Gran Logia Masónica, especie de templo donde se reunieron, para fines un tanto extraños y misteriosos, hombres a quienes se tildaba de incrédulos...." (1960, 30).

80. "[E]n los Estados Unidos se alistaron bajo sus banderas algunos oficiales norteamericanos, varios de nacionalidades diversas—que habían servido en Europa en los ejércitos franceses o ingleses—y una multitud de entusiastas y aventureros de los que por aquella época abundaban en Filadelfia y Baltimore" (2001, 247).

81. For a view of attitudes toward Jews in the early United States, see Pencak.

82. See Cooper, "On Commerce," 478.

83. For a helpful discussion, see Hauser (Vol. 3).

84. Fischer shows that this description of a "Protestant culture" does not take into account different attitudes toward the book, as shown by Puritans in New England (who encouraged mass literacy) and Anglican Virginians (who restricted literacy to a few).

85. See my article "Formación cultural."

86. "The Challenge."

87. Heredia gave a long biographical description of Olavide in the *Diario de Gobierno* (28 abril, 1839), which García Garófalo Mesa reproduces (1949, 677–681).

88. "¡Monstruo de la guerra! Tu cabeza está adornada con treinta diademas; tú dominas la Europa con un haz de cetros en las manos; tú estás rodeada de las palmas de la Gloria; pronúncianse alrededor de ti los nombres pomposos de valor, de firmeza, de patriotismo; no caminas sino acompañada de una ruidosa música; tú ofreces a los ojos deslumbrados la pompa de las tiendas, los penachos, las garzotas flotantes, y la frente brillante con lo más escogido de la raza humana. Yo veo el esplendor de las armas, la marcha igual y rápida de tus caballos, que relinchan, y cuyos impacientes pies cavan la tierra. Veo los vestidos realzados con planchas de oro, y con los rayos del sol que juegan en el voluble acero. Miro los hombres de mejor presencia,, y los laureles que recogen. . . . Pero . . . si mi mano levanta un poco la soberbia cortina que te cubre, ¿qué veré yo? Heridas, sangre, llagas horribles, cuerpos mutilados, trozos de hombres, convulsiones de la rabia. . . . Una humana carnicería: después de esto las lágrimas de las esposas, de las madres, de los hijos, de los amigos. . . .

"Qué me importa tu coloso horrible que pisa al mundo? No miro a tu lado sino el cuchillo exterminador, que destroza el seno de las naciones. Yo te acuso en nombre de la humanidad, te cito ante su tribunal, rompo tus manifestos; yo atribuyo tu origen a los siglos de ferocidad en que nada distinguía al hombre del bruto. . . . La moral de las naciones se ha hecho para atemorizar a la autoridad de las armas, para disipar la atmósfera que rodea los tronos, para envilecer al ambicioso bajo sus coronas, para hacer a los usurpadores, a los conquistadores, y a los Reyes, hambrientos de riquezas tan despreciables, como son odiosos,, y en fin para ilustrar al hombre, y abrir los ojos del universo sobre esta preocupación destructiva, que arruina el poder real del hombre, lo opone a sí mismo, y contradice el plan que la naturaleza había formado para la paz, y su felicidad" (73–76).

89. *TLS*, p. 8.

Appendix A

BOOKS MATHEW CAREY OFFERED FOR SALE IN THE *AURORA GENERAL ADVERTISER,* APRIL 7, 1815

The titles appear as listed in the newspaper. Then, for this advertisement and for the book list in Appendix B, I place in parentheses what I think is the likely edition (sometimes I have guessed and sometimes I have had to conclude failure), having consulted the following bibliographies and catalogues: Francisco Aguilar Piñal's *Bibliografía de autores españoles del siglo XVIII.* 9 vols. (Madrid: C.S.I.C., 1991); Antonio Palau y Dulcet's *Manual del librero hispanoamericano; bibliografía general española e hispano-americana desde la invención de la imprenta hasta nuestros tiempos.* 28 vols. 2ª ed. (Barcelona: Librería Palau, 1954–1955); José F. Montesinos's *Introducción a una historia de la novela en España en el siglo XIX. Seguida del esbozo de una bibliografía española de traducciones de novelas, 1800–1850.* (Madrid: Ed. Castalia, 1980); and the online catalogues of the Library of Congress, the University of California State Library System, the Biblioteca Nacional (Madrid), the Bibliothèque Nationale (Paris), and the British Library.

——— BOOKS LISTED FOR SALE ———

Historia crítica de España. 20 vols. (*Historia crítica de España y de la cultura española. Obra compuesta y publicada en italiano de Juan Francisco Masdeu.* Madrid: A. de Sancha, 1783–1807.)

Obras de Quevedo. 11 vols. (*Obras* [Francisco] de Quevedo. Madrid: Antonio de Sancha, 1791, 11 vols.)

Teatro historico crítico de la eloquencia espanola. 4 vols. (*Teatro histórico crítico de la eloquencia española*, Antonio de Capmany y de Montpalau. Madrid: A. de Sancha, 1786–1794.)

Veladas de la quinta. 3 vols. (*Veladas de la quinta o novelas e historias sumamente útiles para las madres de familia.* Mme. Stephanie Felicité de Genlis, trad. de don Fernando Gilman. Madrid: González, 1788; 3ª ed. Madrid: Collado, 1804.)

Obras poeticas de don Vicente de la Huerta, 2 vols. (*Obras poéticas de Don Vicente García de la Huerta.* 2ª ed. Madrid: Pantaleón Aznar, 1786.)

Romances de Germania. 1 vol. (*Romances de germanía de varios autores, con el vocabulario por la orden del a.b.c. Para declaración de sus términos y lengua. Compuesta por Juan Hidalgo. El discurso de la expulsión de los Gitanos, que escribió el doctor Don Sancho de Moncada . . . y los romances de la germanía que escribió Don Francisco de Quevedo.* Madrid: Don Antonio de Sancha, 1779.)

El tesoro español. 1 vol. (*Tesoro del Parnaso español, poesías selectas castellanas, desde el tiempo de Juan de Mena hasta nuestros días.* Ed. Manuel José Quintana. 4 vols. Perpiñan: J. Alzine, 1817.)

La Araucana. 2 vols. (*La Araucana.* Alonso de Ercilla y Zúñiga. Madrid: Antonio de Sancha, 1776.)

La Constante Amarilis. 1 vol. (*La Constante Amarilis.* Christóbal Suárez de Figueroa. Madrid: A. de Sancha, 1781.)

Don Quixote de la Mancha. 4 vols. (*Vida y hechos del Ingenioso Hidalgo Don Quixote de la Mancha.* Miguel de Cervantes. 4 vols. Madrid: Joachín de Ibarra, 1771, 1780, 1782; Burdeos: Juan Pinard, 1804; Madrid: Viuda de Barco López, 1808.)

Obras jocosas de Quevedo, 6 vols. (*Obras jocosas y poesías escogidas.* Francisco de Quevedo. 6 vols. Madrid: Villalpando, 1796.)

La Galatea de Cervantes, 2 vols. (*Los seis libros de la Galatea.* Miguel de Cervantes. 2 vols. Madrid: Don Antonio de Sancha, 1784.)

Viage al parnaso por Miguel de Cervantes, 1 vol. (*Viage al Parnaso, compuesto por Miguel de Cervantes Saavedra. Publícanse ahora de nuevo una tragedia y una comedia, inéditas del mismo Cervantes La numancia, El trato de argel.* Madrid: J. Ibarra, 1784.)

Parnaso español, colección de poesias, 9 vols. (*Colección de poesías escogidas de los más célebres poetas castellanos*, ed. José López de Sédano. Madrid: J. Ibarra, 1768–1778.)

Obras escogidas de Quevedo, 2 vols. (*Obras escogidas.* Francisco de Quevedo. 2 vols. 2nd ed. Madrid: Fermín Tadeo Villalpando, 1794.)

Eusebio por don Pedro Montengon, 4 vols. (*Eusebio. Parte primera [a quarta], sacada de las memorias que dexó él mismo.* Pedro Montengón. Madrid: G. García, 1807–1808.)

Compendio de la historia de España por don Francisco de Isla, 2 vols. (*Compendio de la historia de España*. Padre [Jean-Baptiste Philpoteau] Duchesne, trad. por Francisco de Isla. Madrid, Imprenta Real por Pedro Pereyra, 1799.)

La Música, poema por don Tomas de Iriarte, con laminas finas, 1 vol. *(La Música*, Tomás de Iriarte. Venezia: Stampería de A. Curti q. Giacomo, 1789.)

Historia de la vida de Ciceron por don Joseph de Azara, con laminas finas, 4 vols. (*Historia de la vida de Marco Tulio Cicerón, escrita en inglés por Conyers Middleton; traducida por Nicolas de Azara*, Madrid: Imprenta Real, 1790.)

El Secretario del comercio. 1 vol.

Compendio de la vida y hechos de Calliostro. 1 vol. (*Compendio de la vida y hechos de Joseph Balsamo llamado Conde Calliostro. Que se ha sacado del proceso formado contra él en Roma el año de 1790 y que puede servir de regla para conocer la índole de la secta de los francmasones.* Giovanni Barberi. Barcelona: Viuda Piferrer, 1790; Sevilla: Imprenta de Vázquez e Hidalgo, 1791.)

Secretos raros de artes y oficios. 2 vols. (*Secretos raros de artes y oficios. Obra útil a toda clase de personas.* Madrid: Imprenta de Villalpando, 1806–1807.)

La independencia de la costa firma. 1 vols. (*La independencia de la costa firme, justificada por Thomas Paine treinta años ha, extracto de sus obras, traducido del inglés al español por D. Manuel García de la Sena.* Philadelphia: T. y J. Palmer, 1811.)

Gonzalo de Cordoba o la conquista de Granada, 2 vols. (*Gonzalo de Córdoba o la conquista de Granada*, Jean Pierre Claris de Florian, traducción de José López de Peñalver. Madrid: Juan López de Peñalver, 1804.)

Expedicion de los Catalanes y Aragoneses contra Turcos y Griegos, 1 vol. (*Expedición de los Catalanes y Aragoneses contra Turcos y Griegos*. Francisco de Moncada. Madrid: Imprenta de Sancha, 1805.)

La religión. Poema de Racine, traducido por don Bernardo de Calzada, 1 vol. (*La religión. Poema de Luis Racine, traducido en endecasílabos castellanos por D. Bernardo María de Calzada.* Madrid: Imprenta Real, 1786.)

Itinerario de Roma, 2 vols. (*Itineraire instructif de Rome ancienne et moderne*, nov. ed. Mariano Vasi. Rome: L'auteur, 2 vols. 1806; *Itinerario istruttivo de Roma a Napoli* [*Itinéraire instructif de Rome a Naples, ou description générale . . . de cette ville et de ses environs.* 2 vols. Rome, 1813].)

El director de los niños para aprender a deletrear y leer, por don Carlos Le Brun, 1 vol. (*El director de los niños para aprender a deletrear y leer.* Philadelphia: Imprenta de Mateo Carey, 1811.)

Appendix B

SUPLEMENTO AL *NOTICIOSO GENERAL*, NUM. 52 DEL MIERCOLES 1° DE MAYO DE 1822*

En la librería de Recio, Portal de Mercaderes, se hallan de venta las obras siguientes, todas de las ediciones más modernas:

Agricultura de Herrera, aumentada con los descubrimientos modernos. (*Agricultura general, que trata de la labranza del campo y sus particularidades, crianza des animales, propriedades de las plantas que en ella se contienen y virtudes provechosas a la salud humana. Compuesta por Alonso de Herrera y los demas autores, que hasta agora han escrito de esta materia, cuyos nombres y tratados van a la vuelta de esta hoja.* Madrid: D. Josef de Urrutia, 1790.)

Almacen de chanzas y veras. (*Almacén de chanzas y veras para instrucción y recreo. Obra escrita en metros diferentes por E.A.P.* Madrid: Imprenta de Aznar, 1802.)

Misales de cámara, media cámara y en cuarto, comunes y con santos franciscanos.

Artes de Nebrija. (*De institutione grammaticae libri quinque. Los cinco libros de Elio Antonio de Nebrija, añadida la traducción al castellano en verso y en prosa de los Géneros, Pretéritos y Supinos de los verbos y de los Libros cuarto y quinto por Don Rodrigo Oviedo.* Madrid: Sump. Regiae Societatis, 1817.)

Colección de muestras de escribir por Tosío y por Zafra. (See below, Torcuato Torío de la Riva.)

Táctica de caballería con láminas. (*Primera parte de la táctica de la caballería inglesa, traducida al castellano por S. Whitingham y R. Ramonet.* Algeciras: 1811.)

---

*Supplement to the *Noticioso General*, No. 2, Wednesday, May 1, 1822.

Torío. *Arte de escribir, ortologia y diálogos de calograrfía.* (*Arte de escribir por reglas y con muestras, según la doctrina de los mejores autores antiguos y modernos, extranjeros y nacionales: Acompañado de unos principios de Aritmética, Gramática y Ortografía castellana, Urbanidad y varios sistemas para la formación y enseñanza de los principales caracteres que se usan en Europa.* Torcuato Torío de la Riva. Madrid: Viuda de Joaquín Ibarra, 1798, 2ª ed. 1802; *Ortología.* Madrid: Ibarra, 1804, 1818).

El Gerundio del Padre Isla, 4 tomos (*Historia del famoso predicador Fray Gerundio de Campazas, por el Padre Isla.* Madrid: Imprenta que fue de Fuentenebro, 1813; Barcelona: Imprenta del Gobierno Político Superior, 1820.)

Nisten, *Manual de medicina práctica.* (*Compendio de toda la Medicina Práctica, Compuesto por Laurencio Heister. Traducido y añadido por el Doctor N.N. y lo publica D. Andrés García Vázquez.* 2 vols. Madrid: Pedro Marín, 1776.)

Filosofia Lugdunense. 5 tomos. (*Lógica parlamentaria. Biblioteca de jurisprudencia, filosofía e historia.* William Gerard Hamilton. Madrid: 18–).

Viage de Anarcarsis á Grecia y Asia. 7 tomos. (*Viage del joven Anarcharsis a la Grecia a mediados del siglo quarto antes de la era vulgar, por Juan Jacobo Barthelemi, traducido del francés al castellano.* Madrid: Imprenta de Collado, 1813.)

Ortografía de la lengua castellana por la Academia. (*Ortografía de la lengua castellana. Por la Real Academia Española.* Madrid: Imprenta Real, 1815.)

Semanas Santas por Rigual y por Villanueva. (*Historia cronológica del pueblo hebreo: de su religión y gobierno político. Historia sagrada de la vida, pasión, muerte y resurrección de Jesu-Christo, sacada de los Santos Evangelios. Explicación de las ceremonias, y disciplina eclesiástica de la Semana Santa.* José Rigual y Ferrer. Madrid: Imprenta de Pedro Marín, 1779.)

Capmani, *Diccionario frances-espanol; y Espanol-frances* por Nuñez Taboada. 2 tomos, edicion de 1820. (*Nuevo Diccionario francés-español. En éste van enmendados, corregidos, mejorados y enriquecidos considerablemente los de Gattel y Cormon, por Antonio de Capmany.* Madrid: Sancha, 1805; 2ª ed. 1817; *Diccionario español–francés, francés–español.* Melchor Emmanuel Núñez Taboada. 3ª ed. Barcelona, 1840.)

Coloquios con Jesucristo Sacramentado.

Fábulas de Fedro, por Oviedo. (*Fábulas de Phedro, liberto de Augusto, traducidas al castellano en verso y prosa, con la explicación de los accidentes de cada palabra, a fin de facilitar su inteligencia en el grado posible, por Don Rodrigo de Oviedo.* 2ª ed. Madrid: Imprenta de José Martín Avellano, 1819.)

Ulloa del Rosario. (*Arco-iris de paz: cuya cuerda es la consideración y meditación para rezar el Santísimo Rosario de Nuestro Señora, compuestas por Fray Pedro de Santa María y Ulloa.* Madrid: Plácido Barco Pérez, 1800.)

Gramática de Iriarte. (*Gramática latina*. Juan de Iriarte. 3ª ed. Madrid: Imprenta Real de la Gazeta, 1775).

Richerand, *Fisiologia* en castellano, 4 tomos. (*Nuevos elementos de fisiologia, por el caballero [Anthelme] Richerand*. Madrid: Francisco Martínez Dávila, 1821.)

Cepero, *Lecciones constitucionales.*

Bueno, *Prontuario de química*. (*Prontuario de química, farmacia y materia médica*. Pedro Gutiérrez Bueno. Madrid: Villalpando, 1815.)

Almeida, *Tesoro de paciencia*. (*Tesoro de paciencia, o consuelo del alma atribulada en las meditaciones de las penas del Salvador*. Teodoro de Almeida. Madrid: 1793.)

Verdejo Paez, *Geografia*. (*Principios de geografía astronómica, física y política, arregladas en los últimos tratados de paz, según el estado actual de Europa*. Francisco Verdejo Páez. Madrid: Imprenta de Repullés, 1818.)

Sturm, *Reflexiones sobre la naturaleza*, 6 tomos. (*Reflexiones sobre la naturaleza, o consideraciones de las obras de Dios en el orden natural: escritas en alemán para todos los días del año. Por H.S.S. Sturm, traducidas al francés, y de éste al castellano*. 2ª impresión, corregida y aumentada. Madrid: Don Benito García y Compañía, 1803.)

Marina, *Teoría de las Córtes*, 3 tomos, edicion de 1820. (*Teoría de las Cortes o grandes juntas nacionales de los reinos de León y Castilla. Monumentos de su constitución política y de la soberanía del pueblo. Con algunas observaciones sobre la lei fundamental de la monarquía española . . . de 1812*. Francisco Martínez Marina. Madrid: Impr. de Fermín Villalpando, 1813.)

Arbiol, *Familia regulada*. (*La familia regulada con doctrina de la sagrada escritura y santos padres de la Iglesia Católica; para todos los que regularmente componen una casa seglar, a fin de que cada uno en su estado y en su grado sirva a Dios Nuestro Señor con toda perfección y salve su alma*. Antonio Arbiol, Impresión quinta, ilustrada y corregida por su autor. Madrid: Thomas Rodríguez Frías, 1725.)

Cuarto tomo de la *Fisiolofia* de Dumas. (*Principios de fisiología, o introducción a la ciencia experimental, filosófica y médica del hombre vivo, por el Ciud. Carlos Luis Dumas, traducida por Don Juan Vicente Carrasco*. Madrid: Imprenta de Don Mateo Repullés, 1804.)

Breviarios comunes y franciscanos.

Garcia, *Geografia*. 2 tomos. (*Nuevos elementos de geografía general astronómica, física y política para servir de base a la educación de la juventud*. Juan Justo García. 2 vols. Salamanca: Imprenta de D. Vicenta Blanco, 1818–1819.)

Diarios de las Córtes de España.

Ordenanzas militares. (*Colección general de las ordenanzas militares, sus innovaciones, y aditamentos, dispuesta . . . con separación de clases, por . . . Joseph Antonio Portugués*. Madrid: Imprenta de Antonio Marín, 1764–1765.)

Castro, *Reformacion cristiana*. (*Reformación christiana: así del pecador como del virtuoso*. Francisco de Castro. Madrid: Imprenta de Benito Cano, 1785.)

Formularios para juicios de conciliación, retencion de efectos y demas. Obra muy útil á toda clase de personas, pero con especialidad a los alcaldes y escribanos. (*Formulario de los juicios de conciliación: retención de efectos y demás en que los alcaldes constitucionales pueden tomar providencias provisionales, con arreglo al decreto 201 de 9 octubre de 1812; o sea reglamento de las audiencias y juzgados de primera instancia*. Madrid: Oficina de D. Francisco Martínez Dávila, 1820.)

Filangieri, *Ciencia de la legislación*. 10 tomos. (*Ciencia de la legislación, traducida del italiano por D. Jaime Rubio, corregida y añadida*. Cayetano Filangieri. 10 vols. 3rd ed. Madrid: Imprenta de Núñez, 1822.)

Wattel. *Derecho publico*. 4 tomos. (*Instituciones sobre el derecho público, sacadas de las obras del chanciller Enrique Francisco d'Aguesau*. México: M. Ontiveros, 1813.)

Biblia en latín y castellano, 15 tomos.

Curso de política constitucional por Benjamin Constant, en castellano, 3 tomos. (*Curso de la política constitucional por Benjamin Constant, traducido libremente al español por Marcial Antonio López*. Burdeos: Imprenta de Lawalle Jóven, 1823, 2ª ed. 3 vols.)

Kempis, en latin y en castellano. (*De Contemptu Mundi*. Palau says Latin editions generally have no date; *De la imitación de Cristo o menosprecio del mundo, traducido por Fr. Luis de Granada*. Tomás de Kempis. Madrid: Sancha, 1821.)

Jaquier, *Filosofía*, 4 tomos. (*Institutiones Philosophicae*. Francisco Jacquier. 4 vols. Valentiae: 1769.)

Obras de Cadalso. 3 tomos: (*Obras del coronel Don Joseph Cadalso*. 3 vols. Madrid: Don Mateo Repullés, 1803.)

Bichat, *Anatomia general*. 4 tomos. (*Anatomía general: aplicada a la fisiología y a la medicina*. Xavier Bichat. Madrid: Imprenta de Francisco de la Parte, 1814.)

Jesus moribundo. (*Jesús moribundo*. Valencia: Los Hermanos de Orga, c. 1794.)

El cantor practico. (*El práctico cantor en el ministerio de la iglesia, obra de castellano y figurado*. D. Daniel Travería. Madrid: García y Cía, 1804.)

Decretos de las Córtes. Tomo 6.

Aforismos de Boerhaave, en castellano, por Lavedan, un tomo 1817. (*Aphorismos de cirugia*. Herman Boerhaave. 8 vols. Madrid: Imprenta de Pedro Marín, 1774–1788.)

Diarios comunes y franciscanos en 12 y en 16, 1817.

Montesquieu, *Espíritu de las leyes con su elogio, análisis, defensa, las observaciones de Condorcet, y los comentarios del Conde Destut de Traci, Par de*

Francia, arreglados á los progresos que han hecho las luces en los últimos 50 años, 5 tomos en castellano, edicion de 1821. (*Comentario sobre el Espíritu de las leyes de Montesquieu*. Antoine Louis Claude, comte Destutt de Tracy. Burdeos: Imprenta de Lavalle joven, 1821.)

Centellas. *De ayudar á bien morir*. (*Prácticas de visitar los enfermos y ayudar a bien morir*. Balthasar Bosch Centellas y Cardona. Madrid: Oficina de Joachín Ibarra, 1759.)

Colección de autores latinos para el uso de las escuelas pias.

Bell. *Curso completo de cirugia*. 5 tomos. (*Sistema completo de Cirugía. Traducido del inglés por Santiago García*. Benjamin Bell. 6 vols. Madrid: Imprenta de Repullés, 1813.)

Bell. *De Lue Venérea*. 2 tomos. (*Tratado de Bienorrhagia y de la Lue venérea. Traducido del inglés con notas por Santiago García*. Benjamin Bell. Madrid: Imprenta de Manuel González, 1793.)

Furcroy. *Sistema de los conocimientos químicos*. 10 tomos. (*Sistema de los conocimientos químicos, y de sus aplicaciones a los fenómenos de la Naturaleza y del Arte, obra escrita en francés por A.F. Fourcroy, y trasladada al castellano por D. Pedro María Olive y D. Gregorio González Azaola*. Madrid: Imprenta Real, 1803–1809).

Diccionario de Balbuena, cuarta edicion. (*Diccionario universal . . . latino–español, dispuesto por Manuel de Valbuena*. 4ª ed. Madrid: Imprenta Real, 1819.)

Las siete partidas del sabio Rey Don Alonso, con la glosa de Gregorio Lopez. 4 tomos. folio. (*Las Siete Partidas del Sabio Rey D. Alonso el Nono, copiadas de la edición de Salamanca del año de 1555, que publicó el Sr. Gregorio López*. Valencia: Benito Monfort, 1767, 5 vols.)

Año Cristiano, adicionado por los Padres Centeno y Roxas con el índice. 19 tomos. (*Año cristiano, o Exercicios devotos para todos los días del año, escrito en francés por Juan Croiset, traducido al castellano por Josef Francisco de Isla y adicionado por Pedro Centeno y Juan Fernández de Roxas*. Madrid: Imprenta de la Real Compañía, 1804.)

Arte de tocar la guitarra por Ferrandier. (*Arte de tocar la guitarra española por música*. Fernando Ferandière. Madrid: 1799.)

Salsas. *Catecismo predicable*. 5 tomos, cuarto. (*Catecismo pastoral y prontuario moral sagrado de platicas doctrinales y espirituales; sobre todos los puntos de la doctrina christiana, apoyado en la Sagrada Escritura, Santos Padres y Doctores Catolicos*. Pedro Salsas y Trillas. Madrid: Imprenta de la viuda e hijo de Marín, 1795-1801, 5 vols.)

Ligorio. *Visitas al Santísimo y á la Santísima Virgen*. (*Visitas al ssmo. Sacramento y a María Santísima para todos los días del mes; actos de preparación y de acción de gracias para la sagrada comunión/obra compuesta en italiano por Alonso de Liguori; vertida al español por un sacerdote del oratorio de S. Felipe de Neri de Barcelona*. México: Oficina de Arizpe, 1818.)

Física de Brison. (*Diccionario universal de física. Escrito en francés por M. Brisson, traducido al castellano por los doctores D.C.C. y D. F.X.C.* Mathurin Jacques Brisson. 10 vols. Madrid: Imprenta de Benito Cano, 1796–1802; *Tratado elemental o, principios de física, fundados en los conocimientos más ciertos así antiguos como modernos y confirmados por la experiencia*. 4 vols. Madrid: Imprenta de la Administración del Real Arbitrio de Beneficencia, 1803–1804.)

Vidas de los mártires. 13 tomos en castellano. (*Vidas de los padres, mártires y otros principales santos; deducidas de monumentos originales y de otras memorias auténticas, ilustradas con notas de historiadores y críticos juiciosos y modernos; corregidas y aumentadas por manuscritos del mismo autor*. Alban Butler. Valladolid: Viuda e hijos de Santander, 1789–1792.)

Dios inmortal. (*Dios inmortal padeciendo en carne moral* [¿?] *o la pasión de Cristo, traducido del latín por el Dr. D. Francisco Patricio de Berguizas*. Madrid: Imprenta Real, 1807.)

Ordenanzas del Consulado de Bilbao, añadidas. 1819 (*Copia a la letra de los capítulos 9, 10, 11, 14 y 17 de las reales ordenanzas del Consulado de la villa de Bilbao; por real cédula de diciembre de 1737*. Guadalaxara: Mariano Valdés, 1796.)

Simon de Nantua ó el mercader forastero. Obra compuesta por el célebre Jussieu, para instrucción de la juventud, que por unanimidad de votos, obtuvo en 1818 el premio de la academia en Paris, un tomo, traducido al castellano. (*Simón de Mantua, traducido del francés*. Torcuato Torío de la Riva. Laurent de Jussieu. Madrid: Ibarra, 1819.)

Pablo y Virginia, con láminas. (*Pablo y Virginia, traducido en español por Don Josef Miguel Aléa*. Bernardin de Saint-Pierre. Madrid: Pantaleón Aznar, 1798; Madrid: B. García, 1800; Valencia: I. Mompié, 1816.)

Fray Luis de Granada, *Meditacion*. (*Libro de la oración, y meditación en el qual se trata de la consideración de los principales Misterios de nuestra Fe*. Madrid: Imprenta de la Compañía, 1815; Cervera: Imprenta de la Real y Pontificia Universidad por Josef Casanova, 1816.)

Maclovia y Federico, *Minas del Tirol*. (*Maclovia y Federico, o, Las minas del Tirol*. Louise Marguerite Jeanne Madeleine Brayer de Saint-Leon. Valencia: I. Mompié, 1816.)

Voz de la naturaleza. (*Voz de la naturaleza. Memorias o anécdotas curiosas e instructivas, de Don Ignacio García Malo*. Gerona: Imprenta de Blas S–, 1793; Madrid: Aznar, 2ª impresión, 1803–7 vols.)

La Carolina Lichefield. (*Carolina de Lichtfield, puesta en castellano por D.F.D.O*. Isabelle de Bottens. 2ª impresión. Madrid: Imprenta Real, 1802.)

Viacrucis esplanado.

Sala, *Instituciones Romano-Hispanae.* (*Institutiones romano-hispanae.* Juan Sala Banuls. 2 vols. Valencia: Salvador Fauli, 1788–1789.)

Atala, amores de dos salvages en el desierto. (*Atala o los amores de dos salvajes en el desierto, traducción hecha libremente del francés al español por D.T.T.d.l.R.* [Torcuato Torío de la Riva]. François René Chateaubriand. 2ª ed. Barcelona: Sierra y Martí, 1808.)

Cartas del Conde Cavarrus. (*Cartas sobre los obstáculos que la naturaleza, la opinión y las leyes oponen a la felicidad pública.* Francisco, conde de Cabarrús. 3ª ed. Madrid: Imprenta de Burgos, 1820; Valencia: Imprenta de I. Mompié, 1822.)

Celia y Rosa. (*Celia y Rosa, novelas escritas . . . por madame de Renneville y trads. por D.J.M.A.* 2 vols. Mme. Sophie Renneville Senneterre. Valencia: Esteban, 1817.)

Larraga, cuarta vez, ilustrado. (*Promptuario de la theología moral: compuesto primeramente por Francisco Larraga, después reformado y corregido en algunas de sus opiniones . . . y ahora últimamente acabado de reformar, añadir y reducir a mejor método, orden y conexión de doctrinas en todos los demás tratados y materias por don Francisco Santos y Grosin . . . nuevamente corregido, retocado y añadido por el mismo autor.* Barcelona: Imprenta de los Consortes Sierra y Martí, 1797.)

Febrero. *Librería de escribanos y materia criminal* por Villanova, 11 tomos, cuarto. (*Librería de escribanos, e instrucción jurídica theórico práctica de principiantes.* José Febrero. 7 vols. Madrid: Imprenta de Pedro Marín, 1789–1790.)

Ideker, *La fe triunfante,* idem. (*La fe triunfante, o, Carta a la junta llamada el Gran Sanhedrin de los Judíos de París y a todo el pueblo hebreo esparcido por el mundo.* Juan Joseph Heydeck. Madrid: Imprenta Real, 1815.)

Colección de seguidillas, tiranas y polacas para cantar á la guitarra. 2 tomos. (*Colección de las mejores coplas de seguidillas, tiranas y polacas que se han compuesto para cantar a la guitarra.* Don Preciso. 2 vols. Madrid: Repullés, 1815–1816.)

Almacen de fruslerias. 2 tomos. (*Mis pasatiempos: almacén de fruslerías agradables.* Cándido María Trigueros. 2 vols. en uno. Madrid: Viuda de López, 1804.)

Ramillete de divinas flores

Wuotres, *Exposicion de la doctrina.* 4 tomos, cuarto. (*Historia de las variaciones de las iglesias protestantes: y Exposicion de la doctrina de la iglesia Cathólica, sobre los puntos de controversia . . .* Jacques Benine Bossuet. 4 vols. Madrid: Antonio Fernández, 1786.)

Colon, *Juzgados militares*, tercera edicion, 4 tomos. (*Compendio de los juzgados militares para el uso de los corregidores y alcaldes de los pueblos de España*. Félix Colón de Larriátegui. 4 vols. Valencia: Impr. de M. Domingo, 18–.)

Lecciones de política y derecho público para instrucción del pueblo mexicano, un tomo en 8, pasta. (*Lecciones de política y derecho público para instrucción del pueblo mexicano*. Juan María Wenceslao Barquera. México: Impr. de Doña Herculana del Villar y socios, 1822.)

Iraisos, *De ceremonias*, en un tomo. (*Directorio de sacrificantes: instrucción theori-práctica acerca de las rúbricas generales del missal, ceremonias de la missa rezada y cantada, oficios de Semana Santa y de otros días especiales del año; con un índice copiosíssimo de decretos de la Sagrada Congregación de Ritos, y algunas notas para su mejor inteligencia*. Fermín de Irayzos. 2ª impresión. Madrid: Imprenta y Librería de Joseph García Lanza, 1757.)

La Matilde ó el subterraneo, 3 tomos, 12. (*Camila o El subterráneo*, anonymous, published first in Paris, 1803; *Matilde*, trad. por M. García Selto. Mme. Marie Risteau Cottin. 3 vols. Madrid: Brugada, 1821 [¿?].)

La Noche entretenida, un tomo. (*La noche entretenida*. D.J.M.H. Madrid: Viuda e hijo de Marín, 1798.)

Sermones de Macillou, 11 tomos, 4.

Año panegírico, 6 tomos.

Prontuario de los ayudantes generales y agregados á los estados mayores por Pablo Thiebault. (*Prontuario de los ayudantes generales y agregados a los estados mayores de división de los exércitos, traducido por F.S. y F*. Tarragona: Brusi, 1810.)

Pastorales de Benedicto XIV, 2 tomos, cuarto. (*Pastoral de Ntro. Ssmo. Padre Benedicto XIV de gloriosa memoria: siendo cardenal arzobispo de la Santa Iglesia de Bolonia, e instrucciones eclesiásticas para su diócesis*. 2 vols. 5ª impresión. Madrid: Imprenta Real, 1787.)

Sermones del Santísimo Sacramento del Altar, un tomo, cuarto.

Poesias de Goveo. (*Mis amores o poesías líricas*. Gregorio Isaac Díaz de Goveo. Madrid: 1805.)

Poesias de Arellano. (*Poesías varias*. Vicente Rodríguez de Arellano y el Arco. Madrid: Repullés, 1806.)

Poesias de Doña Rosa Galvez. (*Obras poéticas*. María Rosa Gálvez de Cabrera. 3 vols. Madrid: Imprenta Real, 1804.)

Obras políticas de Don Diego Saavedra, 11 tomos, 8. (*República literaria/ Obras de don Diego de Saavedra Faxardo*. Madrid: Benito Cano, 1789-1790, 11 vols.)

Colección de filósofos moralistas antiguos, 6 tomos, 12. (*Colección de filósofos moralistas antiguos*. Trad. por Enrique Ataide y Portugal. 2 vols. Madrid: Aznar, 1802–1803.)

Burriel, *Cartas eruditas y criticas*, un tomo cuarto. (*Cartas eruditas y críticas del P. Andrés Marcos Burriel, de la extinguida Compañía de Jesús.* Madrid: Imprenta de la viuda e hijo de Marín, 1775.)

Aforismos de cirugia de Boerhaave, por Van-swieten, 8 tomos, cuarto.

Historia del Emperador Carlo Magno, un tomo, 8. (*Historia del emperador Carlo Magno, en la qual se trata de las grandes proezas, y hazañas de los doze pares de Francia, y de cómo fueron vendidos por el traydor de Ganalon, y de la cruda batalla que huvo Oliveros con Fiérabras de Alexandria, hijo del Almirante Balan.* Jean Baignon. Barcelona: A. Arroque, 17–.)

Belarmino, *Declaracion copiosa de la doctrina cristiana*, 1 tomo, 8. (*Declaración copiosa de la doctrina christiana: compuesta por orden del beatísimo padre Clemente VIII de feliz memoria.* Roberto Francesco Romolo Bellarmino. Cervera: Imprenta de la Pontificia y Real Universidad, 1779.)

El Sacerdote santificado, 2 tomos, 8. (*El Sacerdote santificado en la administración del sacramento de la penitencia: cartas sobre el modo práctico de administrar el santo sacramento de la penitencia con provecho propio, y de los penitentes.* Madrid: Plácido Barco López, 1789.)

Directorio politico de alcaldes constitucionales para el ejercito de las conciliaciones y juicios verbales. (*Directorio político de alcaldes constitucionales: para el ejercicio de las conciliaciones, juicios verbales, y otras funciones de su instituto, puesto en estilo de diálogo para la más fácil instrucción de todos los que tengan que formalizar alguna demanda.* Juan Wenceslao Barquera. México: Oficina de Juan Bautista de Arizpe, 1820.)

Appendix C

SPANISH-LANGUAGE BOOKS PRINTED BY ACKERMANN, ADVERTISED IN 1826 IN *CURIOSIDADES PARA LOS ESTUDIOSOS*, SOLD IN LONDON IN SU REPOSITORIO DE ARTES, AND IN MEXICO, COLOMBIA, BUENOS AIRES, CHILE, PERU, AND GUATEMALA

El Mensagero, por D. Jose Blanco White. Toda la colección.
Museo universal de ciencias y artes, por J.J. de Mora, redactado bajo un nuevo plan. Numero 10.
Correo literario y politico de Londres. Periodico Trimestre, particularmente destinado a la America que fue Española, en el cual se presenta un cuadro sucinto de Acaecimientos Politicos, y de Composiciones y Noticias relativas a la Literatura y a las Artes. Redactado por J.J. Mora.
No me olvides, Colección de Composiciones por J.J. de Mora. El tercer tomo.
Viage pintoresco a las Orillas del Ganges y del Jumna, en la India.
Carta sobre la educación del bello sexo.
Memorias de la revolucion de Megico, y de la Espedicion del General Mina.
Gimnastica del bello sexo.
El Español por Blanco White.
Teología natural, por Paley.
La gastronomía, o los placeres de la mesa.

Gramatica inglesa, por D. Jose de Urcullu.
Catecismo de gramatica latina, por J.J. de Mora.
La venida del Mesias en gloria y majestad, con varios discursos en defensa del autor. En tres tomos, 8vo.
Historia antigua de Megico, por Clavigero, traducida del italiano por J.J. Mora, con excelentes estampas y un mapa.
Elementos de la ciencia de hacienda, por D. Jose Canga Arguelles.
Obras liricas, de D. Leandro Fernandez de Moratin.
Descripcion abreviada del mundo.
Catecismo de geografia.
———*quimica.*
———*agricultura.*
———*industria rural y economica.*
———*historia de los imperios antiguos.*
———*historia de Grecia.*
———*historia romana.*
———*historia del Bajo Imperio.*
———*historia moderna, Parte I.*
———*historia moderna, Parte II.*
———*astronomia.*
———*gramatica castellana.*
———*economia politica.*
———*mitologia*, por D. J. de Urcullu.
———*aritmetica comercial*, por el mismo.
———*historia natural*, por el mismo.
———*retorica*, por el mismo.
———*moral*, por el Dr. J.L. de Villanueva.
———*geometria elemental*, por D. Jose Nunez Arenas.
De la administración de la justicia criminal en Inglaterra, por Cottu. Traducida al castellano por el autor del *Espanol* y de las *Variedades*.
Viage pintoresco por las orillas del Sena.
Viage pintoresco por las orillas del Rin.
Noticias de las Provincias Unidas del Rio de la Plata, por D. Ignacio Nuñez.
Ivanhoe, Novela por autor de *Waverley* y del *Talisman*.
El Talisman. Cuento del tiempo de las Cruzadas, por el autor de *Waverley*, *Ivanhoe*, &
Cuentos de duendes y aparecidos, compuestos con el obgeto espreso de desterrar las preocupaciones vulgares de apariciones. Adornados con seis estampas iluminadas. Traducidos del ingles por D. Jose de Urcullu.
El Padre Nuestro del Suizo, ilustrado con estampas, y sus esplicaciones.
Dios es el amor mas puro, mi oracion y mi contemplación. Con muchisimas estampas y oraciones para la Misa. Traducido por D. Jose de Urcullu.

Cuadros de la historia de los arabes. Dos tomos en 12mo.
Elementos de dibujo.
Elementos de perspectiva.
La soledad, por Young; traducida al castellano.
Meditaciones poeticas, por J.J. de Mora, con estampas.
Manual de medicina domestica, 12mo.
Curiosidades para los estudiosos.
Elementos de esgrima.
Lecciones de moral, virtud y urbanidad, por D. Jose Urcullu.
Trescientas sentencias arabes; Quinientas maximas y pensamientos de los mas celebres autores antiguos y modernos; y cincuenta pensamientos originales del que ha redactado los anteriores.
Recreaciones geometricas.
Recreaciones arquitectonicas.
Nuevo silabario de la lengua castellana.
La batalla de Junin, Canto a Bolivar, por J.J. Olmedo, con tres estampas.
La nueva muñeca, con seis estampas.
Muestras de letra inglesa.
Trages de boda de las principales naciones.
Himno a Bolivar, Poesia de J.J. de Mora, musica del Caballero Castelli.
Himno a Victoria, por los mismos.
Himno a Bravo, por los mismos.
No me olvides, Cancion por los mismos.
La mariposa. Cancion por los mismos.
Amor es mar profundo, Bolero a duo, por los mismos.
El pescador, Cancion por los mismos.
Vista de Lima por el lado del este.
Vista de las montanas principales del mundo.
Triunfo de la Independencia americana.
Registros para libros, en 10 estampas.
Un mapa grande de la republica de Megico.
Dos vistas de Megico, iluminadas.

—— EN PRENSA ——

Diccionario latino-espanol, de Valbuena, con muchas adiciones.
Gramatica latina, por Yriarte.
Elementos de equitación, que contienen un tratado sobre las diferentes castas de caballos, sus enfermedades, y proporciones.

Appendix D

CATALOGUE OF SPANISH BOOKS AND MANUSCRIPTS, PRINTED IN WILLIAM ROBERTSON'S *HISTORY OF AMERICA*, 1803 EDITION

Documentation is original to the catalogue, and I have not corrected misspellings. References alongside some entries refer to the following: *Delle navigationi et viaggi raccolte da m. Gfo. Battista Ramusio*. Giovanni Battista Ramusio. (Venetia: Apressi I. Givnti, 1606); Melchisedec Thevenot, *Recueil de voyages de Mr. Thevenot*. (Paris: Chez E. Michallet, 1681); Andrés González de Barcia Carballido y Zúñiga. *Historiadores primitivos de las Indias Occidentales que juntó, traduxo en parte, y sacó a luz, ilustrados con eruditas notas, y copiosos índices*. (Madrid: 1749, 3 vols.); Awnsham Churchill. *A Collection of Voyages and Travels, some now first printed from original manuscripts*... (London: 1704, 1744–1746; 1752); *Colección de documentos: tocantes a la persecución que los regulares de la Compañía suscitaron y siguieron tenazmente por medio de sus jueces conservadores, y ganando algunos ministors* [sic] *seculares desde 1644 hasta 1660 contra... Bernardino de Cárdenas, religioso antes del orden de S. Francisco, obispo de Paraguay*... (Madrid: Imprenta real de la Gaceta, 1768–1770, 4 vols.); Simon Grynaeus, *Novis Orbis, id est, Navigationes prima, in Americam: quipus adiunximus Gasparis Varrerii Discursum super Ophra regione*. (Roterodami: apud Johannem Leonardi Berewout, 1616).

Acarete de Biscay, *Relation des Voyages dans la Rivière de la Plata, & de la par Terre au Perou*. Exst. Recueil de Thevenot, Part IV.
———. *A Voyage up the River de la Plata, and thence by Land to Peru*. 8 vo. London, 1698.
Acosta (P. Jos. de), *Historia Natural y Moral de las Indias*. 4to. Madrid, 1590.

———. (Joseph de) *Histoire Naturelle & Moral des Indes tant Orientales qu'Occidentales*. 8 vo. Paris, 1600.

———. *Novi Orbis Historia Naturalis & Moralis*. Exst. in Collect. Theod. de Bry, Pars IX.

———. *De Natura Novi Orbis*, Libri duo, & de procuranda Indorum Salute, Libri sex, Salmant. 8 vo. 1589.

———. (Christov.) Tratado da las Drogas y Medecinas de las Indias occidentales, con sus Plantas Dibuxadas al vivo. 4to Burgos, 1578.

Acugna (P. Christoph.) *Relation de la Rivière des Amazones*. 12 mo. Tom. ii. Paris, 1682.

Acugna's *Relation of the great River of the Amazons in South America*, 8 vo. Lond. 1698.

Alarchon (Fern.) *Navigatione a Scoprere il Regno di sette Città*. Ramusio, III, 363.

Albuquerque Coello, (Duartè de) *Memorial de Artes de la Guerre del Brasil*, 4to. Mad. 1634.

Alcafarado (Franc.) *An Historical Relation of the Discovery of the Isle of Madeira*. 4to. Lond. 1675.

Alçedo y Herrera (D. Dionysio de) *Aviso Historico-Politico-Geografico, con las Noticias mas particulares del Peru, Tierra Firmé, Chili, y nuevo Reyno de Granada*. 4to. Mad. 1740.

———. *Compendi Historico de la Provincia y Puerto de Guayaquil*. 4to. Mad. 1741.

———. *Memorial sobre diferentes Puntos tocantes al estado de la Real hazienda, y del Comercio, & en las Indias*. fol.

Aldama y Guevara (D. Jos. Augustin de) *Arde* [sic] *de la Lengua Mexicana*. 12 mo. Mexico, 1754.

Alvarado (Pedro de) *Dos Relaciones a Hern. Cortes Referiendole sus Expediciones y Conquistas en varias Provincias de N. Espagna*. Exst. Barcia Historiad. Primit. tom i.

———. *Lettere due*, &. Exst. Ramus, iii, 296.

Aparicio y Leon (D. Lorenzo de) *Discurso Historico-Politico del Hospital San Lazaro de Lima*. 8vo. Lim. 1761.

Aranzeles Reales de los Ministros de la Real Audiencia de N. Espagna, fol. Mex, 1727.

Argensola (Bartolome Leonardo de) *Conquistas de las Islas Malucas* fol. Mad. 1609.

———. *Anales de Aragon* fol. Saragoca, 1680.

Arguello (Eman.) *Sentum Confessionis* 12mo. Mex. 1703.

Arriago (P. Pablo Jos. de) *Extirpacion de la Idolatria de Peru* 4to. Lima, 1621.

Avendagno (Didac.) *Thesaurus Indicus, ceu generalis Instructor pro Regimine Conscientiae, in ius quae ad Indias spectant*, fol. 2 vols. Antwerp, 1660.

Aznar (De Bern. Fran.) *Discurso tocante a la real hazienda y administracion de ella*, 4to.

Bandini (Angelo Maria) *Vita e Lettere di Amerigo Vespucci*, 4to. Firenze, 1745.

Barcia (D. And. Gonzal.) *Historiadores Primitivos de las Indias Occidentales*, fol. 3 vols. Madrid, 1749.

Barco-Centinera (D. Martin de) *Argentina y Conquista del Rio de la Plata Poema*. Exst. Barcia *Historiad*. Primit. III.

Barros (Joao de) *Decadas de Asia*, fol. 4 vols. Lisboa, 1682.

Bellesteros (D. Thomas de) *Ordenanzas del Peru*, fol. 2 vols. Lima, 1685.

Beltran (P.F. Pedro) *Arte de el Idioma Maya reducido a sucintas reglas, y Semilexicon*, 4to. Mex. 1746.

Benzo (Hieron.) *Novi Orbis Historae-De Bry America* Part IV, V, VI.

Betancurt y Figueroa (Don Luis) *Derecho de las Iglesias Metropolitanas de las Indias*, 4to. Madr. 1637.

Blanco (F. Matias Ruiz) *Conversion de Piritu de Indios Cumanagotos y otros*. 12mo. Mad. 1690.

Boturini Benaduci (Lorenzo) *Idea de una nueva Historia general de la America Septentrional, fundada sobre material copiosa de Figuras, Symbolas Caracteres, Cantares y Manuscritos de Autores Indios*, 4to. Mad. 1746.

Botello de Moraes y Vasconcellos (D. Francisco de) *El Nuevo Mundo Poema Heroyco*, 4to. Barcelona, 1701.

Botero Benes (Juan) *Description de Todas las Provincias, Reynos, y Ciudades del Mundo*. 4to. Girona, 1748.

Brietius (Phil.) *Paralela Geographiae Veteris & Novae*. 4to. Paris, 1648.

Cabeza de Baca (Alvar, Nugnez) *Relacion de los Naufragios*. Exst. Barcia *Hist*. Prim. tom. i.

_____. *Examen Apologetico de la Historica Narration de los Naufragios*. Exst. Barcia *Hist*. Prim. tom. i.

_____. *Commentarios de lo succedido durante su gubierno del Rio de la Plata*. Exst. ibid. Cabo de Vacca *Relatione de*. Exst. Ramus. III.. 310.

Cabota (Sebast.) *Navigazione de*. Exst. Ramus, II, 211.

Cadamustus (Aloysius) *Navigatio ad Terras incognitas*. Exst. Nov. Orb. Grynaei, p. 1.

Calancha (F. Anton. de la) *Cronica moralizada del Orden de San Augustin en el Peru*. fol. Barcelona, 1638.

California—*Diario Historico de los Viages de Mar y Tierra hechos en 1768, al Norte de California di orden del Marques de Croix Vi-rey de Nueva Espagna*, etc. MS.

Calle (Juan Diaz de la) *Memorial Informatorio de lo que a su Magestad Provien de la Nueva Espagna y Peru.* 4to. 1645.

Campomanes (D. Pedro Rodrig.) *Antigüedad Maritima de la Republica de Cartago, con el Periplo de su general Hannon,* traducido e illustrado, 4to. Mad. 1756.

———. *Discurso sobre el fomento de la Industria popular.* 8vo. Mad. 1774.

———. *Discurso sobre la Educacion popular de los Artesanos.* 8vo. 5 vol. Mad. 1775&.

Caracas—*Real Cedula de Fundacion de la real Compagnia Guipuzcoana de Caracas.* 12mo. Mad. 1765.

Caravantes (Fr. Lopez de) *Relacion de las Provincias que tiene el Gobierno del Peru, los Officios que en el Provien, y la Hacienda que alli tiene su Magestad, lo que se Gasta de ella y le queda Libre, &&. Dedicado al Marques de Santos Claros,* Agno, de 1611, MS.

Cardenas y Cano (Gabr.) *Ensayo Cronologico para la Historia general de la Florida.* fol. Mad. 1733.

Carranzana (D. Gonçales) *A Geographical Description of the Coasts, & of the Spanish West Indies,* 8vo. Lond. 1740.

Casas (Bart. de las) *Brevissima Relacion de la Destruycion de las Indias.* 4to. 1552.

———. *Narratio Iconibus illustrata per Theod. de Bry.* 4to Oppent. 1614.

———. *An Account of the first Voyages and Discoveries of the Spaniards in America.* 8vo. Lond. 1693.

Cassani (P. Joseph) *Historia de la Provincia de Compagnia de Jesus del Nuevo Reyno de Granada.* fol. Mad. 1741.

Castanheda (Fern. Lope de) *Historia do Descobrimento & Conquista de India pelos Portugueses.* fol. 2 vol. Lisbon, 1552.

Castellanos (Juan de) *Primera y Secunda de las Elegias de Varones Illustres de Indias.* 4to. 2 vol. Mad. 1589.

Castillo (Bernal Dias del) *Historia Verdadera de la Conquista de Nueva Espagna.* fol. Mad. 1632.

Castro, Figueroa y Salazar (D. Pedro de) *Relacion di su ancimiento* [sic] *y servicios,* 12mo.

Cavallero (D. Jos. Garcia) *Brieve* [sic] *Cotejo y Valance de las pesas y Medidas di varias Naciones, reducidas a las que Corren en Castilla.* 4to. Mad. 1731.

Cepeda (D. Fern.) *Relacion Universal del Sitio en que esta fundada la Ciudad de Mexico.* fol. 1637.

Cieça de Leon (Pedro de) *Chronica del Peru,* fol. Sevill. 1533.

Cisneros (Diego) *Sitio, Naturaleza y Propriedades de la Ciudad de Mexico,* 4to. Mexico, 1618.

Clemente (P. Claudio) *Tablas Chronologicas, en que contienen los Sucesos Ecclesiasticos y Seculares de Indias.* 4to Val. 1689.

Cogullado (P. Fr. Diego Lopez) *Historia de Yucatan*. fol. Mad. 1688.

Collecao dos Brives Pontificios e Leyes Regias que forao Expedidos y Publicadas [sic] *desde o Anno 1741, sobre a la Liberdada des Pessoas bene e Commercio dos Indos de Bresil.*

Colleccion General de las Providencias hasta aquí tomadas par el Gobierno sobre el Estragnimento, y Occupacion de Temporalidades de los Regulares de la Compagnia, de Espagna, Indias, &. Partes IV, 4to. Mad. 1767.

Colon (D. Fernando) *La Historia del Almirante, D. Christoval Colon*. Exst. Barcia *Hist*. Prim. I, i.

Columbus (Christ.) *Navigatio qua multas Regiones hactenus incognitas invenit*. Exst. *Nov. Orb.* Grynaei, p. 90.

Columbus (Ferd.) *Life and Actions of his Father Admiral Christoph. Columbus*. Exst. Churchill's *Voyages*, II, 479.

Compagnia Real de Comercio para las Islas de Sto. Domingo, Puerto-rico y la Margarita. 12mo.

Compendio General de las contribuciones y gastos que ocasionan todos los effectos, frutos, caudales, &. que trafican entre los reynos de Castilla y America. 4to.

Concilios Provinciales Primero y Segundo celebrados en la muy Noble y muy leal Ciudad de Mexico en los Agnos de 1555 & 1565. fol. Mexico, 1769.

Concilium Mexicanum Provinciale tertium celebratum Mexici, Anno 1585, fol. Mexici, 1770

Continente Americano, Argonauta de las costas de Nueva Espagna y Tierra Firme, 12mo.

Cordeyro (Antonio) *Historia Insulana das ilhas a Portugas sugeytas no Oceano Occidental*. fol. Lisb. 1717.

Corita (Dr. Alonzo) *Breve y sumaria Relacion de los Segnores, manera y Differencia de ellos, que havia en la Nueva Espagna, y otras Provincias sus Comarcanas, y de sus Leyes, Usos y Costumbres, y de la Forma que tenian en Tributar sus Vasallos en Tiempo de su Gentilidad, &.* MS, 4to. pp. 307.

Coronada (Fr. Vasq. de) *Sommario di due sue Lettere del Viaggio fatto del Fra. Marco da Nizza alle sette Città de Cevola*. Exst. Ramusio III, 354.

―――. *Relazion Viaggio alle sette Città*. Ramusio III, 359.

Cortes (Hern.) *Quattro Cartas dirigidas al Emperador Carlos V. en que ha Relacion de sus Conquistas en la Nueva Espagna*. Exst. Barcia *Hist*. Prim. tom. i.

Cortessi (Ferd.) *De insulis nuper inventis Narrationes ad Carolum V*. fol. 1532.

Cortese (Fern.) *Relacioni, &.* Exst. Ramusio III, 225.

Cubero (D. Pedro) *Peregrinacion del Mayor Parte del Mundo*, Zaragoss. 4to. 1688.

Cumana-Govierno y Noticia de. fol. MS.

Davilla Padilla (F. Aug.) *Historia de la Fundacion y Discurso de Provincia de St. Jago de Mexico.* fol. Bruss. 1625.

———. (Gil Gonzalez). *Teatro Ecclesiastico de la Primitiva Iglesia de los Indias Occidentales.* fol. 2 vols. 1649.

Documentos tocantes a la Persecucion, que los Regulares de la Compagnia suscitaron contra Don B. de Cardenas obispo de Paraguay. 4to. Mad. 1768.

Echaveri (D. Bernardo Ibagnez de) *El Reyno Jesuitico del Paraguay.* Exst. tom. iv. *Colleccion de Documentos,* 4to. Mad. 1770.

Echave y Assu (D. Francisco de) *La Estrella de Lima convertida en Sol sobre sur tres Coronas.* fol. Amberes, 1688.

Eguiara El Egueren (D. Jo. Jos.) *Bibliotheca Mexicana, sive Eruditorum Historia Virorum in America Boreali natorum, &.* tom. prim. fol. Mex. 1775. (N.B.: No more than one volume of this work has been published.)

Ercilla y Zuniga (D. Alonzo de) *La Araucana. Poëma Eroico.* fol. Mad. 1733.

———. ——— 2 vols. 8vo. Mad. 1777.

Escalona (D. Gaspar de) *Gazophylacium Regium Peruvicum,* fol. Mad. 1775.

Faria y Sousa (Manuel de) *Historia del Reyno de Portugal,* fol. Amber. 1730.

Faria y Sousa, *History of Portugal from the first Ages to the Revolution under John IV.* 8vo. Lond. 1698.

Fernandez (Diego) *Prima y secunda Parte de la Historia del Peru.* fol. Sevill. 1571.

Fernandez (P. Juan Patr.) *Relacion Historial de las Missiones de los Indias que claman Chiquitos.* 4to. Mad. 1726.

Feyjoo (Benit. Geron) *Espagnoles Americanos-Discurso VI. del tom. iv. del Teatro Critico.* Mad. 1769.

———. *Solucion del gran Problema Historico sobre la Poblacion de la America/ Discurso XV, del tom. v. de Teatro Critico.*

Feyjoo (D. Miguel) *Relacion Descriptiva de la Ciudad y Provincia Truxillo del Peru,* fol. Mad. 1763.

Freyre (Ant.) *Piratas de la America.* 4to.

Frasso (D. Petro) *De Regio Patronatu Indiarum,* fol. 2 vols. Matriti, 1775.

Galvao (Antonio) *Tratado dos Descobrimentos Antigos y Modernos,* fol. Lisboa, 1731.

Galvano (Ant.) *The Discoveries of the World from the first Original unto the Year 1555.* Osborne's Collect. II, 354.

Gamboa (D. Fran. Xavier de) *Comentarios a los ordenanzas de Minas.* fol. Mad. 1761.

Garcia (Gregorio) *Historia Ecclesiastica y Seglar de la India Oriental y Occidental, y Predicacion de la Santa Evangelia en ella.* 12mo. Baeca, 1626.

———. (Fr. Gregorio) *Origen de los Indios del Nuevo Mundo.* fol. Mad. 1729.

Gastelu (Anton. Velasquez) *Arte de Lengua Mexicana.* 4to. Puibla de los Angeles. 1716.

Gazeta de Mexico pos los Annos 1728, 1729, 1730. 4to.
Girava (Hieronymo) *Dos Libros de Cosmographia.* Milan, 1556.
Godoy (Diego) *Relacion al H. Cortes, que trata del Descubrimiento de diversas Ciudades, y Provincias, y Guerras Guerras que tuio con los Indios.* Exst. Barcia *Hist.* Prim. tom. i.
Godoy *Lettere a Cortese, &.* Exst. Ramusio III, 300.
Gomara (Fr. Lopez de) *La Historia general de las Indias.* 12mo. Anv. 1554.
_____. *Historia general de las Indias.* Exst. Barcia *Hist.* Prim. tom. ii.
Gomara (Fr. Lopez de *Chronica de la Nueva Espagna ò Conquista de Mexico.* Exst. Barcia *Hist.* Prim. tom. ii
Guatemala/Razon puntual de los succesos mas memorabiles, y de los estregos y dannos que ha padecido la rindad [sic] *de Guatemala.* fol. 1774.
Gumilla (P. Jos.) *El Orinoco illustrado y defendido; Historia Natural, Civil, y Geographica de este Gran Rio,* etc. 4to. 2 tom. Mad. 1745.
_____. *Histoire Naturelle, Civile, et Geographique de l'Orenoque. Traduite par M. Eidous.* 12mo. tom. iii. Avig. 1758.
Gusman (Nugno de) *Relacion scritte in Omitlan Provincia de Mechuacan della maggior Spagna nell 1530.* Exst. Ramusio III. 331.
Henis (P. Thadeus) *Ephemerides Belli Guiarancici, ab Anno 1754.* Exst. *Colleccion general de Docum.* tom. iv.
Hernandes (Fran.) *Plantarum, Animalium & Mineralium Mexicanorum Historia.* fol. Rom. 1651.
Herera (Anton. de) *Historial general de los Hechos de los Castellanos en las Islas y Tierra Firma de Mar Oceano.* fol. 4 vols. Mad. 1601.
_____. *Historia General, &.* 4 vols. Mad. 1730.
_____. *General History, &.* Translated by Stephens, 8vo. 6 vols. Lond. 1740.
_____. *Descriptio Indiae Occidentalis.* fol. Amst. 1622.
Huemez y Horcasitas (D. Juan Francisco de) *Extracto de los Autos de Diligencias y reconocimientos de los rios, lagunas, vertientes, y desaguas de Mexico y su Valle. &.* fol. Mex. 1748.
Jesuitas—*Colleccion de las applicaciones que se van haciendo de los Cienes* [sic], *casas, y Coligios que fueron de la Compagnia de Jesus, expatriados de estos Reales dominios.* 4to. 2 vols. Lima, 1772 y 1773.
Jesuitas/*Colleccion General de Providencias hasta aquí tomadas por el Gobierno sovre el Estrannamiento y Occupacion de temporalidades, de los Regulares de la Compagnia de Espagna, Indias, e Islas Filipinas.* 4to. Mad. 1767.
_____. *Retrato de los Jesuitas formado al natural.* 4to. 2 vols. Mad. 1768.
_____. *Relacion Abbreviada da Republica que os Religiosos Jesuitas estabeleceraon* [sic]. 12mo.
_____. *Idea del Origen, Gobierno,* etc. *de la Compagnia de Jesus.* 8vo. Mad. 1768.

Laevinius (Apollonius) *Libri V. de Peruviae Invention. et rebus in eadem gestis.* 12mo. Ant. 1567.

Leon (Fr. Ruiz de) *Hernandia, Poëma Heroyco de Conquista de Mexico.* 4to. Mad. 1755.

Leon (Ant. de) *Epitome de la Bibliotheca Oriental y Occidental, Nautica y Geografica.* fol. Mad. 1737.

Lima. *A true Account of the Earthquake which happened there.* 28th October 1746. Translated from the Spanish, 8vo. Lond. 1748.

Lima Gozosa, Description de las festibas Demonstraciones, con que esta ciudad Celebrò la real Proclamacion de el Nombre Augusto del Catolico Monarcho D. Carlos III. Lima, 4to. 1760.

Llano Zapata (D. Jos. Euseb.) *Preliminar al Tomo I. de las Memorias Historico-Physicas. Critico-Apologeticas de la America Meridional.* 8vo. Cadiz, 1759.

Lopez (D. Juan Luis) *Discurso Historico Politico en defenco* [sic] *de la Jurisdicion Real.* fol. 1685.

Lopez (Thom.) *Atlas Geographico de la America Septentrional y Meridional.* 12mo. Par. 1758.

Lorenzana (D. Fr. Ant.) Arzobispo de Mexico, ahora, de Toledo. *Historia de Nueva Espagna, escrita por su Esclarecido Conquistador Hernan Cortes, Aumentada con otros Documentos y Notas.* fol. Mex. 1770.

Lozano (P. Pedro) *Description Chorographica, del Terretorios, Arboles, Animales, del Gran Chaco, y de los Ritos y Costumbres, de las innumerabiles Naciones que la habitan.* 4to. Cordov. 1733.

――――. *Historia de la Compagnia de Jesus en la Provincia del Paraguay.* fol. 2 vols. Mad. 1753.

Madriga (Pedro de) *Description du Gouvernment du Perou.* Exst. Voyages qui on servi à l'établissement de la comp.. des Indes. tom. ix. 105.

Mariana (P. Juan de) *Discurso de las Enfermedades de la Compagnia de Jesus.* 4to. Mad. 1763.

Martinez de la Puente (D. Jos.) *Compendio de las Historias de los Descubrimientos, Conquistas, y Guerras de la India Oriental, y sus Islas, desde los Tiempos del Infante Don Enrique de Portugal su inventor.* 4to. Mad. 1681.

Martyr ab Angleria (Petr.) *De Rebus Oceanicis & Novo Orbe Decades tres.* 12mo. Colon. 1574.

――――. *De Insulis nuper inventis, & de Moribus Incolorum.* Ibid. p. 329.

――――. *Opus Epistolarum.* fol. Amst. 1670.

――――. *Il Sommario cavato della sua Historia del Nuevo Mundo.* Ramusio III, i.

Mata (D. Geron. Fern. de) *Ideas politicas y morales.* 12mo. Toledo, 1640.

Mechuacan—*Relacion de las Ceremonias, Ritos, y Poblacion de los Indios de Mechuacan hecha al I.S.D. Ant. de Mendoza Virrey de Nueva Espagna.* fol. MS.

Melendez (Fr. Juan) *Tesoros Verdaderos de las Indias Historia de la Provincia de S. Juan Baptista del Peru, del Orden de Predicadores.* fol. 3 vols. Rom. 1681.

Memorial Ajustado por D.A. Fern. De Heredia Gobernador de Nicaragua y Honduras. fol. 1753.

Memorial Adjustado contra los Officiales de Casa de Moneda a Mexico de el anno 1729. fol.

Mendoza (D. Ant. de) *Lettera al Imperatore del Discoprimento della Terra Firmè della N. Spagna verso Tramontano.* Exst. Ramusio III, 355.

Mendoza (Juan Gonz. de) *Historia del gran Reyno de China., con un Itinerario del Nuevo Mundo.* 8vo. Rom. 1585.

Miguel (Vic. Jos.) *Tablas de los Sucesos Ecclesiasticos en Africa, Indias Orientales y Occidentales,* 4to. Val. 1689.

Miscellanea Economico-Politico, &. fol. Pampl. 1749.

Molina (P.F. Anton.) *Vocabulario Castellano y Mexicano,* fol. 1571.

Monardes (El Dottor) *Primera y Segunda y Tercera Parte de la Historia Medicinal, de las Cosas que se traen de neustras [sic] Indias Occidentales, que sirven en Medicina.* 4to. Sevilla, 1754.

Moncada (Sancho de) *Restauracion Politica de Espagna y deseos Publicos.* 4to. Mad. 1746.

Morales (Ambrosio de) *Coronica General de Espagnia.* fol. 4 vols. Alcala, 1574.

Moreno y Escaudon (D. Fran. Aut.) *Description y Estado del Virreynato de Santa Fè. Nuevo Reyno de Granada, &.* fol. MS.

Munoz (D. Antonio) *Discurso sobre economia politica.* 8vo. Mad. 1769.

Nizza (F. Marco) *Relatione del Viaggio fatta per Terra al Cevole, Regno di cette Città.* Exst. Ramus. III, 356.

Nodal/*Relacion del Viage que hicieron los Capitanes Barth. y Gonz. de Nodal al descubrimiento del Estrecho que hoy es nombrado de Maire, y reconocimiento del de Magellanes.* 4to. Mad.

Noticia Individual de los derechos según lo reglado en ultimo proyecto de 1720. 4to. Barcelona, 1732.

Nueva Espagna/*Historia de los Indios de Nueva Espagna dibidida en tres Partes. En la primera trata de los Ritos, Sacrificios y Idolatrias del Tiempo de su Gentilidad. En la segunda de su maravillosa Conversion a la Fè, y modo de celebrar las Fiestas de Nuestra Santa Iglesia. En la tercera del Genio y Caracter de aquella Gente; y Figuras con que notaban sus Acontecimientos, con otras particularidades; y Noticias de las principales Ciudades en aquel Reyno. Escrita en el Agno 1541 por uno de los doce Religiosos Franciscos [sic] que primero Passaron a entender en su Conversion.* MS. fol. pp. 618.

Ogna (Pedro de) *Arauco Domado.* Poëma, 12mo. Mad. 1605.

Ordenanzas del Consejo real de las Indias, fol. Mad. 1681.

Ortega (D. Casimiro de) *Resumen Historico del primer Viage hecho alrededor del Mundo,* 4to. Mad. 1769.

Ossorio (Jerome) *History of the Portuguese, during the Reign of Emmanuel.* 8vo. 2 vols. Lond. 1752.

Ossorius (Hieron.) *De rebus Emmanuelis Lusitaniae Regis,* 8vo. Col. Agr. 1752

Ovalle (Alonso) *Historica Relacion del Reyno de Chili,* fol. Rom. 1646.

———. *An Historical Relation of the Kingom of Chili.* Exst. Churchill's Collect. III, i.

Oviedo y Bagnos (D. Jos.) *Historia la Conquista y Publicacion ce Venezuela* [sic]. fol. Mad. 1723.

Oviedo *Sommaria, &.* Exst. Ramusio III, 44.

Oviedo (Gonz. Fern. de) *Relacion Sommaria de la Historia Natural de los Indias.* Exst. Barcia Hist. Prim. tom. i.

Oviedo, *Historia Generale & Naturale dell Indie Occidentale.* Exst. Ramusio III, 74.

———. *Relatione della Navigatione per la Grandissima Fiume Maragnon.* Exst. Ramus. III, 415.

Palacio (D. Raim. Mig.) *Discurso Economico Politico,* 4to. Mad. 1778.

Palafox y Mendoza (D. Juan) *Virtudes del Indios o Naturaliza y Costumbres de los Indios de N. Espagna,* 4to.

———. *Vie de Venerable Dom. Jean Palafox Eveque de l'Angelopolis.* 12mo. Cologne, 1772.

Pegna (Juan Nugnez de la) *Conquista y Antiguedades de las Islas de Gran Canaria.* 4to. Mad. 1676.

Pegna Montenegro (D. Alonso de la) *Itinerario para Parochos de Indios, en que tratan les materias mas particulares, tocante a ellos para su buen administración.* 4to. Amberes, 1754.

Penalosa y Mondragon (Fr. Benito de) *Cinco Excellencias del Espanol que des peublan* [sic] *a Espagna.* 4to. Pampl. 1629.

Peralta Barnuevo (D. Pedro de) *Lima fundada o Conquista del Peru, Poëma Eroyco.* 4to. Lima, 1732.

Peralta Calderon (D. Mathias de) *El Apostol de las Indias y nueves gentes San Francisco Xavier de la Compagnia de Jesu Epitome de sus Apostolicos hechos.* 4to. Pampl. 1665.

Pereire de Berrido (Bernard.) *Annaes Historicos do estado do Maranchao.* fol. Lisboa, 1749.

Peru/*Relatione d'un Capitano Spagnuolo del Descoprimento y Conquista del Peru.* Exst. Ramus. III. 371.

Peru/*Relatione d'un Secretario de Franc. Pizzarro della Conquesta del Peru.* Exst. Ramusio III, 371.

———. *Relacion del Peru,* MS.

Pesquisa de los Oydores de Panama contra D. Jayme Mugnos, &. pro haverlos Commerciado illicitamente en tiempo de Guerra. fol. 1755.

Philipinas—*Carta que escribe un Religioso antiguo de Philipinas, a un Amigo suyo en Espagna, que le pregunta el Natural y Genio de los Indios Naturales de Estas Islas.* MS, 4to.

Piedrahita (Luc. Fern.) *Historia general de las Conquistas del Nuevo Reyno de Granada.* fol. Ambres.

Pinelo (Ant. de Leon) *Epitome de la Bibliotheca Oriental y Occidental en que se continen los Escritores de las Indias Orientales y Occidentales.* fol. 2 vols. Mad. 1737.

Pinzonius socius Admirantis Columbi/Navigatio et res per eum repertae. Exst. Nov. Orb. Grynaei, p. 119.

Pizarro y Orellana (D. Fern.) *Varones Illustres del N. Mundo.* fol. Mad. 1639.

Planctus Judorum Christianorum in America Peruntina. 12mo.

Puente (D. Jos. Martinez de la) *Compendio de las Historias de los Descubrimientos de la India Oriental y sus Islas.* 4to. Mad. 1681.

Quir (Ferd. de) *Australis Incognita; or, a new Southern Discovery, containing a fifth Part of the World lately found out.* 4to. Lond. 1617.

Ramusio (Giov. Battista) *Raccolto delle Navigazioni e Viaggi.* fol. 3 vols. Venet. 1588.

Real Compagnia Guipuzcoana de Caracas. Noticias historiales Practicas, de los Successos y Adelantamientos de esta Compagnia desde su Fundacion en 1728 hasta 1764. 4to. 1765.

Recopilacion de Leyes de los Reynos de las Indias. fol. 4 vols. Mad. 1756.

Reglamento y Aranceles Reales para el Comercio de Espagna a Indias. fol. Mad. 1778.

Relazione d'un Gentiluomo del Sig. Fern. Cortese della gran Città Temistatan, Mexico, et delle altre cose della Nova Spagna. Exst. Ramus. III, 304.

Remesal (Fr. Ant.) *Historia general de las Indias Occidentales y particular de la Governacion de Chiapa y Guatimala.* fol. Mad. 1620.

Ribadeneyra (D. Diego Porticuelo de) *Relacion de Viage desde que salio de Lima, hasta que llegò a Espagna.* 4to Mad. 1657.

Ribandeneyra y Barrientos (D. Ant. Joach.) *Manuel [sic] Compendio de el Regio Patronato Indiano.* fol. Mad. 1755.

Ribas (Andr. Perez de) *Historia de los Triumphos de Nuestra Sta. Fè, entre Gentes la mas Barbaras, en las missiones de Nueva Espagna.* fol. Mad. 1645.

Riol. (D. Santiago) *Representacion a Philipe V. sobre el estado actual de los Papeles universales de la Monarchia,* MS.

Ripia (Juan de la) *Practica de la Administracion y cobranza de las rentas reales.* fol. Mad. 1768.

Rocha Pitta (Sebastiano de) *Historia de America Portougueza [sic] des de o Anno de 1500 du su Descobrimento ate o de 1724.* fol. Lisboa, 1730.

Rodriguez (Manuel) *Explicacion de la Bulla de la Santa Crusada.* 4to. Alcala, 1589.

Rodriguez (P. Man.) *El Maragnon y Amozonas, Historia de los Descubrimientos, Entradas y Reduccion de Naciones.* fol. Mad. 1684.

Roman (Hieron.) *Republicas del Mundo.* fol. 3 vols. Mad. 1595.

Roma y Rosell (De Franc.) *Las segnales de la felicidad de Espagna y medios de hacerlas efficaces.* 8vo. Mad. 1768.

Rosende (P. Ant. Gonz. de) *Vida del Juan de Palafox Arzobispo de Mexico.* fol. Mad. 1671.

Rubaclava (Don Jos. Gutierrez de) *Tratado Historico Politico, y Legal de el commercio de las Indias Occidentales.* 12mo. Cad. 1750.

Ruiz (P. Ant.) *Conquista Espiritual hecha por los Religiosos de la Compagnia de Jesus, en las Provincias de la Paraguay, Uraguay, Parana y Tape.* 4to. Mad. 1639.

Salazar de Mendoza (D. Pedro) *Monarquia de Espagna.* tom. i, ii, iii, fol. Mad. 1770/

—— y Olarte (D. Ignacio) *Historia de la Conquista de Mexico - Segunda Parte.* Cordov. 1743.

—— y Zevallos (D. Alonz. Ed. de) *Constituciones y Ordenanzas antiguas Agnadidas y Modernas de la Real Universidad y estudio general ste* [sic] *San Marcos de la Ciudad de los Reyes del Peru.* fol. En la Ciudad de los Reyes, 1735.

Sanchez (Ant. Ribero) *Dissertation sur l'Origine de la Maladie Venerienne, dans laquelle on preuve qu'elle n'a point été portée de l*"*Amerique.* 12mo. Paris, 1765.

Sarmiento de Gomboa (Pedro de) *Viage al Estrecho de Magellanes* [sic]. 4to. Mad. 1768.

Santa Cruz (El Marques) *Comercio Suelto y en Companias General.* 12mo. Mad. 1732.

Santo Domingo, Puerto Rico, y Margarita, Real Compagnia de Comercio. 12mo. 1756.

Schemided (Ulderico) *Historia y Descubrimiento del Rio de la Plata y Paraguay.* Exst. Barcia *Hist. Prim.* tom. iii.

Sebara da Sylva (Jos. de) *Recueil Chronologique & Analytique de tout ce qu'a fait en Portugal la Société dite de Jésus, depuis son Entrée dan ce Royaume in 1540 jusqu'à son Expulsion 1759.* 12mo. 3 vols. Lisb. 1769.

Segni (D. Diego Raymundo) *Antiquario Noticiosa General de Espagna y sus Indios.* 12mo. 1769.

Sepulveda (Genesius) *Dialogus de justis belli causis, praesertim in Indos Novi Orbis.* MS.

—— (Jo. Genesius) *Epistolarum Libri VII.* 12mo. Salam. 1557.

Sepulveda de regno, *Libri III.* 12mo Ilerdae, 1570.

Seyxas y Lovero (D. Fr.) *Theatro Naval Hydrographico.* 4to. 1648.

———. *Descripcion Geographica y Derrotera de la Region Austral Magellanica.* 4to. Mad. 1690.

Simon (Pedro) *Noticias Historiales de las Conquistas de Tierra Firmè en las Indias Occidentales.* fol. Cuenca, 1627.

Solarzano y Pereyrra (Joan.) *Politica Indiana.* fol. 2 vols. Mad. 1776.

———. *De Indiarum jure, sive de justa Indiarum Occidentalium Gubernatione.* fol. 2 vols. Lugd. 1672.

———. *Obras Varias posthumas.* fol. Mad. 1776.

Solis (D. Ant. de) *Historias de las Conquistas de Mexico.* fol. Mad. 1684.

———. *History of the Conquest of Mexico - Translated by Townsend.* fol. 1724.

Soto y marne (P. Franc. de) *Copia de la Relacion de Viage que desde la ciudad de Cadiz a la Cartagena de Indias hizo.* 4to. Mad. 1753.

Spilbergen et Le Maire *Speculum Orientalis Occidentalisque Navigationum.* 4to. L. Bat. 1619.

Suarez de Figueroa (Christov.) *Hechos de D. Garcia Hurtado de Mendoza.* 4to. Mad. 1613.

Tanco (Luis Bezerra) *Felicidad de Mexico en la admirable Aparicion de N. Signora di Guadalupe.* 8vo. Mad. 1745.

Tarragones (Hieron. Gir.) *Dos Libros de Cosmographia.* 4to. Milan, 1556.

Techo (F. Nichol. de) *The History of the Provinces Paraguay, Tucuman, Rio de la Plata, &.* Exst. Churchill's Coll. VI. 3.

Torquemada (Juan de) *Monarquia Indiana.* fol. 3 vols. Mad. 1723.

Torres (Sim. Per. de) *Viage del Mundo.* Exst. Barcia Hist. Prim. III.

Torres (Franc. Caro de) *Historia de las Ordenes Militares de Santiago, Calatrava y Alcantara, desde su Fundacion hasta el Rey D. Felipe II. Administrador perpetuo dellas.* fol. Mad. 1629.

Torribi (P.F. Jos.) *Aparato para la Historia Natural Espagnola.* fol. Mad. 1754.

———. *Dissertacion Historico Politica y en mucha parte Geographica de las Islas Philipinas.* 12mo. Mad. 1753.

Totanes (F. Sebastian de) *Manual Tagalog para auxilio de Provincias de las Philipinas.* 4to Samplai en las Philipinas, 1745.

Ulloa (D. Ant. de) *Voyage Historique de l'Amerique Méridionale.* 4to. 2 tom. Paris, 1752.

———. *Noticias Americanas, Entretenimientos Physicos-Historicos, sobre la America Meridional y la Septentrional Oriental.* 4to Mad. 1772.

Ulloa (D. Bern. de) *Restablecimiento de las Fabricas, trafico, y comercio maritimo de Espagna.* 12mo. 2 vols. Mad. 1740.

——— (Franc.) *Navigazione per scoprire l'Isole delle Specierie fino al Mare detto Vermejo nel 1539.* Exst. Ramus. III, 339.

——— (D. Bernardo) *Rétablissement des Manufactures & du commerce d'Espagne.* 12mo. Amst. 1753.

Uztariz (D. Geron.) *Theoria y Practica de Commercio & de Marina.* fol. Mad. 1757.

_____. *The Theory and Practice of Commerce, and Maritime Affairs.* 8vo. 2 vols. Lond. 1751.

Verages (D. Thom. Tamaio de) *Restauracion de la Ciudad del Salvador y Baia de Todos Sanctos en la Provincia del Brasil.* 4to. Mad. 1628.

Vargas Machuca (D. Bern. de) *Milicia y Descripcion de las Indias.* 4to. Mad. 1699.

Vega (Garcilasso de la) *Histoire de la Conquête de la Floride.* Traduite par Richelet, 12mo. 2 tom. Leyd. 1731.

_____. *Royal Commentaries of Peru,* by Rycaut, fol. Lond. 1688.

Vega (L'Ynca Garcilasso de la) *Histoire des Guerres Civiles dos Espagnoles dans les Indes,* par Baudouin, 4to. 2 tom. Paris, 1648.

Veitia Linage (Jos.) *The Spanish Rule of Trade to the West Indies.* 8vo. Lond. 1702.

_____. *Declamation Oratoria en Defensa de D. Jos. Fern. Veitia Linage.* fol. 1702.

_____. *Norte de la Contratacion de las Indias Occidentales.* fol. Sevill. 1672.

Venegas (Miguel) *A Natural and Civil History of California.* 8vo. 2 vols. Lond. 1759.

Verazzano (Giov.) Relazione delle Terra per lui Scoperta nel 1524. Exst. Ramusio III, p. 420.

Vesputius (Americus) Duae Navigationes sub auspiciis Ferdinandi, &. Exst. De Bry *America* Pars X.

_____. *Navigatio prima, secunda, tertia, quarta.* Exst. Nov. Orb. Grynaei, p. 155.

Viage de Espagna. 12mo. 6 tom. Mad. 1776.

Victoria (Fran.) *Relationes Theologicae de Indis & de jure belli contra eos.* 4to. 1765.

Viera y Clavijo (D. Jos.) *Noticias de la Historia general de las Islas de Canaria.* 4to. 3 tom. Mad. 1772.

Villalobos (D. Juan de) *Manifiesto sobre in introducción de esclavos negros en las Indias Occidentales.* 4to. Sevilla, 1682.

Villagra (Gasp. de) *Historia de Nueva Mexico Poëma.* 12mo. Alcala. 1610.

Villa Segnor y Sanchez (D. Jos. Ant.) *Theatre Americano. Descripcion general de los Reynos y Provincias de la Nueva Espagna.* fol. 2 tom. Mex. 1746.

_____. *Res puesta sobre el precio de Azogue.* 4to.

Vocabulario Brasiliano y Portugues. 4to. MS.

Ward (D. Bernardo) *Proyecto Economico sobre la población de Espagna, la agricultura en todos sus ramos, y de mas establecimientos de industria, comercio con nuestra marina, arreglo de nuestra [sic] intereses en America, libertad del comercio en Indias, &.* 2 vols. 4to. MS.

Xeres (Franc. de) *Verdadera Relacion de la Conquista del Peru y Provincia de Cuzco. Embiada al Emperador Carlos V.* Exst. Barcia *Hist.* Prim. tom. iii.

———. *Relatione, &&.* Exst. Ramusio III. 372.

Zarate (Aug. de) *Historia del Descubrimiento y Conquista de la Provincia del Peru.* Exst. Barcia *Hist.* Prim. tom. iii.

———. *Histoire de la Decouverte & de la Conquête du Perou.* 12mo. 2 tom. Paris, 1742.

Zavala y Augnon (D. Miguel de) *Representacion al Rey N. Segnor D. Philipe V. dirigida al mas seguro Aumento del Real Erario.* No place, 1732.

Zevallos (D. Pedro Ordognuez de) *Historia y Viage del Mundo.* 4to. Mad. 1691.

BIBLIOGRAPHY

PRIMARY SOURCES

I have only listed those authors and works considered in detail. Others are mentioned in the text or footnotes.

Manuscripts

Thomas Robeson letters, Lea and Febiger Collection, File 227B, Incoming Correspondence
Carey and Lea letters, Lea and Febiger File of Outgoing Correspondence

Newspapers

Aguila Mexicana (Mexico City, April, 1823–1828).
The Aurora, The General Advertiser (Philadelphia, 1790–1814).
Aurora de Chile, Periódico ministerial y político (Feb. 13, 1812–April 1, 1813). Modern paleographic edition by Julio Vicuna Cifuentes (Santiago de Chile, Imprenta Cervantes, 1903).
El Federalista (Mexico City, June 24, 1823–October 14, 1823).
El hombre libre (Mexico City, 1822–April 1, 1823).
El Iris (Mexico City, 1826). Ed. facsimilar. Intro. María del Carmen Ruíz Castañeda, estudio Luis Mario Schneider (México: UNAM, Instituto de Investigaciones Bibliográficas, 1986).
El Redactor Mexicano (Mexico City, 1814).
El Sol (Mexico City, 1822–1828).
Miscelánea de literatura, ciencias y artes. (Mexico City, October 1823–1828).
Semanario Político y Literario (Mexico City, 1820–1822).

Other Primary Sources

Actas de las Cortes de Cádiz. 2 vols. Pról. Enrique Tierno Galván. Madrid: Taurus, 1964.

Alamán, Lucas. *Historia de México desde los primeros movimientos que prepararon su Independencia en el año de 1808 hasta la época presente*. 5 vols., 1852. México: Instituto Cultural Helénico, Fondo de Cultura Económica, 1985. [edición facsimilar].

Alcalá Galiano, Antonio. *Literatura española siglo XIX. De Moratín a Rivas*. Trad., introducción y notas de Vicente Lloréns. Madrid: Alianza Editorial, (1834), 1969.

Annals of the Congress of the United States (17th Congress, Second Session, 1822–1823). Washington, DC: Gales and Seaton, 1855.

Barère de Vieuzac, Bertrand. *La libertad de los mares, o el govierno Inglés descubierto. Traducida libremente del francés al castellano por dr. Carlos Le Brun*. Filadelfia: Juan F. Hurtel, 1820... (On the cover: To the philosopher of Montecello, Thomas Jefferson, ex-president of the United States.)

Barry, Edward. *The elements of Spanish and English Conversation: with new, familiar, and easy dialogues, designed particularly for the use of schools*. Philadelphia: Carey & Lea, 1822.

———, trans. *El monitor de los Masones Libres; o Ilustraciones sobre la Masonería, por Tomás Smith Webb, Gran Maestro Pasado de la Gran Logia de Rhode Island. Traducido del Inglés al Español*. Philadelphia: H.C. Carey & I. Lea, 1822.

———, trans. *El solitario, o el misterioso del monte. Novela escrita en Francés por El vizconde de Arlincourt, traducida al Inglés, y de Este al Español por* ... Filadelfia: Imprenta de H.C. Carey y I. Lea, 1822. (Original: *Le Solitaire*, by Charles Victor Arlincourt, Vicomte d'Prevot; translated to English as *The Renegade* and *The Recluse*.)

———, trans. *Jachin y Boaz; o una Llave auténtica para la puerta de Francmasoneria, tanto antigua, como moderna. Por un caballero de la Logia de Jerusalén. Traducida al español por* ... Shoemaker attributes the work to "R.S." Filadelfia: H.C. Carey & I. Lea, 1822.. Published in English, in London by W. Nicoll in 1762 as: *Jachin and Boaz; or, An authentic key to the door of free-masonry, Calculated not only for the instruction of every new-made mason; but also for the information of all who intend to become brethren ... Illustrated with an accurate plan of the drawing on the floor of a lodge. And interspersed with a variety of notes and remarks, necessary to explain and render the whole clear to the meanest capacity. By a gentleman belonging to the Jerusalem Lodge*.

———, trans. *La librería Masónica y general Ahiman Rezon; conteniendo una delineación de los verdaderos principios de Francmasonería, especulativa y operativa, religiosa y moral. Compilada de los escritos de los autores más aprobados, con notas y observaciones casuales. Por Samuel Cole, P.M. de las logias de Concordia y Cassia, P.G.S. de la G.L. de Meriland. T.T.C.M. &. In principio erat sermo ille, et sermo ille erat apud Deum, erat que ille sermo Deux. Evangelio de Sn. Juan. Al principio a la verdad irá con él, por caminos torcidos, y la pondrá miedo y temor, y en su disciplina le atormentará hasta tanto que se confíe de su ánimo, y le haya tentado en sus leyes; y volverá otra vez a él derechamente, y le alegrará y le revelará sus secretos. Eclesiástico. Traducida al Español por Eduardo Barry.* Philadelphia: H.C. Carey & I. Lea, 1822.

———, trans. *La vida de Jorge Washington, comandante en gefe de los egércitos de los Estados Unidos de América, en la Guerra que estableció su independencia; y su primer presidente. Escrita en inglés por David Ramsay M.D., y traducida al español por . . .* Filadelfia: Imprenta de R. Desilver., 1826.

———, trans. *Observations on the political reforms of Colombia. By J.M. Salazar, Translated from the manuscript by Edward Barry.* Philadelphia: W. Stavely, 1828.

———, trans. *Sandoval, or The Freemason: A Spanish Tale, by the author of "Don Esteban."* by Valentín Llanos Gutiérrez. 2 vols. New York: E. Bliss and E. White; Philadelphia: H.C. Carey and I. Lea, Sleight & Tucker, 1826.

Bolívar, Simón. *El Libertador. Writings of . . .* Edited by David Bushnell; Translated by Frederick H. Fornoff. New York: Oxford University Press, 2003.

Bustamante, Carlós María. *Diario histórico de México (Dic. 1822–Agosto, 1841).* Ed. arreglada por Elías Amador. Tomo I (1822–1823). Zacatecas: Tip. de la Escuela de Artes y Oficios de la Penitenciaría, a cargo de J. Ortega, 1896.

Capmany y Montpalau, Antonio de. "*The Anti-Gallican Sentinel . . . Dedicated to all nations, Translated from the Spanish by a Gentleman of this City.*" New York: printed for Ezra Sargeant, 1809; second part printed by Fry and Kammerer in Philadelphia, 1810. First published in Madrid in 1808, dedicated to Lord Holland. The original Spanish version is available in an edition by Françoise Etienore. London: Tamesis, 1988.

Carey, Mathew. "Autobiography." *The New England Magazine* Vol. 5, July–Dec., 1833; Vol. 6, Jan.–June, 1834; Vol. 7, July–Dec., 1834; reprinted New York: AMS Press, 1965.

———. *Desultory Facts, and Observations Illustrative of the Past and Present Situation and Future Prospects of the United States: Embracing A View of the Causes of the Late Bankruptcies in Boston. To Which is Annexed, A Sketch of The Restrictive Systems of The Principal Nations of Christendom by A Pennsylvanian.* Philadelphia: H.C. Carey & I. Lea, 1822.

Constitución de los Estados Unidos, traducida del inglés al español por Jph. Manuel Villavicencio. Philadelphia: Imprenta de Smith & M'Kenzie, 1810.

Declaraciones de los derechos del hombre en sociedad. México: Oficina de José María Ramos Palomera, 1822.

de la Torre, Villar, Ernesto, ed. *Juan Schmaltz y su misión en México*. La Habana: n.p., 1957.

Derechos del hombre y del ciudadano. Ed. Pedro Grases, estudio preliminar por Pablo Ruggeri Parra. Caracas: Academia Nacional de la Historia, 1959.

Eymeric, Nicolau. *Manual de inquisidores*. Trad. ed. by José Marchena Ruíz. Mompellier: Imprenta de Feliz Aviñon, 1821; reprinted in Barcelona: Editorial Fontamara, 1974, 1982.

Fernández de Lizardi, José Joaquín. *Obras*. 14 vols. México: UNAM, 1968–1997.

Fernel, F.A. *Curiosidades para los estudiosos, sacadas de los tesoros más auténticos de artes, ciencias, naturaleza, biografía, historia, y literatura en general del ingles, con un gran número de notas instructivas y explicativas por . . .* Londres: R. Ackermann, Impreso por Carlos Wood, 1826.

Foronda, Valentín de. *Apuntes ligeros sobre la nueva constitución, proyectada por la Majestad de la Junta Suprema española, y reformas que intenta hacer en las leyes*. Philadelphia: Thomas y Jorge Palmer, 1809.

———.*Carta sobre lo que debe hacer un príncipe que tenga Colonias a gran distancia*. Philadelphia: n.p., 1803.

———. *Cartas para los amigos y enemigos de . . . , encargado de negocios y cónsul general de S.M.C. Fernando VII, cerca de los Estados Unidos de la América Septentrional, relativas a lo acontecido en España con el motivo de haber nombrado el emperador Napoleón I a su hermano Joseph rey de las Españas e Indias*. Philadelphia: Thomas y Jorge Palmer, 1808. (A third edition was published in 1809, 39 pp., including additional material, also by the Palmer firm.)

———. *Cartas presentadas a la Sociedad Filosófica de Philadelphia*. Philadelphia: Thomas y Guillermo Bradford, 1807.

García de Sena, Manuel. *La independencia de la costa firme justificada por Thomas Paine treinta años ha*. Filadelfia: T. y J. Palmer, n.d.

———. Trans. of John M'Culloch's *Concise History of the United States from the Discovery of America up until 1807, Historia concisa de los Estados Unidos desde el descubrimiento de la América hasta el año de 1807*. Filadelfia: T. y J. Palmer, 1812.

Grégoire, Henri-Baptiste, Abbé. *Apologie de Barthélemy de Las Casas, évêque de Chiappa, par le citoyen G.; lu al l'Institut Nacional le 22 Florel al an 8*. Paris: Badouin, 1802.

Gutiérrez, Luis. *Cornelia Bororquia, o La víctima de la Inquisición*. Paris, 1801. Modern edition by Gérard Dufour. Alicante: Instituto Juan Gil-Albert, 1987.

Henderson, James. *Representación a los Americanos del Sud y Mexicanos; Para disuadirles de que concedan Ventajas Comerciales a otras Naciones, en perjuicio de Inglaterra, por causa de su Retardo en reconocer su Independencia; cuyo Retardo se halla explicado, en los Principios bien fundados de Integridad y Honor Nacional. Con un Examen rápido de varios acontecimientos importantes* [sic], *y rasgos patrióticos, que han distinguido sus respectivas revoluciones. Por* . . . London: W. Marchant,, Ingram-court, Fenchurch-Street for J.M. Richardson, 23 Cornhill; and J. Hatchard, Piccadilly, 1822.

Jicoténcal. 2 vols. Published anonymously. Filadelfia: Guillermo Stavely, 1826. Modern edition by Luis Leal and Rodolfo J. Cortina attributed to Félix Varela. Houston: Arte Público Press, 1995; English translation by Guillermo I. Castillo-Feliú. Austin: University of Texas Press, 1999.

Jordan, John. *Dangers of foreigners and foreign commerce in the Mexican States: Useful information to all travelers in that country, and especially to the merchants of the United States; and equally important to the cabinets of Washington, London, and to the congress of Tacubaya.* Philadelphia: P. M. Lafourcade, 1826.

Juan, Jorge y Antonio Ulloa. *Discourse and Political Reflections on the Kingdoms of Peru. Their Government, Special Regimen of Their Inhabitants, and Abuses Which Have Been Introduced into One and Another, with Special Information on Why They Grew Up and Some Means to Avoid Them.* Edited by John J. Tepaske and Besse A. Clement. Norman: University of Oklahoma Press, 1978.

———. *Noticias secretas de América, sobre el estado naval, militar, y político de los reynos del Perú y provincias de Quito, costas de Nueva Granada y Chile: Gobierno y regimen particular de los pueblos de indios. Cruel opresión y extorsiones de sus corregidores y curas: Abusos escandalosos introducidos entre estos habitantes por los misioneros: Causas de su origen y motivos de su continuación por el espacio de tres siglos. Escritas fielmente según las instrucciones del Excelentísimo Señor Marqués de la Ensenada, primer secretario de estado, y presentadas en informe secreto a S.M.C. El Señor don Fernando VI. Por don Jorge Juan, y don Antonio de Ulloa. Sacadas a luz para el verdadero conocimiento del gobierno de los españoles en la América Meridional, por don David Barry.* Londres: Imprenta de R. Taylor, 1826.

Knox, Vicesimus. *El espíritu del despotismo, traducido del Inglés, y dedicado al Excelentísimo Señor Don Simón Bolívar, Presidente de la República de Colombia, por Eduardo Barry.* Filadelfia: Imprenta de H.C. Carey y I. Lea, 1822. (Originally published in English in London in 1795, republished in London in 1821.)

L.F.E. (pseudonym "El Durangüeño"). "Centinela contra los seductores." México: no printer, No. 2, no date.

La Galatea de Miguel de Cervantes, imitada, compendiada, concluída por Jean Pierre Claris de Florian, Traducido por D. Casiano Pellicer. Philadelphia: Imprenta de M. Carey, 1810.

La vida de Lazarillo de Tormes, y de sus fortunas y adversidades, por Don Diego Hurtado de Mendoza. Nueva edición. Filadelfia: Imprenta de Matías Carey e Hijos, 1821.

Las Casas, Fray Bartolomé de. *Breve relación de la destrucción de las Indias Orientales . . . Impresa en Sevilla. Reimpresa en Londres y ahora en Filadelfia*. Filadelfia: Juan F. Hurtel, 1821.

———. *In Defense of the Indians*. Published first in Latin and translated by John Phillips, published in London. Modern facsimile edition by Colin Steele (n.p.: Oriole, 1972); also translation by Stafford Poole, C.M. DeKalb: Northern Illinois Press, 1992.

Llorente, Juan Antonio. *Aforismos políticos, escritos en una de las lenguas del norte de la Europa*. México: Reimpresos en la Oficina de D. Mariano Ontiveros, impresos en Madrid, 1821.

———. *Apología católica del proyecto de constitución religiosa, escrito por un Americano*. San Sebastián: Baroja, 1821.

———. *Carta escrita a un americano sobre la forma de gobierno que para hacer practicable la constitución y las leyes, conviene establecer en Nueva España atendida su actual situación*. San Sebastián: Baroja, 1821.

———. *Discurso heráldico sobre el escudo de armas de España, leído . . . en el mes de julio del año 1808. Lo publica su autor D.J.A.L. (Llorente)*. Madrid: Impr. de T. Albán, 1809.

———. *Discursos sobre una constitución religiosa, considerada como parte de la civil nacional*. Paris: Imprenta de Stahl, 1819. Reprinted in 1820 in Paris in French by L.E. Herhan, "Projet d'une constitution religieuse, considérée comme faisant partie de la constitution civile d'une nation libre indepéndante, écrit par un Americain. Publié avec une préface, par Dom Jean-Antoine Llorente".

———. *Disertación sobre el poder que los reyes españoles ejercieron hasta el siglo duodécimo en la división de opisbados, y otros puntos conecsos de disciplina eclesiástica: con un apéndice de escrituras en que constan los hechos citados en la disertación*. Madrid, reimpresa en México en la oficina del ciudadano Alejandro Valdés, 1826.

———. *Histoire critique de l'Inquisition d'Espagne, depuis l'époque de son établissement par Ferdinand V, jusqu'au règne de Ferdinand VII, tirée des pieces originales des archives du Conseil de la Suprême, et de celles des tribunaux subalternes du Saint-Office. Par . . . Traduite de l'espagnol, sur le manuscrit et sous les yeux de l'auteur, par Alexis Pellier*. Paris: Treuttel et Würtz, 1817–1818. Translated into English and published in 1826 in Philadelphia by T.B. Peterson and brothers, and in New York (translated by "an American") by G.C. Morgan.

———. *Leyes del Fuero-Juzgo, o Recopilación de las leyes de los Wisi-Godos españoles, titulada primeramente "Liber judicum"*. Madrid: Imprenta de Hernández Pacheco, 1792.

———. *Memoria histórica sobre qual ha sido la opinión nacional de España acerca del tribunal de la Inquisición*. Madrid: Imprenta de Sancha, 1812.

———. *Noticia biográfica (Autobiográfica)*. Critical note by Antonio Márquez, bibliographical essay by Emil van der Vekene. Madrid: Taurus, 1982.

———. *Pequeño catecismo sobre la materia de concordatos. Escrito en francés y traducido al español por José Mariano Ramírez Hermosa*. México: Mariano Galván Rivera, 1826.

Mease, James. *The Picture of Philadelphia, giving an account of its origin, increase and improvements in arts, sciences, manufactures, commerce and revenue. With a compendious View of Its Societies, literary, benevolent, patriotic, and religious. Its police— the public buildings—the prison and penitentiary system—institutions, monied and civil— museum*. Philadelphia: B. & T. Kite, 1811.

Mier, Servando Teresa de. *Cartas de un americano, 1811–1812*. Intro. by Manuel Calvillo. México: SEP, 1987.

———. *Historia de la revolución de Nueva España*. Ed. A. Saint Lu y M.C. Benassy-Berling, prefacio de David A. Brading. Paris: Publications de La Sorbonne, 1990.

———. *Memoria político-instructiva enviada desde Filadelfia en agosto de 1821 a los gefes independientes del Anáhuac, llamado por los españoles Nueva España*. Philadelphia: Juan F. Hurtel, 1821.

———. *Memorias*. 2 vols. Ed., prólogo de Antonio Castro Leal. México: Ed. Porrúa, 1971; *The Memoirs of* . . . Ed. Susana Rotker, trans. Helen Lane. Oxford, UK: Oxford University Press, 1998.

———. *Obras completas*. 4 vols. Intro., recopilación, edición y notas de Jaime E. Rodríguez O. México: UNAM, 1988.

Miranda, Francisco. *The Diary of . . . Tour of the United States, 1783–1784*. Edited by William Spence Robertson. New York: The Hispanic Society of America, 1928.

Neuman, Henry. *A new dictionary of the Spanish and English languages, wherein the words are currently explained, agreeably to their different meanings, and a great variety of terms, relating to the arts, sciences, manufactures, merchandise, navigation, and trade, elucidated. Compiled from the most valuable works of English and Spanish writers*. Vol. I. Philadelphia: Printed for A. Small and H.C. Carey & I. Lea, 1823.

Newman, Henrique. *Diccionario Nuevo de las dos lenguas Española e Inglesa; que contiene las significaciones de sus voces con sus diferentes usos. Y los términos, de artes, ciencias, oficios, manufacturas, comercio, y marina, que* se usan en las dos lenguas. Compilado de los mejores autores Españoles e Ingleses. Tomo II, Filadelfia: Impreso a costa de Abraham Small, y H.C. Carey y I. Lea, 1823.

O'Conway, Santiago Matthias. *Hispano–Anglo Grammar, containing the definitions, structure, inflections, referents, arrangement, concord, government and combination of the various classes of words in the Spanish language. An appropriate vocabulary, familiar phrases, dialogues, and a complete index.* Philadelphia: Thomas Dobson, 1810.

———. *Rasgos históricos y morales; sacados de autores célebres de diversas naciones y destinados para la instrucción y entretenimiento de los estudiantes del idioma español.* Philadelphia: Thomas and William Bradford, 1809.

Olavide, Pablo de. *El desafío, Novela. Por Don Atanasio Céspedes y Monroy.* Philadelphia: Imprenta de M. Carey, 1811.

———. *La paisana virtuosa. Novela. Por Don Atanasio Céspedes y Monroy.* Philadelphia: Imprenta de M. Carey, 1811.

———. *La presumida orgullosa. Novela. Por Don Atanasio Céspedes y Monroy.* Philadelphia: Imprenta de M. Carey, 1811.

———. *Obras selectas.* Ed. Estuardo Núñez. Lima: Banco de Crédito del Perú, 1987.

Ortiz de Ayala, Tadeo. *México considerado como nación independiente y libre.* Burdeos: Carlos Lawalle Sobrino, 1832. Modern Edition: Prólogo de Fernando Escalante Gonzalbo. México: Conaculta, 1996.

Paine, Thomas. *El derecho del hombre para el uso y provecho del género humano. Compuesto por Don Tomás Paine, Miembro de la Convención nacional de Francia; Secretario del Congreso, durante la Guerra de América; autor de la obra, intitulada* Common Sense (Sentido Común), &&. Traducida del inglés por Santiago Felipe Puglia. Filadelfia: Matías Carey e Hijos, 1821. Reprinted by H.C. Carey & Lea, 1822,

———. *Rights of Man, Common Sense.* Edited by Michael Foot. New York: Alfred A. Knopf, 1994.

———. *The Thomas Paine Reader.* Edited by Michael Foot and Isaac Kramnick. London: Penguin, 1987.

Poinsett, Joel Roberts. *Notes on Mexico, Made in the Autumn of 1822, Accompanied by An Historical Sketch of the Revolution, and Translations of Official Reports on the Present State of That Country.* Philadelphia: H. C. Carey & I. Lea, 1824; modern edition, New York: Praeger, 1969.

Pretensiones de los anglo-americanos. México: Oficina de D. Alejandro Valdés, 1820.

Puglia, James Philip. *El desengaño del hombre, compuesto por Santiago Felipe Puglia, Maestro de la lengua castellana en esta metrópoli. Feliz quien llega a conocer por qué el hombre afecta amor, justicia y fe. El autor.* Filadelfia: F. Bailey, 1794; republished in Philadelphia by H.C. Carey y I. Lea, 1822.

———. *The Federal Politician, by . . . Teacher of the Spanish and Italian Languages, and author of the Spanish work entitled "El desengaño del hombre" or The man undeceived*. Philadelphia: Francis Robert Bailey, 1795.

Quince días en Londres, o sea corto viage de un francés a Inglaterra a fines de 1815, traducido al Castellano. México: reimp. Oficina del Aguila, dirigida por José Ximeno, 1826.

Quirós, José María. *Guía de negociantes. Compendio de la legislación mercantil de España e Indias*. México: UNAM, (1810) 1986.

———. *Memorias políticas y económicas del Consulado de Veracruz, 1796–1822*. Ed. Javier Ortiz de La Tabla Duccase. Sevilla: Escuela de Estudios Hispano-Americanos, CSIC, 1985.

Ramos Arizpe, Miguel. *Memorial on the Natural, Political and Civil State of the Province of Coahuila, One of the Four Provinces of the East, in the Kingdom of Mexico*. Philadelphia: Printed by G. Palmer for John Melish, 1814. The Spanish original is available in a modern edition by W. Michael Mathes. Guadalajara: Ayuntamiento, 1991: *Memoria que el Doctor D. Miguel Ramos Arizpe, cura de Borbon, y diputado en las presentes Cortes Generales y extraordinarias de España por la provincia de Coahuila, una de las cuatro internas del Oriente en el Reyno de Mexico, presenta a el augusto Congreso sobre el estado natural, politico, y civil de su dicha provincia, y las de el Nuevo Reyno de Leon, Nuevo Santander, y los Texas, con exposición de los defectos del sistema general, y particular de sus gobiernos, y de las reformas, y nuevos establecimientos que necesitan para su prosperidad*.

Reglamento para el comercio libre, 1778. Madrid: Imprenta de Pedro Marín, 1778; modern ed., Sevilla: Escuela de Estudios Hispano-americanos, CSIC, 1979.

Robertson, William. *The History of America*. 10th ed., 4 vols. London: printed by A. Strahan for A. Strahan, T. Cadell Jun. and W. Davies; Edinburgh: E. Balfour, (1777) 1803.

Robinson, William Davis. *Memoirs of the Mexican Revolution; including a Narrative of the Expedition of General Xavier Mina. To which are annexed Some Observations on the Practicability of Opening a Commerce between the Pacific and Atlantic Oceans, through the Mexican Isthmus, in the Province of Oaxaca, and at the Lake of Nicaragua; and On the Vast Importance of Such Commerce to the Civilized World*. 2 vols. London: Lackington, Hughes, Harding, Mavor, & Lepard, 1821.

Rocafuerte, Vicente. *Bosquejo ligerísimo de la revolución de Mégico, desde el grito de Iguala hasta la proclamación imperial de Iturbide. Por un verdadero americano*. Philadelphia: Imprenta de Teracrouef y Naroajeb, 1822. Facsimile edited by Luz María y Miguel Angel Porrúa, prologue by Horacio Labastida Muñoz. México: Porrúa, 1984.

———. *Ensayo político: El sistema colombiano, popular, electivo y representativo es el que más conviene a la América Independiente*. New York: Imprenta de A. Paul, 1823.

———. *Ideas necesarias a todo pueblo americano independiente, que quiere ser libre*. Philadelphia: D. Huntington, 1821, 180 pp., reprinted after the Philadelphia edition in Puebla in 1823 "en la oficina de P. de la Rosa, impresor del gobierno," 227 pp.

Roscio, Juan Germán. *El triunfo de la libertad sobre el despotismo en la confesión de un pecador arrepentido de sus errores políticos, y dedicado a desagraviar en esta parte a la religión ofendida con el sistema de la tiranía*. Filadelfia: Thomas H. Palmer, 1817; 2a ed. Filadelfia: Impr. de M. Carey e Hijos, 1821. Facsimile ed., with "prólogo, cronologia y bibliografia de Domingo Miliani". Caracas: Biblioteca Ayacucho, 1996.

———. *Homilía del Cardenal Chiaramonte, Obispo de Imola, actualmente Sumo Pontífice Pío VII, dirigida al pueblo de su Diócesis en la República Cisalpina, el día del nacimiento de J.C. Año de 1797. Traducida del francés al español por un Ciudadano de Venezuela en la América del Sur, que la publica rebatiendo con ella un papel del mismo Papa en favor de Fernando VII, contra los insurgentes de las llamadas Colonias españolas.*. Filadelfia: J.F. Hurtel, 1817; M. Carey, 1821.

Rousseau, Jean Jacques. *El contrato social; o Principios del derecho político. Nueva ed., revista y corregida*. Filadelfia: Imprenta de M. Carey e Hijos, 1821, 1822.

S., P.F. "Respuesta a las imposturas de un folletista español. O sea Tapaboca al Libelista autor del anónimo publicado en Filadelfia intitulado: Manifiesto a los hombres de la injusticia que llama justicia el Dr. D. Manuel de la Bárcena. Carta a un amigo". México: Imprenta de Doña Herculana del Villar y Socios, 3 octubre, 1822.

Varela, Félix. *El Habanero*. Philadelphia: Stavely y Bringhurst, 1824–1826. Modern edition edited by José M. Hernández. Miami: Universal, 1997.

Volney, C.F. *Ruins, or Meditations on the Revolution of Empires*. Boston: Charles Gaylord, 1835. Modern edition by Robert D. Richardson, Jr. 2 vols. New York: Garland, (1791) 1979.

———. *Sistema politico moral . . . La lei natural, o Catequismo del Ciudadano Francés, compuesto por . . . , y traducido del Francés al Castellano por Santiago Felipe Puglia*. Philadelphia: Mathew Carey e Hijos, 1821. Modern edition, *La loi naturelle ou Catéchisme du citoyen français* by Gaston-Martin. Paris: Librairie Armand Colin, 1934.

Von Humboldt, Alejandro. *Cartas americanas*, edited by Charles Minguet, trad. Marta Traba. Caracas: Ayacucho, 1980.

———. *Personal Narrative of Travels to the Equinoctial Regions of the New Continent during the Years 1799–1804*. Translated from the French original by Helen Maria Williams. Carlisle, PA: printed for Mathew Carey by George Philips, 1815.

———. *Political essay on the kingdom of New Spain, containing researches relative to the geography of Mexico, the extent of its surface and its political division into intendancies, the physical aspect of the country, the population, the state of agriculture and manufacturing and commercial industry, the Canals projected between the South Sea and Atlantic Ocean, the crown revenues, the quantity of the precious metals which have flowed from Mexico into Europe and Asia, since the discovery of the new continent, and the military defence of New Spain by . . . with physical sections and maps, founded on astronomical observations, and trigonometrical and barometrical measurements.* New York: I. Riley, 1811, 2 vols.; taken from the four-volume London translation by John Black, 1811, and published originally in French in Paris in 1811.

—— SECONDARY SOURCES ——

Adams, Henry. *History of the United States of America during the Administration of Thomas Jefferson.* New York: Library of America, 1986.

Adorno, Rolena. "Washington Irving's Romantic Hispanism and Its Columbian Legacies."In *Spain in America, The Origins of Hispanism in the United States*, edited by Richard L. Kagan. Urbana, IL: University of Illinois Press, 49–105.

Aguilar Piñal, Francisco, *Bibliografía de escritores españoles del siglo XVIII.* 9 vols. Madrid: CSIC, 1983.

———. *Cándido María Trigueros: Un escritor ilustrado.* Madrid: CSIC, Instituto de Filología, 1987.

Aguirre, Robert D. *Informal Empire, Mexico and Central America in Victorian Culture.* Minneapolis: University of Minnesota Press, 2004.

Aguirre Elorriaga, Manuel. *El Abate de Pradt en la emancipación hispanoamericana (1800–1830).* Caracas: Universidad Católica Andrés Bello, Instituto de Investigaciones Históricas, 1983.

Alcides Reissner, Raúl. *El indio en los diccionarios, Exégesis léxica de un estereotipo.* México: Instituto Nacional Indigenista, 1983.

Alonso Seoane, María José. "Los autores de tres novelas de Olavide", *Actas de las IV Jornadas de Andalucía y América en el siglo XVIII* (pp., 1–22). Sevilla: Escuela de Estudios Hispano-Americanos de Sevilla, 1985.

Altamirano, Carlos y Jorge Myers. *Historia de los intelectuales en América Latina.* Buenos Aires: Katz, 2008.

Alvarez de Miranda, Pedro. "Sobre el 'quijotismo' dieciochesco y las imitaciones reaccionarias del *Quijote* en el primer siglo XIX", *Dieciocho* 27 (2004): 31–45.

American Art: 1750-1800, Towards Independence. Edited by Charles F. Mongomery and Patricia E. Kane. New Haven, CT: Yale University Art Gallery, NY Graphic Society, Victoria and Albert Museum, 1976.

Amory, Hugo and David D. Hall. "Afterword." *A History of the Book in America*, vol. 1. The Colonial Book in the Atlantic World, edited by Hugh Amory and David D. Hall. Cambridge, UK: Cambridge University Press, American Antiquarian Society, 2000, 477–485.

Anderson, Benedict. *Imagined Communities, Reflections on the Origin and Spread of Nationalism.* London: Verso, (1983) 1985.

Anna, Timothy E. *The Mexican Empire of Iturbide.* Lincoln, London: University of Nebraska Press, 1990.

Arteta, Begoña, ed. *Primera exposición de arte prehispánico por William Bullock.* México: Universidad Autónoma Metropolitana, Unidad Azcapotzalco, 1991.

Ayers, Edward L. "Antebellum Era." *The Oxford Companion to United States History*, edited by Paul S. Boyer. New York: Oxford University Press, 2001, 37–38.

Baer-Wallis, Friederike. "They 'Speak Irish but Should Speak German': Language and Citizenship in Philadelphia's German Community, c. 1800 to 1820." *PMHB (The Pennsylvania Magazine of History and Biography)* 128 (2004): 5–33.

Báez Macías, Eduardo. *Jerónimo Antonio Gil y su traducción de Gerard Audran.* México: UNAM, 2001.

Baker, Maury Davidson, Jr. "The U.S. and Piracy during the Spanish American Wars of Independence." PhD diss., Duke University, 1946.

Barragán Barragán, José. *Temas del liberalismo gaditano.* México: UNAM, 1978.

Barrenechea, José Manuel. *Valentín de Foronda, reformador y economista ilustrado.* Prólogo Ernest Lluch Vitoria: Diputación Foral de Alava, 1984.

Bauer, Ralph. "Notes on the Comparative Study of the Colonial Americas, Further Reflections on the Tucson Summit," *Early American Literature* 38 (2003): 281–304.

———. *The Cultural Geography of Colonial American Literatures, Empire, Travel, Modernity.* Cambridge, UK: Cambridge University Press, 2003.

Baur, John E. "The Evolution of a Mexican Foreign Trade Policy, 1821–1828," *The Americas* 19 (1963): 225–261.

Belaúnde, Víctor Andrés. *Bolívar and The Political Thought of the Spanish American Revolution.* New York: Octagon Books, (1938) 1978.

Benavides, M. y C. Rollán. *Valentín de Foronda, Los sueños de la razón.* Madrid: Ed. Nacional, 1984.

Benot, Yves. *Diderot: del ateísmo al anticolonialismo.* Trans. Sergio Fernández Bravo. México: Siglo XXI, 1973.

Benson, Nettie Lee. *La diputación provincial y el federalismo mexicano*. México: El Colegio de México, UNAM, 1994.

———, ed. *Mexico and the Spanish Cortes, 1810–1822. Eight Essays*. Austin: Universisty of Texas Press, 1966.

———. "Territorial Integrity in Mexican Politics." *The Independence of Mexico and the Creation of the New Nation* (275–307), edited by Jaime E. Rodríguez O. Los Angeles, Irvine: UCLA Latin American Center, 1989.

———. "The Plan of Casa Mata." *HAHR* 25 (1945): 45–56.

Berruezo León, María Teresa. *La lucha de Hispanoamérica por su independencia en Inglaterra, 1800–1830*. Madrid: Instituto de Cultura Hispánica, 1989.

Bosch García, Carlos. *Problemas diplomáticos del México independiente*. México: UNAM, 1986.

———, ed. *Documentos de la relación de México con los Estados Unidos. I. El mester politico de Poinsett (Noviembre de 1824-Diciembre de 1829)*. México: UNAM, 1983.

Bowman, Charles H., Jr. "The Activities of Manuel Torres as Purchasing Agent, 1820-1821." *HAHR* 48 (1968): 234–246.

Brack, Gene M. *Mexico Views Manifest Destiny, 1821–1846, An Essay on the Origins of the Mexican War*. Albuquerque: University of New Mexico Press, 1975.

Brading, David A. *The First America, The Spanish Monarchy, Creole Patriots and the Liberal State, 1492–1867*. Cambridge: Cambridge University Press, 1991.

Bradsher, Earl L. *Mathew Carey, Editor, Author and Publisher, A Study in American Literary Development*. New York: Columbia University Press, 1912.

Branson, Susan and Leslie Patrick. "Etrangers dans un Pays Etrange: Saint-Domingan Refugees of Color in Philadelphia." In *The Impact of the Haitian Revolution in the Atlantic World*, edited by David P. Geggus. Columbia: University of South Carolina Press, 2001, 193–208.

Brickhouse, Anna. *Transamerican Literary Relations and the Nineteenth-Century Public Sphere*. Cambridge: Cambridge University Press, 2004.

Brooks, Van Wyck. *The World of Washington Irving*. New York: E.P. Dutton & Co., 1944.

Brown, H. Glenn and Maude O. Brown. *A Directory of the Book-Arts and Book Trade in Philadelphia to 1820, Including Painters and Engravers*. New York: The New York Public Library, 1950.

Bueno, Salvador. "Sobre el posible autor de la novela *Xicotencatl*" *Revista de literatura cubana* 11 (1992): 105–107.

Bullock, Steven C. *Revolutionary Brotherhood: Freemasonry and the Transformation of the American Social Order, 1730–1840*. Chapel Hill: University of North Carolina Press, 1996.

Cañizares-Esguerra, Jorge. *Nature, Empire, and Nation, Explorations of the History of Science in the Iberian World*. Stanford: Stanford University Press, 2006.

Canny, Nicholas and Anthony Pagden. *Colonial Identity in the Atlantic World, 1500–1800*. Princeton: Princeton University Press, 1987.

Carrasco Puente, Rafael. *La prensa en México, Datos históricos*. Pról. María del Carmen Ruíz-Castañeda. México: UNAM, 1962.

Carreño, Alberto María. *La diplomacia extraordinaria entre México y Estados Unidos, 1789–1947*. Vol. 1, 2ª ed. México: Ed. Jus, 1961.

Castañeda, Carmen. "Libros para todos los gustos: la tienda de libros de la imprenta de Guadalajara, 1821". *Empresa y Cultura en tinta y papel (1800–1860)*. Coord. general Laura Beatriz Suárez de la Torre, ed. Miguel Angel Castro. México: Instituto de Investigaciones Dr. José Maria Luis Mora, UNAM, 2001, 245–257.

Castañeda, Carmen y Myrna Cortés, coord. *Del autor al lector*. México: CIESAS, CONACYT, Miguel Angel Porrúa, 2002.

Castañeda García, Carmen, Luz Elena Galván Lafarga, Lucía Martínez Moctezuma, coord. *Lecturas y lectores en la historia de México*. México, Zamora, Cuernavaca: CIESAS, El Colegio de Michoacán, Universidad Autónoma del Estado de Morelos, 2004.

Castro-Klarén, Sara and John Charles Chasteen, ed. *Beyond Imagined Communities, Reading and Writing the Nation in Nineteenth-Century Latin America*. Washington, D.C., Baltimore: Woodrow Wilson Center, The Johns Hopkins University Press, 2003.

Catálogo comentado del acervo del Museo Nacional de Arte (Escultura, Siglo XIX), ed. Esther Acevedo, Jaime Cuadriello, Fausto Ramírez, Angélica Velásquez Guadarrama. México: CONACULTA, 2001.

Catálogo de la Colección Lafragua de la Biblioteca Nacional de México, 1821–1853. Coord. Lucina Morena Valle. México: UNAM, 1975.

Catalogue of Mexican Pamphlets in the Sutro Collection, 1623-1888, With Supplements, 1605–1887. San Francisco: California State Library, Sutro Branch, 1939–1941; Kraus reprint, New York, 1971.

Chartier, Roger. *El juego de las reglas: lecturas*. México: Fondo de Cultura Económica, 2000.

———. *The Order of Books*. Trans. Lydia G. Cochrane. Stanford: Stanford University Press, (1992) 1994.

Chávez, Thomas E. *Spain and the Independence of the United States, An Intrinsic Gift*. Albuquerque: U of New Mexico Press, 2002.

Chevigny, Bell Gale and Gari Laguardia, ed. *Reinventing the Americas: Comparative Studies of Literature of the United States and Spanish America*. Cambridge: Cambridge University Press, 1986.

Clark, John G. *New Orleans: An Economic History, 1718–1812*. Baton Rouge: Lousiana State University, 1970.

Clark de Lara, Belem y Elisa Speckman Guerra, eds. *La república de las letras. Asomos de la cultura escrita del México decimonónico*. 3 vols. México: UNAM, 2005.

Clarkin, William. *Mathew Carey, A Bibliography of His Publications, 1785–1824*. New York: Garland, 1984.

Clasicismo en México. México: Malibu: Centro Cultural, J. Paul Getty Museum, 1990.

Classical Taste in America, 1800–1840. Edited by Wendy A. Cooper. Baltimore: The Baltimore Museum of Art, Abbeville Press, 1993.

Cohen, Margaret and Carolyn Dever, ed. *The Literary Channel, The International Invention of the Novel*. Princeton: Princeton University Press, 2002.

Coil, Henry Wilson, comp. *Coil's Masonic Encyclopedia*. New York: Macoy Publishing and Masonic Supply Co., 1961.

Colley, Linda. "The Sea Around Us." Review of Bernard Bailyn's *Atlantic History: Concept and Contours*. New York Review of Books, June 22, 2006, 43–45.

Colón, María Luisa. "Impresos en español publicados en Filadelfia durante los años 1800 a 1835". PhD diss., Catholic University, 1951.

Connaughton, Brian. *Dimensiones de la identidad patriótica: Religión, política y regiones en México, Siglo XIX*. México: Universidad Autónoma Metropolitana, Unidad Iztapalapa, 2001.

_____. "Los lindes teóricos de una inquietud de época: Cádiz y las lecturas paradigmáticas de la década independentista". En *Independencia y Revolución: pasado, presente y futuro*. Gustavo Leyva, Brian Connaughton, Rodrigo Díaz, Nestor García Canclini, Carlos Illades (coord.). México: Fondo de Cultura Económica, Universidad Autónoma Metropolitana, 2010, 108–143

_____. "Voces europeas en la temprana labor editorial mexicana, 1820-1860." *Historia mexicana* 219 (2006): 895–946.

Conway, Christopher B. *The Cult of Bolívar in Latin American Literature*. Gainesville: University Press of Florida, 2003.

Cooper, James Fenimore. *The American Democrat and Other Political Writings*, edited by Bradley J. Birger and John Willson. Washington, DC: Regnery, 2000.

Cordero Aroca, Alberto P., coord. *Documentos políticos de Don Vicente Rocafuerte*. Guayaquil: n.p., 1997.

Costeloe, Michael P. "William Bullock and the Mexican Connection." *Mexican Studies/ Estudios Mexicanos* 22 (2006): 275–309.

Cuevas, P. Mariano, S.J. *Historia de la Iglesia en México*. El Paso, TX: Editorial "Revista Católica,"1928.

Cussen, Antonio. *Bello and Bolívar, Poetry and Politics in the Spanish American Revolution*. Cambridge: Cambridge University Press, 1992.

Daniels, Christine and Michael V. Kennedy. *Negotiated Empires, Centers and Peripheries in the Americas, 1500–1820*. New York: Routledge, 2002.

Darnton, Robert. *The Business of the Enlightenment, A Publishing History of the Encyclopedie 1775–1800*. Cambridge: Harvard University Press, 1979.

———. *The Literary Underground of the Old Regime*. Cambridge: Harvard University Press, 1982.

Davidson, Cathy. *Revolution and the Word, The Rise of the Novel in America*. New York: Oxford University Press, 1986.

———, ed. *Reading in America, Literature & Social History*. Baltimore: The Johns Hopkins University Press, 1989.

Davis, William C. *The Pirates Laffite, The Treacherous World of the Corsairs of the Gulf*. New York: Harcourt, 2005.

Dawson, Frank Griffith. *The First Latin American Debt Crisis, The City of London and the 1822–25 Loan Bubble*. New Haven: Yale University Press, 1990.

De Bufanda, J.M. *Index Librorum Prohibitorum, 1600–1966*. Montreal: Université de Sherbrooke, Mediaspaul, Librairie Droz, 2002.

Defourneaux, Marcelin. *Inquisición y censura de libros en la España del siglo XVIII*. Trans. J. Ignacio Tellechea Idígoras. Madrid: Taurus, (1963) 1973.

de la Torre Villar, Ernesto. *Breve historia del libro en México*. México: UNAM, 1990.

Delgado Carranco, Susana María. "Las primeras discusiones en torno a la libertad de imprenta: El *Diario de México (1811–1815)*. In *Empresa y cultura en tinta y papel (1800–1860)*. Coord. general, Laura Beatriz Suárez de la Torre, ed. Miguel Angel Castro. México: Instituto de Investigaciones Dr. José María Luis Mora, UNAM, 2001, 473–488.

———. *Libertad de imprenta, política y educación: su planteamiento y discusión en el Diario de México, 1810–1817*. México: Instituto Mora, 2006.

de los Reyes, Guillermo. "'El compás y la escuadra': The Influence of Catholicism and Masonry in the Formation of Mexican Political Thought" Translated by Craig Dennison. In *Recovering Hispanic Religious Thought and Practice of the United States*, edited by Nicolás Kanellos. Newcastle: Cambridge Scholars Publishing, 2007, 8–24.

del Palacio Montiel, Celia. "Imprentas e impresores de Veracruz, 1795-1850", *Empresa y cultura en tinta y papel (1800–1860)*. Coord. General, Laura Beatriz Suárez de la Torre, ed. Miguel Angel Castro. México: Instituto de Investigaciones Dr. José María Luis Mora, UNAM, 2001, 171-191.

de María y Campos, Armando. *Manuel Eduardo de Gorostiza y su tiempo. Su vida, su obra*. México: n.p., 1959.

Denslow, Ray V. *Freemasonry in the Western Hemisphere.* n.p.: 1953.
de Onís, José. *The United States as Seen by Spanish American Writers (1776–1890).* New York: Hispanic Institute in the United States, 1952.
———. "Valentín de Foronda's Memoir on the United States of North America, 1804." *The Americas* 4 (1948): 351–387.
"Desaguiliers." "Freemasonry in Mexico. Its Origin, &. Illustrated by Original Documents, Not Heretofore Published." *Mason Review* (August, October, 1858, Cincinnati, Ohio).
Descriptive Catalogue of the Documents relating to the history of the U.S. in the Papeles Procedentes de Cuba deposited in the Archivo General de Indias at Seville. Edited by Roscoe R. Hill. Washington, DC: Carnegie Institution of Washington, 1916.
Dessens, Nathalie. *From Saint-Domingue to New Orleans, Migration and Influences.* Gainesville: University Press of Florida, 2007..
Diner, Hasia R. *The Jews of the United States, 1654–2000.* Berkeley: University of California Press, 2004, 2006.
Documentos relativos a la Independencia de Norteamérica existentes en archivos españoles. Vol. 3, 2 numbers, Archivo Histórico Nacional, ed. Pilar León Tello, con la colaboración de Concepción Menéndez y Carmen Herrero; Vol. 5, 2 numbers, Archivo General de Simancas, ed. María Francisca Represa Fernández, Carlos Alvarez García y Miguel Represa Fernández, bajo la dirección de Amando Represa Rodríguez. Madrid: Ministerio de Asuntos Exteriores, 1976.
Domínguez Michael, Christopher. *Vida de Fray Servando.* México: Ediciones Era, CONCULTA, INAH, 2004.
Dufour, Gérard. *Juan Antonio Llorente en France, 1813–22: contribution a l'étude du liberalisme crétien en France et en Espagne au début du XIXe siècle.* Genève: Librairie Droz, 1982.
Dunkerley, James. *Americana, The Americas in the World, around 1850.* London: Verso, 2000.
Dykstra, Kristin. "On the Betrayal of Nations: José Alvarez de Toledo's Philadelphia *Manifesto* (1811) and *Justification* (1816)." *The New Centennial Review* 4 (2004): 267–305.
Echeverria, Durand. *Mirage in the West, A History of the French Image of American Society to 1815.* Princeton: Princeton University Press, 1957.
Elliott, J.H. *Do the Americas Have a Common History?* Providence, RI: The John Carter Brown Library, 1998.
———. *Empires of the Atlantic World, Britain and Spain in America, 1492–1830.* New Haven: Yale University Press, 2006.
Encina, Francisco A. "The Limited Influence of the Revolution." In *The Origins of the Latin American Revolutions, 1808-1826,* edited by R.A. Humphreys and John Lynch. New York: Alfred A. Knopf, 1965, 106–110.

An Encyclopedia of Freemasonry and Its Kindred Sciences. Edited by Albert G. Mackey. New York, London: The Masonic History Co., 1917.

Fabian, Bernhard. "English Books and Their German Readers."In *The Widening Circle, Essays on the Circulation of Literature in Eighteenth-Century Europe*, edited by Paul J. Korshin.. Philadelphia: University of Pennsylvania Press, 1976.

Fauchon, Pierre. *L'abbé Grégoire, le prêtre-citoyen*. Tours: Editions de la Nouvelle République, 1989.

Febvre Lucien and Henri-Jean Martin. *The Coming of the Book, The Impact of Printing 1450–1800*. Trans.by David Gerardo, edited by Geoffrey Nowell-Smith and David Wootton.. London: Verso (1958) 1986.

Fernández-Armesto, Felipe. *The Americas: A Hemispheric History*. New York: Modern Library, 2003.

Fischer, David Hackett. *Albion's Seed*. New York: Oxford University Press, 1989.

———. *Liberty and Freedom, A Visual History of America's Founding Ideas*. New York: Oxford University Press, 2005.

Fisher, Lillian Estelle. *The Background of the Revolution for Mexican Independence*. Boston: Christopher Publishing House, 1934.

———. *Commercial Conditions in Mexico at the End of the Colonial Period*. Reprinted from *New Mexico Historical Review*. Santa Fe: no publisher, 1932.

Florescano Mayet, Sergio. *El camino México-Veracruz en la época colonial*. Xalapa: Universidad Veracruzana, Centro de Investigaciones Históricas, 1987.

Fontana, Josep. *La crisis del Antiguo regimen, 1808–1833*. Barcelona: Crítica, (1979) 1992.

Fraser, Ronald. *Napoleon's Cursed War, Popular Resistance in the Spanish Peninsular War, 1808–1814*. London: Verso, 2008.

Frasquet, Ivana. "Cádiz en América: Liberalismo y Constitución." *Mexican Studies/Estudios mexicanos* 20 (2004): 21–46.

Freemasonry in Pennsylvania 1727–1907, As Shown by the Records of Lodge No. 1. F. and A.M. of Philadelphia. Philadelphia: Norris S. Barratt and Julius F. Sachse, 1919.

Fuentes, Juan Francisco. "Leyenda y realidad de un abate revolucionario." In *Liberales, agitadores y conspiradores*. Coord. Isabel Burdiel, Manuel Pérez Ledesma. Madrid: Espasa, 2000, 47–71.

Fuentes Mares, José. *Poinsett, Historia de una gran intriga*. México: Ed. Jus, 1951.

Garate, Justo. *El Caballero Valentín de Foronda "Ilustrado" Alavés*. Separata from *Boletín "Sancho el Sabio"* Año XVIII, Tomo XVIII, 1974, 581–620.

García Garófalo Mesa, M. *Vida de José María Heredia en México, 1825–1839*. México: Ed. Botas, 1949.

García Malo, Ignacio. *Voz de la naturaleza*. Selección, estudio de Guillermo Carnero. Madrid: Tamesis, 1995.

Gaxiola, Francisco Javier. *Poinsett en México (1822–1828) Notas de un libro inconcluso*. Pról. José Elguero. México: Ed. "Cultura", 1936.

Gómez Alvarez, Cristina y Guillermo Tovar de Teresa. *Censura y revolución. Libros prohibidos por la Inquisición de México (1790–1819)*. Madrid: Trama editorial, Consejo de Crónica de la Ciudad de México, 2009.

Gómez de Enterria, Josefa. *Voces de la economía y el comercio en el español del siglo XVIII*. Alcalá: Universidad de Alcalá, 1996.

———. "Notas sobre el vocabulario del comercio en el siglo XVIII. Algunos problemas neológicos". *Dieciocho* 20.1 (1997): 85–96.

Gómez Imaz, Manuel. *Los periódicos durante la guerra de independencia (1808–1814)*. Madrid: Tipografía de la Rev. de Arch. Biblio. y Museos, 1910.

González Acosta, Alejandro. *El enigma de Jicoténcal. Estudio de dos novelas sobre el héroe de Tlaxcala*. México: UNAM; Instituto Tlaxcalteca de Cultura, Gobierno del Estado de Tlaxcala, 1997.

González Casanova, Pablo. *La literatura perseguida por la Inquisición*. México: Grijalbo, (1958) 1992.

——— y José Miranda. *Sátira anónima del siglo XVIII*. México: Fondo de Cultura Económica, 1953.

González Palencia, Angel. *Estudio histórico sobre la censura gubernativa en España, 1800–1833*. 3 vols. Madrid: Tipografía de Archivos, 1933.

Grases, Pedro. "El círculo de Filadelfia", *Obras* 3. Caracas, Barcelona, México: Seix Barral, (1981): 280–283.

———. *El viajero Francisco Depons*. Caracas: Banco Central de Venezuela, 1960.

——— y Alberto Harkness. *Manuel García y la Independencia de Hispanoamérica*. Caracas: Publicaciones de la Secretaría General de la Décima Conferencia Interamericana, 1953.

Green, James N. "From Printer to Publisher: Mathew Carey and the Origins of Nineteenth-Century Book Publishing." In *Getting the Books Out, Papers of the Chicago Conference on the Book in 19th-Century America*. Washington: Library of Congress, 1987, 26-44.

———. *Mathew Carey, Publisher and Patriot*. Philadelphia: Library Co. of Philadelphia, 1985.

Green, Stanley C. *The Mexican Republic: The First Decade (1823–1832)*. Pittsburgh: University of Pittsburgh Press, 1987.

Griffin, Charles C. "Privateering from Baltimore during the Spanish American Wars of Independence." *Maryland Historical Magazine* 35 (1940); 1–25.

Gross, Robert A. and Mary Kelley, eds. *A History of the Book in America, An Extensive Republic, Print, Culture, and Society in the New Nation, 1790–*

1840. Vol. 2. Chapel Hill: University of North Carolina Press, American Antiquarian Society, 2010.

Gruesz, Kirsten Silva. *Ambassadors of Culture, The Transamerican Origins of Latino Writing*. Princeton: Princeton University Press, 2002.

Guerra, François-Xavier. *Modernidad e independencias. Ensayos sobre las revoluciones hispánicas*. México: Ed. MAPFRE, Fondo de Cultura Económica, (1992) 2000.

Guía del Archivo de la Antigua Academia de San Carlos, 1801–1843. México: UNAM, 1972.

Guide to the Manuscript Collections of the Historical Society of Pennsylvania. Philadelphia: HSP, 1991.

Guimerá Ravina, Agustín. *Burguesía extranjera y comercio atlántico, La empresa comercial irlandesa en Canarias (1703–1771)*. Santa Cruz de Tenerife: Consejería de Cultura y Deportes, Gobierno de Canarias, CSIC, 1985.

Guiot de la Garza, Lilia. "El Portal de Agustinos; un corredor cultural en la ciudad de México", *Empresa y Cultura en tinta y papel (1800–1860)*. Coord. general Laura Beatriz Suárez de la Torre, ed. Miguel Ángel Castro. México: Instituto de Investigaciones Dr. José María Mora, UNAM, 2001, 233–243.

Gutiérrez Lorenzo, María del Pilar, coord. *Impresos y libros en la historia económica de México (siglos XVI–XIX)*. Guadalajara: Universidad de Guadalajara, 2007.

Gutjahr, Paul C. *An American Bible, A History of the Good Book in the United States, 1777–1880*. Stanford: Stanford University Press, 1999.

Guzmán, Martín Luis. *Filadelfia, Paraíso de conspiradores y otras historias noveladas*. México: Compañía General de Ediciones, 1960.

———. *Javier Mina, Héroe de España y de México*. México: Fondo de Cultura Económica, 1990; México: Ed. Planeta de Agostini, CONACULTA, 2001.

Hale, Charles A. *Mexican Liberalism in the Age of Mora, 1821–1853*. New Haven: Yale University Press, 1968.

Hall, David D. "Introduction." In *A History of the Book in America. Vol. One, The Colonial Book in the Atlantic World*, edited by Hugh Amory and David D. Hall. Cambridge: Cambridge UP, American Antiquarian Society, 2000, 1–25.

Hanke, Lewis. *Bartolomé de las Casas, An Interpretation of His Life and Writings*. The Hague: Martinus Nijhoff, 1951.

Hauser, Arnold. *The Social History of Art*. 4 vols. Trans. Stanley Godman. New York: Vintage, 1951.

Henson, Margaret Swett. *Juan Davis Bradburn: A Reappraisal of the Commander at Anáhuac*. College Station: Texas A & M University Press, 1982.

Hernández C., Roberto. *Los primeros pasos del arte tipográfico en Chile y especialmente en Valparaíso . . . Camilo Henríquez y la publicación de la "Aurora de Chile"*. Valparaíso: Imprenta Victoria, 1930.

Herr, Richard. *The Eighteenth-Century Revolution in Spain*. Princeton: Princeton University Press, (1958) 1973.

Humphreys, R.A. and John Lynch. *The Origins of the Latin American Revolutions, 1808–1826*. New York: Alfred A. Knopf, 1965.

Huss, Wayne A. "Pennsylvania Masonry: An Intellectual and Social Analysis, 1727–1826." PhD diss., Temple University, 1984.

Iguíniz, Juan B. *La imprenta en la Nueva España*. México: Ed. Porrúa, 1938.

Indice de las Gacetas de literatura de México de José Antonio Alzate y Ramírez. Coord. Ramón Aureliano, Ana Buriano, Susana López. México: Instituto Mora, 1996.

Isenberg Nancy. *Fallen Founder: The Life of Aaron Burr*. New York: Viking, 2007.

Jackson, Joseph. *Encyclopedia of Philadelphia*. 4 vols. Harrisburg: National Historical Assoc., 1931.

Jackson, Leon. *The Business of Letters, Authorial Economies in Antebellum America*. Stanford: Stanford University Press, 2008.

Jacob, Margaret C. *Living the Enlightenment, Freemasonry and Politics in Eighteenth-Century Europe*. New York: Oxford University Press, 1991.

―――. *The Origins of Freemasonry, Facts & Fictions*. Philadelphia: University of Pennsylvania Press, 2006.

Jiménez Codinach, Guadalupe. "La insurgencia de los nombres". In *Interpretaciones de la Independencia de México*. Coord. Josefina Zoraida Vázquez. México: Nueva Imagen, 1997, 103–122.

―――. *La Gran Bretaña y la Independencia de México, 1808–1821*. Trans. by Mercedes Pizarro Suárez e Ismael Pizarro Suárez. México: Fondo de Cultura Económica, 1991.

―――. *México en 1821: Dominique de Pradt y el Plan de Iguala*. México: Universidad Iberoamericana, 1982.

Johns, Adrian. *The Nature of the Book, Print and Knowledge in the Making*. Chicago: University of Chicago Press, 1998.

Johnson, Julie Greer, ed. *The Book in the Americas. The Role of Books, Printing in the Development of Culture and Society in Colonial Latin America. Catalogue of an Exhibition*. Bibliographical Supplement by Susan L. Newbury. Providence, RI: The John Carter Brown Library, 1988.

―――. *Satire in Colonial Spanish America: Turning the New World Upside Down*. Austin: University of Texas Press, 1993.

Kagan, Richard L., ed. *Spain in America, The Origins of Hispanism in the United States*. Urbana, Chicago: University of Illinois Press, 2002.

Kalman, Judy. *Writing on the Plaza, Mediated Literacy Practices among Scribes and Clients in Mexico City*. Cresskill, NJ: Hampton, 1999.

Kanellos, Nicolás. "José Alvarez de Toledo y Dubois and the Origins of Hispanic Publishing in the U.S." *Early American Literature* 43 (2008): 83–100.

———. "A Socio-Historic Study of Hispanic Newspapers in the U.S." In *Recovering the U.S. Hispanic Literary Heritage*, edited by Ramón Gutiérrez and Genaro Padilla. Houston: Arte Público Press, 1992, 107–128.

——— with Helvetia Martell. *Hispanic Periodicals in the United States. Origins to 1960. A Brief History and Comprehensive Bibliography*. Houston: Arte Público Press, 2000.

Karp, Abraham J. "Overview: The Synagogue in America — A Historical Typology." In *The American Synagogue, A Sanctuary Transformed*, edited by Jack Westheimer. Hanover: Brandeis University Press, University Press of New England, (1987) 1995.

Kaser, David. *Messrs. Carey & Lea of Philadelphia, A Study in the History of the Booktrade*. Philadelphia: University of Pennsylvania Press, 1957.

Kaufmann, William W. *British Policy and the Independence of Latin America, 1804–1828*. New Haven: Yale University Press, 1951.

Kinane, Vincent. "'Literary Food' for the American Market: Patrick Byrne's Exports to Mathew Carey." Reprinted in. *Proceedings, American Antiquarian Society* 1 (2) (1994): 315–332.

Kramnick, Isaac, ed. *The Federalist Papers (James Madison, Alexander Hamilton, John Jay)*. London: Penguin, (1788) 1987.

Kraus, Michael. *The Atlantic Civilization, Eighteenth-Century Origins*. Ithaca: Cornell University Press, 1966.

Las academias de arte (VII Coloquio Internacional en Guanajuato). México: UNAM, 1985.

La diplomacía mexicana. 3 vols. México: Secretaría de Relaciones Exteriores, 1910.

Ladd, Doris. *The Mexican Nobility at Independence, 1780–1826*. Austin: University of Texas Press, 1976.

Lanning, John Tate. *Academic Culture in the Spanish Colonies*. Port Washington, NY: Kennikat Press, (1940) 1971.

Lazo, Rodrigo. *Writing to Cuba, Filibustering and Cuban Exiles in the United States*. Chapel Hill: University of North Carolina Press, 2005.

Lee, Jean Gordon. *Philadelphia and the China Trade, 1784–1844*. Philadelphia: Philadelphia Museum of Art, 1984.

Lenz, Hans. *Historia del papel en México y cosas relacionadas, 1525–1950*. México: Miguel Angel Porrúa, 1990.

Leonard, Irving. *Books of the Brave*. Introduction by Rolena Adorno. Berkeley: University of California Press, (1949) 1992.

——— and Robert S. Smith. "A Proposed Library for the Merchant Guild of Veracruz, 1801." *HAHR* 24 (1944): 84–102.

Little, Nigel. *Transoceanic Radical, William Duane: National Identity and Empire, 1760–1835*. London: Pickering & Chatto, 2007.

Lloréns, Vicente. *Liberales y románticos. Una emigración española en Inglaterra (1823–1834)*. Madrid: Ed. Castalia, (1954) 1979.

Loera, Jorge Enrique, coord. general. *Las aduanas de México*. México: Centro de Investigación Aduanera y de Comercio Internacional, A.C., 2000.

Lopez, François. "La librería madrileña al final del Antiguo Regimen". *Dieciocho* 27 (2004): 17–29.

Los precursores ideológicos de la Guerra de Independencia, La Masonería en México, Siglo XVIII. Tomo 2. Introduction by Nicolás Rangel. México: Archivo General de la Nación, 1932.

Loughran, Trish. *The Republic in Print, Print Culture in the Age of U.S. Nation Building, 1770–1870*. New York: Columbia University Press, 2007.

Lovett, Gabriel H. *Napoleon and the Birth of Modern Spain*. 2 vols. New York: New York University Press, 1965.

Macdonell, Diane. *Theories of Discourse: An Introduction*. New York: Basil Blackwell, 1986.

MacKay, Ruth. *"Lazy, Improvident People." Myth and Reality in the Writing of Spanish History*. Ithaca: Cornell University Press, 2006.

Mackey, Albert G. *Encyclopedia of Freemasonry and Its Kindred Sciences, Comprising the Whole Range of Arts, Sciences and Literature as Connected with the Institution*. Philadelphia: McClure Publishing Co., 1917; new and revised ed. New York: The Masonic History Co., 1917, 2 vols.

Manet/Velázquez: The French Taste for Spanish Painting. Edited by Gary Tinterow and Genevieve Lacambre. New York: The Metropolitan Museum of Art, Yale University Press, 2003.

Manning, William R. *Diplomatic Correspondence of the United States Concerning the Independence of the Latin American Nations*. 3 vols. New York: Oxford University Press, 1925.

Mateos, José María. *Historia de la Masonería en México*. México: "La Tolerancia," 1884.

McClenachan, Charles T. *History of the Most Ancient and Honorable Fraternity of Free and Accepted Masons of New York from the Earliest Date*. 4 vols. New York: Grand Lodge, 1888.

McCullough, David. *John Adams*. New York: Simon & Schuster, 2001.

McKenna, John J. "The Translations of José Marchena: A Force for Humanism in Eighteenth-Century Spain." *Dieciocho* 5 (1983): 18–33.

McKenzie, D. F. *Bibliography and the Sociology of Texts*. Cambridge: Cambridge University Press, (1986) 1999.

McKitterick, David. *Print, Manuscript and the Search for Order, 1450–1830*. Cambridge: Cambridge University Press, 2003.

McMichael, Andrew. *Atlantic Loyalties: Americans in Spanish West Florida, 1785–1810*. Athens: University of Georgia Press, 2008.

Medina, José Toribio. *Historia del Tribunal del Santo Oficio de la Inquisición en México*. México: Miguel Angel Porrúa, (1905) 1987.

―――. *La imprenta en México (1539–1821)* 8 vols. México: UNAM, (1911) 1989.

―――. *La imprenta en Oaxaca, Guadalajara, Veracruz, Mérida y varios lugares*. México: UNAM, (1904) 1991.

Mejía Sánchez, Ernesto. *Las Casas en México, 1566–1966*. México: UNAM, 1967.

Mencken, H.L. *The American Language, An Inquiry into the Development of English in the United States*. New York: Alfred A. Knopf, (1919) 1945.

Menéndez y Pelayo, Marcelino. *Historia de los heterodoxos españoles*. México: Ed. Porrúa, (1882) 1983.

Miquel i Verges, José María. *Diccionario de insurgentes*. México: Ed. Porrúa, 1980.

Miranda, José. *Humboldt y México*. México: UNAM, 1962.

Monroy Castillo, María Isabel. *Sueños, tentativas y posibilidades, Extranjeros en San Luis Potosí, 1821–1845*. San Luis Potosí: Colegio de San Luis, Archivo Histórico del Estado de San Luis Potosí, 2004.

Montesinos, José F. *Introducción a una historia de la novela en España en el siglo XIX. Seguida del esbozo de una bibliografía española de traducciones de novelas, 1800–1850*, 4ª ed. Madrid: Ed. Castalia, 1980.

Moore, Ernest R. "José María Heredia in New York, 1824-1825." *Symposium* 5 (Nov. 1951): 256–291.

Morton, Ohland. *Terán and Texas, A Chapter in Texas-Mexican Relations*. Introduction by Eugene C. Barker. Austin: Texas State Historical Assoc., 1948.

Mulford, Carla. "Radicalism in Joel Barlow's The Conspiracy of Kings (1792)." In *Deism, Masonry and the Enlightenment*, edited by J.A. Leo Lemay. Cranbury, NJ: Associated University Presses, 1987, 137–157.

Murphy, Martin. *Blanco White, Self-banished Spaniard*. New Haven: Yale University Press, 1989.

Neal, Clarice. "Freedom of the Press in New Spain, 1810–1820." In *Mexico and the Spanish Cortes, 1810–1822*, edited by Nettie Lee Benson. Austin: University of Texas Press, 1966, 37–112.

Núñez, Estuardo. *El nuevo Olavide, Una semblanza a través de sus textos ignorados*. Lima: n.p., 1970.

Osorio Romero, Ignacio, et al. *La tradición clásica en México*. México: UNAM, 1991.

Palmer, Timothy. "José Alvarez de Toledo." In *Handbook of Texas*, Wikipedia.

Parada, Alejandro E. *El mundo del libro y de la lectura durante la época de Rivadavia. Una aproximación a través de los avisos de La Gaceta Mercantil*

(1823–1828). Cuadernos de Bibliotecología No. 17. Buenos Aires: Universidad de Buenos Aires, Instituto de Investigaciones Bibliotecológicas, 1998.

Parmenter, Mary Fisher, Walter Russell Fisher and Lawrence Edward Mallette. *The Life of George Fisher (1795–1873) and The History of the Fisher Family in Mississippi*. Jacksonville, FL: The H. & W.B. Drew Col, 1959.

Parry, J. H. *Trade and Dominion. The European Oversea Empires in the Eighteenth Century*. London: Phoenix Press, (1971) 2000.

Pasley, Jeffrey L. *"The Tyranny of Printers" Newspaper Politics in the Early American Republic*. Charlottesville, London: University of Virginia Press, 2001.

Peale, Charles Willson. *The Selected Papers of… and His Family*. 4 vols. Edited by Lillian B. Miller. New Haven: Yale University Press, Smithsonian Institution, 1996.

Pencak, William. *Jews and Gentiles in Early America, 1654–1800*. Ann Arbor: University of Michigan Press, 2005.

Perdices Blas, Luis. *Pablo de Olavide (1725–1803), El Ilustrado*. Madrid: Editorial Complutense, 1993.

Pérez Firmat, Gustavo, ed. *Do the Americas Have a Common Literature?* Durham: Duke University Press, 1990.

Pérez Marchand, Monelisa Lina. *Dos etapas ideológicas del siglo XVIII en México a través de los papeles de la Inquisición*. México: El Colegio de México, Centro de Estudios Históricos, (1945) 2005.

Peters, Edward. *Inquisition*. New York: Free Press, 1988.

Peterson, Brent O. *Popular Narratives and Ethnic Identity, Literature and Community in Die Abendschule*. Ithaca: Cornell University Press, 1991.

Platt, D.C.M. *Latin America and British Trade 1806–1904*. London: Adam and Charles Black, 1972.

Pradells Nadal, Jesús. *Diplomacia y comercio. La expansión consular española en el siglo XVIII*. Alicante: Universidad de Alicante, Instituto de Cultura "Juan Gil Albert," 1992.

Prideaux, S.T. *Aquatint Engraving. A Chapter in the History of Book Illustration*. London: W.G. Foyle, (1909) 1968.

Proceedings of the Grand Lodge of Texas, from its organization in the city of Houston Dec., A.D. 1837, A.L. 5837, to the close of the Grand Annual Communication held at Palestine Jan. 19, A.D. 1857, A.L. 5857. Galveston: Richardson & Co., 1857.

Racine, Karen. *Francisco de Miranda, A Transatlantic Life in the Age of Revolution*. Wilmington, DE: SR Books, 2003.

Rees, Peter. *Transportes y comercio entre México y Veracruz, 1519–1910*. México: SEP, 1976.

Remer, Rosalind. *Printers and Men of Capital, Philadelphia Book Publishers in the New Republic*. Philadelphia: University of Pennsylvania Press, 1996.

Reprint of the Minutes of the Grand Lodge of Free and Accepted Masons of Pennsylvania. Comp. Joshua L. Lyte. Vol. IV (1817–1822). Philadelphia: Grand Lodge, 1898.

Reséndez, Andrés. *Changing National Identities at the Frontier, Texas and New Mexico, 1800–1850.* (Cambridge: Cambridge University Press, 2005.

Reyna, María del Carmen. "Impresores y libreros extranjeros en la ciudad de México, 1821–1853", *Empresa y cultura en tinta y papel (1800–1860),* coord. Laura Beatriz Suárez de la Torre, ed. Miguel Angel Castro. México: Instituto de Investigaciones Dr. José María Luis Mora, UNAM, 2001, 259–271.

Riaño de la Iglesia, Pedro. *La Imprenta en la Isla Gaditana durante la Guerra de la Independencia: Libros, folletos y hojas volantes (1808-1814). Ensayo bio-bibliográfico documentado.* 3 vols. Ed. a cargo de José Manuel Fernández Tirado y Alberto Gil Novales. Madrid: Ediciones Orto, 2004.

Ricardo, José G. *La imprenta en Cuba.* La Habana: Editorial Letras cubanas, 1989.

Rich, Paul, Guillermo de los Reyes, and Antonio Lara. "Smuggling Masonic Books to Mexico: A Philadelphia Publisher and the Inquisition." *Heredom* 6 (1997): 121–130.

_____ and Antonio Lara. "The Mystery of Mathew Carey: Continuing Adventures in Masonic Bibliography." *Heredom* 8 (1999–2000): 219–223.

Ríos, Eduardo Enrique. *El historiador Davis Robinson y su aventura en Nueva España.* México: Antigua Librería Robredo, 1939.

Rippy, J. Fred. *Joel R. Poinsett, Versatile American.* Durham: Duke University Press, 1935.

Ritter, Abraham. *Philadelphia and Her Merchants.* Philadelphia: n.p.,1860.

Rives, George Lockhart. *The United States and Mexico, 1821–1848.* New York: Charles Scribner's and Sons, 1918; Kraus reprint 1969, 2 vols.

Rodríguez Cepeda, Enrique. "Los *Quijotes* del siglo XVIII." Part 1 in *Cervantes* 8 (1988): 61–108; Part 2 in *Hispania* 71 (1988): 752–779.

Rodríguez O., Jaime E. "The Constitution of 1824 and the Formation of the Mexican State." In *The Origins of Mexican National Politics, 1808–1847,* edited by Jaime E. Rodríguez O. Wilmington, DE: SR Books, 1997, 65–84.

_____. *The Emergence of Spanish America, Vicente Rocafuerte and Spanish Americanism, 1808–1832.* Berkeley, Los Angeles, London: University of California Press, 1975.

_____. "Mexico's First Foreign Loans." In *The Independence of Mexico and the Creation of the New Nation,* edited by Jaime E. Rodríguez O. Los Angeles, Irvine: UCLA Latin American Center, 1989, 215–235.

Roeber, A. Gregg. "German and Dutch Books and Printing." In *A History of the Book in America,* Vol. 1. The Colonial Book in the Atlantic World,, edited by Hugh Amory and David D. Hall. Cambridge: Cambridge University Press, American Antiquarian Society, 2000, 298–313.

Rojas, Rafael. *La escritura de la Independencia, El surgimiento de la opinión pública en México.* México: Taurus, CIDE, 2003.

Roldán Vera, Eugenia. *The British Book Trade and Spanish American Independence, Education and Knowledge Transmission in Transcontinental Perspective.* Aldershot, Hampshire, UK: Ashgate, 2003.

———. "Useful Knowledge for Export." *In Books and the Sciences in History,* edited by Marina Frasca-Spada and Nick Jardine. Cambridge: Cambridge University Press, 2000, 338–353.

———. "Libros extranjeros en Hispanoamérica independiente: de la distribución a la lectura." María del Pilar Gutiérrez Lorenzo, coord. *Impresos y libros en la historia económica de México (siglos XVI–XIX).* Guanajuato, Guadalajara: Universidad de Guadalajara, 2007, 187-213.

Rowe, Kenneth Wyer. *Mathew Carey, A Study in American Economic Development.* Baltimore: Johns Hopkins University Press, 1933.

Rydjord, John. *Foreign Interest in the Independence of New Spain, An Introduction to the War for Independence.* New York: Octagon, (1935) 1972.

Salvucci, Linda K. "Atlantic Intersections: Early American Commerce and the Rise of the Spanish West Indies (Cuba)." *Business History Review* 79 (2005): 781–810.

———. "Merchants and Diplomats: Philadelphia's Early Trade with Cuba," http://www.hsp.org. March 28, 2006.

Santana, Arturo. *José Alvarez de Toledo, El revolucionario cubano en las Cortes de Cádiz y sus esfuerzos por la emancipación de las Antillas.* San Juan, PR: Centro de Estudios Avanzados de Puerto Rico y el Caribe, 2006.

Sarrailh, Jean. *La España Ilustrada de la segunda mitad del siglo XVIII.* Trans. Antonio Alatorre. México, Madrid, Buenos Aires: Fondo de Cultura Económica, (1954) 1974.

Scharf, J. Thomas and Thompson Westcott. *History of Philadelphia, 1609–1884.* 3 vols. Philadelphia: L.H. Everts & Co., 1884.

Schmidt, Rachel. "La ilustración gráfica y la interpretación del *Quijote* en el siglo XVIII", *Dieciocho* 19 (1996): 203–235.

Schumacher, María Esther, comp. *Mitos en las relaciones México-Estados Unidos.* México-Secretaría de Relaciones Exteriores, Fondo de Cultura Económicas, 1994.

Seminario de Historia de la Educación en México. *Historia de la lectura en México.* México: El Colegio de México, 1988.

Sepinwall, Alyssa Goldstein. *The Abbé Grégoire and the French Revolution, The Making of Modern Universalism.* Berkeley: University of California Press, 2005.

Sevilla Soler, María Rosario. *Las Antillas y la independencia de la América Española (1808–1826)*. Madrid, Sevilla: CSIC, Escuela de Estudios Hispano-Americanos de Sevilla, 1986.

Shafer, Robert J. *The Economic Societies in the Spanish World*. Syracuse: Syracuse University Press, 1958.

Shields, David S. "Eighteenth-Century Literary Culture." In *A History of the Book in America. Vol. 1 The Colonial Book in the Atlantic World*, edited by Hugh Amory and David D. Hall. Cambridge: Cambridge University Press, American Antiquarian Society, 2000, 434–476.

Shoemaker, Richard H. *A Checklist of American Imprints*. Metuchen, NJ: Scarecrow Press, 1967.

Simmons, Merle E. *Santiago F. Puglia, An Early Philadelphia Propagandist for Spanish American Independence*. Chapel Hill: UNC Department of Romance Languages, 1977.

———. "Spanish and Spanish American Writer Politicians in Philadelphia, 1790-1830." *Dieciocho* 3 (1980): 27–39.

Solís, Ramón. *El Cádiz de las Cortes*. n.p.: Silex, 1987.

Solís Vicarte, Ruth. *Las sociedades secretas en el primer gobierno republicano, 1824–1828, según el Diario Histórico de C.M. de Bustamante*. México: A.S.B.E., 1997.

Sollors, Werner, ed. *Multilingual America, Transnationalism, Ethnicity and the Languages of American Literature*. New York: New York University Press, 1998.

Sommer, Doris. *Foundational Fictions*. Berkeley, Los Angeles: University of California Press, 1991.

———. *Proceed with Caution when Engaged by Minority Writing in the Americas*. Cambridge: Harvard University Press, 1999.

Spell, Jefferson Rea. "An Illustrious Spaniard in Philadelphia, Valentín de Foronda." *Hispanic Review* 4 (1936): 136–140.

———. *Rousseau in the Spanish World Before 1833: A Study in Franco-Spanish Literary Relations*. New York: Octagon Books, (1938) 1973.

St. Clair, William. "Afterwords." Review of *The Edinburgh History of the Book in Scotland*. TLS, April 10, 2009, 7–8.

Stein, Stanley J. and Barbara H. Stein. *Apogee of Empire, Spain and New Spain in the Age of Charles III, 1759–1789*. Baltimore: Johns Hopkins University Press, 2003.

Stern, Madeline B. *Nicolas Gouin Dufief of Philadelphia: Franco-American Bookseller 1776–1834*. Philadelphia: Philobiblon Club, 1988.

Stolley, Karen. "Writing Back to Empire: Juan Pablo Viscardo y Guzmán's 'Letter to the Spanish Americans'." In *Liberty! Egalité! ¡Independencia! Print Culture, Enlightenment, and Revolution in the Americas, 1776–1838*.

Worcester: American Antiquarian Society, 2007, 117–132; also *Proceedings of the American Antiquarian Society* 116, Part 2 (2006), 337–352.

Stroud, Patricia Tyson. *The Man Who Had Been King, The American Exile of Napoleon's Brother Joseph*. Philadelphia: University of Pennsylvania Press, 2005.

Suárez de la Torre, Laura Beatriz, coord.. *Empresa y cultura en tinta y papel (1800–1860)*, ed. Miguel Angel Castro. México: Instituto de Investigaciones Dr. José María Luis Mora, UNAM, 2001.

Tanck Estrada, Dorothy. *La educación ilustrada (1786–1836)*. México: El Colegio de México, 1977.

———. "Las escuelas Lancasterianas en la ciudad de México". *Historia Mexicana* 88 (abril–junio, 1973): 494–514.

Taylor, Diana. "Remapping Genre through Performance: From 'American' to 'Hemispheric' Studies." *PMLA* 122 (2007): 1416–1430.

Tenenbaum, Barbara A. *México en la época de los agiotistas, 1821–1857*. México: Fondo de Cultura Económica, 1985.

Theroux, Manon. Unpublished checklist. Sterling Memorial Library, Yale University.

Thomas, Isaiah. *The History of Printing in America. With a Biography of Printers and an Account of Newspapers*. New York: Weathervane, (1810) 1970.

Toll, Ian. *Six Frigates: The Epic History of the Founding of the U.S. Navy*. New York: W.W. Norton & Co., 2006.

Torales Pacheco, Josefina Maria Cristina. *Ilustrados en la Nueva España, Los socios de la Real Sociedad Bascongada de los Amigos del País*. México: Real Sociedad Bascongada de los Amigos del País, Colegio de San Ignacio de Loyola Vizcaínas, Universidad Iberoamericana, 2001.

———. "La familia Yraeta, Yturbe e Ycaza. In *Familias novohispanas, Siglos XVI al XIX, Seminario de Historia de la Familia*. México: Centro de Estudios Históricos, Colegio de México, 1991, 181–202.

Torre, Jose R., ed. *The Enlightenment in America, 1720–1825*. 4 vols. London: Pickering and Chatto, Ashgate, 2008, 181–202.

Torres Puga, Gabriel. *Los últimos años de la Inquisición en la Nueva España*. México: CONACULTA, INAH, Miguel Angel Porrúa, 2004.

Tracy, James D., ed. *The Political Economy of Merchant Empires, State Power and World Trade, 1350–1750*. Cambridge: Cambridge University Press, (1991) 1997.

Ugalde, Luis, S.J. *El pensamiento teológico-político de Juan Germán Roscio*. Caracas: La Casa de Bello, 1992.

Unzueta, Fernando. "Subjectivity and Olavide's Sentimental Novels." In *Foucault and Latin America*, edited by Benigno Trigo. New York: Routledge, 2002, 185–196.

Valenzuela Arce, José Manuel, coord. *Los estudios culturales en México*. México: Fondo de Cultura Económica, 2003.

Valle, Enid. "La duplicación en *El incógnito o el fruto de la ambición* de Pablo de Olavide y Jáuregui". *Dieciocho* 21 (1998): 195–208.

Velasco Toro, José y Luis Alberto Montero García, coord. *Economía y espacio en el Papaloapan veracruzano, Siglos XVII–XX*. México: Gobierno del Estado de Veracruz, 2005.

Velleman, Barry L. *Andrés Bello y sus libros*. Caracas: La Casa de Bello, 1995.

Villoro, Luis. *El proceso ideológico de la Revolución de Independencia*, 2ª ed. México: UNAM, 1977.

Visiones de la Guerra de Independencia. Comp. Jacobo Dalevuelta y Manuel Becerra Acosta. México: Talleres Gráficos de la Nación, 1929.

Vogeley, Nancy. "Actitudes en México hacia la Inquisición: el pro y el contra, 1814, 1824". *Revista de la Inquisición* (Madrid) 11 (2005): 223–243; Shorter version: "Mexican Attitudes Toward the Inquisition: Two Views, 1814, 1824." *Dieciocho* 23 (2000): 91–96.

———. "Defining the 'Colonial Reader': *El Periquillo Sarniento*." *PMLA* 102 (1987): 784–800.

———. "Formación cultural después de la Independencia: Una revista literaria mexicana, 1826". *Estudios* (Caracas) 5 (1995): 79–90.

———. "Heredia y el escribir de la historia" in *La imaginación histórica en el siglo XIX*, edited by Lelia Area and Mabel Moraña. Rosario: UNR Editora, 1994, 39–6.

———. *Lizardi and the Birth of the Novel in Spanish America*. Gainesville: University Press of Florida, 2001.

———. "Llorente's Readers in the Americas.".In *Liberty! Égalité! ¡Independencia!: Print Culture, Enlightenment, and Revolution in the Americas, 1776–1838*. Worcester: American Antiquarian Society, 2007, 155–173; also *Proceedings of the American Antiquarian Society* 116, Part 2 (2006): 375–393.

———. "Lo práctico por lo teórico: Lecciones de París para los americanos en transición". *Independencia y Revolución: Pasado, presente y futuro*, edited by Gustavo Leyva, Brian Connaughton, Néstor García Canclini, Carlos Illades. México: Fondo de Cultura Económica, Universidad Autónoma Metropolitana, Iztapalapa, 2010, 144–173.

———. "Mexican Readings of Hugh Blair's *Rhetoric*." *Dieciocho* 21 (199): 153–165.

———. "Introduction." "Satire and Decolonization." *The Mangy Parrot*. Trans. by David Frye Cambridge, MA: Hackett, 2004, xi–x xix.

———. "Spanish-Language Masonic Books Printed in the Early U.S." *Early American Literature* 43 (2008): 337–360.

———. "Two Arguments for the Spanish Authorship of *Gil Blas*: Francisco de Isla and Juan Antonio Llorente." *PMLA* 125 (2010): 454–466.

———. *Un manuscrito inédito de poesías de José Joaquín Fernández de Lizardi. Estudio de la literatura en manuscrito en el México de la Independencia.* México, Berkeley: UNAM, Bancroft Library, 2003.

Wainwright, Nicholas B. *Andalusia, Countryseat of the Craig Family and of Nicholas Biddle and His Descendants.* Philadelphia: HSP, 1976.

———, ed. *Paintings and Miniatures at the Historical Society of Pennsylvania,* rev. ed. Philadelphia: HSP, 1974.

Warren, Richard A. "Displaced 'Pan-Americans' and the Transformation of the Catholic Church in Philadelphia, 1789–1850." *The Pennsylvania Magazine of History and Biography* 128 (2004): 343–366.

Weber, David J. *The Spanish Frontier in North America.* New Haven: Yale University Press, 1992.

Webster, C.K., ed. *Britain and the Independence of Latin America, 1812–1830.* 2 vols. Oxford: Oxford University Press, 1938.

Wertheimer, Eric. *Imagined Empires: Incas, Aztecs and the New World of American Literature, 1771–1876.* Cambridge: Cambridge University Press, 1999.

Wheaton, Barbara Ketcham. *Savoring the Past, The French Kitchen and Table from 1300 to 1789.* New York: Touchstone, 1983.

Whitaker, Arthur P. *The United States and the Independence of Latin America, 1800–1830.* Baltimore: Johns Hopkins University Press, 1941; reprinted W.W. Norton, 1964.

Williford, Miriam. *Jeremy Bentham on Spanish America. An Account of His Letters and Proposals to the New World.* Baton Rouge: Louisiana State University Press, 1980.

Wold, Ruth. *Diario de México: Primer Cotidiano de Nueva España.* Madrid: Ed. Gredos, 1970.

Wood, Sarah F. *Quixotic Fictions of the USA, 1792–1815.* Oxford: Oxford University Press, 2006.

Zahar Vergara, Juana. *Historia de las librerías de la ciudad de México, evocación y presencia.* México: UNAM, 2000.

Zalce y Rodríguez, Luis J. *Apuntes para la historia de la masonería en México.* 2 tomos México: Taller Tipográfico de la Penitenciaría del Distrito Federal, 1950.

Ziga, Francisco y Susano Espinosa. *Adiciones a la imprenta en México de J. Toribio Medina.* México: UNAM, 1997.

INDEX

A
La Abeja, 242
Academia de San Carlos, 237
Ackermann, Jorge, 225
Ackermann, Rudolph, 225, 233, 245
Adams, John, 45, 58, 236, 245
Adams, John Quincy, 56, 86, 183
Adams-Onís Treaty, 42, 52
Agnosticism, 26, 162, 206
Aguila Mexicana, 235
El Aguinaldo, 72
Ahiman Rezon, 177
Alamán, Lucas, 119, 195, 239
Alcalá Galiano, Antonio, 242
Aldama, Col., 117–118, 125, 282
Alea, Josef Miguel, 39
Alonso Seoane, María José, 49, 264, 271, 272
Alvarado, Francisco, 204
Alvarado, port of, 1, 84, 109, 110, 113, 115, 116, 117, 128, 121, 122, 123, 124, 127, 129, 130, 131, 132, 134, 137, 138, 139, 143, 144, 146, 181, 185, 186, 191, 199, 238
Alvarez de Toledo, José, 53, 54, 55
Alzate y Ramírez, José Antonio, 192
America, 2, 9, 13, 18, 20, 21, 22, 35, 41, 43, 45, 48, 50, 53, 56, 57, 63, 67, 68, 69, 71, 72, 77, 80, 87, 117, 139, 173, 202, 205, 207, 224, 225, 226, 227, 229, 235, 237, 241, 245, 246, 277, 283, 286, 288
    definition of, 22

American Bible Society, 139
American Tract Society, 23
Amory, Hugh, 17
Anáhuac, 117, 126
Anderson, Benedict, 4
Aranda, conde de, 169
Arate de Peralta, José, 133
Arden, Daniel, 73
Ariza, Angel Benito de, 134
Arte de armas, 116, 117
Articles of Confederation, 56, 63, 183, 234
Atala, 83, 189
Aurora General Advertiser, 38, 67, 86, 263
Austin, Stephen, 81, 134, 191, 238
Ayers, Edward L., 4

B
Bache, Benjamin Franklin, 202
Bailey, Lydia, 73
Baltimore, 40, 41, 49, 58, 73, 74, 113, 119, 123, 130, 169, 173, 174, 190, 235, 247
    Daily Advertiser, 235
Barclay, Herring, Richardson & Co., 173
Barère de Vieuzac, Bertrand, 10, 67, 158, 236
Barlow, Joel, 45, 49
Barry, David, 70, 71
Barry, Edward, 41, 71
    indiscretion, 70, 111

life, 69,
translation work, 63, 67, 68, 69, 70, 130, 138, 177
Barry family, 70, 119, 120
Barry, James, 70, 119, 172
Basan, Señor, 118, 138, 185
Bauer, Ralph, 17, 31
Beethoven, Ludwig von, 252
Bello, Andrés, 205, 225, 237
Benoit, A.V., 196
Bentham, Jeremy, 225, 243
Berruezo León, María Teresa, 119, 120, 224
Bible, 37, 38, 124, 139, 200, 246
Bibliography, 17, 18
Biblioteca Americana, 225
Bibliothèque de l'homme publique, 186
Biddle, Nicholas, 50
Bielfeld, Baron de, 58, 199
Biggs, James, 45
Bill of Rights, 56, 201
Blanco White, José, 162, 205, 225
Blocquerst, Andrew, 78
Boccaccio, 225
　Decameron, 225
Bolívar, Simón, 48, 63, 83, 87, 158, 174, 205, 207, 224, 235, 239
Bonaparte, José, 47, 49, 50, 61–62, 158, 190, 195, 200, 229
Bonaparte, Napoleon, 46, 49, 133
Books, 6, 8, 38, 138, 223, 226, 233, 239, 242, 249
　attitudes of Latin American scholarship toward, 18–20
　attitudes of U.S. scholarship toward, 17–20
　as commodities, 6, 239–243, 249
　differences between the U.S. and Mexico toward, 241–242, 244–246, 251
　as diplomatic overtures, 240, 247, 249, 251
　traffic in, 3, 8, 38, 87, 125, 175, 240, 243
Boston, 45, 46, 49, 177, 235
Bourbon Family, 43, 175, 204, 237
Boyd, Rev. H., 49
Boyle, P., 44

Brackenridge, Henry Marie, 53
Bradburn, John Davis, 74, 112, 113, 122, 126, 138, 173, 182, 190, 191, 233
Bradford, Thomas, 39, 78
Bradford, William, 39, 78
Bradford and Inskeep, 49
Bravo, Nicolás, 141, 182
Brazil, 156
Brickhouse, Anna, 17
Brown, Jerry, 5
Bryant, William Cullen, 23, 77
Buenos Aires, 61, 67, 192, 226, 234, 243
　constitution of, 137
　sale of Spanish-language books printed by Ackermann, 225–226, 233
Buffon, Comte de, 45, 48, 173
Bullock, William, 227
Burke, William, 205, 206
Burr, Aaron, 52,
Bustamante, Carlos María, 113–115, 124, 141, 143, 166, 187, 192, 201, 235, 248
　El Juguetillo, 201
Byrne, Patrick, 36, 37
Byron, Lord, 35, 48

C
Cadalso, José, 233
　Noches lúgubres, 233
Cádiz, 48, 68, 72, 84, 87, 111, 169, 179, 180, 187, 192, 197, 198, 199, 200, 201, 202, 203, 204, 205, 206, 238, 248
　Cortes de, 44, 47, 187, 197, 200, 204, 238
Cadwalader, General Thomas, 50
Calderón de la Barca, Pedro, 43
Campomanes, count of, 60, 200, 284
　"Discurso sobre el fomento de la industria popular," 200
　"Discurso sobre la educación popular," 200
Canary Islands, 70
Candio, Mariano, 120, 127
Cañizares-Esguerra, Jorge, 17

330

INDEX

Canny, Nicholas, 25
Capmany y Montpalau, Antonio de, 46, 47, 48, 61, 186, 264, 268
Caracas, 61, 161, 205
Carey, Henry Charles, 37, 68
Carey, James, 58
Carey, Mathew, 1, 7, 35, 170, 183, 185, 188, 207–208
  business history, 1, 7, 9, 16, 35–45, 53, 56, 62, 63, 67, 68, 71, 78, 85, 120, 127, 130, 134, 138, 139, 140, 143, 144, 145, 146, 147, 157, 159, 163, 171, 172, 176, 177, 179, 180, 184, 189, 196, 206, 245, 263–265
  Carey and Lea business, 1, 3, 9, 10, 28, 37, 68, 69, 72, 73, 74, 85, 109, 110, 113, 131, 144, 147, 187, 239, 240, 242, 244, 248
  "Desultory Facts, and Observations," 170
  life story, 35–42, 207, 208
  pamphlets, 8, 35, 37, 42, 53, 58, 63, 69, 85, 87, 120, 179, 194, 203, 250
Carleton, Henry, 52
Carlos III, 163
Carlos IV, 58, 142
Carrasco Puente, Rafael, 269
Carroll, John, 70
Carta de Tallibran, 116, 117
Castañeda, Carmen, 19, 24
Castillo, Florencio, 126, 284
Castillo, J.G., 177
Catalogue of Spanish Books, 226, 281
Catholicism, 21, 179, 182, 196, 206, 207
  history of Maryland, 10, 41
Cerneau, Joseph, 177
Cervantes, Miguel de, 43, 188, 264
  Don Quijote, 49, 120, 131
  La Galatea, 40, 126, 131
Céspedes, Manuel de, 40, 133
Céspedes y Monroy, Atanasio, 40
  see Pablo de Olavide
Cevallos, Pedro de, 46, 204
Charleston, 53, 184
Chartier, Roger, 19
Chávez, Thomas E., 43
Chew, William White, 87

Chile, 12, 16, 70, 71, 119, 137, 202
  Aurora de Chile, 13, 202
  constitution of, 137
  sale of Spanish-language books printed by Ackermann, 277–279
Chinese miners, railroad workers, 21
Christophe, Henri, 159
Civil War, 4, 22
Clark, John G., 35, 184
Clarkin, Wiliam, 35, 184
Classicism, 237
  Neoclassicism, 237
Clavijero, Francisco Javier, 48, 172
  The History of Mexico, 48
Clavijo y Fajardo, José, 25, 41,
Clay, Henry, 40
Clinton, DeWitt, 62
Cole, Samuel, 41, 69, 82, 177, 232, 264, 267, 269, 271, 273, 274, 277, 281
Collado, José, 196
Colman, George, 40
Colombia, 58, 137, 175, 238
  constitution of, 137
  sale of Spanish-language books printed by Ackermann, 277–279
Commerce, 6, 39, 47, 48, 60, 68, 117, 170, 173, 175, 176, 183, 188, 196, 228, 247, 248, 249
  as communication, 5
  contraband, 175, 199, 240
  debate over tariffs vs. free trade, 170, 171, 198, 208
  as index of a nation's maturity, 8
  language of, 60
  as means to national unity, 10
  as moral tool, 7, 158, 164, 167, 172, 188
  opium, 15, 71
  piracy, 7, 172, 241
  slavery, 3, 22, 39, 240
Communication, 4, 21, 82, 138, 158, 197, 208
Compendio de la vida y hechos de Joseph Balsamo llamado Conde Calliostro, 176, 265
Condillac, Etienne Bonnot de, 58
Congress of Aix-la-Chapelle, 46

INDEX

Congress of Vienna, 51, 83
Connecticut, constitution of, 63
Constant, Benjamin, 194, 264, 270
Cookery, book on, 130, 137, 138, 159, 186
Cooper, James Fenimore, 23, 249
Coppinger, José, 85
Copyright laws, 6, 35
Cornelia Bororquia, 121, 124, 187, 188, 189
   Luis Gutiérrez, 187
Cortés, Eugenio, 47, 53, 54, 56, 84, 86, 117, 181, 187, 190, 198, 200, 203, 204, 232, 238, 269, 282, 285
Coxe, Tenche, 69
Crukshank, James, 45
Crukshank, Joseph, 45
Cuba, 6, 54, 55, 69, 70, 77, 85, 87, 109, 172, 176, 186, 238, 240
Cubí y Soler, Mariano, 41
Curiosidades para los estudiosos, 225

D

Darnton, Robert, 17, 24
Davis, William C., 51, 70, 74, 112
Dawson, Thomas, 120, 121, 124, 127
De Glock D'Obernay, Joseph, 181
de Pauw, Cornelius, 48, 173
de Silver, Robert, 56, 78, 120
de Tracy, Destutt, 234, 271
Declaration of Independence, 56, 63, 137, 183, 234
Declaration of the Rights of the Several States, 137
Decolonization, 10, 171, 249
Defoe, Daniel, 189
Deforneaux, Marcelin, 196
Deism, 181
Delaware River valley, 20
Delolme, Jean Louis, 126, 136
Depons, François Raymond Joseph, 50
Depuis, C.F., 196
Dermott, Laurence, 177
Desnoues, Joseph, 57, 177
Destutt de Tracy, Antoine Louis Claude, 234
Diario de México, 26, 59, 190, 192, 201, 246

Diario literario de México, 192
Dick, Juan Henrique, 225
Dido, 139
Dobson, Thomas, 41
Duane, William, 78, 86, 87, 202
Dublin, 35, 36
Dufief's Book Store, 121, 187
Dumoland, Mr., 62
Dunn, Nathan, 71
du Pont de Nemours, E.I., 184

E

Earle, Edward, 49
Early American Literature, 20
Echávarri, José Antonio, 122, 135
Edward Earle, Eastburn, Kirk and Co., 49
The Edinburgh Review, 225
Elliott, John H., 21
England, 67–68, 175, 177, 224–228, 236
Enlightenment, 2, 4, 11, 13, 24, 25, 26, 43, 46, 58, 60, 162, 169, 170, 198, 231, 239, 243, 249
Epistemology, 26
Ercilla, Alonso de, 49, 264, 286
Erie Canal, 71
El Español, 205, 225
El Español Constitucional, 204, 205, 225
El Espectador Sevillano, 169
El Espíritu del despotismo, 56, 63, 66, 68, 158
Espíritu de los estatutos y reglamentos de la orden francmasónica, 177
Estatutos generales de la masonería escocesa, 177
Esteva, José Ignacio, 185
Eymeric, Nicolau, 196

F

Fagoaga, Carlos, 114
Febre, Lucien, 19, 273
The Federalist Papers, 136, 235, 248
El Federalista, 234
Feijoo, Benito, 61
Female Tract Society, 73
Fernagus, J.L., 38

INDEX

Fernández Armesto, Felipe, 21
Fernández de Lizardi, José Joaquín, 60, 168, 180, 192, 193, 197, 232
   Correo semanario, 232
   El Pensador Mexicano, 201
Fernando VII, 49, 58, 61, 64, 164, 196, 247
Fernel, F.A., 225
Filangieri, Gaetano, 42, 186, 270
Fischer, David Hackett, 20, 250
Fisher, George, 181, 182
Florian, Jean Pierre Claris de, 40, 62
Florida, 41, 44, 50, 52, 85
   acquisition of, 52
Follin, George, 73, 109, 110, 143, 144, 179, 180, 184, 185
Foronda, Valentín de, 12, 58, 59, 60, 61, 62, 85, 236
   "Apuntes ligeros," 61
   "Carta sobre lo que debe hacer un príncipe," 59
   "Cartas para los amigos y enemigos," 61, 62
   "Cartas presentadas a la Sociedad Filosófica de Philadelphia," 60, 62
   life of, 57–62
   "Observaciones," 59
France, 12, 25, 35, 40, 43, 45, 47, 49, 57, 58, 69, 158, 166, 174, 175, 185, 187, 195, 196, 205, 225, 228, 229, 232, 233, 236, 238
   desire to enter the Mexican markets, 175, 228
   philosophers, 1, 11, 12, 164, 165, 198, 224
   printers, 121, 187, 228
   revolution, 19, 243
Franklin, Benjamin, 35, 43, 60, 192, 202
Freemasonry, 69, 82
   see Masonry
Fry, William, 49
Fry and Kammerer, 47, 48
Fuentes, Juan Francisco, 78, 263, 287

G

G. Keatinge and L. Frailey, 190
Gaceta de Caracas, 205
Gacetas de literatura de México, 192
Galli, Florencio, 237
Gálvez, Bernardo de, 43, 274
García, Francisco (General), 135
García de Sena, Manuel, 63, 67, 135
Gaxiola, Francisco Javier, 191
Gelone, V. de, 38
The General Advertiser, 67, 263
Gilpin, Joshua and Thomas, 73
Ginés de Sepúlveda, Juan, 80
Girard, Stephen, 50, 76, 238
Globalization theories, 17
Godoy, Manuel de, 169, 199, 203, 287
Goethe, Johann Wolfgang von, 252
Goldsmith, Lewis, 190
   see "Stewarton"
Gómez, Esteban, 166
Gómez, José Ignacio, 205
Gómez de Enterría, Josefa, 60
González Casanova, Pablo, 17, 167
Grattan, William (Guillermo), 41, 57, 78
Graves, Richard, 49
Great Britain, 38, 71
Green, James N., 207
Grégoire, Henri (abbé), 78, 80, 82, 83, 163
Grotuis, Hugo, 186
Gual, Pedro, 158
Guatemala, 57
Guerin, Bertrand, 169
Guerra, François Xavier
Guerrero, Vicente, 141, 142, 190
Gutiérrez de Lara, Bernardo, 54
Guzmán, Martín Luis, 247
   Javier Mina, Heróe de España y México, 247
   Philadelphia, Haven for Conspirators, 247

H

Haiti
   revolution in, 21, 80, 159
Hall, David D., 17
Hamilton, Alexander, 12
Hapsburg family, 204, 237
Hardig, James, 77
Harvard College, 4

Havana, 43, 54, 73, 77, 116, 119, 132, 133, 146, 147, 190, 240
Hayley, William, 49
Henderson, James, 228
Henríquez, Camilo, 13
Heredia, José María, 57, 235, 237, 242, 237, 289
   Elements of General History (Alexander Fraser Tytler), 242
   El Iris, 237, 242
   La Minerva, 242
Herrera, José Manuel, 51, 172, 267, 282
Hibernian Society, 37, 208
Hidalgo, Miguel, 81, 162 162, 197, 201, 224, 232, 264
Highlander, 111, 117
Hispanic vogue in U.S., 42–50
Hispano-Anglo Grammar, 41
Historical Society of Pennsylvania, 1
History of America, 53, 226, 281–295
The History of North and South America, 53
Hogan, William, 85, 111
El hombre libre, 234
Hopkinson, Joseph, 50
House, E.G., 49, 111, 134
Howe, John, 73
Humboldt, Alexander von, 51, 126, 142, 239
   Personal Narratives of Travels, 73
   Political Essay on the Kingdom of New Spain, 51, 192
Hunt, Leigh, 35, 39
Huntington, D., 49
Hurtel, Juan F., 56, 57, 67, 78, 80

I
Ideology, 11–16
Ilustraciones de masoneria, 177
Immigration, 20, 50, 225
Imprenta de York, 161
Imprenta Liberal de Moreno Hermanos, 81
Indian Queen Tavern, 185
Inquisition, 4, 15, 25, 26, 40, 44, 62, 85, 118, 124, 157, 158, 159, 161, 162, 167, 168, 176, 187, 188, 193, 194, 195, 196, 197, 201, 202, 202, 203, 229, 232, 233, 239, 250

Irana y Torre, José Isidro, 155
   see Antonio José Ramón de Irisarri, 119
Ireland, 35, 38, 207, 208
Irisarri, José Antonio, 119
Irvine, Baptist, 87
Irving, Washington, 23, 50
Iturbe, Gabriel de, 59
Iturbide, Agustín de, 1, 14, 55, 57, 77, 84, 115, 117, 119, 125, 126, 128, 133, 135, 141, 142, 143, 155, 156, 157, 172, 173, 174, 180, 190, 232

J
J.A.C., 204
J. Kingsland & Co., 177
Jachin y Boaz, 68, 177, 187
Jaudenes y Nebot, Josef de, 49
Jay, John, 234
Jefferson, Thomas, 12, 40, 49, 52, 59, 183
Jesuits, 227
Jews, 83, 129
Jicoténcal, 20, 28, 77, 78, 79
John Adams, 130, 140
John Carter Brown Library, 16
John West and Co., 49
Johns, Adrian, 24
Jordan, John, 247
   Dangers of foreigners and foreign commerce in the Mexican States, 247
Journalism, 8, 9, 23, 78, 169, 251
Jouy, Etienne, 73
Jovellanos, Gaspar Melchor de, 12, 14, 169
   Delincuente honrado, 233
Juan, Jorge y Antonio de Ulloa, 70
   Noticias secretas de América, 70
Juárez, Benito, 161
Junta de Sevilla, 61
Justine, 44

K
Kanellos, Nicolás, 17
Kinane, Vincent, 37
Kite, Benjamin and Thomas, 49
Knox, Vicesimus, 63

INDEX

Kotzebue, August Friedrich Ferdinand von, 49
Kramnick, Isaac, 248

L

La Dulce, 126, 131, 138, 188
Lady Morgan, 184
Lafayette, Marquis de, 35
Lancaster, Joseph, 124
    Lancasterian School, 124, 139
Lang and Ustick, 76
Lanuza, Cayetano, 78, 79, 233
    Lanuza y Mendia, 233
Las Casas, F. Bartolomé de, 55, 78, 80–82, 155, 232
Laussel, Juan, 159
Le Brun, Charles, 61, 67, 68, 128, 134, 197
    El director de los niños, 41, 67, 265
    Retratos políticos, 67
    translation of *La Libertad de los Mares*, 61, 63
Lea, Isaac, 1, 41, 68, 69, 70, 72, 109, 110, 112, 131, 134, 143, 144, 145, 147, 157, 171, 180
Lee, Jean Gordon, 71
Leonard, Irving, 17
Letters (as genre), 156
Letters of Eloisa y Abelardo, 136
Lewis, Matthew Gregory, 49, 190
La librería Masónica, 69, 137, 177
La Libertad de los Mares, 63, 64, 131, 171, 242
Library of Congress, 16, 232, 263
Linati, Claudio, 237
Lista, Alberto, 169
Llamos Gutiérrez, Valentín, 69
Llorente, Juan Antonio, 82, 156, 162, 187, 196, 229, 231, 232
    Aforismos políticos, 231
    Apología católica, 232
    Carta escrita a un Americano, 156, 232
    Colección diplomática, 232
    Discursos sobre una constitución religiosa, 231
    Disertación sobre el poder, 232
    Histoire de la Inquisición d'Espagne, 229
    Leyes del Fuero Juzgo, 229
    life of, 82, 229–232
    Pequeño catecismo sobre la materia de concordatos, 232
    Proyecto de una constitución religiosa, 57, 232
    Retrato político de los papas, 232
Lockhart, Andrew, 119, 120
London, 11, 24, 25, 36, 38, 44, 45, 47, 51, 53, 55, 59, 63, 70, 74, 76, 78, 80, 84, 119, 139, 155, 162, 172, 192, 204, 205, 224, 225, 226, 227, 228, 229, 230, 232, 237, 242, 245, 277
Longfellow, Henry Wadsworth, 23
Lope de Vega, 40
Lord and Lady Holland, 225
Lorenzana, Cardinal Francisco Antonio, 172
Louisiana, 41, 52, 55
    Louisiana Purchase, 2, 42, 52

M

Machiavelli, Niccolò, 42
Madrid, 12, 44, 51, 76, 155, 156, 169, 186, 188, 203, 225, 227, 229, 231, 232, 233, 243, 251
Maldonado, Francisco Severo, 157
Malo de Luque, Eduardo (duque de Almodóvar), 196
Malsain, 109, 110, 125, 126, 144
Mantilla, Pedro de, 186
Manuscripts, 48, 204
Manual masónico, 177
Marchena, José, 195, 196
Marino Faliero, Doge of Venice, 35
Marmontel, Jean François, 40, 58
Marqués del Valle, 122, 172
Mary Washington, 109, 110, 111, 125, 143, 144
Masonry, 68, 69, 71, 86, 116, 146, 176, 177, 179, 180, 180, 181, 182, 183, 184, 185, 206, 207
    attitudes toward in Mexico, 9, 69, 124, 125, 128, 179, 182, 185, 187, 206
    catechisms, 110, 137, 225, 233, 246
    lodges—Scottish, York, 179, 180, 182

335

INDEX

newspapers, 8, 21, 23, 37, 38, 55, 63, 145, 147, 169, 192, 197, 201, 202, 203, 225, 225, 234, 235, 242
schools, 124
McKean, Sally, 49
McKean, William, 144
   McKean and Pennoyer, 110, 144
McKenzie, D.F., 18, 24
McQueen, William, 140
M'Culloch, John, 63
Meade, Richard, 54, 86, 87, 111, 113, 117
Mease, James, 37
Medina, José Toribio, 16
Mejía, Félix (or Megía), 62
Melish, John, 48
Memoirs of the Mexican Revolution, 70, 74
Menéndez Pelayo, Marcelino, 196
Mexicana, 111, 120, 127, 139, 146
Mexico, 1, 2, 3, 4, 9, 12, 14, 15, 16, 19, 21, 22, 23, 25, 27, 28, 37, 39, 42, 46, 51, 52, 53, 54, 55, 56, 57, 60, 62, 68, 70, 71, 72, 73, 74, 76, 76, 77, 78, 81, 81, 81, 81, 83, 84, 86, 87, 109, 112, 113, 114, 116, 117, 118, 119, 120, 122, 123, 124, 125, 126, 127, 128, 129, 130, 131, 132, 133, 134, 138, 139, 141, 145, 155, 156, 157, 158, 159, 159, 159, 161, 162, 163, 166, 167, 168, 169, 171, 172, 173, 174, 175, 177, 179, 180, 182, 183, 184, 185, 185, 187, 188, 189, 190, 190, 191, 191 192 194, 195, 197, 199, 201, 202, 203, 204, 205, 206, 207, 223, 224, 225, 226, 227, 228, 229, 232, 233, 234, 235, 236, 236, 237, 238, 239, 239, 240, 241, 242, 243, 244, 245, 246, 247, 248, 251, 285, 287, 289
Acapulco, 171, 199
Alvarado, 84, 115, 181, 185, 186, 199, 204, 238
attitudes toward the U.S., 3, 5, 58, 84, 115, 174, 183, 206, 234, 235, 237, 238, 239, 247
brigands, 122, 130, 132, 175
Congress of Chilpancingo, 161
domestic print industry, 194, 206, 232, 242
Guadalajara, 82, 231
Isthmus of Tehuantepec, 76
Mexico City, 26, 81, 82, 83, 114, 115, 118, 119, 122, 123, 124, 143, 155, 156, 161, 172, 189, 191, 194, 205, 206, 225, 231, 234, 235, 236, 240, 242, 246
Oaxaca, 161, 166
politics, 14, 55, 62, 67, 84, 135, 142, 155–159, 162–166, 180, 192, 195–204
Perote, 122
public discourse, 7, 193, 195, 200, 208
Puebla, 81, 122
Punto Altesardo, 125
statistics for imports, 16
Tampico, 134, 140, 141, 174, 175, 199, 238
Tlacotalpan, 116, 123, 125
Veracruz, 7, 171, 181, 184–191, 199, 240
Yucatán, 199
Michelena, José Mariano, 114
Mier, F. Servando Teresa de, 55, 56, 72, 74, 76, 80, 81, 83, 84, 85, 111, 114, 115, 141, 180, 189, 191, 199, 203, 205, 224
   life, 55, 83–85
   Memoria político-instructiva, 84, 203
Mier y Terán, Manuel de, 191
Miliani, Domingo, 161
Mill, James, 205, 225
Milnor, Rev. Dr. James, 139
Mina, Xavier, 74, 112, 113, 143, 173, 247
Miquel i Verges, José María, 115, 148
Miranda, Francisco de, 16, 40, 45, 59, 158, 224, 225
Miranda, José, 17
Miscelánea de literatura, ciencias y artes 235
Mississippi River, 21, 43, 52, 56
Molière, (Jean Baptiste Poquelin), 49
Molinos, Miguel de, 49
El Monitor de los Masones Libres, 68, 137, 177–178, 180

Monitor, o Guía de los Francmasones utilísimo, 177
Monroe, James, 51, 54, 58, 67, 174
Monroe Doctrine, 2, 10, 23, 174
Montagu, Lady Mary, 50
Monte, Domingo del, 57
Montengón, Pedro, 76
Montesquieu, Charles Louis de Secondat, 186, 194, 196, 234, 270
Mora, José María Luis, 234
Moreau, L., 52, 82
Morelos, José María, 51, 162, 197, 224
Morgan Dorsey, 73, 127, 144, 145
Morgan, William, 177
Morín, Esteban, 177
Mowry, Juan, 46
Munroe, Francis, and Parker, 46
Murtra, Cristóbal, 77
Museo universal de ciencias y arte, 226

N
NAFTA, see North American Free Trade Agreement, 5
Napoleon, 80, 111, 133, 163, 190, 202, 203, 235, 237
see Bonaparte, Napoleon
Nation formation, 13–14
Necker, Jacques, 186
Neuman, Henry, or Newman, Henry, 41, 69, 124, 131, 143
New Castle, Delaware, 1, 111, 187
New England, 4, 10, 20, 21
New Jersey, 50, 63
constitution of, 63
New Orleans, 43, 46, 52, 55, 56, 58, 71, 73, 74, 109, 145, 147, 159, 163, 173, 174
L'Argus, 235
New York, 10, 20, 35, 36, 41, 44, 46, 49, 49, 50, 57, 58, 73, 77, 78, 79, 119, 126, 139, 145, 169, 177, 180, 181, 190, 233
Newport, Rhode Island, 58, 83
Nicaragua, 158, 289
Nolan, Philip, 191
Nolasco Palmer, Pedro, 77
Norfolk, Virginia, 58
North American Free Trade Agreement, 5

Noroña, Miguel Cabral, 55, 58, 247
Noticioso General, 194, 267
Novels, 127, 150, 188–189, 247

O
Ocios de españoles emigrados, 226
O'Conway, Matthias James (Santiago), 39, 41, 73
Olavide, Pablo de, 40, 188, 189, 233, 251
see Atanasio Céspedes y Monroy
El desafío, 40, 251, 252
El Evangelio en triunfo, 233
La dulce venganza, 131
La paisana virtuosa, 40, 233
Lecturas útiles y entretenidas, 188
Oledo, Juan, 161
Onís, Luis de, 53, 54, 55, 58, 247
Ontiveros, Mariano, 81, 82
O'Reilly, Felipe, 119
Ortega, Juan Gualberto, 289
Ortiz de Ayala, Tadeo, 119

P
P.F.S., 155, 156
Pagden, Anthony, 25
Paine, Thomas, 10, 15, 49, 63, 161, 169, 189, 197, 207, 250, 265
Common Sense, 56, 63, 84
Rights of Man, 68, 69, 110, 131, 143, 157, 169, 171, 189, 205
Palmer, George, 38, 77
Palmer, Thomas H., 39, 77, 78, 163, 176
Pamphlets (as genre), 204
Paper, 3, 16, 36, 38, 63, 73, 117, 120, 121, 123, 125, 138, 140, 189, 193, 197, 240
attitudes toward, 189
production, 73
Paris, 26, 40, 45, 51, 63, 73, 78, 80, 82, 83, 187, 189, 203, 228, 229, 232, 240
Parrott, William, 187
Partidas, 198
Patrick, Leslie, 36
Paul, Abraham, 39, 57
Paul et Virginie, 39, 189, 194

INDEX

Peale, Charles Willson, 50, 69, 227
Pellicer, Casiano, 40
Penn, William, 164, 236
Pennoyer, James, 110, 144
Pennsylvania, 44, 50, 76, 164, 237
  constitution of, 63
Pennsylvania Academy of Fine Arts, 50
Peru, 4, 82, 225
  sale of Spanish-language books printed by Ackermann, 277
Philadelphia, 1, 3, 10, 19, 23, 28, 36, 37, 38, 39, 40, 41, 42, 43, 44, 45, 46, 47, 48, 49, 50, 53, 54, 55, 56, 57, 58, 60, 61, 62, 67, 68, 69, 70, 71, 72, 73, 74, 76, 77, 78, 80, 81, 82, 83, 84, 85, 86, 87, 109, 110, 115, 116, 118, 121, 125, 131, 134, 144, 147, 155, 158, 159, 161, 163, 166, 176, 181, 183, 184, 187, 190, 194, 197, 199, 202, 206, 208, 227, 233, 234, 235, 236, 238, 242, 246, 247
  center of Freemasonry, 176
  geography of, 124
  Hispanic vogue in, 42–50
  myth of, 23, 39, 76, 166, 246, 247
  tolerant spirit of, 44, 56, 59, 83, 85
Philadelphia Company of Booksellers, 38
  manifesto of, 38, 201
Philippines, 158, 188
Phillips, George, 73
Picornell y Gomila, Juan Antonio, 54, 158, 164
Picture of Philadelphia, 37
Pignatelli, Gen., 47
Poinsett, Joel, 15, 122, 130, 136, 140, 141, 143, 171–175, 176, 181, 182, 185, 186, 191, 194, 195, 233, 238
  Notes on Mexico, 171
  report on Mexico's bookstores, level of literacy, 194–195
Political-Moral System, 110
Pope Alexander VI, 164
Porlier, Juan Díaz, 166
Porter, David, 50
Postcolonialism, 27, 248–253

Pradt, Dominique Georges Frédéric (abbé de), 46, 118, 166, 170, 196
  La Europa y la América, 118
Press freedom, 2, 28, 167, 179, 194, 195, 197, 198, 200, 201, 202, 206, 235
Preston, William, 177, 201
Priestley, Joseph, 45
Printing, U.S., 4, 23, 233
  in Dutch, 8, 20, 25, 243
  as economic boon, 4, 37, 223
  French, 8, 231
  Gaelic, 8
  German, 8, 21, 41, 50, 228
  Hebrew, 8, 21, 49, 62, 83
  history of, 4, 243
  Indigenous language, 8
  Latin, 8
  as tool for political consolidation, 4, 8–9, 245, 246
  Welsh, 8, 21
Printing, Mexico, 4
  criollo psychology, 156, 244
  history of, 81, 186, 203
  press freedom, 128, 206
Protestantism, 21, 26, 49, 202, 206, 227
Pufendorf, Samuel von, 186
Puglia, James Philip, 46, 63, 67, 68, 110, 157, 180, 236, 242, 247
  El desengaño del hombre (Man Undeceived), 68, 110, 125, 126, 131, 143, 158, 159
  The Federal Politician, 159

Q

Quakers, 10, 71, 76
Quince días en Londres, o sea corto viage de un francés a Inglaterra, 228
Quintana, Manuel, 169
Quirós, José María, 240
  Guía de negociantes, 240

R

Radcliffe, Ann, 187, 189
Radway, Janice, 20
Ramos Arizpe, Miguel, 48, 114, 238

338

INDEX

Ramsay, Andrew Michael, 179
Ramsay, David, 68
Raynal, Guillaume Thomas (abbé), 12, 170, 196
  Histoire philosophique et politique, 196
Readers
  American characteristics, 243–248, 250
  prescriptions for reading, 165, 167, 246
  reception theories, 19
Real Academia de Bellas Artes y Ciencias (Bordeaux), 58
Real Academia Española, 60, 268
Recio, Manuel, 122, 123, 126, 138, 139, 192, 193, 194, 197, 206, 233, 236, 245
Recueil Précieux de la Maçonnerie, 176
"Reflexiones imparciales sobre la francmasoneria," 58, 176
Remer, Rosalind, 36
Reportorio Americano, 225
Republicanism, 3, 11, 15, 56, 78, 83, 86, 181, 183, 208, 236, 237, 241
Revillagigedo, Conde de, 159
Revista trimestre de Filadelfia, 235
Reyes, Don Manuel, 116, 117, 125, 191
Rhees, Morgan, 76
Ricardo, José G., 77
Richardson, Samuel, 189
Riego, Rafael de, 186, 196
"Rights of Man and the Citizen," 205
Riley, Capt., 117, 118, 124, 139, 140, 185
Riley and Souberville, 121, 134, 138, 145, 146
Rivera, Martín, 161
Robert Staples & Co., 173
Robertson, William, 226, 227, 281
  History of America, 53, 281
  "Catalogue of Spanish Books and Manuscripts," 226
Robeson, Thomas W., 1, 2, 3, 7, 10, 12, 22, 109, 110, 111, 116, 117, 125, 155, 157, 158, 159, 161, 166, 172, 175, 176, 179, 180, 181, 184, 187, 188, 189, 190, 191, 195, 197, 224, 227, 233, 236, 240, 242, 244, 245, 251
Robeson and Paul, 184
Robeson/Carey letters, 3, 4, 7, 9, 22, 23, 24, 26, 52, 56, 61, 70, 71, 72, 73, 109–147, 155, 156, 161, 171, 184, 185, 191, 193, 233, 238, 239, 248
  contrast with Ackermann business in Latin America, 170, 185, 186, 233, 245–246
  significance, 7, 8, 9, 10, 26, 28, 37, 87, 156, 206, 223, 233, 248, 250
Robespierre, Maximilien, 56
El Robiespierre Español, 203
Robinson, Howland, Miller and Hutchens, 49
Robinson, William Davis, 51, 70, 74, 76, 85, 119
  A Cursory View, 74
  Memoir addressed, 74
  Memoirs of the Mexican Revolution, 74, 76
Rocafuerte, Vicente, 55, 56, 67, 77, 80, 86, 114, 124, 139, 166, 174, 183, 194, 226, 239, 248, 249
  Bosquejo ligerísimo, 55, 77
  Ensayo politico, 56, 192
  Ideas necesarias, 55, 183, 194
  Lecciones para las escuelas, 124
Roche, Daniel, 19
Rodríguez, Simón, 83
Romanticism, 49, 237
Roscio, Juan Germán, 10, 55, 56, 72, 76, 87, 159–166, 167, 168, 197, 205, 206, 207, 224, 236, 239, 250
  Homilía del Cardenal Chiaramonte, 56, 163
  life, 162–166
  Triumph of Liberty over Despotism, 110, 131, 159, 160, 161, 163, 169, 197, 234
Rousseau, Jean Jacques, 1, 10, 16, 45, 59, 61, 63, 65, 136, 138, 158, 159, 161, 164, 165, 191, 196, 207, 234, 239, 250
  Social Contract, 44, 59, 65, 77, 110, 122, 131, 157, 169, 205, 236

INDEX

Ruinas de Palmira, 116, 136, 138
Ruíz de Padrón, Antonio José, 43, 44, 232
Russia, 38, 68, 226

S
S. Marks, 177
Sade, Marquis de, 44
Saint-Pierre, Bernardin de, 39, 272
Salazar, José María, 87
San Juan de Ulúa, 76, 81, 85, 114, 115, 117, 121, 122, 140, 186
Santa Anna, Antonio López de, 1, 135, 140, 173, 180, 227
Sánchez, Gen. Epitacio, 142
Sanromán, Urano, 82
Santamaría, Miguel de, 114, 115, 126, 172, 186
Santo Domingo, 41, 54, 141, 177, 189, 193
Sargeant, Ezra, 46
Satire, 17, 167–169, 205
Savannah, 83, 172
Say, Jean-Baptiste, 170, 265
Schmaltz, Juan, 15, 121, 174, 175, 176, 238
Schulze and Dean, 80
Science, 8, 9, 18, 24, 25, 26, 37, 122, 164, 168, 225, 245
Scio, P. Felipe, 124, 139
Scotland, 35, 36, 396
Scott, Walter, 19, 35, 69, 189
  Waverley, 27, 189
Scottish Lodge, 179, 180, 181, 182, 234
A Seaman's Manual, 110, 127
Sedella, Antonio, 55
Semanario Patriótico, 169
Semanario Político y Literario, 234
Senda de las Luces Masónicas, 177
Shaler, William, 54
Shields, David S., 17
Skerrett, J.H.A., 49
Small, Abraham, 78
Smith, Adam, 170, 186, 198, 226
  Wealth of Nations, 12
Smith, Dennis, 113, 130, 186
Smith and M'Kenzie, 49
Snowden, Richard, 53

Sociedad de Amigos del País, 58
El Sol, 62, 124, 234, 242
El solitario, o el misterioso del monte, 68
Sollors, Werner, 17
Sommer, Doris, 17
Southey, Robert, 39, 49, 189, 225
Spain
  Cádiz publications, 202–206
  constitution of 1812, 53–54, 166
  language usage in, 165, 192
  Peninsular War, 51, 59, 74, 203, 225
  politics, 40, 42, 46, 47, 49, 50–63, 67, 87, 196, 206, 237
  printing, 127, 130, 156, 158, 164, 169, 187, 189, 205, 227, 232
Spell, Jefferson Rea, 196
Spirit of Despotism, 63, 66
Spottvogel, Thaddeus, 41
St. Clair, William
Stavely, William, 20, 62, 77, 78
  Stavely and Bringhurst, 57
Stewarton, 190
  see Lewis Goldsmith
Stoughton, Mathilda, 49
Style, literary, 6, 8, 9, 10, 17, 18, 20, 23, 24, 27, 35, 36, 38, 49, 59, 72, 78, 116, 167, 169, 188, 188, 197, 208, 226, 228, 235, 237, 242, 244, 251, 251
Suárez de la Torre, Laura Beatriz, 19
Sue, Eugène, 19
Sutro Library, 81, 156, 180, 204, 228, 232
Swift, Jonathan, 189
Syria, 45

T
"El Tapatío," 235
Tenney, Tabitha, 49
Texas, 52, 54, 55, 80, 113, 119, 134, 143, 173, 191, 233, 237
Thomas, Isaiah, 4
Thomas and Whipple, 49
Thompson, Allen, 116, 134, 144, 145, 147, 184, 185
Ticknor, George, 50
Torre, José R., 155
Torres, Manuel, 48, 53, 58, 84, 86

Torróntigui, María Trinidad, 133, 134
Tovar y Salcedo, Antonia, 68, 69
Translation, 39, 40, 41, 45, 48, 56, 60, 61, 121, 126, 130, 131, 139, 159, 163, 169, 177, 180, 189, 195, 196, 197, 200, 201, 205, 225, 229, 234, 235, 238, 242, 243, 245, 246
  business of, 62–71
Treaty of Ghent, 2, 52
Trinidad, 70, 77

U
United Mining Association, 239
United States, 1, 2, 3, 5, 7, 8, 9, 10, 12, 15, 16, 17, 18, 19, 20, 21, 22, 23, 24, 28, 35, 36, 37, 38, 39, 40, 41, 42, 43, 44, 45, 47, 48, 50, 51, 52, 53, 54, 55, 56, 57, 58, 59, 60, 62, 63, 67, 68, 69, 70, 71, 73, 74, 81, 82, 83, 84, 85, 86, 87, 113, 115, 117, 121, 124, 130, 133, 139, 157, 161, 169, 170, 171, 173, 174, 175, 181, 182, 183, 186, 189, 190, 191, 199, 205, 207, 208, 223, 224–243, 244, 247, 248
  Constitution, 2, 56, 63, 137, 183, 201, 234, 238

V
Valdés, Alejandro, 81, 156, 206
Valero, Fernando, 57
Varela, Félix, 57, 183, 238
  El Habanero, 57, 238
Vargas Llosa, Mario, 78, 170
Variedades, o Mensagero de Londres, 225
Vaughan, John, 60
Velázquez de la Cadena, Mariano, 41
Venegas, Francisco Xavier (viceroy), 201, 202
Victoria, Guadalupe, 57, 140, 180,
La vida de Jorge Washington, 68
La vida de Lazarillo de Tormes, 78, 126, 131
Vidaurre, Manuel Lorenzo de, 57
Virgen de Guadalupe, 201
Virgen de los Remedios, 201
Virginia, 10, 20, 50, 226
  constitution of, 63, 72, 246

Viscardo, Juan Pablo, 44, 189, 205, 226
  Carta a los españoles Americanos, 226
Volney, C. F., 45, 126, 127, 179, 180, 181, 196, 234
  La loi naturelle ou Catéchisme du Citoyen François, 45, 46, 68, 179, 250
  Ruins, or Meditations on the Revolution of Empires, 45, 180, 187
Voltaire, 40, 116, 117, 136, 138, 191, 196
von Campe, Joachim Heinrich, 57
A Voyage to Abyssinia, 73

W
War of 1812, 51, 52, 73
Warden, David Bailie, 234
Warner, John (consul), 15, 73, 109, 129, 130, 133, 144, 145, 152, 184, 186, 187, 199, 226, 236, 240, 247
Washington, George, 2, 121, 127, 234, 235, 236, 238, 246
  Farewell Address, 137
  pictures of, 127, 184
Webb, Thomas Smith, 68, 177
Webster, Noah, 21
Weems, Mason Locke, 72, 111, 245
Wells and Lilly, 73
West, John, 49
West Point, 42
The Westminster Review, 225
Wilcocks, James, 129, 248
Wilkinson, James, 52, 116, 134, 143, 172, 185, 190, 191
Wood, C., 232
Wordsworth, William, 237

Y
Yanes, Francisco Javier, 48
Yard, James, 48
Yrujo, marqués de Casa (Martínez de Irujo y Tacón, Carlos), 49, 58, 70

Z
Zea, Francisco Antonio, 228
Zozaya, Manuel, 174